EDWARD THOMAS
A Portrait

25 & 26 -V. 16.

'No one cares less than I,
Nobody knows but God,
Whether I am ~~xxxxx~~ destined to lie
Under a foreign clod'
Were the words I made to the
    bugle call in the morning

But laughing, storming, scorning,
Only the bugles know
What the bugles say in the morning,
And they do not care, when they blow
~~The same call they~~
The call that I heard & made words
        to early this morning

A first draft from Edward Thomas's notebook.

EDWARD THOMAS

★

A Portrait

R. GEORGE THOMAS

Cobwebs and wholesome dust we needed some of both in the corners of our minds. They mature the wine of the spirit perhaps . . . Unfortunate (we thought) is he who has no dusty and never-explored recesses in his mind.

(Edward Thomas, *Pater,* 173–4)

CLARENDON PRESS · OXFORD
1985

Oxford University Press, Walton Street, Oxford OX2 6DP
Oxford New York Toronto
Delhi Bombay Calcutta Madras Karachi
Kuala Lumpur Singapore Hong Kong Tokyo
Nairobi Dar es Salaam Cape Town
Melbourne Auckland
and associated companies in
Beirut Berlin Ibadan Nicosia

Oxford is a trade mark of Oxford University Press

Published in the United States
by Oxford University Press, New York

British Library Cataloguing in Publication Data
Thomas, R. George
Edward Thomas: a portrait.
1. Thomas, Edward, 1878–1917—Biography
2. Poets, English—20th century—Biography
I. Title
821'.912   PR6038.H55Z/
ISBN 0-19-818527-8

Library of Congress Cataloging in Publication Data
Thomas, R. George.
Edward Thomas: a portrait.
Includes bibliographies and index.
1. Thomas, Edward, 1878–1917—Biography.   2. Authors,
English—20th century—Biography.   I. Title.
PR6039.H55Z89 1985   821'.912 [B]   85-3060
ISBN 0-19-818527-8

Set by Cotswold Typesetting Ltd.
Printed in Great Britain at
the University Press, Oxford
by David Stanford
Printer to the University

Acknowledgements

THIS portrait of Edward Thomas relies heavily on the kindness of people and institutions who possess a large quantity of original source material: a list is given in the appendix on sources. I owe a special debt of gratitude to the late Helen Thomas, to her daughters Bronwen (now dead) and Myfanwy, the active president of the Edward Thomas Fellowship, to the poet's grandson Edward, to his nephews Edward and David, and to the many relations and friends who in the early 1960s supplied me without stint from their reminiscences of the poet. The late Rowland L. Watson and his widow Cherry allowed me generous access to the wide-ranging material he had acquired as Secretary to the Edward Thomas Memorial Fund. These were all invaluable aids freely given.

My best thanks for permission to publish some of this material are now due to them and to the following: the Bodleian Library, Oxford; the Colbeck Collection, University of British Columbia, Vancouver; Dartmouth College Baker Library, Hanover, New Hampshire; Battersea Public Library; University College Library, Cardiff; the Lockwood Memorial Library, State University of New York at Buffalo; the University of Durham Library; Humanities Research Center, the University of Texas at Austin; Mr Gervase Farjeon and the Oxford University Press; Professor Emeritus Gwyn Jones and *The Welsh Review*; Mr Norman Colbeck, Mr Alan Anderson, and Mr Anthony Berridge. I am grateful for the award of an Emeritus Fellowship by the Leverhulme Trust which enabled me to visit libraries in North America and provided me with necessary research assistance. The Faculty of Arts at my own college has helped me materially to begin the assembling of a major Edward Thomas Collection there. Mrs Irene Fawcett and Miss Kim Scott Walwyn gave me their best help during the final preparation of the typescript and throughout Mr John Bell has supported me with wise advice, meticulous criticism, and sympathetic understanding. The errors and blemishes that remain are entirely my own.

The presentation of Welsh place-names and personal names was a shade perplexing. An orthodox system of Welsh orthography had not been established in Thomas's day and, I believe, he was influenced to some extent in his own practice by his friend Gwili, the Welsh theologian and scholar-bard; but he was a little inconsistent. I have adopted throughout the current English form of Welsh place-names as given in the Index to *The Times Concise Atlas of the World* and have silently amended Thomas's variations. To his English friends he explained that the 'f' in the names of Merfyn and Myfanwy were pronounced as 'v' and, normally, he used the anglicized form when writing about them to those friends, although within the family (except for a short period in 1914–15) the Welsh form 'Merfyn' was used consistently. I have used 'Merfyn' in the narrative, while keeping Thomas's varying spelling in quoted letters.

For the student of Edward Thomas five books are indispensable: Helen Thomas, *As It Was* and *World Without End*; Eleanor Farjeon, *Edward Thomas: The Last Four Years*; John Moore, *The Life and Letters of Edward Thomas*; and, to a lesser degree, Robert P. Eckert, *Edward Thomas: A Biography and a Bibliography*. They are either first-hand accounts of the events they describe or well-attested narratives written when the authors were in direct contact with those who had known Thomas well. In this picture I have not drawn on these records except when they alone could fill out the sketch. They still remain primary sources of information and guides to our understanding of this strange personality who commands increasingly the attention of a younger generation as remote from his day as light is from twilight or rest from unrest:

> Under the heavens that know not what years be
> The men, the beasts, the trees, the implements
> Uttered even what they will in times far hence—
> All of us gone out of the reach of change—
> Immortal in a picture of an old grange.

Llanishen, Cardiff   R. George Thomas

Contents

List of Illustrations

CHAPTER 1

The Heritage

THE woods seem but just freed from the horror of primeval sea, if that is not primeval sea washing their bases. Capella hangs low, pale, large, moist and trembling almost engulfed between two horns of the wood upon the headland, the frailest beacon of hope, still fluttering from the storm out of which the land is emerging. Then, or at home looking at a map of Britain, the West calls, out of Wiltshire and out of Cornwall and Devon beyond, out of Monmouth and Glamorgan and Gower and Caermarthen, with a voice of dead Townsends, Eastaways, Thomases, Phillipses, Treharnes, Marendaz, sea men and mountain men.

Westward, for men of this island, lies the sea; westward are the great hills. In a mere map the west of Britain is fascinating. The great features of that map, which make it something more than a picture to be imperfectly copied by laborious childish pens, are the great promontories of Caernarvon, of Pembroke, of Gower and of Cornwall, jutting out into the western sea, like the features of a grim large face, such a face as is carved on a ship's prow.... To the eyes of a child they stand for adventure. They are lean and worn and scarred with the strife and watching. Then gradually into the mind of the child comes the story that justifies and, still more, inspires and seems to explain those westward-pointing promontories. For, out towards them continually have the conquered races of the world retreated, and their settlements give those corners a strangeness and a charm to our fantastic sympathies. Out from them conquerors in their turn have gone to found a legend like the Welsh Madoc, an empire like the men of Devon. The blood of conquered and conqueror is in our veins, and it flushes the cheek at the sight or thought of the west. Each man of us is as ancient and complicated, as lofty-spired and as deep-vaulted as cathedrals and castles of old, and in those lands our crypts and dark foundations are dimly remembered.

Edward Thomas wrote these words in 1908, at a period of comparative ease and tranquillity, when he had gone about the South Country

these twenty years and more on foot, especially in Kent between Maidstone and Ashford and round Penshurst, in Surrey between London, Guildford and Horley, in Hampshire round Petersfield, in Wiltshire between Wootton Bassett, Swindon and Savernake. The people are almost foreign to me, the more so because country people have not yet been thrown into quite the same confusion as townspeople, and therefore look awkwardly upon those who are not in trade—writing is an unskilled labour and not a trade—not on the land, and not idle. . . . Yet is this country, though I am mainly Welsh, a kind of home, as I think it is more than any other to those modern people who belong nowhere. . . . These are the 'home' counties. A man can hide away in them. The people are not hospitable, but the land is.

This concern with his own roots was a frequent preoccupation in his writing. In spite of the touches of mystification he employed in many autobiographical references scattered through twenty years of publishing, it is possible to detect the complicated temperament he had inherited. But this is only one side of the picture. In verse and prose he was hell-bent on facing himself when things were out of joint; the scalpel-probe is counterbalanced by the unlearned, incurious manner in which he found deepest ease and joy out of doors—a way of healing he had discovered early in life, although he did not consider himself a naturalist.

Philip Edward Thomas was born in London on 3 March 1878 at 10 Upper Lansdowne Road North, now 14 Lansdowne Gardens, just off South Lambeth Road, where his parents occupied rooms let by a Mrs Legge. It was their first London home after their marriage in Wales some time in 1874–5. His father, Philip Henry Thomas, had distinguished himself in a Civil Service Examination (Executive Branch) and had been posted to a staff clerkship for light railways and tramways at the Board of Trade. According to family tradition, Mr Thomas (1854–1920) had once been a pupil-teacher in his home town of Tredegar, a flourishing iron and coal community. The poet's grandfather, Henry Thomas, was a fitter by trade and followed a typical path of migration in the early nineteenth century. Like many Welshmen in and around the Neath and Swansea valleys, he had made his way from the more rural communities of West Glamorganshire and Carmarthenshire, up the valleys towards Brecon, and then moved eastwards towards the concentration of new industries at Dowlais, Merthyr, Rhymney, Tredegar, Beaufort, Ebbw Vale, and Pontypool. From this area, at the heads of the East Glamorgan and West Monmouthshire valleys, some moved later southwards towards Newport.

This first wave of West Walians to the new industrial areas of north-eastern South Wales brought a distinctive radical, nonconformist, and Welsh-speaking element to a pastoral community that had remained largely conservative and unchanged from the late seventeenth century and was slowly losing the old Welsh language—rapidly so in Monmouthshire—and along with it any acute sense of separate national identity. The racial mixture was soon to be sharpened, as the mid-century railway boom got under way, by new waves of immigrants from

Ireland, the Forest of Dean, Herefordshire, and Somerset; but already the social, political, and religious pattern of the new South Wales and the eastern valleys of Monmouthshire had been firmly set for another century.

Henry Thomas and his son, Philip Henry, were probably Welsh speakers who both married women from Gwent. The poet's paternal grandmother, Rachel Phillips, was a native of Abertillery (or Blaenau Gwent) where a native Welsh tradition had survived, as it had in the Tredegar of her youth. She eventually carried the Welsh language with her, later in life, to the clannish Welsh community that developed around the Great Western Railway works in Swindon. For Henry Thomas had left Tredegar for railway employment in Swindon and one of his sons, the Uncle Harry who features in the Swindon holidays described so lovingly in *The Childhood of Edward Thomas,* was a fitter at the Swindon GWR works until he set sail for South Africa in 1891. The poet never knew his grandfather, who 'had long been dead' when Edward first visited his father's mother at Swindon in 1888.

The Eastaway and Treharne names still retained in the Thomas family indicate that originally the family came from the coastal region of Glamorgan between Neath and Gower. Cross-channel traffic between South Wales and the coast from Weston to Ilfracombe, with settlement of Somerset and Devon families along the Welsh coast, is attested in the parish records that survive from the seventeenth century. The use of 'Treharne Thomas' as a family name was preserved in the Pontardulais cousins with whom Edward spent his Oxford long vacations. They too were a family of skilled craftsmen and, like so many of the first two generations of South Wales industrial settlers, retained a small interest in country matters, raising pigs and often keeping a pony or two on the outskirts of their villages.

Little is known about Philip Henry Thomas's life and career before he settled down in Lambeth with his Newport-born wife Elizabeth, grand-daughter of Alderman William Townsend (1795–1877) on her father's side and a sea-captain named Marendaz on her mother's side. In his *Edward Thomas* (1937), Judge Robert P. Eckert—who corresponded frequently with the poet's maternal aunt, Margaret Townsend, and his youngest brother, Julian—describes the father as a 'practical, self-made man . . . a short, stocky Welshman, a dark, good-looking man'. Margaret Townsend had spend some time helping her sister with the large growing family, especially during the frequent pregnancies, and she had lived with the poet's mother in Stow Hill, Newport, until the move to

London. Margaret certainly visited 'Edwy' (the family name for the poet) at Oxford and corresponded with him subsequently from the USA until his death.

She probably supplied the adjective 'practical' for Eckert. I was once told that Philip Henry Thomas, while preparing himself for the Civil Service examination, had followed his period as a pupil-teacher with a post connected with the railways which were expanding rapidly in industrial South Wales in the 1860s and 1870s. His third son, Theodore, eventually became technical head of London Transport; Ernest, the second son, trained to become an art teacher but spent most of his life in industrial design and advertising; the poet, too, possessed strong, capable, craftsman's hands and the poet's daughter, Myfanwy, still treasures many examples of her father's skill as a carpenter and metal worker. Her brother, Merfyn, began training with his uncle as a motor engineer and eventually became a technical journalist.

In the half-fictional *The Happy-Go-Lucky Morgans,* and in the pruned record of *The Childhood,* Thomas has left detailed accounts of his extending interest in 'Butterflies, Moths and Pigeons', in fishing, in birdnesting of all kinds, with the skills and making of implements that accompanied these activities. It is surprising how little the poet's father shared in these games and sports, which could have helped form a natural bridge of intimacy with his six sons as they began to go their several ways.

The father's preparation for the Civil Service Examination—probably as rigorous an academic test as the external London matriculation examinations of the first forty years of this century—had given him command of three languages, Latin, French, and German, and a powerful interest in political and philosophical topics. His impact on one side of the new society he had entered in the Battersea district is recorded in an obituary tribute in the *Clapham Observer, Tooting and Balham Times* of Friday 24 December 1920:

By the death, at the age of 66, of Mr. Philip Henry Thomas which took place after a long illness, on Saturday the 18th instant, at his residence at 13 Rusham Road, Battersea loses a citizen who has been active for 40 years in championing the cause of Liberalism in this borough. . . . Coming to London as a young clerk attached to the Board of Trade, it was not long before he began to take an interest in political affairs, and his remarkable gift for public speaking was developed at the old Battersea Parliament, to which belonged many men who have since played important roles in public life . . . including Stanley (now Lord) Buckmaster, John Burns and Horatio Bottomley. . . . Although invited by the Liberal Party to be their candidate for the Clapham Division 20 years ago or more, [he] was unable to accept the invitation, and contented himself with speaking for the Liberal or Progressive candidate at every available opportunity in many elections. On his retirement from the Civil Service six years ago ... he became President of the Clapham Liberal Association, and at the General Election of 1916 was the chosen parliamentary candidate for the new constituency of South Battersea where he put up a strong fight against odds for what he firmly and honestly believed to be the right. He lost two sons in the Great War.... Besides his political activities Mr. Thomas also found time for lecturing on literary, philosophical and ethical subjects in many parts of the country, and at one time he lectured almost every Sunday in the Town Hall for the Battersea Ethical Society. He was a brilliant speaker and lecturer. Latterly he became prominent in Positivist circles and occupied until recently the pulpit at the little-known Church of Humanity in Holborn. His sympathies were also with the poor and the oppressed, and in him Democracy has lost an intellectual, enlightened and patriotic advocate of England's faith, honour and advancement.

When Edward was two, and a second child was expected, Mr Thomas moved house (the number cannot now be traced) to Wakehurst Road, one of the rows of recently built small houses parallel to Battersea Rise and between Clapham and Wandsworth commons. There Ernest, Theodore, and Reginald were born within six years, but Edward's recollections of this time are sketchy. Before his tenth birthday, with another child (Oscar) on the way, the family moved yet again to 61 Shelgate Road, a much larger detached house four streets nearer to Battersea Rise and Wandsworth Common. Near to a school and a cemetery and with an older house (with its orchard and coachhouse) at the end of the road, this spacious house remained Edward's home until he left Oxford. His father was now well-established in his career and though never affluent they were comfortably off. Edward recalls his earliest years at Wakehurst Road:

I have only one clear early glimpse of my father—darting out of the house in his slippers and chasing and catching a big boy who had bullied me. He was eloquent, confident, black-haired, brown-eyed, all that my mother was not. By glimpses I learnt with awe and astonishment that he had once been of my age. ... I can hear but never see him telling me for the tenth or hundredth time the story of the Wiltshire moonrakers ... and many another comic tale or rhyme. ... [My parents] were sober reverent people without a creed, though their disbelief in Hell and the Devil almost amounted to a creed. My father and I made merry over the Devil and the folly of believing in him as we supposed many did. He used to try different chapels or different preachers, sometimes taking me with him, more especially when he had become an almost weekly attendant at a Unitarian Chapel. . . . Chapel and Sunday-school were to me cruel ceremonious punishments for the freedom of Monday to Saturday. . . . The best of life was passed out of the house and out of school.

Otherwise, in these early years before the age of twelve, the references to his father are few and nebulous: 'My mother played the piano a little; my father sang "Bonny Mary of Argyle" to her accompaniment.' 'The pleasure of being top, and nothing else, except the interest of my father, made me do such homework as I did in the evenings. . . . My father made me attend evening lectures for a time on sound, light, and heat—with no effect.'

A little later, two references uncover a less severe view of P. H. T. After a talk with his mother about misuse of pocket-money, in order to buy new pigeons, 'I confessed. My father spoke to me angrily. As I hated anger and blame, I became wretched. The result was that very soon indeed afterwards my father came with a very sad but kind face in to the room where I sat alone and told me he was sure I should not do that sort of thing again. His shaking hands with me made me feel half hero, half saint. Naturally I did not do quite that sort of thing again.' Edward entered Battersea Grammar School as a 'free scholar'. One master

earned respect and obedience without fear from nearly all his class, by being a just, quiet, serious man, even of speech and kindly. . . . With slow wrinkling his stiff face relaxed now and then into a feminine tender smile. After a time I found myself frequently addressing him as 'Father', so naturally did he touch the gentle docile side of me. The one time I ever cried in school was when he blamed me with a severity that seemed to hurt him. . . . My father probably went over the [Shakespeare] plays with me when I was doing my home-work, but his taste was for directly elevating philanthropic and progressive literature. Or was it only with a view to inspiring a love of virtue that he read 'Abou Ben Adhem' and how he 'loved his fellow men.'

There follows an account of Edward's slight involvement in his father's political activities, especially his schoolboy advocacy during the Home Rule election when his 'enthusiasm pleased my father'. But from the same Grammar School period Edward recalls in detail 'the Sunday dinner anger, which became almost a regular thing', with the boys tittering and refusing to discuss the topic of the morning's sermon until they received a lecture or abuse from their father, at this 'almost the only meal as a rule which the whole family had together'.

Philip Henry expected a late-Victorian respectable pattern of behaviour from his sons. Edward, school apart, was living a much more exciting life at the ramshackle, free-and-easy household of a friend, and exploring the common around his home in ever-increasing circles in the company of a few youths of similar tastes. The qualities of independence, singularity of viewpoint, and readiness to move far afield in pursuit of his inner wishes (a characteristic of his father's early career) were beginning to appear in the son. Three of Edward's brothers (Ernest, Theodore, and Julian) recorded brief memories of their eldest brother in 1947. They recall his taste for long walks of twenty to twenty-five miles in rural settings away from Battersea, his passion for fishing in ponds and canals, and his accurate enlightening knowledge of birds, trees, insects, and flowers. Their recollections also emphasize his aloofness, shyness, sudden love of fun, and self-contained nature. They give no sense of a close-knit family unit, but they make it quite clear that when Edward writes of adventures in and around London commons, or at Swindon, the word 'we' invariably includes one of them. He was diffident—unlike Ernest who was good at all games—and preoccupied with his country pursuits, but they found him companionable; himself capable of long hours of solitude, he could always find acquaintances ready to share his company for a time; but only a few dedicated companions shared his exacting singleminded concentration on these occupations. He has recalled drily that as a schoolboy he found it easy to get his own way. His own statements, supported by his brothers', disclose a resilient, self-reliant nature counterbalancing his sensitive response to the natural world.

Photographs and recollections confirm that in features and colouring he resembled his mother. She was hesitant, shy, reserved, 'more than pretty' in the eyes of the 'eldest son she loved best of her many sons'. *The Childhood*, with its insistence on only those memories that could be recalled clearly, supports Eckert's belief that there was a silent but complete understanding between them:

My mother I can hardly see save as she is now while I am writing. [In 1913.] I cannot see her but I can summon up her presence. She is plainest to me not quite dressed, in white bodice and petticoat, her arms and shoulders rounded and creamy smooth. My affection for her was leavened with lesser likings and with admiration. I liked the scent of her fresh warm skin and supposed it unique. Her straight nose and chin made a profile that for years formed my standard. No hair was so beautiful to me as hers was, light golden hair, long and rippling. Her singing at fall of night, especially if we were alone together, soothed and fascinated me, as though it had been divine, at once the mightiest and the softest sound in the world. Usually perhaps there was a servant, but my mother did everything for us in the house, made many of our clothes and mended them, prepared and gave us food, tended us when sick, comforted us when cold, disappointed, or sorrowful. The one terrible thing I witnessed as a small child was my mother suddenly rising from the dining-table with face tortured and crying, 'I am going to die'. My father took her on his knee and soothed her. . . . For her younger sister I felt a similar affection and admiration. . . . She sang livelier songs, e.g. from *Patience,* than my mother ever did. But she did not know our ways and her complaints or corrections were harsh by comparison with my mother's.

The Thomas household had five sons by the time Edward was ten years old. Welsh servants and mother's helps came and went, and some he 'admired and enjoyed admiring for their sweet looks or language or presence. The only woman I had anything to do with regularly was my mother, and except at meals and bed time I did not see much even of my mother. Occasionally we played cards or draughts together in the evening.' On Sunday, sitting between his father and mother in the Unitarian chapel, he only knew that

where people were sad and solemn I was overcome, half-suffocated by the sadness and the solemnity. What was read and preached was to me airy nothing. I knew of no virtues except truthfulness, obedience, self-sacrifice, total abstinence from alcoholic drinks. . . . As for self-sacrifice it was mostly incredible. But I liked to please my mother and keep undisturbed the love that was between us. I sometimes did little unexpected kind things out of my tenderness for her, and was always glad to be the one to take up tea for her if she was unwell, and so on, or to help her with the housework when she was servantless. . . . My mother never attempted to add to the religion of the chapel. On the contrary she roused my indignation at the two conspicuously Christian aunts who had made her childhood in that dark house at Newport miserable. If she or I had taken more trouble I might have been convinced that all religious people were cruel hypocrites.

The Childhood makes only three other references to his mother. One is a brief account of the birth at home of the sixth son, Julian: the others refer to her active role as intermediary between the sons and the father. One passage, when Edward was a scholar at Battersea Grammar School, sums up the general atmosphere of 61 Shelgate Road, as the poet recalled it twenty years later:

We had very few visitors, none to turn us inside out. Once a lady and a daughter, remote cousins or friends of friends, came, and the girl left me with a yearning heart for some days and a curiosity for years like my curiosity about the lost childish books. Christmas was eagerly awaited for, but the day itself meant chiefly watching for the postman, disappointment, chapel, a heavy dinner and crackers, some squabbling comparisons of our presents, tea . . . supper . . . The disappointment is vivid yet of the Christmas day when the postman arrived at last, hours late, and brought me only a long narrow box of crackers. We children gave no presents to one another or to our parents: we were content to send out a few picture cards paid for by our parents, to people who would send us cards. The faculty for ceremony or festival was not in any of us. Our boy friends seldom came to the house. Nor were we very anxious that they should, knowing that we should be constrained by the presence of father or mother. For we had one way at home, another abroad.

He had severely limited the scope of his autobiography: 'I depict not what I *was* but what I see when I look back', he told Eleanor Farjeon. *The Childhood,* perhaps, gives too joyless a picture of the tendrils of home that Thomas brought with him from boyhood.

In his sixteenth year he had the confidence to begin to write descriptive nature essays for publication in journals and newspapers. In this he was encouraged by the Unitarian minister Mr Tarrant and a new friend, the literary critic James Ashcroft Noble. Such tangible paid recognition of Edward's literary interests gained the approval of his father, who had himself remained a dedicated, aloof, self-improving student at home while his sons gave full rein to their athletic, roaming, rumbustious interests 'abroad'. Mr Thomas wished his sons to enjoy the best education he could provide, partly as a means of fulfilling their intellectual potential, but even more as a necessary upward step on the social-economic scale. Edward recalls this attitude clearly among the Swindon-Welsh cronies of his paternal grandmother: 'They used to remark how well my father was doing, my grandfather who had long been dead having only been a fitter'. The fear of a 'few stern five minutes' with his father, who wanted him to leave Battersea Grammar School for the neighbouring public school St. Paul's, and had arranged for him to have special lessons in Latin verse and in Greek, kept him steadily at school work, although he knew he 'could do better at lessons if I wished'.

His vital interest was exploring the countryside with his school friend Arthur Hardy, as he records it in *A Sportsman's Tale*: 'We had spent the best ten years of life together and after that saw one another about twice a year . . . Most of those ten years which had bound us together were spent out of doors.' They had first met on a school paperchase when they strayed off course and returned late after nightfall.

From that year onward we two went through most of the stages into which the ordinary man's love of Nature is divided. First the wild unconscious play when we hardly distinguished between the open fields and the neighbourhood of towns except that we preferred the fields. Then, very soon, the hunting stage when we deliberately played at savages. Then the time of collecting eggs, flowers and insects, of stuffing birds and animals. And not long before we left school, the poetical stage when we read poetry out of doors, or rather I did, while he listened. There was not a poet's emotion which we did not heartily believe ourselves to share, evoked by the poem but not imitated from it. What had come to the poets in their most serene or passionate moments we glided into as easily as we gathered flowers for Maud or Blanche or Mabel, as we lay in the grass with our eyes divided between the books, the land and the clouds.

From the hundreds of volumes at home, including Shakespeare, Chaucer, Spenser, Shelley, Keats, Byron, Tennyson, and Browning, the boys were encouraged to learn selected poems for recitation; but Edward does not record where he had found and read Darwin's *Descent of Man* and books of travel, sport, and natural history, especially the many copious draughts of Richard Jefferies. It seems safe to assume that Jefferies, like Waterton, Buckland, Wallace, and Charles Kingsley, would have been on his father's shelf. Mr Thomas was a Comtean Positivist.

The gilt-edged selection from Tennyson into which he dipped, before reading him more extensively (around his fifteenth year), belonged to his mother. Edward's early memories are softer in tone when they describe his visits with her to relations in the Welsh Border counties and especially to Herefordshire. From *The Childhood,* and even more from some conversations I recorded with the poet's second cousin (T. Treharne Thomas) in 1966-7, there are hints that Mrs Thomas's family proudly preserved the memory of Alderman Townsend and his descendants: the Tedmans at a vicarage in Much Birch, near Hereford; another great-uncle at Limpley Stoke near Bath with an interest in the development of Edward's French grammar; and many more who had either been abroad and returned to moderate affluence in the Border counties (according to Mr T. T. Thomas's recollections) or had settled abroad in Africa or in the USA, like Edward's aunt Margaret. She had received a sound enough education to act as a governess to children with parents overseas and, later, as a secretary-companion to American ladies. There are substantial hints that if paternal family experience encouraged Edward to extend his interests, both in preparing for a career and in his natural history pursuits, along practical and fact-gathering lines, the subtler influence of his mother and her family gave approval to the sudden spurt of interest in the affective literature of Richard Jefferies and, even more, to the reading of poetry for its own sake. When he wrote *The Childhood* at the age of thirty-five, Thomas associated this sudden interest in poetry with a sex-stirred liking for a 'tall thin freckled girl of about my own age with good rather large features, dark hair and grey eyes, and an austere expression'.

The double-sided nature of the sixteen-year-old boy who arrived in the History Eighth at St. Paul's among a group of conventionally well-educated youths two years his senior—who seemed to him grimly earnest and thinking only of work and success and speaking in more refined voices than he was used to—is clearly shown by Thomas's two attempts at writing fiction, *The Happy-Go-Lucky Morgans* (1913) dedicated to 'My Father and my Mother' with its epigraph from Hardy, 'But now—O never again', and an unpublished work of 'Fiction' (his title) which he abandoned in the early summer of 1914. The novel is a curious mixture of autobiography, fantasy, speculation about poetry, and Welsh legends (modelled obliquely on the *Arabian Nights*) that begins as a 'story of Balham and of a family dwelling in Balham who were more Welsh than Balhamilish'. Initially it gives a fairly accurate account of the Jones family who are described briefly in *The Childhood*. This factual structure is intermingled with anecdotal family memories of the once popular London Welsh poet Lewis Morris, with some echoes of the people who encouraged Edward in his earliest published writings, and with an even more substantial use of Welsh and Swindon topics now missing from the numerous notebooks. The tone of the descriptions and conversations of Mr Morgan of Abercorran House and his curiously assorted friends (Aurelius, Mr Torrance and Mr Stodham) is cheerfully loving in its recall of the London commons and the Wiltshire and Welsh countryside upon which Edward was to draw for much inner satisfaction throughout his adult life. Equally necessary to the book's structure is the character of the housekeeper Ann, a straightforward transfer of Edward's own mother into the world of the kitchens of his cousins in Pontardulais with their attractive young women and idealized Welsh 'Mams'. Ann stands for all the women of common-sense, warm affection, and practical piety that Edward repeatedly attempted to sketch realistically or to record in dream-like settings in his essays and sketches. She supplies the book's hasty conclusion after the death at Lydiard Constantine of Philip—a partial picture of one side of the Battersea Grammar School Edward:

At this point the people of Abercorran House—even Jessie and Aurelius—and the dogs that stretched out in death like blessedness under the sun, and the pigeons that courted and were courted in the yard and on the roof, all suddenly retreat from me when I come to that Spring in memory; a haze of ghostly, shimmering silver veils them; without Philip they are as people in a story whose existence I cannot prove. The very house has gone. The elms of the Wilderness have made coffins, if they were not too old. Where is the pond and its lilies? They are no dimmer than the spirits of men and children. But there is always Ann.

Ann, in 1913, would have been the same age as Edward's mother and, from family hearsay, Ann's sentiments resemble closely the practical, optimistic piety of Mary Elizabeth Thomas.

The Happy-Go-Lucky Morgans is in no way a conventional novel. As far as one can tell from his letters, he was pleased with it although it did not sell. The book adds a distinctive, more cheerful gloss to the boyhood and early youth of a precocious young writer who later, on his own testimony, suffered bouts of depression of different degrees of intensity from the age of sixteen onwards. Gradually, in the novel, the friends of the Morgans grew up and 'acquired preferences which were not easily to be adapted to that sunny, untidy house . . . They said it was different: but they were wrong; it was they themselves were different; the Morgans never changed. In this way young men of the neighbourhood discovered that they were no longer boys. They could no longer put up with that careless hullabaloo of lazy, cheerful people, they took offence at the laziness, or else at the cheerfulness.' We are left in no doubt that the author, from first to last, approves the viewpoint of the people of Abercorran House. The additional Celtic (and gypsy-like) lore he draws upon to fill out a flimsy plot is firmly placed within the suburban London life between Clapham Junction and Richmond Park.

The one exception is the final chapter, 'The Poet's Spring at Lydiard Constantine'. Writing this from the standpoint of the narrator (Arthur) looking back to the sixteenth (and last) year of Philip, the youngest child of the Morgan household, we are told that Arthur kept a diary of that year—as indeed Edward had kept such a diary and later printed it in *The Woodland Life*. Again, in reference to Philip's new-found love of poetry and Shelley, driving out his old enthusiasm for birdnesting, Arthur states 'I have beside me the book which taught Philip this sad bliss, this wisdom. The fly-leaves are entirely covered by copies in his handwriting of the best-loved poems and passages [of Shelley].' This notebook survives and its dated notes can be checked against Arthur's account of the spring spent at Lydiard Constantine. In the novel, Philip became ill and was left behind there to die while Arthur returned to London and began a new course of study. Philip died and was buried at Lydiard Constantine, near

Swindon. In some obscure way Thomas recognized (in 1913) that his decision to become a writer at the age of sixteen closed the door on a career that would have pleased his father. There are no overt clues to help us. The nearest we get is Helen Thomas's introduction to the 1932 edition of *The South Country* about the life he had chosen, often suffering 'despair and humiliation', but always finding in the country 'the comfort he so passionately sought'. The eighty notebooks in the Berg Collection refer to a process of discovery, loss, and rediscovery throughout his writing life. But there is no unequivocal statement as to why or how his life took a firm direction at this time. Philip, perhaps, stands in part for his earlier carefree schoolboy self between the age of eleven and fifteen—the 'foolish years' was his later name for them. The open nature of this schoolboy Philip Edward Thomas, with his ready absorption in the Morgans' sporting activities, held some charm for the disappointed middle-aged writer. The positive outlook of the Morgan family—based on a real-life family—is present even in the mysterious final chapter, with its faint suggestion of the Arabian Nights:

We were not merely ready to welcome strange things when we had walked half a mile up a lane and met no man, but we were in a gracious condition for receiving whatever might fall to us. We did not go in search of miracles, we invited them to come to us. What was familiar to others was never, on that account, tedious or contemptible to us. I remember that when Philip and I first made our way through London to a shop which was depicted in an advertisement, in spite of the crowds on either hand all along our route, in spite of the full directions of our elders, we were as much elated by our achievement as if it had been an arduous discovery made after a journey in a desert. In our elation there was some suspicion that our experience had been secret, adventurous, and unique. As to the crowd, we glided through it as angels might.

Sometimes in our rare London travels we had a glimpse of a side street, a row of silent houses all combined as it were into one gray palace, a dark doorway, a gorgeous window, a surprising man disappearing . . . We looked, and though we never said so, we believed that we alone had seen these things, that they had never been seen before. We should not have expected to see them there if we went again. Many and many a time have we looked, have I alone in more recent years looked, for certain things thus revealed to us in passing.

In his recall of clearly remembered events in *The Childhood* Thomas was determined not to be led astray by reverie and adult speculation. His method was to include the remembrance of moods and apprehensions as well as images and incidents. In these autobiographical investigations, he seems to follow an aim he had noticed in *L'Intelligence des Fleurs* where, at times, Maeterlinck 'seems to be striving to look at scientific facts in a poetical manner.... He advocates the instinct, the imagination, the unconsciousness, by means of the intelligence which he esteems so far beneath them. . . . His detached, even, and quite uncontroversial manner makes him a valuable auxiliary of liberal thought.' Thomas presents his own pre-adolescent boyhood in a similar spirit. The boy's hedonistic love of naturalist pursuits is linked to a sense of oneness and wonder, if only at rare recorded moments. The significance of such insights was reinforced later by his reading of Jefferies' *Amateur Poacher* and *The Story of My Heart*. Holidays spent in Swindon or Wales, a time of freedom from the severities of classroom timetables and disciplines, gave opportunities for naturalistic pursuits in a setting more favourable even than the widening circle of his weekend and holiday explorations of London and Surrey commons with Arthur Hardy or his own brothers, themselves an essential escape from domesticity, homework and discipline.

Swindon and, by extension, the Jefferies country around Coate won a permanent place in Thomas's life because of the indissoluble friendship that developed between him and the old man called 'Dad' Uzzell. Here was a character, like his Uncle Harry, who offered a way of life quite different from the one Mr Thomas hoped to provide for his six sons. Dad Uzzell appears in many guises in Thomas's stories, and travel books; parts of him—and stories told by him—are an important strand in some of the wayfaring characters found in the pre-enlistment poems. In *As It Was* Helen has left her own warm-hearted account of the 'tiny honeymoon' she and Edward stole and spent in 'the cottage of his old gamekeeper friend' Dad and his wife Granny. But in the Colbeck Collection there is a manuscript of about 2,300 words which Edward wrote in 1895; it is corrected in his much later handwriting and is entitled 'Dad'. The following extracts from it, written before Edward had met Helen Noble but after he had left St. Paul's, catches the effect the old man had upon the young would-be writer:

We were roach fishing, larking about perhaps more than anything else, and could catch nothing; you see it was a scorching day and the water bright and clear as crystal. Suddenly with a tremendous stroke an old man close by threw a tiny fish up in the air and down it fell. It was Dad.... Then we had a little talk, but it did not end there. Chance acquaintance like this ripened into friendship. We found he had a whole store of out of door knowledge which he was quite ready to impart.

In spite of his clothes—what difference did clothes ever make in a good strong man—he looked a finely made fellow, and we became secretly his admirers. No man at his age ever had a straighter back, that we were sure of, straight and strong, it was as the ground ash stick he always carried. His clear steel blue eyes looked you full in the face without a spark of insolence. It was a kind intelligent eye too, though he could twist a rabbit's neck on occasion with the nonchalance of a professional poacher. Time had left few furrows on that bull strong face, sunburnt like his sinewy neck. . . . He used to tell us with a sparkle of pride of enormous weights lifted by him in his youth, and of fights where he felled a man like a bullock. Recalling the mad days of youth in fact, a fierceness almost brutal, showed itself, and destroyed the symmetry of his face. In such moments he was not himself, for age had quelled the turbulent spirit, and tamed what must have been a fierce temper indeed. . . .

But in knowledge of nature beyond that required in poaching—which is very considerable—Dad was even more erudite. He had climbed trees for the blue hawk's nest, and knew its eggs and their markings; the hawfinch, that parrot of the woods with its strange cry and saucer nest, was common in his time. He knew exactly where to look for the nest of any bird we were likely to come across and by certain local circumstances was unerringly guided to a nest hidden deep perhaps in a thorn bush. . . . One failing he had in common with most labourers on the soil, much inaccuracy in bird nomenclature. Thus he thought there were two distinct birds, chaffinch and pie finch, and yet called them indiscriminately twinks or pinks! . . . Bird notes, not songs, he could emulate to the life, and had I believe made use of this faculty in trapping birds. The hollow note of the bullfinch that is almost ventriloquial in its effect, came as easily from his lips as the chuckle of a jackdaw or the chiding of a sparrow hawk at its prey. I remember being highly amused at his rendering of a young rook's cry whilst gobbling a worm: it was perfectly true to nature. . . . Such were only a few of the multitude of his accomplishments.

By pointing out a flower or describing a rarity he could make a walk supremely interesting and was indeed a charming companion on any expedition in the fields. There was not a herb or flowering plant of any sort to be met on our walks that he did not know, and hardly one that was not invaluable as a remedy for some complaint. He certainly had no intention of allowing the old lore concerning herbs to die out. Dried specimens of any sort were always kept by him and roots of many more. Such knowledge as he was full of is fast decaying and it is interesting to come across this old exponent of time-honoured homely skill. He might have made a doctor as well as a poacher. . . .

In modern history as it affected his class he was well informed as ever, and had a memory overflowing with detail. He was bitter against the Church and State though a more truly orthodox man never breathed, and insisted that there was a separate system of law for rich and poor. When bread was a shilling a loaf and men earned less than ten shillings from a long week's work, his father or some other relation was among the most bitterly rebellious against a system that could tolerate such things. Every man poached then, and his family with the rest. He remembers hearing it said that each man in one gang at least vowed to kill or disable the keepers if they attempted to thwart their attacks on the game. It was a wild time, and even the old women were poachers, he said, with the aid of a harmless looking dog that barked only when they reached the cottage with a fresh killed rabbit. Latterly Dad had sobered much when he was no longer able to perform his old feats of strength and daring. To make amends perhaps for the past he had turned tee-totaller and finally Salvationist. It was a strange step from poacher to street corner preacher, but was doubtless sincere. He was loud against 'these new religions'; his woodland life and really intense sympathy with Nature could not overcome his adherence to traditional views of religion.

Dad Uzzell, as much as the writer Ashcroft Noble, was a powerful formative influence on Thomas in the eighteen months between his abandoning St. Paul's and entering Oxford. Edward, according to his younger brother's memories, had always shown a rebellious independance of spirit against domestic or external authority. The example of Dad Uzzell was before him for the rest of his life.

This self-confessedly wilful boy always contrived to have a great deal of his own way and seemed able to follow his bent whenever the weather permitted. In the long darker evenings, school and home life brought together (however unwillingly at first) the complementary joys of reading and the learning of languages, which led in late adolescence to a much-praised gift for descriptive writing based on his explorations and observations of the natural world. He was establishing a pattern of behaviour that with minimal alterations was to become essential to his habitual well-being: long walks with a selected companion, in place of the organized games and sports of boyhood and middle-school days; the acquisition of semi-rural skills—fishing, bird nesting, skinning pelts, skilful carpentry, well-arranged collecting of eggs and butterflies and specimens; and, always, the adventure of trespass and unusual exploration that was, in some frenetic way, aimed at the rapid expansion of suburban villa London into older, more rural surrounding communities. As his own prose essays on 'Nature' were being admired by the adolescent girls in the Young People's Guild at the Unitarian chapel, and approved by the minister, by his father and by Ashcroft Noble, and eventually published in sectarian and national journals, Edward discovered the English poets, first slowly under imposition and then, in a rush, in his father's wide-ranging library.

This boy, in spite of a studious shyness with most adults and many girls, had somehow acquired a self-confidence based, not so much on achievement in games or school work, but on a sense of the rightness of what he was doing with his own free time. As he explored Merton, Wimbledon, or south and east of South Croydon with Arthur Hardy, 'We had no single definite object now that no eggs were to be found. Talking, and looking at the earth and the sky, we just walked about until it was dark. Students we were not: nothing was pursued to the uttermost. We merely became accustomed to the general life of the common birds and animals, and to the appearances of trees and clouds and everything upon the surface that showed itself to the naked eye'. He wrote the last words of *The Amateur Poacher*—a gospel, an incantation—as an epigraph on all his own books. His self-asssurance comes out now in his attitude to school work: 'I did not like not being able to answer a question, particularly if another boy could'.

Edward learned his lessons quickly, but he was never happy in the various schools to which his father sent him. Probably he resented and resisted the thrust of his father's ambition for all his sons, but especially for Edwy, the eldest, so obviously gifted with the academic ability for professional or 'establishment' success. (Unfortunately, there is no hint of the conversations that took place at this time between Lloyd George and Mr Thomas as they took their daily morning walk 'across the park' from the underground station at Westminster.) While Edward kept himself out of trouble with parents and schoolmasters without extending himself, he never, not even at St. Paul's, acquired the social ease of his schoolfellows. The History Eighth, which had assimilated G. K. Chesterton and E. C. Bentley immediately before Thomas's short stay there, could not quite swallow him, nor he them. A public school was more alien to his nature than his father realized: this son was not cut out for a smooth ascent of the ladder of preferment.

The 'foolish years' as a Battersea Grammar school boy confirmed certain attitudes that Edward Thomas never abandoned and that he passed on to his children. He held on to his love of unregimented activity in the open air, away from encroaching London suburbia, and he cherished a sense of belonging to another country—Cambria or Gwalia, Glamorgan or Gwent—in addition to the still strange city he was slowly beginning to explore along both banks of the Thames. This dual heritage sharpened the sense of himself as a fused centre between the dream world of a long-vanished civilization and the natural world he observed scientifically. Supported by a work ethic to which his father gave eloquent support in lectures and in writing, he acquired imperceptibly habits of concentrated intellectual enquiry. From his mother, and her more easy-going and less consciously nonconformist relations, he found sanctions for that profound exploration of sensations that were given early expression in his gift for 'Composition'. His sense of the long, mixed past of his own family, and the need to rebel against the purpose—if not the pattern—of his upbringing, left him neither passionately involved in everyday things, nor yet coldly indifferent to the other people. The *persona* of 'the Watcher', which dominates his best writing, was already being formed: his way forward lay somewhere between social openness and egotistical restlessness. He makes the point in *The Childhood*, as he describes his half-holiday explorations with Arthur Hardy: 'We merely became accustomed to the general life of the common birds and animals'. These purposeful wanderings in nearby London commons were the nearest he could come to the idealized world he had found in *The Amateur Poacher:* 'What I liked in the books was the free open-air life, the spice of illegality and daring, roguish characters—the opportunities so far exceeding my own, the gun, the great pond, the country home, the apparently endless leisure—the glorious moments that one could always recapture by opening the *Poacher*—and the tinge of sadness here and there as in the picture of the old moucher perishing in his sleep by the lime kiln, and the heron flying over in the morning indifferent.' These experiences he could share with Dad Uzzell, but not with his own father. Following his nature, and before his sixteenth birthday, Edward Thomas had somehow combined a love of nature and of literature, twin aspects of realized contemplation that were to characterize his life as a writer of prose and verse.

CHAPTER 2

St. Paul's and Helen Noble

'SEEN through the Willow-tree' was the title given by Edward Thomas to an unpublished, corrected, but incomplete essay dated 24 December 1902. Underneath he added 'which would be a good title for my next book or for all my work'. The essay evokes the second phase of his life between his fifteen months at St. Paul's School from January 1894 until Easter 1895, his courtship and marriage to Helen Noble, his three years at Oxford from October 1897 to June 1900, his year as a poverty stricken journalist in London, and his determined move to Bearsted in September in 1901:

There is a willow before my house. It is covered in ivy by day and by night in mystery and when I lie in bed I see men and women through it passing by. I see it fantastically in the pages of books I read and in a true sense I see life through the leaves of the willow tree. It is I suppose an ordinary willow. In summer it is not so dense but that I can find the blackbird wherever it sings among its branches and not in Winter so agile but that its changing patterns are conspicuous against the sky, its sound an appreciable susurration using the harp strings of the wind. And always in its straight bole I have a stop watch to tell me whether the slowest clouds are sliding and at what a pace a storm is travelling. From my childhood days it was little more than a map, a puzzling weaver, a many tailed whip in the hands of the north wind. On its bush I once traced a gracious face that soothed some half-controlled tears, and once a leer that agitated some nervous mood of loneliness. But the leer and the face have gone. Nor has anything quite so definite taken their place. How often I have watched, nay studied it, and wasted more honest words upon it than I can [on] most men! . . .

I have hinted that the dawn has many times come to me through the leaves of the willow, but it is less the tree itself nowadays that transmits things seen to my mind—than something of which the willow is a visible type. I saw once the head of a dear friend among the leaves and was less astonished at what first seemed an apparition than by his disentangling himself and in the flesh bidding his good morning, so accustomed was I to looking for my thoughts and news among the leaves.

Men and books I see through Nature in the first place . . .

Edward Thomas's fifteen months at St. Paul's helped to shape the early pattern of his life as a writer:

I was considered to excel in this form of rhetoric. So seriously, too, did I take myself in it, that from the time I was sixteen I found myself hardly letting a week pass without writing one or two descriptions—of a man, or a place, or a walk—in a manner largely founded on Jefferies' *Amateur Poacher*, Kingsley's *Prose Idylls,* and Mr. Francis A. Knight's weekly contributions to the *Daily News,* but doubtless with tones supplied also by Shelley and Keats, and later on by Ruskin, De Quincey, Pater, and Sir Thomas Browne . . . While I was afflicted with serious English composition and English literature, I was reading Scott, Fenimore Cooper, Henty, and the travellers, because I loved them; I was also thinking and talking in a manner which owed little to those dignified exercises, though the day was to come when I spoke very much as I wrote . . . There is no doubt that my masters often lent me dignity and subtlety altogether beyond my needs. ('How I Began', January 1913.)

When Edward Thomas entered the History Eighth at St. Paul's in January 1894, he was at least seventeen months younger than the seven pupils who had joined the class in the previous July or September and who were to leave it the following June. We have reports of his school progress for the two half-years ending July 1894 and December 1894 (he left school at Easter 1895 before the July report). The reports by his form master R. F. Cholmeley are in typical school-report phraseology:

July 1894. *Latin*—Much to learn: starts a long way behind the rest:—works well. *French*—Weak as yet. *Divinity and English Literature*—very fair *Mathematics*—Weak. *Map Drawing*—Very Fair. *General Remarks*—Does his work very steadily; backward in languages, but gets on. I wish he seemed to take more interest in life generally.

December 1894. *Classics*—Backward; improves, Greek very little. *French*—knows little, improving. *Mathematics*—Fair, making some progress. *Drawing*—Good. *General Remarks:* I should say quite the ablest in the form considering his age. He has no taste for languages, but his history is very good. I wish he were a more sociable person.

Both reports square with the poet's clinical memory later in *The Childhood*. He felt isolated. He travelled to and from home alone, and soon he decided to eat a few buns in the classroom while reading Jefferies, or else to have lunch outside school. He was not asked to play games because he was excessively shy and unaccustomed to Rugby football, although he had played soccer and cricket at Battersea Grammar School, but without the distinction of his second brother Ernest. No one at St. Paul's shared his interest in natural history and 'the naturalists, whom these boys knew nothing of. "What are you reading, Thomas?" asked one of the boys who already wore a scholar's gown. "*The Gamekeeper at Home*", said I. "The gamekeeper's place is in the woods," said he. And I kept silence, not venturing to remark that the woods were his home.' Often, a victim of his paralysing shyness, he walked along the far side of the Thames, 'sometimes in such wretchedness that I wanted to drown myself'. He realized that his own interests were not favoured at school by boys or masters:

I felt unimportant, isolated, out of place, and only not despised because I was utterly unnoticed. . . . I had now a faint ambition, both definite and indefinite, to do something in connection with learning or literature. My father wished me to try for a history scholarship and I occasionally read as hard as it was possible to do without any interest in history beyond the attempt to memorize facts. . . . I never had any grounds for differing from the historian I had last read. The other boys either had enormous appetites for books of many kinds, or they had native wit. I seemed to have nothing.

But when the two scholars had gone up to Oxford, 'I began to be near the top of the form . . . but still everything at school was an aimless task performed to the letter only. It cost me many night-hours the more because I was reading of one thing and thinking of another.' He had failed to gain a scholarship to St. Paul's and one assumes that his father decided that his son's lack of ambition and apparent aimlessness about a career did not justify the money spent on a schooling that should naturally lead to Oxford or Cambridge, and thereafter to the Civil Service. After fifteen months Edward left St. Paul's on the tacit understanding that he would read at home for the competitive administration examinations of the Civil Service.

Edward Thomas's own narrative of his public-school days is substantiated by memoirs collected in the late 1940s by Rowland Watson and partially supported by reading between the lines of the 'Fiction' which Thomas abandoned in 1914.

In 1945, Lucian Oldershaw, with E. C. Bentley a member of the History Eighth at St Paul's when it was first created in July 1893, recalled Thomas at school and during his early days at Oxford:

Thomas was two years younger than I and I never met him till the year I left St. Paul's School (1894). The meeting to me was memorable. It took place at the house of my friend R. E. Vernede, himself a poet of some promise and a novelist of some performance who was also killed in the '14–18' war. We had talked books and Thomas and I left together and went on talking books. We walked for hours about the streets of Notting Hill and talked and talked. What we talked about (it was mainly the classical poetry of the eighteenth century!) did not seem to matter much. I felt we were communing with something deeper than words. I felt something of the same awe and excitement I had experienced four years before when tramping round and round Warwick Gardens with Chesterton, debating the execution of Charles I. Here was someone who ought to have been a member of the Society that G. K. C. had dominated at St. Paul's from 1891 to 1893. When we parted about midnight, physically tired but spiritually exalted, I found myself quoting what I could recall of Keats' sonnet, a new planet had swum into my ken. I feel today the excitement of that encounter almost as keenly as I did when it took place over fifty years ago.

Despite its eulogistic tone Oldershaw's memory seems more credible than E. C. Bentley's half-humorous, half-invented sketch of Thomas aged sixteen during his first half-year at St. Paul's: 'It was Walker [Frederick Walker, the High Master] too, who had made this possible by creating the "History Eighth", the first recruits to which included my friend Oldershaw and myself, soon to be joined by an exceptionally reserved and quiet boy who usually had in his pocket a rat or so, and a few snakes, which he would shut in his desk with books, and occasionally peep at stealthily—Edward Thomas the poet.'

Few Pauline contemporaries noticed the change in Thomas from an animal carefreeness into the youth who 'had quite a number of temptations to print, and at the age of fifteen easily gave way'. Mr. Tarrant, the minister of the Unitarian church which the Thomas family now attended regularly, had encouraged Edward in his outdoor tastes with much kindness and persuaded the editor of a children's paper to print his early holiday-task descriptions of country walks:

But like all other grown-up people he inspired me with discomfort, strangeness, a desire to escape . . . However, I think the minister had something to do with the essays I wrote and the natural history notes I kept day by day besides the almost daily entries in a general diary . . . My father wanted me to go on to a Public School and I received special lessons in Latin Verse and in Greek . . [My father] used to talk to me of books and take me to lectures. At Kelmscott House I heard Grant Allen recommending State endowment of literary genius: I saw William Morris and I was pleased and awed. But nothing I ever heard at home attracted me to literature or the arts.

One significant external event which placed the attraction of a literary career before the young essayist was the minister's decision to introduce Mr and Mrs Philip Henry Thomas to the family of James Ashcroft Noble, the critic and journalist. Noble had returned in 1894 from Liverpool to London and, after some months attending the fashionable Bloomsbury Square chapel where Stopford Brooke preached to a large intellectual gathering, had decided to join the Unitarian chapel close to their new suburban home at 6 Patten Road, Wandsworth Common. Mr Tarrant—kindly portrayed in *The Happy-Go-Lucky Morgans* as Mr Stodham—later introduced Edward to Mr Noble (the father of his future wife) who was slowly dying of a malignant, tubercular throat disease but was still actively engaged as 'Paul Pelican', an influential journalist and critic. Frequent visits to the Noble home, across Wandsworth Common, began in early April 1895 before Edward celebrated his release from St. Paul's with a three-day walk from London to Marlborough in order to spend the summer term with his paternal grandmother at Swindon. From there he made frequent visits to Jefferies' Coate Farm and Reservoir, to well-off Townsend cousins in Clifton, and to the neighbouring Downs. He returned to Surrey on 21 July 1895. Apart from a family holiday at Eastbourne during the last fortnight in August, he remained at Battersea Rise until he revisited his relations at Swindon from 15 February to 28 March 1896, when he broke off his stay in order to visit Mr Noble. But Noble was in the last week of his life, and proved too ill to see his favourite pupil or to hear read the letter of sympathy and comfort which Edward had sent him.

The 1895 visit to Swindon, in place of the summer term at St. Paul's, repeats an earlier pattern in Edward's life between schools before he won a scholarship to Battersea Grammar School and while his youngest brother Julian was born into the already over-crowded house at 61 Shelgate Road. Then he caught glimpses of the freer way of life of his father's bachelor brother and, as he explored and fished along the canal, got to know Dad Uzzell who remained a surrogate father-figure for the rest of Edward's life. But during this 1895 Swindon visit Edward kept the detailed diary of 'Field Notes' that was later incorporated into *The Woodland Life*. His articles on 'Nature' topics, too, had begun to appear in the various journals where Noble had influence, *New Age,* the *Speaker,* and the *Globe*. Probably the idea of collecting the articles and publishing a book with Mr Noble's own publishers, Blackwoods, was beginning to take shape even before Easter 1895. Certainly Edward's last (and only surviving) letter to the critic suggests that the period of mentorship had lasted for a reasonable time, probably at least a year. It records, too, the young pupil's development from an observer—of plants, birds, trees and animals—into a detached recorder of what he had seen. ('Your good influence and help has sometimes drawn me from the enwrapping pleasure of scenes which before held me alone with them.') After the August family holiday at Eastbourne, 'Edwy' became a frequent welcome visitor to Mr Noble's friendly house. The father found him a ready substitute for his own dead infant son, Philip, and often called the young writer 'Phil'. The mother, who attracted and welcomed happy young men to the house, was a little put out by Edwy's rather shy and serious manner. The elder Noble daughter, Irene, was already launched on her own secretarial career and, at this time, was a close friend of the writer, Richard le Gallienne, a protegé of her father. The youngest daughter Mary, a gifted academic in later life, was still at one of the Girls' Public School Trust schools at Wimbledon, and the only son, Lancelot, was at Merchant Taylors' School. Helen, the second daughter, had left the Wimbledon school when she was sixteen and was at home helping her mother to run the house and, as his fatal illness developed, to assist in nursing her father, to whom she was particularly close.

As the friendship between father and youth developed, Helen frequently ran from the kitchen to open the door to him and occasionally saw him out. For Ashcroft Noble had never forbidden his study to children, and Helen later recalled seeing Edward at the end of a visit still standing by a bookcase and reluctant to leave. After one such visit she insisted on a chaste goodbye kiss. Her father encouraged Edward to take the freedom- and country-loving Helen on one of his famous long walks in and around London and Surrey commons. Eventually, after one false start, when Edward assumed (wrongly) that Helen would not come, they set off in late November '95 for a short walk to Wimbledon, followed four days later by a trip to Croydon. Thereafter Helen frequently walked to meet him or to accompany him on his return home across Wandsworth Common and on January 1896 they had their first long walk to Richmond. In the Diary included in *The Woodland Life* Edward notes under 7 January 1896: 'Year opens mild, with the happy songs of blackbird and thrush thick in the woods; green shoots rising everywhere; all life is quick and glad; the fallow deer idle in the tempered sun under the oaks at Richmond, or sip the water through budding buttercups and weeds. Wood-pigeons crowd to the oaks at sundown, chattering loudly'. In his notebook under 9 January is the single phrase 'Richmond w. HN.' Before he left for his six weeks stay in Swindon that spring he had first called her 'sweet', she recalled four months later, 'in the little passage, near the willows, near the farm' on Wandsworth Common. They corresponded regularly while he was away, although her mother had forbidden it. Arthur Hardy, Edward's close Battersea school friend and constant country companion, was a welcome visitor to 6 Patten Road. He acted as go-between postman, and from time to time he walked with Helen across and around the Common and talked to her a great deal about Edward. Helen believed that their acquaintance would ripen into a warm friendship, equalling her affection for Jane Aldis, but did not believe that she and Edward could ever fall in love, so convinced was she of her own 'ordinariness'. Arthur assured her she was 'quite decent' and that Edward would stick to her. Helen, however, was still imprisoned in the fears and longings that had marked her life during the first years of puberty and was obsessed with the idea that she would never marry and have children. In six letters from Swindon Edward poured out to her his hopes, his feelings, and his frustrations, and sent poems addressed to her.

A week after Edward's return from Swindon in March 1896 Mr Noble died. Edward's parents sent their condolences, attended the ceremony at chapel and graveside, and Mrs Thomas visited the widow. Edward, too, was a frequent and welcome visitor, for Mrs Noble, and her children, were fully aware of his special place in Ashcroft Noble's affection. Mrs Noble gave Helen, as a keepsake, Edward's last letter to her father. Helen and Edward now met frequently on the Common, and she visited her father's grave with him as he tended it with wild flowers. After a fortnight's visit with her mother to her aunt Mrs Poole at Ramsgate, Helen decided that she must earn some money and, if possible, live away from home where her mother's grief-stricken restrictions and excessive dependency—so she thought—would curtail that freedom of action and expression in which her father had encouraged her. Apparently, too, Mrs Noble was becoming dubious about the friendship with Edward and the consequences that might follow the hasty pell-mell nature of her second daughter.

The Nobles were not well off, and Helen's departure as a nursemaid to the Webbs at 9 Lancaster Place, Cliftonville, Margate, seemed a welcome relief to the widow. Edward was still living at home, preparing without a coach for the Civil Service examination. He was equally busy with his nature walks (frequently with Arthur Hardy), writing papers for acceptance or rejection by the *Globe*, the *Academy* and the *Speaker* (earning $22\frac{1}{2}$ guineas by June), but, most significantly of all, as he later obliquely confessed in 'How I Began', writing almost daily letters to Helen. Their fiercely preserved notion of honest, controlled friendship had moved sharply into an expression of mutual love—symbolized, as Helen insisted in all this early correspondence, by the purity and truthfulness of their kisses. In deference to her mother's prudent requests Helen had asked him to write only one letter a week. None of Edward's have survived, but to judge from the cross-references in the forty-five extant replies from Helen—which Edward preserved carefully and in order for the rest of his life—he wrote about sixty between 15 May and 27 July 1896. The intensity of their love, and their readiness to speak to each other directly from the heart, fed rapidly on this period of enforced absence, made tolerable—and enhanced—by the writing of letters. (It was a pattern that repeated itself, and Helen often recognized its therapeutic value for herself and Edward at moments of difficulty throughout their married life.) During the month after her father's death each of them had discovered the need to explore hitherto suppressed areas of feeling and half-knowledge that stood between them and a clearer knowledge of the selves they were now fully determined to offer to each other. For Edward it was the third of many stages on his career as a writer:

Myself and English, as she is taught in schools, came to a conflict and gradually to a more and more friendly agreement through the necessity of writing long letters daily to one who was neither a schoolboy nor an elder, the subject of the letters being matters concerning nobody else in the world. Now it was that I had a chance of discarding or of adapting to my own purpose the fine words and infinite variety of constructions which I had formerly admired from afar off and imitated in fairly cold blood.

There was little cold blood about the topics discussed in these Margate letters. Edward was eager to see and to understand the precise nature and functioning of female anatomy and physiology; Helen, with equal insistence on their purity of motive and the intense trust in him that love had given her, was surprised by joy, sustained by daydreams of their future Eden together, and fired by his frank letters with their confessions of his adolescent fight against erections, nocturnal emissions, and occasional masturbation. She gave him all that she knew—chiefly from conversations with her close friend, Jane Aldis, and from a small book on physiology belonging to her father which she read secretly until it was removed. They believed in exact equality between man and woman. They showed little regard for the ceremony of church weddings, although they both hoped to find some form of acceptable New Testament-based belief for themselves without benefit of clergy; they believed, in Lamarckian fashion, that the physical match and spiritual preparation of parents would ensure a 'better' offspring, as one essential step to a better world. Edward, a great believer in cold baths and the restorative power of long walks (of between 25 and 50 miles), began to use dumb-bells in order to tone up his body and produce more muscles. Helen used some of her earnings to hire a bathing machine and develop her swimming. Above all she sought—and hoped—to prepare herself in every way for modern motherhood, free of the restrictions that had marked her own unhappy upbringing. Under Edward's direction she shared his reading: some Shelley, some Byron, Milton, more Wordsworth, Ruskin, Carlyle and always, Jefferies. (Helen introduced him to *The Story of My Heart*.) She sympathized with and approved of, if never quite comprehended, Edward's intense love of the special happiness that he found in the heart of the country when absorbed with his rare intensity in sights, sounds, and scents. He sent her some of his notes of what he had seen in their walks and frequently let her see his 'papers' before they were copied out for the editors. She sent him one long descriptive prose account, but kept her own poems to herself.

This exploratory phase of their amorous correspondence was interrupted on 23 June. Edward and Arthur Hardy were spending a short farm holiday at Horsmonden, a 2½ hour train journey away from Margate. Helen got away for one day and they spent nine hours together in the open air. She had set off from Margate before eight o'clock and for a short time she fell asleep in his arms. They picnicked, and explored the countryside not too far from Lambkin Farm, still quite unaware of the passionate natures they kept in check. ('To lie innocently then with you seems my ideal for the present', Helen wrote in August.) They must have talked long and hard about their future, and from now on Helen believed that other people would probably regard them as being 'engaged'—a term she hated because of the overtones of male dominance and female sexual ignorance that went with it. When she returned to Margate after 10.30 that night she found a letter from Edward, posted before they had met, awaiting her. She assured him that his apprehensions about her travelling late at night were quite unfounded: she and her sisters had been allowed to travel about unaccompanied in Southport and London since the age of twelve or thirteen.

Until Helen spent a week at home in early October, they did not meet again for four months; and when the Webb family were at Rotherfield for two months in August and September, there are no letters or notebooks to fill the gap. Except for a few letters from Helen to Jane Aldis, there is nothing until January 1897. Edward returned to his 'little study at home' and, with her encouragement, began serious study for the Civil Service examination. She knew that he 'ought always to live in the country; and someday you will with me'; for the present, she encouraged him to carry out his father's plans. 'Be brave and strong at your work, dear. I mean your examination work, for in your other work you need no encouragement, for you like it so much as it is yourself finding expression in words.' She hopes ('in a money sense') that he will 'get the Civil Service post. Nice to have a little money to spare above the necessaries of life.' (A wry comment from two young people who sometimes had to delay posting letters until they could find a few pennies for stamps.) 'When I first knew you, you would have been full of despair and melancholy at the thought of clerical life, but now though there is a faint hint of it you are full of hope and joy.' She asks him to recognize his father's wisdom in trying to encourage him to work for a steady position and shares his anxiety about delays with Blackwoods, over the publication of *The Woodland Life*. Impulsive by nature and eager to experience fully the love that she knows will be hers for life, Helen is scrupulous in her demands on his friendship and earnest in her desire to learn by his side. The 'H. T.' who wrote *As It Was* and *World Without End* can be heard just beneath the surface of these youthful letters written nearly thirty years before. While Helen's day was filled by the demands of her young charges and the vain attempts of Mrs Webb to train her in some orderliness in domestic affairs, Edward continued to tend her father's grave. He was still a favourite with her sisters and brother and he was Helen's principal source of news about her home. His moods, as reflected in her letters, remained volatile and while he continued his triple tasks—preparation for the examination, deciding the final shape of his first book, and producing a spate of articles, many of which were published—there are continuous references in her letters to his indifferent health and to his repeated determination to live chastely with her until circumstances alter.

The pattern of their future life together was already taking shape. Helen believed unshakeably in his genius and was determined to enable him to realize his potential as a writer—a poet, like Shelley, she believed at this time—without sacrificing her own strong desire for freedom of independent action, untrammelled by the stuffy conventions of the elders she suspected of hypocrisy. She wished to offer herself in complete love, without demanding in return any limit to his interest in other people. So convinced was she that 'Love conquers all' that she was prepared at all times to forgo conventional ties if they interfered with his development. Her faith in him was severely tested later, especially in

1908 and again in 1913; but she drew on deep reservoirs of resilience until the anxieties of his last year as a soldier began to sap her energies as housekeeper, mother, and gardener. Although he made a huge bonfire of his papers and correspondence in 1916, and kept it going for a few days, Edward preserved all her letters along with his notebooks. They were part of the story of his heart and, re-read now, one recognizes that the Helen Noble of these letters is incorporated in part into the texture of poems like 'After you speak' and 'And you, Helen':

> I would give you back yourself,
> And power to discriminate
> What you want and want it not too late, . . .
> And myself, too, if I could find
> Where it lay hidden and it proved kind.

Her letters, like his own comment in 1913 on his letters to her, suggest that at eighteen he had begun for her eyes alone the long process of self-discovery with assured confidence of her support. The following extracts from one letter portray the Helen recalled by Eleanor Farjeon in 1958: 'Of her he said: "During the nine months before her baby is born, her face is one perpetual smile. My wife could be the happiest woman on earth—and I won't let her." He said she wrote better letters than any woman he knew—"only it is a different letter each time you read it." '

I have said nothing of your letter. What indeed can I say. All the most lovely words of love and passion could not express one tenth of what I feel for you. And your letter is you . . . You have my soul now, all my thoughts are yours; only a short time before you can have all of me, even my poor body which I now strive to make purer and better, healthier and stronger for that time. But before that time comes we must often be together. If possible we must spend that time at Coate [where Edward then was], and now I long to go to Horsmonden, for every place where you have lived and been happy, is to me dearer than any others. And yet, though I feel so sure that we shall spend a lovely but short time together somewhere alone, yet when I think calmly I grow despairing, for if I went to stay with you, anywhere in the same house and alone, nothing would induce mother to believe me really innocent and pure in heart. It would break her heart. And it is not that she knows me to be bad or weak, or you either, but her conventional mind could not grasp that a thing so often impure, can be made absolutely and perfectly pure. Yet somehow we *must* do it . . . What an exquisite verse from Shelley you quoted. It makes me long for a complete collection so that I might read on, especially the verse you mention but do not quote. Do you know sweetheart I have often wondered since I knew about things whether a brother or sister ever did love with such a love as ours.

Oh I used to think 'how beautiful' if such a thing were possible, but I had no idea that such love was thought vile. It seems so natural and pure, so perfect. It is too pure for this impure world, therefore they condemn it as vile. Tell me more of it . . . I must say my thoughts to you. Did you know I feel that if I thought (and if you ever did, I should know it as soon as the thought had crossed your brain) you doubted my perfect love, truth, sincerity and striving for goodness, I must indeed give up all the good I have gained, and gain daily, by your love and mine. I should become bad, selfish, a curse to myself and to all who knew me. Life for me would be empty and not life, a mere dragging on of weary time, perhaps not that. I feel like a wretched bird here, taken from its loved mate and caged, trying to sing cheerfully to its poor lonely loved one, but failing fearfully. . . . I had your last dear letter this morning (Tuesday), and I feel after your loving, passionate one how mine must seem cold. Yet the words you will not count. Only see me as I write this, throbbing with love and passion, yearning to kiss you, to talk with you. And now I have a terrible thing to tell you. Mrs Webb has never paid me. My money was due on the 11th, and when I have posted this, my last stamp will be spent, and I shall have to wait 'till she remembers. So this will have to be my last letter till then. . . . Dearest heart, sweetest one, lover so good and pure, think when indeed we shall both caress a little soul, a little body, ours to love, to form, to live for and love. When each day shall add strength to its limbs, and its love. When its fairness of mind and body shall be our aim in life, when its beauty shall be our pride our joy. Just yours and mine, no one elses. There shall be no shadowy third. We will teach it to be pure as we count pure, not the vile purity of the world. We will teach it to have all beauty, we will teach it that love is the most beautiful thing, and never need wax cold, as years go by. We will teach it to love as we its parents purely *everlasting*. What a future! How sublime, and to you it is as beautiful as to me, else all its beauty would be gone. And now I must say goodbye. . . . P.S. Tell me more of the brother and sister of sweet Shelley. I must save up for all of him. Browning too I want, and Keats.

Helen spoke on to the page, indiscriminately, in ink, in pencil, in her bedroom, out on the park seat while her charges slept, or on the beach after bathing. She keeps nothing hidden from Edward, so confident is she of his love and so secure in her belief in the future that lies before them, unconventional and home-based:

I think I must have suffered as you before I knew of things relating to sex. I am now nineteen and until I was seventeen I was ignorant as any babe. But my ignorance was not only mental torture, but my body seemed to suffer the intensest agony. And when I first got an inkling the little was far worse than none, and I became melancholy and miserable. Neither father nor mother had ever breathed a word, and my first knowledge was thrust upon me—by happening to read quite unwittingly a pamphlet—it was by Stead, exposing and giving such ghastly details of prostitution . . . It pleases me very much here. I have three little girls aged 8, 6 and 4, and one boy of seven, and they bath and dress together. They sleep in the same room with each other, and look beautiful when I am putting them to bed, jumping and hopping about quite naked, rejoicing in the freedom of no clothes. And it makes me wish that it could always be so. But when they get a little older, they will cover their bodies up and the boy shall never again see his sisters' beauty. O! how wicked it all is, how far from any beauty or ideal. I remember once when I was a very little girl. We were living at Southport and we were being bathed by mother before the kitchen fire, and I was getting undressed and being helped with the buttons by the housemaid. And when it came to the last garment, I pulled that off as well, glad as children always are, and I hope always will to be undressed and free, and stood in what Janet calls 'birthday clothes'. And I remember to this day, though I was so small, that mother was very angry with me, for unclothing myself before the servant, who was a very nice girl who had been with us for a long time. And that is how children are brought up. . . . I know plenty of girls who do not know what marriage means until the bond is sealed and there is no escape. Then the facts are burst upon them, and they shrink from their husbands in loathing and horror. Oh Lord! What horrors and impurities and wickedness exist under convention's cloak. At 12 my children shall be told simply and truthfully and clearly what their infant minds can well grasp. The rest a little later. I have suffered too much to let my children face the same suffering. . . . In all you say about parents and children living in sweet sympathy and perfect knowledge of each other, in freedom of speech, comrades, friends confiding in each other, telling all and being listened to, and taught, in all this I entirely and wholly agree. That kind of family life is the ideal, the only real family life, the one to which I aspire. . . . Again I agree with you when you say that equality of husband and wife is an absolute necessity to the well-being of the family. . . . The kind of modesty Tennyson speaks of I hate. It means nothing, it shows nothing, except sometimes betrays its very vileness it would hide. Do you know one of the very first things I noticed and liked in you, was the way you shook one's hand, and looked straight at one as you said goodbye. The 'step demure' and 'downward lids' offend me, and never bring me a sense of virtue . . . I am not really a coward or even a 'nervous' person. Solitude, darkness, or the horrible crowd which one sees always in such places as this never make me the least afraid. . . . Even in little things we agree. I have always hated that vulgar pomp with which the rite of marriage is coupled. It jars against all my ideas of decency, I should hate it. Mother and father were married without any of that kind of thing.

Edward's preservation of these letters uncover the debt he owed to Helen who brought his idealistic, passionate nature—with its violent occasional swings of mood—into closer contact with her own dreams and desires for fulfilment of her love, in perfect sexual freedom between them, leading to motherhood. She tells him all and, one assumes from hints and a few quotations in her letters, he does the same to her. As she uncovered herself to him—'for I love, and there is no loneliness, no misery, no doubt and ignorance, no hoping for that which seems vain as there used to be, but never will be again'—one glimpses the ideal that enabled her to accept without question the life that lay before them. Later, in 1908, they had to plan once again how to combine their joint ideal of a free domestic relationship with the solitude that Edward's nature demanded as a price to be paid for his self-discovery as a writer. Even now, at eighteen, he suspected the dark recesses within some of his moods, so unlike his usual shy, yet company-loving, social manner. Helen was confident that her love would remove all doubts: 'I do not "darkly feel" what it is I love in you. I know it is all of you, body and soul . . . there is nothing dim or mysterious in our love that we cannot fathom or understand.' It was a creed she held tenaciously—sometimes blindly—to the end of her life.

CHAPTER 3

'How I Began'

In his last letter to Ashcroft Noble, Edward tried to express his thanks to the dying man for the new direction he had given to his life:

I would try and tell you what I have been thinking; though I once told you I cried because I was incapable of thought. . . . Your good influence and help has sometimes drawn me from the enwrapping pleasure of scenes which before held me alone with them . . . You had made ways clear which before had been dark or fearful with doubt . . . You have brought life where there was uncertainty . . . perhaps in part you have made me know myself, understood before by you.

Already, in March 1896 it would seem, Thomas had decided on a career as a writer. Seventeen years later, in 'How I Began', he reflected on the process with controlled detachment:

With short intervals, from [eight or nine] onwards I was a writer by choice. I began several diaries, carrying on the entries in some of them as far as February. By the time I was fourteen or fifteen, I did more; I kept a more or less daily record of notable events . . . they were above syntax and indifferent to dignity . . . I was obliged to write essays . . . where I gave myself up to an almost purely artistic rendering of such facts as I remembered, and such opinions as I could concoct by the help of memory, fancy, and the radical and the free-thinking influence of home . . . I virtually neglected in my writing the feelings that belonged to my own nature and my own times of life—an irreparable loss, whether great or not.

Later in his article, he pinpoints 'the necessity of writing long letters daily' to Helen as the beginning of his departure from nature descriptions—initially written as talks to be given to the Young People's Guild at the Unitarian chapel—or his dignified school essays. The letters gave him the chance of 'discarding or of adapting to my own purpose the fine words and infinite variety of constructions which I had formerly admired from afar and imitated in fairly cold blood.'

These early letters to Helen are now lost and are merely reflected in her long replies from Margate and Rotherfield. Undoubtedly they were chiefly concerned with the 'feelings that belonged to his own nature'. They accept that he is to become a writer and a poet. His autobiography—from birth to his entry into St. Paul's and now known as *The*

Childhood of Edward Thomas—ends before Helen entered his life. Two sources throw light on the youthful nature-journalist who became Edward Thomas, prose writer, literary critic, and poet. One is his novel, *The Happy-Go-Lucky Morgans*; the other, an incomplete work entitled *Fiction* which Thomas conceived as a continuation of his *Childhood* autobiography. It was written rapidly (and compulsively) in early 1914, in an attic room in Selsfield House with some resemblance to his own study bedroom at 61 Shelgate Road where his writing began and where Helen later gave birth to his son. He abandoned it after Robert Frost had read the entire work, approving the *Childhood* section but condemning the *Fiction* as too introspective. The unguarded nature of the latter, which was never worked over by Thomas, provides occasional glimpses of the youth who left St. Paul's after his seventeenth birthday in order to achieve a twofold purpose: ostensibly to please his father by attending a few practical evening classes and in the day by preparing himself for some form of Civil Service clerical post; while privately, he sought the freedom of a young nature-writer who was determined to collect his papers into a book. This decision to live by his writing was a necessary element in a personality that established firm contours quite early. How did this early decision come about?

The *Fiction* records part of the rapid maturing, although his growing friendship with Helen Noble lies outside it. The story is carefully dated to support the 'fiction' that the narrator had left grammar school and entered the Civil Service between April 1894 and January 1895. (Helen and Edward began their acquaintance in the autumn of 1895.) It is almost as if Thomas was trying to create, in fiction, an alternative pattern his life might have followed.

Biographical reconstruction based on Thomas's tales and sketches can be a mistaken exercise. His imagination rested firmly on observed fact and carefully preserved records: his extant notebooks abound in transcriptions of scenes and encounters, interlarded with direct quotations from ordinary speech. (One notable relic is the second volume (*Men*) of a two-volume group entitled *Things and Men*; it is full of snippets of conversation and descriptions spread over the period 1897 to 1910, frequently used in his books and papers in order to restrain his fancy and keep his feet firmly on the ground.) Those who know Thomas well, like W. H. Hudson, were convinced that all his fictitious characters were dominated by recognizable traits of Thomas himself. They could hear him speak unequivocally through his characters. Yet in his *Edward Thomas*, R. P. Eckert argues that the young Edward had explored the

Surrey and Wiltshire countryside in solitude with a fantasy companion
called Philip who later reappeared as 'The Other Man' in *In Pursuit of
Spring* and, even more noticeably, in Thomas's early poem *The Other*.
Eckert did not know the real Arthur Hardy's share in these juvenile
expeditions, nor had he seen the then unpublished *A Sportsman's Tale*
which amplifies the sustained friendship between these two Battersea
Grammar School pupils. The fictional Philip—in *The Happy-Go-Lucky
Morgans*—was a compound creation based partly on Ashcroft Noble's
long-dead infant son, also named Philip. The imagined Philip ceases to
exist at the time of the older critic's death; the real tribute to Mr Noble
was Thomas's first book, inscribed to his memory. Ashcroft Noble was
part-owner of the three weeklies that published his 'Paul Pelican' articles
and accepted Thomas's early essays; and he was also connected with the
Edinburgh firm of Blackwood that was to publish those essays in book
form.

How reliable, as an autobiographical source, is *The Happy-Go-Lucky
Morgans*? It certainly draws heavily upon Thomas's memories of people
and incidents from his youth and early student days and many similari-
ties exist between the bookish Mr Torrance and Mr Noble. The narrator
(of the *Morgans*) is called Arthur and it is Arthur who survives the death
of Philip and goes on to become a writer of some undefined kind on the
model of *David Copperfield* and *Great Expectations*. The places inhabited
by these characters are drawn directly from Edward's first-hand observations around Wandsworth, and on holidays spent in Wiltshire and West
Wales. The world of this novel is as much his country as the wild, half-
derelict countrified pockets around the rapidly developing suburbia of
Wimbledon, Kensington, and Battersea which the fictitious Philip and
Arthur explored as thoroughly as the real Arthur Hardy and Edward
had explored the parts of London commons which they called 'Our
Country'. Edward's second and third brothers, Ernest and Theodore,
have recorded how occasionally they too shared these nature explorations and fishing expeditions in the London woodlands and around
Swindon. Their memories emphasise his intrepid, iconoclastic, and
freedom-loving wilfulness. Ernest wrote:

The only time we really spent together was in the summer holidays . . . with
our grandmother at Swindon. We went fishing in the Wilts. and Berks. Canal,
but sometimes on blazing afternoons, we would trespass in the fields and
search for eggs. A branch of one tree hung out over a pond ending in a spray of
twigs resting on the water. And there, was a moor-hen's nest and eggs. Edwy
was out on the branch almost within reach of the eggs when we were caught

redhanded by the farmer on horseback . . . The matter was settled by our father
with a donation of 5s. to the local hospital.

Theodore recorded:

For one of so gentle a character he could be extraordinarily defiant of gamekeepers, and threatening letters to my father passed on to him with added
threats were not of the slightest avail. He did no wilful damage but regarded
himself as entitled to go where he wished for the purpose in his mind without
regard to the rights of ownership and the alleged presence of man traps and
spring guns. He was scornful of the latter. . . . I met him returning from one of
the Penn ponds with the largest pike of the year swinging by his side and a look
of sheer elation on his face. He would be about 16 years old then but his
sources of pleasure changed little with advancing years though his opportunities became less. . . . A large fish on his or my line was always an occasion for
excitement for Edwy and he would jump into the water with his gaff if he
thought it the only way to land it. Weather was no deterrent for him and was
never allowed to interfere with his plans. . . . On his best days Edwy was a good
companion because of his immense knowledge of country sights and sounds.
Even on his worst (silent) days he was easily stirred by the song of a human or a
bird, by the laugh of a woodpecker, the bark of a pheasant, the sight of a rare
butterfly, or the bark of a fox in the darkness—with his easy and melodious way
of putting over his knowledge . . . There was companionship in his silence
because it was born of a deep reserve which required help at times to find
expression.

Throughout his life Edward had a passion for solitary swimming,
often for an hour at a time, in the sea at Felpham in Sussex, in the small
lakes in the Black Mountains, or the larger ones in the Lake District.
Silent and solitary he often was, as Eckert knew from the evidence of
Margaret Townsend, Thomas's aunt, but he was eager at all times to
share his country knowledge with young people. Children particularly
who knew him well, and spent time in his company, invariably recall his
ease of manner with them and his absorption in their pursuits.

Edward was born on the third of March, and the advent of spring is a
constant theme, and symbol of renewal, in everything he has written.
The fictional Eastertide death of Philip at Lydiard Constantine (in
Swindon), leaving the narrator to continue the kind of life that Thomas
himself followed in his preparation for matriculation at Oxford in
October 1897, reads like a youthful reaction to the actual death of
Ashcroft Noble on Good Friday 1896. It is as though Edward, in 1896,
had abandoned the career 'as Philip' which Noble had made smooth for

him as readily as, seventeen years later, he allowed the fictional Philip to
die. In real life, Edward returned unexpectedly from Swindon to visit
the Noble household and, though unable to see his dying mentor,
became a support to Mrs Noble and her daughters, while his friendship
with Helen grew into love. She was determined to leave home; Edward,
according to one of Helen's letters to Janet Aldis, 'hating' his father who
still wished his son to enter the Civil Service in spite of the modest
success of his articles and the prospect of a first book being published.

The sudden death of Philip in the novel is one of the few traceable
references in Thomas's work to the impact of the elder critic's death
upon him and the part it played in hardening his determination to
become a writer. As he says in the *Childhood,* he had his full share of
determined wilfulness to follow his bent. Apart from the stray references
to external events in the letters between Helen and Edward, the incomplete *Fiction* is a fuller guide to the decisions Thomas was making
between Easter 1895 and the summer of 1896 than reinterpretation of
the *Morgans* novel. The plan of his outward life and activities is suc-
cinctly given in the Diary that forms the last third of *The Woodland Life.*

The *Fiction* was planned in three or four parts and I assume that most
of the first and second parts was incorporated into *The Childhood,* the
initial manuscript of which is in a notebook identical with the extant
one, *Fiction* II 'begun 12. iii. 14 Part II begins p. 86'. The preceding
twenty-five pages describe a long walk taken by Philip Parrish (in his
thirteenth year) with his uncle Richard. It includes a first glimpse of
Stonehenge and their eventual arrival at the home of another widowed
uncle, Mr Morgan, who lives at Jefferies farm with his daughter
Catherine. She resembles closely the 'buxom Welsh cousin named
Florence, who was probably eight or nine years my senior', so described
in *The Childhood,* with whom he spent 'the most blissful hours' in
country walks from his grandmother's Swindon home to Shaw or
Lydiard when he was ten or eleven. 'I suppose I had a sort of unfettered
adoration for her without knowing it. I never saw her after that
summer.' Uncle Richard resembles Edward's Uncle Harry and has not a
little of Dad Uzzell in his make-up, too. In the *Fiction,* before he and his
uncle arrive at the farm, Philip the narrator describes the image of
Catherine that remained from the earlier encounter:

I wish I could say exactly what I saw. Paint it I cannot because I am not a
painter. I could not even give instructions to a painter. Neither do I believe that
a painter could have painted it—had he seen what I saw. She was beautiful. She

had dark but glowing brown hair. I had not yet decided whether her eyes were grey or hazel. Yes! she was beautiful but above all she was blessed and kind and sweet, and I never thought of her as beautiful. It was her face chiefly that I saw brightening and fading away in my mind's eye. Or perhaps I ought to say it was her spirit, since it resembled not at all any portrait that could have been painted. And this spirit brought with it a suggestion rather than the clear outline and colour of the mayblossom dress. I saw what she was—what she was to' me—not what she seemed or would have appeared to be in a photograph or common portrait. For it was not pure ocular seeing, or I should have seen her as a girl of the age which I have now reached. She was not that. She was not of any age but an immortal loveliness. The eyes alone could never have given me so profound a sense of Spring, of Maytime and the blossoming of hawthorn upon the heaths and wild cherry at the border of the beech copses. More often than not the face peered at me through leaves. When faintest it was a face imagined among flames.

The story paints an idyllic picture of many meetings and walks between the lad and Catherine before he and Uncle Richard resume their walk and return home, after a brief visit to Philip's brothers who are orphaned and live elsewhere. There follows a winter of adolescent wretchedness and, as *Part III* of the *Fiction* begins, the narrator describes its surviving effect on him still, almost twenty years later in 1914:

I think now that her predominance has done injustice to lesser things in my life, as indeed it may still do. I fear it is even now doing so. It is urging me on over the years bidding me neglect those that were without Catherine, where as I set out to tell the story of my life, the dull with the bright, the gray with the green, all the Sundays Mondays and Tuesdays of it at least sufficiently to suggest them. Moreover if I were to fly *there* what should I do but renew sorrows and incur perhaps insupportable difficulties in attempting to record them. Yet I must still think it my duty, without reconsidering whether or not it be worthwhile, to continue this plain record of what (I know) need not have been plain but for the accident that I am a niggler without impulse, not an imaginative artist. When I get out of my train at Victoria and look about me at the other two hundred—mostly strangers, not least so those whose names as early schoolfellows dawn on me when they disappeared,—I sometimes think that one or two of us ought to speak out instead of just voting and making a remark in the complaint book once or twice a year and writing to a newspaper less often. Therefore I will continue.

When Edward Thomas decided to send *The Childhood* to Eleanor Farjeon for typing, he declared it impossible to recapture precisely 'what he was' as a youth. The *Fiction*, however, reads like an attempt to break out of this self-imposed restriction. Its genesis perhaps was the unsuccessful attempt by Thomas and his walking companion Jesse Berridge, on the journey that became *In Pursuit of Spring,* to collaborate on a fiction that would include a passionate youthful love, courtship, and marriage. There is no evidence among manuscripts and notebooks to decide this point. Undoubtedly, in March 1914, nine days after his thirty-seventh birthday, at one of the lowest ebbs in his fortune (but soon after he had received a grant from the Royal Literary Fund), Thomas speculated in fictional form upon another path his life might have taken if he had left grammar school at sixteen and followed his father's plan of a career in the Civil Service.

The narrator of the *Fiction,* Philip Parrish, is an orphan living with his uncle but with many brothers scattered elsewhere. He has an uncle called Mr Morgan who lives somewhere in Wiltshire and an aunt in Salisbury. The story of *Part III* begins in a London suburb after he leaves grammar school and goes to evening classes:

From that school of mingled games, friendliness and lessons I went with but a short pause to one where lessons were business, and a very serious business indeed since most of the scholars had already begun to work in offices and came here in the evenings to qualify themselves to earn more money and more leisure. In the pause I studied by myself first at home, then at my aunt's home at Salisbury. There it was that I really began to read.

As he explores the poetry of Byron at Salisbury he works hard at his arithmetic and English composition until he is 'chosen as fit to enter the Civil Service, to hold for the rest of my active lifetime the pen that is mightier (when you get a good one) than the sword (when you get a bad one).' The remaining five pages of the manuscript give a dispiriting account of the office life he leads, the sonnets he writes, the girls and prostitutes he sees but does not meet. Some of these pages round off the last bits of *The Childhood* after he had sent the bulk of it, with Frost's approval, to Eleanor Farjeon for typing. The *Fiction* was his last attempt at personal writing in 1914 before he decided, by whatever hidden processes, that the best solution to his apparent obsession with introspection and self-analysis was to cross over into the world of poetry, with its quite different but equally stringent laws and regulations. The *Fiction,* like *In Pursuit of Spring,* unveils areas of experience that he felt compelled to probe, in order to retain his dignity.

The three following quotations, taken from Part II of the manuscript,

recover a few hitherto unsuspected facets of Thomas the young pre-
Oxford writer. One refers to his fourteenth year, a little later than the
visit to Catherine at Jefferies farm, when he had changed greatly.

I had become a good and conscientious boy. Sometimes I used actually to go to
a church in my religion, not to one peopled by a clergyman, choir boys, bald
old men, and ladies with feathers in their hats, but to an empty church. I know
that I went there when the change I have spoken of must have been already
complete. My uncle in the evening had read aloud something where the line
was quoted

                    The child is father to the man

and these words insinuated themselves not into the stony ground and thistles of
my mind but into the dark rich soil that brings forth a hundred fold. The first
result was a dream that very night. In my dream I flew through a twilight until
I reached a forest of enormous trees. Here I alighted and began to walk into the
wood in search of something. Seeking without knowing what and going deeper
into the forest, I noticed that I was not alone. Other boys and girls were flitting
hither and thither among the trees, singly, without a word or a sign of communication with one another. A few were older, many were younger, than I.
Some like myself were looking about them. Others had found what they
sought. These, when I passed them, I saw to be sitting or kneeling beside
cradles, rocking them, or singing, or gazing intently. The children were very
much like the angels of resurrection which I had seen over tombs. What was
inside the cradles at first sight terrified me. Several that I saw were very old
bearded, emaciated and grim and deathlike, instead of babies, grown men. All
were asleep. I was, however, soon relieved. 'The child is father to the man' said
one of the tenders of cradles in a pause in his song. Instantly I understood
everything. These were children tending the men and old men to whom they
were fathers. I was a father. What I was in search of was my son. After some
wandering among nurseless cradles I recognized him by some unsuspected
instinct—a pallid moustached old baby. I bent down to look more closely. With
a scream I hid my eyes. All had been in vain. My son was dead. And here ended
the dream, but not the growth of that seed sown by Wordsworth's poem . . .

He then relates hearing the ringing of a church bell, dressing quickly,
racing towards the nearest church which was shut, not a sound:

I laughed and awoke. It was a dream, but the disappointment and dreariness
remained with me. The words 'The child is father to the man', had haunted me
all the morning. Beginning by a fantastic attempt to construct pedigrees where
sons were their own fathers, I became gradually so involved that I remember
wondering if God the Father were in truth only the child that grew up into
Jesus Christ. That afternoon I meant to search the Bible for information,

though I knew little of it. Every room in the house contained some form of Bible and I took up a large ancient looking one and opened it as if it had been a door into a cave. What I saw and read was 'Our Father which art in Heaven'. I read no more. My curiosity had ceased, swallowed up by a kind of dreamy awe which from that day increased in me very greatly. All that was necessary to bring it on in more or less its full force was the sight of the Bible, its cover or open page, or its mere name, or the sight of a church, or the sound of any bell ringing solemnly, from Big Ben down to the bell of the Sunday muffin men.

The next extract refers to a period in Salisbury when Philip Parrish works eight hours a day in preparation for his Civil Service examination without too many lapses into dreaming. He closes his book at seven and goes walking and then reads. Although 'Milton and Wordsworth exalted me', he eventually buys a complete Byron for two shillings and reads *Childe Harold*.

I actually wanted someone to share the excruciating sad pleasure I got from some of the words. . . . Once I had desired a world made good and right and pure, as I conceived, by a Liberal statesman benevolent and omnipotent. Now I was in a perfect world of ocean, mountains and great waters, of mighty men mightily acting or speaking, Napoleon and Byron himself.

I had discovered that without which life must be worse than death. From that day onwards I was alive. I knew happiness. As I came down into Salisbury that day I knew for the first time that I had been happy. I used the word happy, repeating it to myself through the streets. When I came to the Market Cross I stopped. I had forgotten my way and had to look all round me slowly until I recognized the street which I had used a hundred times before. The fact is that I had never seen it, or known what I was seeing, until that day: . . . Above all the people were strange. The faces of all, of men more than women, and of dark men particularly, puzzled and fascinated and alarmed me. I saw eyes as unkindly as stuffed fox's. What must some of those mouths have said or done! There was something cabalistic about the bandy legs of a road sweeper, who stood with his back to me leaning on his outstretched broom as on a catamaran while he lit his pipe. . . . One beautiful face in a shop brought into my mind an undraped statue I had seen somewhere and we blushed together. And I believed that to others I who looked thus strangely upon them, I also was strange.

A feeling that I was horribly conspicuous made me wish to hide myself. For the people were no longer a negatively friendly element which the individual slid into and out of. . . . Perhaps I discerned something they had in common, but what I saw chiefly was that they were different from me. I was alone. I knew that I was alone, and I found myself saying over my name to myself to intensify my individuality to bring about a conviction that though alone I was strong. Thenceforward I was always wanting to take the joys of solitude and of society in their extreme forms, and was alternatively miserable from the lack of company or the presence of uncongenial company. I remember how both feelings entered into me in the course of one evening. . . . I walked into the town feeling like a pirate or Border robber descending upon capon-fed middlemen, moneylenders, retired or expecting to retire. But with the first dazzle of the lights all was changed. I was depressed. I had no magic that could open to me any one of those dark doors, lighted windows. I was alone and I hated it. I wanted men, yet I looked into the faces and with hatred.

The third section describes Parrish's success in the Civil Service examination and his growing disillusionment with his fellows and the vacuity of their leisure hours:

On hearing that I had a place among successful candidates I was excited with pleasure. I had won a race; I had gratified my aunt and uncle. Above all I was pleased to have assured myself an income exceeding that on which some men had written great poetry, others had done great deeds, many had been free and happy. That I did not care about my work was, I thought, an outrage. It could not get hold of me and stifle me; for it would employ only my hands and a certain section of my knowledge; the rest of me would be free: after office hours my escape would be absolute; and then the holidays would enable me, according to my powers and my wishes, to live another life as different as that of Jekyll from that of Hyde. I did not find, however, among my colleagues many who were conceivably poets, heroes, or exceptionally free men in their holidays and spare time. . . .

Already I think I found it painful to see so much vacuity without leisure, indolence without refinement. The young men of my own age twirling their canes, pushing into one another sideways, tilting one another's hats, made me angry—was it because they at least had achieved contentment, and I only contempt?

There was no misbehaviour. Every one else was virtually a special constable. . . . The women were better. They always had to be constrained in public, Sundays or not; and if anything they were less so on Sunday, when sometimes their clothes were pretty, and at least were seldom black, navy blue or grey as the men's were invariably. . . . I no longer saw them, indeed, as legless beings on self moving pedestals as I had done at Salisbury but from being so constantly restricted in movement it seemed that they must be incapable of movement. Perpendicular without intermission, taking steps of the same length at the same intervals, their arms hanging useless and helpless they were no better than trussed chickens but for their faces which, even in repose, suggested movement no less than a bird's wings. . . . Was I really different? Why could I never go about arm in arm with two or three others and stare at girls? But I could not be content just to walk alongside a pretty one and hear her giggling. In fact the whole scene of bare common and compact streets looked hopelessly inadequate for two sexes of a race that had produced Byron's poetry and might again do something like it. I was writing sonnets myself, but that did not satisfy me. I looked round for a living man to admire and follow. I used to remember that . . .

and there the *Fiction* ends.

The *Fiction* adds a little to one's understanding of what he was becoming in the eighteen months immediately before his courtship of Helen Noble. His passion for his cousin prefigures many subsequent unfulfilled arousals later in his life exactly as, in moments of heightened sensibility, he reveals an almost Puritan recoil from any way of life that was not earnest, spiritually fruitful, and socially useful. Yet he was not a prig. The *Fiction* captures an iron determination to undertake the hard work necessary to realize his own ideals. It suggests, too, the knife-edge path traversed by the adult writer between his overpowering response to physical and natural beauty and the self-defeating sense of unworthiness that he normally characterises, and displays, as a hampering shyness, a fear of rejection. In most of his literary reviewing, the fineness of his critical discrimination and the clarity with which he expresses it draws fruitfully on this special shyness. He refused to be dogmatic, occasionally wrote a modest puff for a friend, was incapable of brashness, and in judgement of people and books had the ability to suspend belief and disbelief. This last quality—encouraged by Ashcroft Noble—he had learned to recognize in himself during the period of growth between the boy naturalist of *The Childhood* and the much-sought-after undergraduate writer of Lincoln College who breathes freely through the ornate pages of his own *Oxford*.

Is the *Fiction* too slight a foundation to build on for some understanding of these intermediate years? Fortunately, in addition to Helen Thomas's absorbing, unselfconscious account of their courtship and the first years of their marriage, letters still survive which chart the growth of love. Here, in sequence, are quotations from Helen's letters to Janet Aldis:

Do you remember Janet?, when I saw you last I told you of a plan I had made, regarding the boy who father is taking up, and who writes Nature sketches. I think it will succeed although it will take ages, for he is fearfully shy, and I am likewise affected. He wants a girl friend and I want a boy friend, and as I like him (or at least what I know of him) and I *think* he likes me, I think it would be good for both of us if we could be friends. I wonder if we shall. (2 January 1896.)

I and the Thomas boy are very slowly making way. He wrote and asked father if I might go out with him on one of his long walks. To my surprise he said I might. So I was in a great state of elation. But to my disappointment Edward never turned up for me. And when he came last night and was asked the reason, he said he never dreamed I would be allowed to come. But he is going to take me some day this week to some lovely woods he knows. Last night I was in a furious rage because Edward asked me to go to his home this afternoon, and he would show me some flowers and nests he thought I would like to see. So I gladly consented. But that little plan was soon put a stop to, for mother would not let me go by myself, and there was nobody to go with me. Did you ever hear such awful tommyrot in your life? I call it very wrong. Mother says What would Mrs. Thomas think? I say if she thought till she was tired, she could not possibly think of any wrong. . . . Isn't it simply ludicrous? Here I am eighteen years old, and in a great state of elation because I was going out with a boy. It is disgusting and immoral and a disgrace. Why we may go walks together, and not go to his house where there is all his family I simply cannot imagine. It is too deep for me . . . I am going to ask Edward what his views on the subject will be. I rather think he will be very broadminded. He looked awfully amazed when mother said I could not go with him to see his books. (6 January 1896.)

Your remarks about Edward pleased too. Whatever made you think that the idea—of course quite impossible, though for the sake of argument we will not imagine it so—myself and Edward going away together was simply unconventional. Nothing was further from my thoughts; my reason would be simply enjoyment, and if it was the most commonplace thing to do my delight would not be decreased one bit. The novelty or improperness of the idea is not its alarm . . . You scoff at me and my 'one' man friend, you who have so many, but dear girl I have learnt more in the short time of my friendship with Edward, more of the world, of men as distinct from women, and man as an individual than in all my life I have learnt before. You and Osman, you and the Fry, though you have told me of your perfect freedom and exchange of ideas etc. were never freer than Edward and I. Sometimes I wonder that I can speak to him as I do, never before having known a boy, and having only you at times to 'let out' on. Already this freedom has benefited him, and when I know of the good I have done him, I feel that freedom is the only way to greater purity . . . All this is feeble no doubt, my words I mean. I only wish I had the power of putting down my thoughts in clear and sensible language. (27 July 1896.)

These quotations—and many more letters to Edward—amplify, in their chatty, less intense manner, the picture of early courtship recalled by Helen in 1924-6 in *As It Was* and *World Without End*. Edward acknowledges her effect on him in a letter—one of numerous happy, affectionate letters to 'My dearest Friend'—from his lodgings at 113 Cowley Road, Oxford, 29 January 1898 (the third of his letters to her after his return to Oxford for the Lent Term):

Take care of yourself my dearest friend. I often fear for you in many ways, quite unreasonably it may be. Don't go about much; no late returning in crowded streets from Earl's Court or elsewhere; no dissipating jabber and smoking and drinking with the Andrews [where Helen was employed]. *By the way, do you drink wine when I am not here?* I would much rather you did not. Probably you do not care enough for it to create a liking and a need, which we shall never be able to satisfy; nevertheless, avoid it unless principle and pleasure and interest all advise it.—It is my great resting place, that you are well: truly it is more than health to me, and gives me an untroubled fancy which is good for my work and my temper. Tell me therefore of it, little one. Even if I seem often cold in my letters and not noticing your words. I have not often coldness with you, sweet heart; yet I often feel that you teach me to love you. You remember, how once in my self-unconfidence, I asked you to take care of me until my age settled into true understanding of love? But I do love without limit or doubt, you only, your body and spirit and memory.

After Edward arrived in Oxford in October 1897, the regular correspondence between him and Helen gives a fairly full picture of his life until he and Helen and their eight-month-old son, Merfyn, settled temporarily in lodgings, first at Atheldene Road, Earlsfield and then, nearer to both their parental homes, at 7 Nightingale Parade, Balham. This same period is also covered by a series of long letters from Edward to Harry Hooton, an older man who had married Janet Aldis and, increasingly, by correspondence between Edward and Ian MacAlister, who became one of Edward's staunchest friends. (There are, too, some revealing letters from Helen to MacAlister.) But there are few definite sources for Thomas's activities—and even less for his thoughts, opinions, and attitudes—during the period between 30 March 1896, the end of his nature diary (the appendix to *The Woodland Life*), and his entry into Oxford. Helen Thomas's *As It Was* is a principal source. The brief memories written for R. L. Watson in the late 1940s by the poet's second and third brothers say nothing about this period.

Some of the experiences drawn upon in the *Fiction* belong to the blank period between October 1896 and January 1897, for which no letters from Edward and Helen survive. When the correspondence resumes in January 1897, the change of mood is evident from a letter Helen sent to Janet Aldis the previous November from Margate:

This letter is going to be devoted to my affairs in connection with Edward . . . the other day he asked me if I thought you would care to go for a walk into the country somewhere. I said I was sure you would, and gave him your address . . . He would not care to take you home to his house to tea, he hates his father so, but I suggested both going to our place, you will do this won't you? The little mother [Mrs Noble] would be so glad to see you both . . . He may be shy at first, but after a while he will get over that: he is not half so shy as he was, of course not.

The dear boy is very passionate, and his love for me making life now utterly happy, at the same time fills me with a sense of great responsibility. But the happiness would not be so intense were this feeling absent. Mother and lots of other people would say we were too young to love truly, they would have us wait for our 'years of discretion'; at what age one is supposed to be abnormally discreet I do not know, all I know is that I have not arrived there yet, and I hope I never will. I do not believe that youth is incapable of true and lasting love . . . I, since the time when I first became morally certain I was in love, seem to have grown years older . . . There is a purpose in living now, a sense of good in living which I did not know before.

I suppose we are what is called engaged, though it is different somehow. We at first wanted to know each other, then knowing became friends, and every day as our knowledge increased, greater liking, deeper sympathy, and so on to love and feeling our love, knowing it to be true, pure, and everlasting; then the desire for the perfect life of unity, and then of giving the world the benefit of our love by a little child. And so for that time we live now, both of us, and we are perfectly happy, and the waiting is not weary, but good and happy for us both.

We are young and youth is said to be fickle, mutable, and we have both looked at the possibility of ourselves not being exceptions to that supposed rule. We cannot imagine it, yet it is possible, and if such a change did come to one of us, there would be pain for both and merely afterwards friendship . . .

Edward never proposed to me, I never 'accepted' him, yet here we are just as much engaged and much more so than lovers of whom I have read. This love was the outcome of our friendship, just as our friendship was the outcome of our acquaintance; there was no break only a very gradual difference. I can hardly remember the first time I felt that we loved each other. It was all perfectly beautifully natural, like the blossoming of a flower.

Helen's mother wished her daughter to return home from the Webb family. There is a hint that the older people generally frowned on meetings between Edward and Helen similar to their innocent day at Horsmonden. Helen was planning to leave Mrs Webb—now safely delivered of her next child—and to seek employment in London and live at home. There was talk of sending Edward for a short health-restoring visit to Swindon. Having opened negotiations with the publishers Blackwood after Mr Noble's death and having agreed to their request that he should supplement his choice of eleven country essays with a diary of his observations 'in English fields and woods' from 1 April 1895 to 30

March 1896, he was busy reading the final proofs of *The Woodland Life*. The nature of his ill health is undisclosed but his 'wild discontent' was finally healed by two events. The first was Helen's return to 6 Patten Road for a ten-day holiday before she began work in London as governess to Horst, the young son of M. and Mme Roman who lived at the Hotel Metropole. The second, referred to obscurely in Helen's last letter from Margate, was Mr Thomas's decision that Edward should not take up a Civil Service post, but instead prepare himself for an Oxford entrance scholarship. Probably Edward, like Parrish in the *Fiction,* had done extremely well in the Civil Service examination and this evidence of his academic ability, together with the favourable critical reception of *The Woodland Life,* convinced his father that Edward was now worthy of financial support. There is no firm evidence either way. Helen never intended her *As It Was* to be an accurate account of their young lives, and there are no letters because they met often. From February '97 onwards Helen is helping him to buy some newly needed textbooks. In April, while on a protracted stay with Janet's parents in Walsall, she complains of his extremely hard work, and in early May she first states that he is working for Oxford entrance.

By now a new restriction had been placed on their friendship by both parents. Helen's new employers departed mysteriously and suddenly, and Helen was sent to Rugby almost at once to help Mrs Sery, an 'excitable, merry French Woman', with her young son. She stayed a week and then joined Janet Aldis for an indefinite visit at her parents' home in Walsall, where Mr Aldis was a housemaster at Queen Mary's School. Returning Edward the proofs of his book, Helen commented: 'This has indeed been a fair spring for us, though they had made it a winter. Poor fools, how can Winter come, when we love.' When she arrived at Walsall, she informed Edward that Mrs Noble, after sending her earlier a 'vulgar and jeering' letter in which 'She does her best to make me doubt you', had forbidden them to meet or correspond until Helen reached years of discretion—her twenty-first birthday on 11 July 1898. Helen regretted giving her consent, because she intended to see Edward and to write to him. She hated even more the absence of honest dealing with her mother. Eventually she gave her mother an undertaking for a limited period and hoped Edward would agree. 'We must hope before you go to Oxford mother will have relented enough at any rate to make writing to you possible.' Edward agreed. He had often, in their earlier correspondence, spoken of a test or ideal that he wished to impose on himself as a rein on his passionate temperament and his over-eager response to

physical beauty and joy. He explained to Helen the painful discomfort of
his frequent erections while they walked together and his determination
to avoid masturbation. The absence of any letters between them from
mid-July until October suggests that they deliberately refrained from
regular letter writing for a time. After early May, Mrs Noble relented to
some extent. Helen was called home to help her sister, Irene, in her
employment and during this ten-week secretarial stint she and Edward
met frequently on the Common as Helen returned from her work. But
difficulties were placed in their way. Helen, having once given her word,
was uneasy about their infrequent meetings and pleaded with him to
support her resolve:

We both have work to do, we each have a duty, yours your work, mine to help
my Mother, and surely our love will help us more than anything to do well.
And our love does not depend on anything, though for years we saw nothing of
each other, still we should love. And I feel if now we deny ourselves our
greatest delight and say our love alone shall make us strong, our strength shall
not depend on anything but our love then indeed I think we shall be creating
an independence of each other, which can only make our binding sympathy
more perfect. . . . For the present, for the 14 months before I am 21 then I have
after much real thought, much consideration decided that it wouild be best for
both of us to be separated . . . I have not a strong mind, or will, nor am I unsel-
fish, and so knowing well my faults I ask you to help me. Consider it all well,
look into yourself, and tell me soon how you feel. Write to me that is best . . .
Come here to see me if you will; mother asks you, and I want you, but it is for
you to come or not as you feel best, or as you like.

Edward accepted the immediate need to support Helen's decision and
maintain Mrs Noble's good opinion of him. A few hasty notes in July
show that he continued to visit 6 Patten Road, and occasionally to have
dinner there, until their separation became a reality, when Helen took
up a resident post as governess with the Wards, at 33 Bath Road,
Bedford and Edward spent August with his father's relations at 17
Woodville Street, Pontardulais, while his younger brothers became
pupils at a small denominational school in Ammanford. In September,
when Edward had any spare time and Helen was free from work, they
met frequently at the National Gallery, where they examined minutely
Greek male and female statues, or at Janet's lodgings. Mindful of the
gaps in his reading, and aware of the range of books in Mr Noble's
library now denied to him, Edward and Helen scoured the second-hand
bookshops for bargains and texts necessary for his matriculation test in
October. The serious business of gaining an Oxford scholarship and

some measure of financial independence had begun and, for a time, gave
Edward the drive necessary to matriculate easily as a non-collegiate
student at Oxford, to live in lodgings there, and to attend a full course of
lectures to prepare himself for an entrance scholarship to Balliol,
Merton, or Lincoln. The self-discipline and lessened dependence on
each other that Helen had hoped for had had some effect on Edward, as
his first letter to Helen from his Oxford lodgings shows:

My dearest friend,
    As yet I can do little more than write comfortable letters containing matter
of fact and ordinary news. For I have so far lived almost wholly the outer life
which is so distressing to think of and to endure. Never, perhaps, have I so lived
for such a long time together. The cause of it is evident enough: such a call on
my brains merely; and of my brains, only that portion which says one and one
made three, says how do you do, says I will now dine. But it is evident it will
soon alter. When I am settled, there is no reason why my life should not be as
placid, and there is much reason why it should be far more placid, than at
home. Until then I wait. Until then my writing to you, my own sweet little
one, must taste even as harsh as my conversation and look now are . . .
    I cannot even tell you how my work will be though I know very certainly
that it will demand long attention if I am to pass Responsions and get a
scholarship. Therefore you will understand short rare letters. (17 October 1897.)

The period of epistolary self-restraint lasted until the beginning of
1898. The schoolboy writer of nature articles had found a new purpose
around which to weave his dreams of a future with his 'anemone
maiden'.
    As his own free reading expanded, with greater leisure and the wealth
of Mr Noble's books, he had begun to match his nature writings against
the ideal world of the nineteenth-century English poets. In one notebook (dated 24 April to 22 June 1897) he had first written an essay on
the 'London Night' and then wrote across it,

This is a mere exhibition of my inability to write plain prose, and more
terribly, my impotence . . . Now I am off to write my sonorous senselessness in
prose. I wonder shall I ever delight, touch, or interest one human soul that is
strange to me? That vanity about captivating girls with my account of the wild
flower is long past. With all my heart I hope for the failure of that first book—
no, volume, of mine, from beginning to end not trash, but heartless pretence.
Do they prate of observation? My dull eyes were better out, than thus to walk
through life, a sort of inferior lynx, a moral mole, or bat.

Such self-disgust appeared to have physical causes or manifestations: a pattern that was to repeat itself at irregular intervals for the next twenty years. In an earlier notebook, dated 10 March '97, he recorded:

My limbs fall in, tremble, yield, I am a wreck, even of what I was last Spring. Today I started under a rainbow, towards one of those western panoramas of pure cloud that rest there in vain, but could not reach. It is hard. For the spirit still is bright and swift, the eye capable of all delight; but what can that avail, when I cannot, here, in the street, submit to my impulse or sensation, but must be a creature of body, where the body is all, the spirit in subjection to it? If I look up to the blue sky, as yet I must when it is blue and bright suddenly, it is in spite of the heavy limb and relaxing back that will drag me down or cause me to hasten home.

Already, at the age of nineteen, he was experiencing the morbidity which occasionally harrassed him and which he described sixteen years later in a chapter on the 'Character' of Keats:

He was himself the first discoverer of that 'morbidity of temperament'. That he did discover it, that he had a wonderful self-knowledge—not mere self-analysis—calm and penetrating, never coldly submissive, is a proof that it was not the whole truth. The morbidity was the occasional overbalancing of his intense sympathy, his greatest passive power. . . . He was for 'a delicious diligent indolence', for a passiveness allowing the intellectual powers to come very gradually to ripeness. When he was in a room with people, unless he was following a definite thought, he was so open to their influence that the identity of everyone pressed on him and annhilated him: . . . At one time he left off animal food, as he said, that his 'teeming brain' might not be in a greater mist than was natural to it. And there seems no doubt that this intense life of the mind often reached a point either of aching or of languor. The word 'ache' is one of his constant, significant words.

This perceptive study makes it clear that Thomas refused to accept the 'morbidity of temperament' as the only key to understanding the man. There is so much of Keats that he admired—his pugnacity, his social concern, his gusto, his direct presentation of the moment's phases of mind and moods of temperament—that one becomes aware of the impress of Thomas's own mind and experience through his comments on Keats: 'Because he was then in the midst of his greatest period, and had to find vent for the pressure of poetry within him, he had to live away from Fanny Brawne, at Shanklin and Winchester: had he been near her long, at this time, love and poetry together, not to speak of the 'hateful literary chit-chat' of Hampstead, would have been insupportable. When he wrote verses directly to her he proved it.'

Keats was written rapidly at Selsfield House in 1913 some months before he began his work there on the *Childhood* and the *Fiction*. Reliving Keats' love for Fanny Brawne, Thomas (away from home and family) was tapping the subterranean channels of his own courtship and early days as a writer. Except in his early letters to Helen, his reticence about his passionate courtship is almost complete—a fact that may explain, if not excuse, the coldness with which many of his friends and family received Helen's slightly idealized accounts of their life together in *As It Was* and *World Without End*. His yearning letters to her from Wales and Oxford corroborate amply her direct narrative of their passionate, loving sexuality. She remembered incidents vividly and, when she wrote her books, she had their letters to each other and all his notebooks (most of which are now in the Berg Collection), carefully dated between November '95 and June '97. The first four are mainly nature observations similar to the Diary printed in *The Woodland Life*. They record on 9 January 1896, 'Richmond with HN' and that 1896 'opened mild with song of Robin and blithe-heart Blackbird', that in April and early May he was 'at Surrey' and the next month he paid visits to Chipstead and Horsmonden. He noted his reading and his earnings: 'Thoreau I am now reading with interest and pleasure. "There can be no very black melancholy to him who lives in the midst of Nature and has his senses still." (*Walden*).' Typically, he notes a list of payments received for journalism, in the first half of 1896: *Globe*—4 guineas for 4 items; *Speaker*—£14.15.0 for 7 items; and *New Age* five at 10/6 each. The fourth and fifth notebook record an extended period (13 June to 14 November 1896) spent successively at London, Horsmonden, Mumbles, Langland Bay, Carswell Bay, Bishopston, and Pwll Du [Gower], and then September spent at Pontardulais. On his return to London he makes the following comment on the period 8 to 14 November, presumably spent with Helen Noble: 'The holiest and best of pleasures. It cannot be forgotten or surpassed though gone for ever. All life quickens. Mine most of all. Why should I not be proud. But I must be. This heat makes me so. Envy and lust and wrong cannot reach such moods.'

Thomas discussed the relationship between love and poetry much later in *Feminine Influence on the Poets*: 'The love-poem is not for the beloved, for it is not worthy, as it is the least thing that is given to her, and none knows this better than she unless it be the lover. . . . It may open with desire of woman, but it ends with unexpected consolation or with another desire not of woman.' He recalls, without explicit statement (though their letters affirm it), the way in which he and Helen interwove poetry with their own voyages of mutual discovery:

We treat them [poems] as parts written for ourselves to act, in the spirit, as they were written by the poet, in the spirit. There is much of the poetry of Shelley and of Spenser, for example, written since they knew a woman, which has no mention of woman, and yet is full of love and fit to awaken and to satisfy love. . . . At this time when youth is most exultant, this poetry is thumbed night and day; a page is opened at random, as Virgil used to be, for a word big with fate.

This is still (in 1910) the unmistakable voice of his early letters to Helen: it confirms the 'David' portrayed in *As It Was*. During their courtship they believed that his true future was to be a poet. Like his father, Edward was a born teacher, and he guided Helen's reading further into his own thorough knowledge of Wordsworth, Shelley, and Byron. Apart from Dickens, their prose reading reflected the radical attitudes of their Unitarian upbringing: Hazlitt, Carlyle, Cobbett, Ruskin, and William Morris besides numerous progressive pamphlets. The influence of Pater—which lies beneath Edward's undergraduate article on the 'Frontiers of English Prose' with its carefully argued refusal to draw distinctions between prose and poetry—developed during his first non-collegiate year at Oxford. Six months before he sat his Final Schools examination, he recorded the change he had observed in '*My Writing*—it seems daily to become poorer though my mind is slowly growing. My letters perhaps improve [these were chiefly those sent to Helen, Harry Hooton and Ian MacAlister], and perhaps indicate the line of my future efforts. But as it is I feel before the world as Sidney before Stella (Sonnet L)

> So that I cannot chuse but write my mind,
> And cannot chuse but put out what I write.'

This twin need to find adequate expression for his own nature, and to share it with others, remained constant for the rest of his life.

CHAPTER 4

The Long Green Day: Oxford 1897–1898

'In Oxford nothing is the creation of one man or one year'; the subtle blend of antiquity and urgent immediate concerns masks the change that nine (or twelve) short terms can make upon the most transient undergraduate. Edward Thomas was no exception to his own precept. A month before he went up in 1897 his father's first cousin (and namesake) had been struck by the lad's awkward manners, silent gaucherie, unsuitable dress, and down-covered chin; three years later Edward returned the visit in a colours blazer, accompanied by his wife and his eight-months-old son. He was now an Oxford graduate with a second class Honours degree awarded in the History schools, who had published a series of papers in London journals during his Oxford career. These were obvious external changes. The less apparent development of character and literary ambition seems adequately chronicled in numerous surviving letters to Helen Noble and to Harry Hooton, soon to be the husband of Janet Aldis. Edward early knew the deficiency of his letters to Hooton: 'It is a weariness to fumble for truth and completeness, and after all to feel the failure at both. Living words alone could speak plain. Truly my living words could vindicate me; ask Helen, if they would not.'

The necessary complement to the epistolary picture of his Oxford life is his own book *Oxford*, published three years after he came down. There his intense affection for the place, its people, its buildings and its surrounding countryside still shines clearly, although Thomas's Oxford is grossly distorted for us today.

Some time ago . . . in a high attic I heard once again the laud or summons or complaint of bells. . . . Once again I felt the mysterious pleasure of being in an elevated Oxford chamber at night, among cloud and star,—so that I seemed to join in the inevitable motion of the planets,—and as I saw the sea of roofs and horned turrets and spires I knew that, although architecture is a dead language, here at least it speaks strongly and clearly, pompous as Latin, subtle as Greek.

No one can walk much in the Oxford country without becoming a Pantheist. . . . Everywhere the fancy, unaided by earlier fancies, sets to work very busily in these fields. I have on several afternoons gone some way towards the beginning of a new mythology, which might in a thousand years puzzle the Germans. The shadowy, half-apprehended faces of new deities float before my eyes, and I have wondered whether Apollo and Diana are not immortal presences wheresoever

there are awful trees and alternating spaces of cool or sunlit lawn. . . . Often I
saw a clean-limbed beech, pale and slender, yet firm in its loftiness, that shook
delicately arched branches at the top, and below held out an arm on which a
form of schoolboys might have sat,—rising out of fine grass and printing its
perfect outlines on the sky,—and I could fancy it enjoyed a life of pleasure that
was health, beauty that was strength, thought that was repose.

From his digs at 113 Cowley Road, Thomas wrote his first letter to
Harry Hooton: 'My dear Mr. Hooton, I matriculated today before the
Vice-Chancellor of the University, and, in consequence, I am left a little
freer of time and heart: for until then, I feared failure in what turned
out to be the easy matric. exam., and worked to the exclusion of almost
all else: which is the explanation of time and heart.' It was the formal
beginning of a lifelong friendship with 'someone more sure and staid',
eight years his senior. During his first term at Oxford Hooton received
long letters on a wide range of topics. They uncover the gap left in
Thomas's intellectual development by the death of Ashcroft Noble and
his own sense of the inadequacy of his preparation for the nine terms
spent at University between October 1897 and his final viva voce examination in July 1900. 'You will purge me and my mood, as my Pater used
to purge my writing of its excess. . . . Restless that I am, I often pray that
someone would cage and rule me entirely. Just as, in writing, I think
little men should be bound to mere journeyman work . . . I have
changed out of the paternal democracy into a conservatism that believes
in Caesar, Pope and the fierce God of Battles—almost.' Many more revelations and assertions were to follow.

He spent the first three terms as a non-collegiate student (a 'tosher'),
preparing himself for Responsions by means of three hours' daily tuition
directed towards entrance scholarships to Balliol in November and
Merton in January (which he failed to win), and then to Lincoln College,
which he won easily in March 1898 because of the mature quality of his
style and approach in the general essay paper. He had failed Responsions
twice, in December and April before the Lincoln examination and he
knew that if he did not pass in June his Oxford career, in spite of his
entrance scholarship, would end abruptly. Edward overworked in his
lonely digs—'the first time I ever truly worked'—and in these early letters
to Hooton he discovered new qualities in his nature. ('Would you believe
me if I called myself a Puritan? I admire the Puritan and Puritanism; and
so far, my maidenly debauchery of habit still leaves me a Puritan in life.
This, however, becomes sheer self-description.') He passed Responsions
that June and began to look forward to the payments he would get for

1. The Thomas Family when Edward was at St Paul's School, c. 1894–5. From left to right: his father, Julian, Ernest, Edward, Reggie, Oscar, Dory (Theodore), and his mother.

2. Edward Thomas on his twentieth birthday, a non-collegiate student at Oxford.

his journalism—especially for his 'prose poems' in the *Speaker*. He and Helen were planning to save money for their future life together.

Six papers had been accepted for publication during his first Oxford year, but he was as little pleased with them as with *The Woodland Life*: 'I am impatient to get to Lincoln College' he wrote to Hooton. 'One thing I hope to get there—religion. I find such a need of that, as an informing spirit in all I do and am. If I can be serious enough, I hope to find satisfaction in the Church of England: it will be my fault if I don't. I want, as Milton says in those pathetic closing lines of his Epic, "a place of rest" . . . I am too doubtful about my own writing to think of making an effort towards completing another volume. I shall wait. Perhaps some good will come of rivalry and comparisons—if there is any for me—at College. I hope so. I have need of such comparison, otherwise my writing is of a hothouse type.' At the end of July, with Responsions successfully behind him as well as a happy celebratory birthday outing for Helen spent with Harry and Janet, Edward was still as hesitant as in his early letters to Hooton: 'May I bring a paper in manuscript and talk it over with you? I am so discontented with my work. Other people's approbation and censure is all insipid and uncritical, so does not help; and I have no ground for confidence in myself. Without my capacity for perseverance in such work as mere dictionary reading, I should despair. I am constantly called a fool, because I have not that literary indigestion which throws up what it feeds on, every week or so.'

He had come a long way, he believed, since the *Speaker* paper (October 1897), 'Shadows of the Hills'. An evocation of his previous summer holiday in Pontardulais, it was the first of many papers about the half-fantasy Malory-like character of a knight called Basil of the Woods or the Knight Solitary: 'all very sublime but a little uninteresting to everyone but myself. As a child of 16, I was supposed to have some gift of description; now I have not a particle of descriptive power. . . . It all rests upon a possible impressionableness in me, and relies a good deal on mystery or mist.' The allegory in 'Shadows of the Hills' is crystal-clear, in spite of the involved style: 'For Nature took him and held him fast like a jealous lover . . . But he might not always meet her calling or her waiting, for men, too, were bidding him to the sound of axe and plough and sword.'

Thomas found himself ill-equipped to answer this bidding call effectively:

This doubt of myself is the more powerful, because I see how all along my senses are so powerful. Everything affects my senses and thereby my soul;

nothing my mind, and thereby my soul. I am impressed like a child by grand
size, grand sound, vastness in anything, infinity: that sums me up. I am like the
cow at the sea shore, bound by the motion of the waves. I am like the child
spell-bound by the accumulated powers of the night,—darkness, the sound of
silence, loneliness, infinite possibility, all mingled in a vast horror. That is what
touches me. In my affections it was the same. I do not mean a sexual strength—
of that I have little—but a union of all my senses simply carries me past all
reflection, sometimes into a beautiful ease, sometimes into filth and futility . . .
But always I am passive. Open to all the influences of Nature and man, but
giving little: running like a senseless stream . . . All I want my writing to be is
modest, restrained, colourful, truthful. . . . For me, I think the last paragraph in
my paper in the *Speaker* of the week before last ['Shadows of the Hills'] was
pretty good; but it ought to be in verse. It is a sort of Addendum to
Wordsworth's 'Ode'—but very erratic and only half true.

He was still writing verses but, according to Hooton's notes, he abandoned them at the end of this year under the influence of Pater. In these
letters to Harry he frequently mentions his excessive response to beauty
in men, women, and children. He had discussed it often with Helen and
both had agreed that such frankness was a necessary act of truth-telling
between them. Even if their love were to die, nothing should disturb
their friendship. A letter to Hooton, describing an early November
Sunday walk in uncongenial company, introduces the topic naturally
and typically:

The only alleviating point in the walk was the number of pretty women and
girls; so as I delight in looking at such, I very rudely looked into the eyes of
those that passed. And I never want really to go beyond looking at them. . . . It
always has been so with me, and will be. Also, in my thought it is neither
vulgar nor stupid.—I get an extraordinary pleasure thus. And let me explain
what I meant by that silly passage in my last letter, about expensively dressed
girls. It was this. My cousins are rather wealthy, and so wear rich dresses, which
I am never tired of hearing—oh, those sounding silks, so uncomfortable, so
gorgeous. Yet I like comfortable dresses, too: why not? All I don't like is, rags, ill
taste, ill-shapes. . . . My feeling for girls has still the same nervous reverence of
childhood or earliest boyhood, rather increased if anything, and only too excessive to be chivalrous. In my childish days I remember I used to fear to touch the
little girls' sleeves; so it is now. If I retain any true innocence it is here.

Impulses of attraction towards beautiful forms or faces troubled him
frequently for the next two years at Oxford. He saw no inconsistency
between such temporary infatuations and the matrimonial ideal he presented now to Hooton, as he had already discussed it with Helen: 'I am

not at all sure that there is anywhere a loftier, while there could be no sweeter, perfection than that of a household'. Helen, too, was frequently informed of his over-readiness to fall in love with an attractive outward appearance, even as he constantly restated his heavy dependence upon his engrossed love for her:

We men, we know not what loftiness we might reach if only for a few small hours we could by carefulness of life, morally and physically so exact ourselves that scarce any utmost purity of air were too perfect for us. Perfect we cannot be, either by accident or ignorance (like your sweet ignorance, little one), or by strenuous effort; but we can be so near perfection that, from our present and ordinary level, that nearness would seem perfection itself. Sweetheart you can almost do this. You can. Nevertheless do not tell me of it, even to confirm me; for it is what we cannot analyse or arrange, any more than the rich simplicity of childhood.

His letters to Helen range freely, without the stilted asides of his early long letters to Hooton. They are a genuine substitute for the talk and shared companionship that was missing from his first year at Oxford.

For during this first term the long regular letters to Harry Hooton appear to be a substitute for letters to Helen and a roundabout way of informing her of his progress. Mrs Noble, he said, thought him completely immoral and his own parents were chary of allowing Helen to visit him in his study bedroom at Shelgate Road as she used to do, although, he informed Harry, 'Mother knows Helen so well and likes her so much.' One of Mr Thomas's conditions, supported by Mrs Noble, was that Edward and Helen should not correspond when he left for Oxford, and they agreed to this for the first term. They made plans to meet in Harry's room sometimes during the Christmas Vacation which Edward devoted to intense preparations for an entrance scholarship to Merton and continuous work at Latin and Mathematics for Responsions. Besides he read Meredith, Hardy, Pater, Jefferies, some Flaubert ('for my French is fairly good'), and began a more careful study of German. When he and Helen could spend time alone, their passionate unconsummated loving convinced him that but for the 'rich simplicity of childhood' that characterized her, her 'capacity for content', her 'virginity of sentiment and soul', their love-making would be dangerous, 'if my nature were more masculine and daring'. The consistency of her love still surprised him. He was consumed with desire for the possession to come and whenever he could he tried to add to the 45/- in the Post Office Savings Bank so that they could spend some time away together with Dad Uzzell. She, he found, 'though bold, how modest . . . just as when first I kissed at your sweet asking, little one, by the winter gorse'. 'I seem to expect the whole happiness and sweetness to come from you', he wrote as he warned Helen that she should find a real need for patience with him. Already, after a few months' acquaintance, he complained to Harry of 'this hideous analysis which so masters me' and he tried to express Helen's profound effect upon him: 'I always wonder when I look at her or think of her. I don't know why—or care. But I always wonder, as if a film had been taken from my eyes and I saw new worlds.'

As always in his letters (even to Helen) self-scrutiny creeps in—one aspect of the puritan streak he recognized in his own nature:

How vain I feel is an attempt for me with all my weight of immorality and worry and dull (not bad) health to sweeten you who are so pure and without care and of bright health. Ignoble creature that I am! Yes, sweetheart, I feel it in several ways; by contrast, for example, with my idyllic dreaming of two or three years ago; there is a change. Not a change of nature, I hope, and believe: still, a development as the World calls it, though I can not think it is development for the better. My youth flies from me, so. No more can I find, if not content, yet a gorgeous enjoyment, in mere dreams, where men have no past. As to dreams, day dreams, not only do they no longer impose upon me an innocent belief, but they become less glorious, less real, less natural, and less frequent. This I perceive plainly. And you? It must be that you also perceive it. Surely you see a difference between me, who wrote long, incoherent, and enthusiastic letters, enjoyed perfectly the songs of birds and the sight of a sundown, believed in the possibility of perfect happiness, perfect beauty, perfect purity, and a perfect world, all perfected, too, by that thing Nature which was so real to me; a difference between me then and thus, and what I am now, dull unenthusiastic, unimaginative, but more coherent and prudent, though still imprudent enough to write such things as that Sonnet, which even you esteem bad, I think. . . . One other thought I will write . . . you are even now as you were, and ever must be, beautiful, pure and passionate. I say this last, only because it is at the bottom of my mind, deep hid and permanent, not because it is least.

As the Lent term progressed, besides his letters to Helen and Harry (containing verses, some of which survive) and his quick recovery from his failure to gain an entrance scholarship to Merton, he had renewed an acquaintance with MacAlister—an old Pauline friend—who visited him each Sunday. Although feeling hard-pressed by the prospect of Responsions (for four days) followed a week later by the Lincoln entrance examination, he became more confident of a future life as an Oxford student and eager to extend his male friendships and meet the challenge of competition from his equals and betters. Between the two examinations he spent a few necessary days of recuperation at Swindon, spending some time with Dad Uzzell. The letter quoted above was begun at Didcot Station, then continued at his Cowley Road digs, and rounded off at the end of the first day of the Scholarship exam after six hours of hard writing. Were he to fail he would be ashamed to show his face at home 'because all failure is probably due to my own indolence and lacking self-control to help myself out of day-dreaming.' After a request for stamps, he describes a few enjoyable, healthy hours out of doors walking with Dad from ten to three without a rest:

We met a country girl, pale faced, delicate, tall, wrapped up to her neck in winter clothes & feeling cold in spite of all; her eyes were timid & weak; evidently she was suffering as girls do, & was going out to get the fresh air. She hardly dared answer the old man's 'Good Morning', and as for me, I expect she was afraid of me. I had such queer desires to speak to her, to give her my flowers, to kiss her hand,—but did not of course, partly from cowardice, partly because she, however innocent, would probably be afraid; and the old man was there, too. But how I longed to be gallant, as they say; to ask her if I might kiss her on both cheeks if I gave her my two violets. Silly that I am! But I am at least honest in this. All simple & partly lovely women attract me, & not merely attract me, but I want to be something to them. Not a dangerous disposition I think; though it might be if my nature were more masculine & daring. Why! I should have been as timid as the girl herself, if she had looked at me! You are not angry or jealous, are you? I could excuse you if you were, too. Tell me if you think it bad. For you know I often wonder what sort of morality it is that keeps men from anything but superficial intercourse with any woman but their wives: yet I hate adultery & all the intermediate stages; and what men of free habits in this way I have known, I have detested. Suffice it, that I had a few moments of fanciful pleasure. I ran back half a mile of road to get a glimpse of her in the distance, though we had passed her half an hour before, & of course she was out of sight on the Downs. She was not at all good-looking, or graceful, or winning, but a mere maiden; possibly not even a country girl, but a London servant at the great house of Burdcrop nearby.

His letters from Oxford in his third term, after gaining the Lincoln History Exhibition, are much shorter, less introspective, and full of details about his writing, his plans for the future, his increased reading but, above all, his growing friendship with MacAlister who felt that 'his intimate outpouring to me was something of a comfort to him'. They talked endlessly at MacAlister's rooms in Merton, where Thomas could also measure himself against two further acquaintances, Fyffe and

Wharton. At last he began to sense that when he entered Lincoln he would keep his end up in spite of the sketchy nature of his post-Pauline preparation for the Oxford Final History Honours School. MacAlister summed up his special quality: 'While I knew more in my narrowly specialised subjects, he was far above me intellectually and in general maturity of mind.' It was a quality often recalled by Oxford contemporaries. 'Three of us were elected to Exhibitions at the same time, and I recall the maturity of his literary powers as contrasted with the callow essays we had to take up to Owen M. Edwards each week.' (Norman G. Brett-James, later Bursar at Lincoln.) MacAlister proved an ideal walking companion on the weekends as they explored Bagley Wood, Godstow Nunnery, the elmy hills of Cumnor and Radbrook, the churchyard at Hinksey with its elms against the sunset. Everywhere, Thomas later recalled, 'a suspected presence of a hidden melodist' as a conversation 'would grow and blossom between Headington and Wheatley or Osney and Eaton.'

His briefer letters to Harry Hooton—avoiding those 'terrible letters I used to throw at you last term as it might be from the fruitless monotony of this place'—now explain his reading. As yet he had not succumbed completely to the seductive prose of Pater and was reading the 'artificial but interesting *Marius*' side by side with Scott, Meredith, Hardy's *Jude,* and Flaubert's letters. He was attracted to the latter's extravagant precepts on style, in contrast to Pater: 'What a small man Pater is. He is always *talking* about style: he has yet words of the absurdest that occur in every page, bland, delicate, dainty; one blushes to read them.' Thomas could now look back on the papers he had begun, or completed and sold in his first two terms, as 'vain stuff' but he continued to write verses, which were sent to Harry and Helen. He detected a slackening off in his examination work, once he had gained his Exhibition—'a moral weakness, neglect of order in my work and play'; often these 'moods' sent him back to his digs almost beside himself. The only cure for the 'silliness of his brain' was to return to reading, or to write an article. He read Johnson's Dictionary because he felt (from Flaubert) that he needed 'a scientific and accurate vocabulary' and, when further stimulated by *Marius,* he asked Helen to read his recent papers aloud to discover if the 'sounds jar'. To her he confessed that he hoped residence at Lincoln would banish his 'moods' and in the same letter he reflected on his own mother's 'love and uncertainty, in her melancholy unconfident way'. Above all, despite frequent irritation with Helen over trivial expenses and her unbusinesslike attitude to her wages, he relied heavily on her temper, 'her genius for joy', to help him break free of these moods. He is 'loyal only to Nature in a vague way'; he reads obscene books and then worries at frequent seminal emissions. 'My nature is fickle—a little insane—and entirely barren in soul' and in these 'moods of distrust' he needs her love. 'How utterly you love life. Nothing lies hidden in you.' As the term draws to an end, his desire for her dominates his letters. He faces their need to use contraceptive devices, but is ignorant of the facts. ('This century, thinks too much, certainly talks too much, of love. Human beings need many things as well as love, if not more.') When Edward invited Harry to Oxford for Eights Week he informed him of his expectations from Lincoln College. In such moments of confession he frequently strikes a prophetic note about his future life as a writer. There is no hint that he would ever abandon his decision to earn his living as a writer. On this he was adamant and unswerving, however much his father might extol the supreme chance at Oxford to make contacts for a future career, as yet undefined.

Edward's first year at Oxford, with its long hours of set daily lectures and prepared reading, its loneliness punctuated by long walks, longer letters, and occasional forays in search of new friendships, formed a gentle transition from the two years of freedom he had enjoyed, since leaving St. Paul's, towards the severer demands that family and social demands were to make upon him. Here were the seeds of inner conflict that were never completely resolved and here, too, especially in his next five terms of collegiate life, Oxford offered him opportunities of escape from the worries of ordinary living. His letters to Helen, in particular, uncover the head for business, the punctilious sense of irritable rightness, and the concomitant sudden bouts of self-distrust that marched alongside his desire for an extended life of idealized perfection, similar to the intense moments of joyful peace he had discovered for himself during walks. He finds his own words for the mood in a letter to Helen on 6 May '98: 'I am glad my unkind letter allowed you nevertheless to write me so sweet a reply, and besides, to be so sweet tempered, and, as I hope, unhurt save for a moment. It was of course not anger. Did I use the word? It was irritation, doubtless the result of some ill doing or extravagance on my own part, making me hate to see its image elsewhere. Yet, as I said, you are not extravagant, I am. That is enough.'

The unkind letter he refers to gives an informed introduction to their subsequent life together and is here given in full with its immediate predecessor. Together they form the best picture of their love as Edward described it to Harry before his life at Lincoln began: 'For some reason or another we are happier now than ever before. It is a happiness so mild and cool that it is like a kind of saintliness after passion: yet it is not satiety . . . for if she has any unhealth, it is from me; and that more of her lips than in her heart.'

113 Cowley Road.
2. v. '98.

The little blue flower, 'robin-run-in-the-hedge', which probably looked like violet on the first, distant glance, is *ground ivy.*

My dearest friend,

And did you have a happy May day? With all the flowers—and the birds—and the presence of the Sea, the purity & brightness of your own heart could surely make a day nearly perfect. I only hope it did not rain, as, for most of the daylight, it did here. Night at any rate you had fine, as we had, with a high clear moon & just a few stars lost here & there among folds of cloud. So I am desiring, though not more than half expecting, a letter tomorrow morning to hear how you spend your day, &, because you were certainly happy, in what ways you directed your happiness. A thousand pities that the child who was probably with you is not something nearer perfection! And I reflect that if you remember to post early, the letter will come here by the first post! I spent a crowded lonely day. It was so funny—as I walked along, rather disconsolate in the rain, at midday, I suddenly recollected it was Mayday, & knowing I ought to be bright & rejoicing I forthwith was so, at least for a time. You with a mind full only of natural & unembarrassing thoughts, & of me, probably awoke early and remembered & rejoiced; perhaps you had even prepared for it, & went happy walks, singing, garlanded. I am almost glad I was not there, lest I should have spoiled your tranquillity. It would have been a richer joy—but, indeed, as I so often tell you, I delight to picture you in a childlike serenity. I hope it was yours.

With all the crowding work, and a little pleasure, too, I would have written to you yesterday, only I partly feared to, because I had a proposal to make, which it would have been unseemly to make the apparent cause of my haste. It was this—you have now, or should have, at least a sovereign left out of your monthly pay & what survived of the 15/- from the Bank; so is it not best to send it all to me at once? Your expenses, beyond stamps, which I can provide for you, will be nothing, I suppose, at Sandgate—no railway fares, &c &c. If this seems well—& why not?—pray send at once. Only, by the way, I see a large number of Scotts here, uniform with yours & mine, at only 1/- each, yet quite clean & good, & not incomplete like those in bookseller's row; of which, would you care for me to buy one or two—Ivanhoe, Nigel &c? I wish I could buy them myself, & had hoped to; but the *Speaker* rejection makes it impracticable. By the way I shall send another paper to Perris at the end of the week. Shall I send this old friend (or enemy)? You see it is much altered, filed and shaped.

Please return it at once, or when sending the postal order. As to the one I sent in before, it was written so quickly, that it could not be good. Perhaps I shall never rewrite it. It is *all* obscure, & *not* purposely either. By the way also, I have begun the Tristram & Isould story, today, after much hesitation, with a snatch of talk between Kheydius & Palomides. I hope I shall be able to compress it sufficiently.

You do seem to be fortunate in going to Sandgate. What a place it is! Here I see few flowers, save such as water bubbles, though the fields & country generally are the richest I have ever seen. I fancy you like a queen—a princess rather—in all those flowers. Would that I were fit to woo you as what you seem & are, sweet heart! Now goodbye! do I not seem happy, or at least sordidly content? Never mind! You will kiss me, or I will kiss you. Sweet little one, I hope you are beautiful now. Goodbye. In life I am your truest fondest friend Edward, and you ever my own sweet little one Helen, anemone maiden. Goodbye, sweet heart. Does this reach you as you come down from bed? I hope you are well & looking forward to the sunshine. Goodbye.

4. v. '98

I have no stamps at all, nor money, here.
If you could send one soon, I should be glad.

It was very mean of me, I know, after the sweet beginning of your letter & the pleasure I had from it, to be very angry at the end. Not only mean; perhaps it was utterly baseless. But unless you spent a lot on flowers and balls for the children and on Mary's birthday present, considering that you had our 15/- and some 5/- or *more* yes more of your own a month ago, on which no calls but fares need have been made, to which was added about 30/- (or more?) lately, and from it all not 30/- was spent on the dress, you should have a sovereign left: add to this the wages of this month to come, and there should remain, after 35/- to the spectacle man, fully a sovereign, which, considering our needs for the future & also your promises, nay, certainties, at which I laughed, should go to the bank. A pretty sentence indeed! but my feathery head is blazing with the stupidity of all this together with my own unamiability and ungentleness of behaviour. I can not help it. I am certain of my facts & calculations; so there are but two alternatives: either you have spent, not extravagantly, since you are not extravagant, but sillily & thoughtlessly, which really is far worse. What your present needs are, is another thing, but surely 10/- should cover them. I won't write a word more now, but go to my work, cool down, go out, and in the evening post this letter with proofs of my regret, though not recantation, and also proofs of some joy or success I may have this afternoon in fields now rejoicing in sunshine after rain,—to delight my own sweet little one, too tolerant, too childishly submissive, not by nature, which would be *weak*, but by love for me, which is *strength*. Goodbye, little one. I hope you are only passingly depressed by my letter & that what I can write later on will erect your spirits. In fact I wrote a song yesterday & if you are good you shall have it, supposing you care.

Believe me, to conclude, tho' I have no business head, for large & lengthy affairs, I am keen enough in figures & small matters, & always was; so that I can not be disputed. If you think me wrong, it simply means you have, as I used to say, let money 'slip through your hands': and remember we cannot afford to despise money. As you do, very beautifully & genuinely, I know & delight to reflect.

Later

I did manage to get out, immediately after dinner, & fortunately, for now I am back, it rains hard, as it has done every day now for a week. Yet it is very beautiful rain, at least in the country, clear, sweet, musical, with a bright sky usually overhead, & oftentimes a rainbow. I think I am in a kinder mood now, and my only worry is that dulness and thickness of brain which I think I have often mentioned before. I fancy it comes from over reading, so I do as little as I can. My relief is a pipe—really it is a relief. Just now, for instance, I could not sit & do nothing, since that only irritates my brain; & it was then only my pipe that enabled me comfortably to read Rousseau's 'Julie; or the New Heloise'. That is a book you must often have heard of—a series of letters between two lovers; Julie and Saint-Preux. They are very pretty, but somewhat ludicrously sentimental; that is, when one reflects that it was Rousseau that wrote them. I suppose you know the old story—French of the 12th century—about Heloise and Abelard and their strange love?

By the way, after writing to you on Sunday, the mood came, and I wrote the story of Kheydius, 12 close pages, straight off, almost satisfactorily, too. It will take me a long time to correct & copy, though: when I have done so, of course you shall have it. I am pleased with what you say of 'The Time after Anemone'. You prove to me that it gives just the very impression I desired. As to the song I talked of—Here it is. If you can see my meaning, it is well. The thing has little music & little choiceness of words, but I fancied at the time it was genuine enough. I can not ask you to *judge*. But is it better than the verses beginning 'Cottage on the Wye'?

> (1) Weary of April's over-sweet—
>   Anemone & Marigold—
>   I turned my feet
>   To her the meek and bold.
>
> (2) 'Let me but speak to thee, or thou
>   To me, unhastily, of naught:
>   Of love not now,'
>   I moaned with heart distraught.

(3) Wistfully smiling, then, she stept
   To lift me with love's best, though
   Looked not, but wept
   And cared not to reply.

(4) Repose restored, oh! cruel bliss—
   To her sweet toil she rose and wove—
   Ah! bitter 'tis (or? And would not kiss.)
   We cannot always love.

One merit it has—each verse is exactly the same in metre & accent. But here I am talking blissfully about myself in the old fashion! And can you pardon me for coming to such a conclusion as that in the last line of my verses? I think it is very true. Now I think I must run away. I will post this at once so that you will have it by tomorrow's first post. I hope it will not prove an utterly hateful letter. Goodbye, sweetheart. The sun shines without rain once more. Will you kiss me, or will you be unkind just a little while? Tell me. In life I am your truest friend Edward, and you ever my own sweet little one Helen, my anemone maid, and dearest friend. Sweet heart, goodbye'.

Edward approached his third attempt to pass Responsions in a confident and relaxed mood. As he 'crammed' his Latin and algebra, he read *Don Quixote* and Boccaccio and set aside time to read twenty pages of Goethe and twenty pages of Malory daily. But a week before the examination he became restless and peevish. He told Helen he must have gone off his head: he had written three lots of verses in one week (including the one on Old Margaret and Headington Hill printed in *Collected Poems*, p. 458). His confidence was justified and in mid-June he is home at 61 Shelgate Road and their correspondence becomes a thin trickle of notes and letter-cards as they make arrangements to meet when Helen is free from her work. Although he had passed Responsions and had few debts at Oxford except for books, his father was already apprehensive about the cost of an Oxford education, with Ernest in his final year of training to be an art-teacher and Reggie with a consuming passion for Shakespeare and the stage, and no other interest. Dory had already begun his motor-engineering apprenticeship, but Oscar and the young Julian, like Reggie, had still to be provided for.

Mr Thomas, as so often before, turned to his relatives for help. Edward and Reggie were to spend six weeks or so with his cousins in Pontardulais, while Ernest and Oscar stayed with relations in Cwmavon. There were plans for the younger children to join Watcyn Wyn's private academy (for ministerial candidates and others) at Ammanford where the Welsh preacher-bard Gwili (the Revd John Jenkins, later Principal of the Baptist Theological College at Bangor and Archdruid of the Gorsedd of the Welsh National Eisteddfod) was a tutor. He and Edward became close friends with a shared interest in poetry, nature-study, fishing, and the classics. Edward was glad to escape from Shelgate Road: his father seemed to undermine his self-confidence and made him out to be 'several kinds of fool'. At the home of his paternal uncle he was very much at home. His aunt had little or no English and Edward the merest smattering of a few isolated Welsh phrases. She hoped he would study regularly in the small front parlour—'the best room'—but he preferred the roomy kitchen with its large table, coal-fired oven, and brass furnishing around the hearth and the hobs and the mantlepiece. This was the hub of her universe and here the family assembled after a day's work, in the coal-mine or (like Edward's beautiful elder female cousin) the local tinworks. Supper was the banquet time for married children and their families. In the mornings he worked in the kitchen while his aunt baked or cooked or sewed; here in the evenings he absorbed the sense of the impact of new industries on an older more settled way of life which, much later, found its way into the stories and sketches of his best Welsh work, *Rest and Unrest* and *Light and Twilight*. Increasingly during the next fifteen years the triangle formed by Swansea, Pontardulais, and Ammanford—with the frowning eminence of Carreg Cennen Castle in the distance—provided him with a retreat and a source of healing as he faltered towards his final realization as a poet.

Apart from their long walks and interminable conversations and evening singsongs, or their expeditions to ancient monuments, he and Gwili and his cousins assisted with the harvest, binding sheaves and even mowing bracken with a scythe. Assured by Helen that their new way of making love brought no ill effects for her ('Happy and bountiful Helen') he wishes her to understand his satisfaction away from her: 'You would laugh to know what my amusements are!—mere jests of the slightest character; rough simple ways; and very little thought. It is certainly good for me physically, though I am a little dubious about its ultimate good. They are too lenient: that makes it flattering. Believe me, these scrappy notes do not represent my feeling which is deep, continuous, and steady.' He seemed to live his life throughout the summer on two levels: with Gwili and in his own writing and deeper probes into Pater's works he was moving towards the standpoint of his article 'The Frontiers of English Prose' (in *Literature,* September 1899), that a 'most noticeable fact is the apparent destruction of the boundaries between poetry and prose, and between verse and prose. . . . Poetry had been too long and too harshly divided from prose.' As far as I can discover, except for the rough translation of a poem by Watcyn Wyn in his *Wales* (1905), there is no further mention of verse of any kind in Edward Thomas's letters after this Long Vacation.

This absorption into a different community, quite other than anything he had experienced since childhood, into which he had the natural right of entry accorded by his Welsh cousins because of the tie of blood, required a few more Long Vacation visits before he could articulate its meaning for his own mature intellectual development. Gwili tried to interpret for him the power of Welsh literature and especially the 'renaissance' of modern Welsh poetry of which he was himself a part, but Edward had only a smattering of Welsh and, judging from rough translations of folksongs and simple lyrics, he was disinclined to carry his studies further. In September he recorded a very detached impression of his stay: 'The Welsh see so clearly, so abundantly, filling every space of air with a lovely form in firm white. Why don't they carve like Greeks? Instead, their poetry, prose and verse is full of pictures.'

He proved much more responsive to Welsh songs and music and, as Gwili's elder sister sang for him and showed a strong interest in him, he assures Helen that he is 'a very harmless fool' and that his known views on promiscuity and marriage have not changed. Although he had kept up his reading—particularly in Greek and French—and written some stories for the *Speaker,* he believed his intellect had been let sleep. If he was ever to be an artist, he should strive for more balance. 'I wish my sight were not so powerful and so cunning. . . . Time always mellows my impressions, if they are not at all strong.' Early in September the four Thomas brothers were told to make ready for the journey home, where Ernest had to re-sit for his Teacher's Certificate, and Edward was left with scarcely a month to reassure Helen of his faithfulness and to make his final preparations before beginning his historical studies with Owen M. Edwards.

He approached his first term at Lincoln College 'fairly well & in exceedingly good temper . . . Human beings have never touched me so nearly as now when "Nature" was so close: I think, too, I never before struck such firm roots into human hearts'. His Welsh cousins and their friends flattered and cosseted him; he was treated as a gentleman-scholar, sharing much of the natural respect of late nineteenth-century Wales for the scholar-preacher-bard, of which his new friend, Gwili, the theologian-bard, was an excellent example. Edward knew he was being pampered and, in his letters to Helen about his friendship with Gwili's sister, he confessed that 'in fact it was partly you that I saw when I held her: I hope I shall never forget her; then I shall feel that it is possible to love another even though I am all and ever yours, little one. But I won't reason on it.'

After his return to London from Pontardulais, Edward and Helen were finding it more difficult than ever to contain their desire for complete sexual union. Before he had gone to Wales, her employers had allowed him to visit Helen in her own room. She was already twenty-one and their self-imposed tests of constraint were severely strained. After their first post-Wales reunion, on the evening of 19 September '98, he wrote to her fearfully about the results of their intimacy:

Dearest Friend—Let me know soon if you are quite well, and tell me just how you are feeling. For I think you cannot help pondering on our meeting last night. And quite rightly. You, poor little one, were the victim of a pure overwhelming desire, and I of a smaller desire by no means pure; and I feel much more abject than if that desire had been satisfied. I was trying to think in the correct way about right and wrong as I travelled home last night. Of course all kinds of schemes came—we would read stiffly together etc. Somehow I feel as if it were purer—certainly it would be honester—'to do the thing we fear'. But nothing of course would induce me to make a miserable thing out of you and a fool of myself. Could we not find out some means? You understand.

He confesses he hasn't the face to make enquiries about methods and means of contraception, even in the most indirect way. Nothing came of his enquiries and the first ten days of October passed uneventfully with his praise of Helen's 'lovely portion of that maidenliness which you shall never lose'. He settled down again to work ('lessons and literature'), with some hours spent at Wimbledon with Arthur Hardy 'in the warmth and strange visible light of the late afternoon', and enjoyed the kindness around 'which I never felt so much as of late, when it looked as if I was soon to cast it away with such apparent rudeness'. He was well received by Mrs Noble and her daughter Mary, and he planned to visit Mr Tarrant, the Unitarian minister, before spending the evening with Harry Hooton. He assured Helen, 'I did not know I loved you so tenderly until this trial, sweetheart'.

Before he left for Lincoln College on 14 October '98, Helen was peremptorily given a week's notice by Mrs Andrews who had secretly been reading Edward's letters and now accused Helen of 'illicit connexion' with him. Helen cheerfully returned home, but apprehensive about the effect of this 'ghastly suspicion' on her hysterical mother. Edward sent to Mrs Andrews 'a short note, fulfilling the two duties, of thanks for her past undoubted kindness, and of a request for a "character" (virtually) when you leave. The note is formal and discreet, I think. As far as I see, all is well: you at any rate are serene. . . . Until we meet, I remain silent—just a little excited, but still secure on what I *know*.' Helen worked out her last week's notice in utter loneliness with the sympathetic support of Janet and Harry Hooton and the staunch championship of Mrs Beatrice Logan who had offered Helen employment with her. Edward, now in Oxford, felt obliged to write home to his mother with full details of the affair and for the next fortnight pondered the steps he should take. 'Is it any good to write to a Solicitor?' he asked Hooton. 'As for me, I can only shrink and plan a slinking away out of sight, since I love life too much to die.' Soon this mood of despair evaporated under the influence of serene letters from Helen, who flourished among the intimate circle of artistic Bohemian young people—including the poet Charles Dalmon and the actor Franklin Dyall—who lived in Hammersmith and spent a great deal of time at Mrs Logan's large house which had been furnished and decorated in William Morris style. Looking back later, Helen recalled three things about this new life, so different from the unhappy days when she and Edward discovered that his passionate letters to her were being read by Mrs Andrews: 'The beauty of it delighted me, and I thought it the perfect setting for these people with their freedom of manner and thought. . . . I look back upon this household as having been—after [Edward]—the strongest influence in my life. [He] used to make fun of their serious cults of purity and freedom and nakedness. . . . They regarded no convention, and I did not see till later that their unconvention was almost as intolerant as my parents' convention.'

Helen stayed with Mrs Logan—who was awaiting a divorce—during Edward's first year at Lincoln. She was now a companion and friend rather than a nursemaid and domestic servant; she prepared herself to run her own household and developed her skills as a needlewoman. Most of all she found there strong support for the mutually independent role of husband and wife that she and Edward had developed over two years of frustration and parental disapproval. Her love for Edward was constant and rocklike: she matured during these months, but she did not change. Like Edward she knew the 'reason why we don't marry is not our immaturity but impecuniousness'.

CHAPTER 5

The Long Green Day: Oxford 1898–1900

THE freshman lights his meerschaum (holding it in a silk handkerchief), and begins to make a plan for three or four years. But he never completes it. He believes Oxford to be as a fine sculptor, and wishes to put himself in its hands in such a way as to be best shapen by the experience, in a 'wise passiveness'. He wants to be a scholar, and fears to be a pedant. He wants to learn a wise and graceful habit with his fellow-men, and fears to be what he hears called a gentleman. He wants to test his enthusiasm and prejudices, and fears to be a Philistine. He wants to taste pleasure delicately, and fears to be a *viveur* or an aesthete. None of these aims is altogether conscious or precise; yet it is some such combination that he sees before him, faint and possible, at the end of three or four years. Nor has he any aim beyond that. He will work, but at what? Neither has he realised that he will be alone and unhelped.

At first the loneliness is a great, and even at times a delirious, pleasure; and whether he is in a church, or in the fields, or among books, it is almost sensual, and never critical. Oxford is, as it were, doing his living for him. He is as powerless to influence the passage of his days as to plan the architecture of his dreams. He only awakens at his meals with contemporaries, and sometimes at interviews with tutors. The former find him dull and superior. The latter tell him that in his work he is indeed gathering honey, but filling no combs; and find him ungainly and vague. He consoles himself with the reflection that he is not becoming a pedant or a careless liver. He writes verses to celebrate the melodious days he lives.

It is an idealized general portrait that fits many an undergraduate past and present, but there is a great deal of Edward Thomas in it. He was two years senior to his fellow History exhibitioners at Lincoln and Brett-James, who recalled the maturity of his weekly essay as contrasted with their 'callow schoolboy essays' goes on to describe his successive rooms as the leading scholar: 'One in the new buildings just beyond the very beautiful fourteenth century kitchen, at least a century older than the College, and another immediately above John Wesley's old study. There he had gathered a charming collection of books of all periods and most varieties, first editions of poets and essayists, books by Isaac Walton, Cobbett, Jefferies and Hudson. One that has always remained very vividly in my memory is a first edition of Sir Walter Raleigh's *History of the World*, in the original leather bindings.'

Edward's first days at Lincoln, clouded over by Helen's dismissal and

the fear of unfounded slander, were less resilient than the two para-
graphs of hindsight from *Oxford*. He felt the days pass like centuries and
believed himself to be 'weak' and his reputation already 'bad'. 'People
think me filthier than my shy talk, and I begin to think I am: for of course
the public school men, with all their knowledge and taste, are filthy.' But
in a few weeks, with Helen quite happily settled with Mrs Logan, he was
getting quite rowdy. He had officiated with the scissors at the cutting of
the odious love-lock of a freshman, had smoked six cigars in one night
and so got them free. He practised with eight-pound dumb-bells each
morning after his cold bath and won a wager about his skill. He went on
the river every afternoon and he rowed in the 'fours' on 28 November.
And with his new knowledge of Wales, he established a special rapport
with Owen M. Edwards, his tutor, who pressed extra work on him for
an early college examination in December and a Law Preliminary
before June, with quite new matter to get up. He was asked to try for the
Lothian Essay prize and assured that the College wished him to continue
writing his papers for 'the *Speaker* etc'. He ends a letter to Hooton in
unusual good spirits: 'Dear Harry, excuse me for being so lighthearted
and so unlike my melancholy self of last year.' Letters to Harry were
now less frequent and, curiously, no letters to Helen exist for this first
term at Lincoln.

His rowing in November was a success. He was awarded colours and
selected as bow for the College Torpid Eight in February. (Thereafter he
could wear the flamboyant blazer, and did.) He was physically much
stronger and proud of his 11½ stone. He passed his college examination
successfully in December but did not give up the 'social habits' his early
despair had driven him to. He offered Hooton examples of 'some interesting developments and opening possibilities in me. For example,
besides what I have mentioned, I can listen to "Circus Girl" music. I can
topple into bed on the verge of drunkenness more than once: swear: use
slang creditably: howl choruses—even the usual foul choruses of the
Varsity (for of course it is a fiction that the Varsity sings "Who is Sylvia!
What is she?"): also I can be heartily sick and well rid of it all, and able
to talk the most modest commonplaces of affection or business at home.'

He was inordinately proud of his physical condition and, when at
home he was confined to bed over Christmas with a severe chill, he took
some laudanum as a short-cut to relieve the attendant depression. Perhaps MacAlister was right to claim that Thomas always found college
life bewildering and that although he attempted a number of uncongenial activities (like rowing) he was something of a misfit: 'In a sense he

was too mature, though he was entirely free from any sort of pose and was indeed modest and distrustful to a fault', he recalled in 1945.

The friendship with MacAlister (a mere acquaintance at St. Paul's) had developed slowly but firmly when Thomas lodged at Cowley Road. Two similar close friendships formed from Lincoln were with older Balliol men: the writer-solicitor E. S. P. Haynes and the strongly political Welshman—a friend of Thomas's relations at Swansea—J. H. Morgan, later a Professor of Politics in London University. Although Haynes competed unsuccessfully for the Newdigate Prize and probably first met Thomas at the literary Davenant Society, both he and Morgan were involved in Oxford Union debates which were dominated at this time by Raymond Asquith, F. E. Smith, and Hilaire Belloc (all three presented in thin disguises in Thomas's *Oxford*). Although his own father was increasingly involved in local politics, Edward kept himself free from political discussions during the long-drawn-out Boer War. He confined his interest in the past to politics and literature. As he explained to MacAlister, who had been a member of the OTC St Paul's and later sought unsuccessfully to enlist for service in South Africa:

I ought to say I do not deny romance to the present, but that I can only enjoy it as romance at a long distance of time; in fact, for me, romance is formed invariably and certainly by the mere condition of remoteness; anything old is romantic to me, nothing that is new. Nor is this the reason for my neglect of the present. I neglect the present because my sole interest is art, of which romance is a portion. . . . (But as usual I am probably using the term romance in an exclusive way, a way that needs definition before it can appeal to others.) I am learning, slowly, that I must never attack the opinions of another, my own being so exactly the result of my peculiar constitution; but must simply work on, leaving the rest not to time, to which of course I make no appeal, but to the few who resemble me, or who will tolerate sincere art, however narrow and egotistic. What I shall always hate is carelessness and insincerity. The fact that most others are careless and insincere in their efforts in my 'line' is what gives me confidence that I shall surpass them.

These Oxford letters to Hooton, MacAlister and, then, to Helen are full of surprises—of news, opinions, and forecasts that remain valid for the rest of his eighteen years of writing. As an undergraduate he had clearly defined the limits of his interests as a writer and had already acknowledged to himself the kinds of populist writing he would not in any circumstances adopt, even to make a tolerably comfortable living for himself and his future family. Assailed by moments of acute melancholy since the age of sixteen, yet buoyed up by moments of intense, serene experience of the seen world, he somehow retained the capacity for sustained hard work whenever he chose to apply himself, and rarely lost confidence in the true worth of the writing he valued. Was this capacity a legacy from his Oxford days? Or did his working methods at Oxford—and especially in the vacations—merely confirm a deep-seated sense of rightness that lay beneath the diffidence of an acute observer? Competition with able contemporaries provided a reliable scale against which to measure his own potential as a writer and give him some confidence. He extended his reading of French literature and of historical records, and strengthened his knowledge of Goethe while he kept up his close reading of Virgil and Horace. To pass the essential Divinity examination he struggled repeatedly with the Greek New Testament and—at the third attempt—passed it in March 1900 just before he sat for his Final schools. Happily, too, the careful preparation made for various papers read before the Davenant Society met with his tutor's full approval. (Edwards believed firmly in the interdependence of literary and historical studies and Thomas responded to his encouragement by passing Moderations at the end of his fifth term and the Preliminary Law Examination in June 1899.)

The Lent Term of 1899 was a complete contrast to his rather lonely life a year earlier; his letters to Helen are brief and scrappy, apart from the affectionate identical coda which concludes each one. Until mid-February he trained hard for the Torpids, eating much larger meals than usual, drinking three or four glasses of port once or twice a week as 'part of the system of training'. He developed his friendships, attended the Arnold Society and the Oxford Musical Club (with Haynes) and, from time to time, entertained his maternal aunt, Margaret Townsend, who was in Oxford as secretary-companion to an American lady visitor. The Lincoln boat did badly on the river, but the eight survived a motion of disgrace at the College Meeting and were not deprived of the right to wear their blazers. Thomas's *Oxford* notebook records a 'Lincoln Smoking Concert—March 1899.'

Scene: the Hall. Band on the dais. Benches all round, chairs in the body.
Music and songs: then Spanish Castanet dance played by band. Interval for wine: everyone returns half-screwed.
Music seems to grow wilder. Candles fall from brackets. Fumes of tobacco and wine. People begin to shout accompaniment, then to throw down candles. Finally the hall was cleared of chairs, and all joined hands and danced madly—the band played fiercely. No light except by the band, the rest in darkness. How the dance ended I don't know.

To the relief of his tutor, Thomas then settled down to a backlog of work; and he prepared a list of requests for presents he wished to receive on 3 March, his twenty-first birthday. Once the rowing was over, he returned to long country walks with his various friends and, by working late, caught up with his essay work, although he judged it

not very good. It is fidgety and interrupted too often by my lust for society, and in other ways: for instance I spent nearly an hour yesterday with a man on my staircase who was very drunk. It was amusing; for he was strong and very merry. We went round to the rooms of men we didn't like and upset them; he got into another man's bed several times; finally I undressed him and he slept from 9 until nearly 10 the next morning. He used to be a friend of Cornish's, and is not a bad fellow; but the virtuous Cornish will scarcely notice him after such exhibitions as last night's. In spite of all, I have done a little writing—at a paper on Merton [in Surrey] which I think I mentioned to you. But I am not satisfied with it. I am eager to begin something else. I am once again tortured into a feeling that I lack subject matter, that my descriptive powers ought to be used as the ornament not the substance of my work.

Writing to Helen two days after his birthday he combined pleasure at his wide range of presents—from his parents and his aunt, Helen and her mother, his brother Julian, some Lincoln friends, and Arthur Hardy—with the sudden tug of his home life, admittedly tinged with some alcoholic remorse:

People seemed to expect me to have a sort of 'bust-up'. I regret to say I bought three bottles of wine and some fruit, with the result that I was upset just as I was with Arthur on the day before Christmas (you remember). It was a pity and caused remorse; but I am very well this morning, only regretting the expense of such ephemeral pleasure,—a regret which I always feel on such occasions. I hope I do not too easily and too thoroughly settle down to the ways of this wonderful place: I think not. How much rather would I have spent quiet hours in the open fields with you; hours of friendly conversation with Arthur; or satisfaction in the smile of Mother and Father. Do not make me long too soon for the pleasure we are to share when time re-unites us, though indeed I long—I burn and quiver—for it, with the thought of your hair, with the thought of your head and its poise.

He warned that his teetotal father should not be told about the wine.

His father believed that by mixing with the best of men at Oxford Edward would find his way into an established profession; and, on his twenty-first birthday, sent him a formal letter of congratulations, with stiff but kindly and sound advice. Edward's life, after two terms, belied such expectations as much as his 'secret and sacred love' of Helen.

What if the honourable ghosts of Oxford frown upon his strange devotions? He is at least living a life that could not persist elsewhere. At chapel, he is reading Theophrastus. He is studying an undercurrent of the Italian Renaissance at a lecture on Thucydides. As if he were to live for ever, and in Oxford, his existence is such that his stay in Oxford or in life becomes precarious. . . . Like a man who should paint an angel and call it a thief, he narrowly pursues his own choicest veiled gifts with a malicious word. In short, his brilliant conversation proves how much easier it is to think what one says than to say what one thinks. Yet is he now a harder student than he has ever been, and allows nothing to disturb him at his books. . . . His conversation becomes gloomy as well as bitter. . . . He is now often reduced to silence among those who sleep well. He no longer pours a current of fresh and illuminating thought upon things which he not only does not understand, but does not care for, in politics or art.

Admittedly the undergraduate he describes with such clear-sighted, detached affection is a composite portrait, but, as Haynes and MacAlister agree, the flavour of his own varied career is ever-present in *Oxford*, one of his most personal books. The significant lacuna is the subterranean life of passion, separate from Oxford, that is laid bare only in his letters to Helen.

During the previous Christmas vacation Edward had overcome his ignorant reluctance to use contraceptive methods instead of the strained almost intolerable love-play he and Helen had previously indulged in. In late February 1899 he asked Helen to 'go again to that shop in Falcon Road before I come back, if I give you a note as before', and she agrees and sends the prepared envelope to him before he leaves Oxford. The last week there was hectic and varied. He read Gautier's *Mademoiselle de Maupin* and found it fiendishly true and honest; he had breakfast with Morgan at Balliol; went for three walks with Haynes, attended a celebratory 'Festivity of Drink' of the Davenant Society on Monday and the College Smoking Concert on Thursday. He had been writing slowly, but with some pleasure, although nothing of his had appeared in the *Speaker* or in *J. C. R.*, a short-lived undergraduate paper edited by an Old Pauline, Lucian Oldershaw. As he answered Helen's replies to his own 'hopelessly voluptuous ones of late' he longed for their reunion: 'Until Saturday, I think and dream of nothing but your breasts, your hair, your eyes in the silent darkness of night. One prayer I have—that you be well and torn by impatience. Thank you for your letters, though I am mean enough to think only of the throbbing bosom, the brain, the tingling limbs that inspired them: wait and I will cling to you and we shall make mighty atonements for time, my own sweet little one.'

During this Easter vacation a child was conceived on one of their long walks 'in the sweet open air'. Two months later, just before his marriage to Helen at Fulham Registry Office, 20 June 1899, Edward asked Harry Hooton to 'forgive all that is to be foregiven,—do not think hardly of me. I love Helen, and that is enough. My only regret is that perhaps the licentious life at Oxford into which—with wine and wild talk, grave and gay—I have entered with all the zest that was to be expected from one who has spent so many years in solitude—that this life may have heated my blood somewhat unnaturally.' Returning to Lincoln for the summer term [1899], Edward had detected hints of unease in Helen's letters, but his chief concerns were with his own paper on 'Prose and Poetry in the Nineteenth Century' for the Davenant Society, with the results of Moderations (which he passed modestly), with writing a paper on 'The Caryatids' for publication, and with the deepening of his friendship with Haynes and Morgan and to a lesser extent, with three Lincoln men, Collins, Davies, and O'Brien.

Early in May Helen spent a day in Oxford. They met at the railway station. Avoiding the city, they walked along the canal and then on and to the river and beyond. In his worst 'colour book' style Edward recalls the path of their walk at the end of his chapter on 'The Oxford Country'—so weaving into his *Oxford* at least one experience which Helen could partially share:

One such footpath I remember, that could be seen falling among woods and rising over hills, faint and winding, and disappearing at last,—like a vision of the perfect quite life. We started once along it, over one of the many fair little Oxford bridges, one that cleared the stream in three graceful leaps of arching stone. The hills were cloudy with woods in the heat. On either hand, at long distances apart, lay little grey houses under scalloped capes of thatch, and here and there white houses, like children of that sweet land—*albi circum ubera nati.* For the most part we saw only the great hawthorn hedge, which gave us the sense of a companion always abreast of us, yet always cool and fresh as if just setting out. It was cooler when a red-hot bicyclist passed by. A sombre river, noiselessly sauntering seaward, far away dropped with a murmur, among leaves, into a pool. That sound alone made tremble the glassy dome of silence that extended miles on miles. All things were lightly powdered with gold, by a lustre that seemed to have been sifted through gauze. The hazy sky, striving to be blue, was reflected as purple in the water. There, too, sunken and motionless, lay amber willow leaves; some floated down. . . .

We could not walk as slowly as the river flowed; yet that seemed the true pace to move in life, and so reach the great grey sea. Hand in hand with the river wound the path, until twilight began to drive her dusky flocks across the west, and a light wind knitted the aspen branches against the silver sky with a crescent moon as troubled tenderly by autumnal maladies of soul, we came to our place of rest,—a grey, immemorial house with innumerable windows.

One wonders what Helen made of the autumnal echoes of this high-piled description which he had to learn to undo over the next decade? Yet he had suspected in Pontardulais, with Coleridge, that 'sight was the most despotic of the senses'.

During their walk, Helen felt convinced that she was carrying a child and assured him of her happiness. They made no plans for marriage, then, but discussed various possibilities. Recently, Helen and her sisters had received legacies of £150 each, still controlled by Mrs Noble and the family solicitor. Edward was in debt for wine, clothes, and books and was quite unable to save from his exhibition or his father's allowance. Mr Thomas had insisted that Edward should contribute some part of his literary earning to the household expenses until he reached twenty-one. Edward had deposited the remainder in the Post Office Saving Bank and had encouraged Helen to open an account. Neither of them foresaw any financial difficulties ahead, but they intended to conceal their marriage because they believed that Mr Thomas would withdraw his allowance and bring Edward's Oxford career to an end. In May he paid two visits to Helen who still worked and lived with Beatrice Logan at 23 St. Peter's Square, Hammersmith. Mrs Logan was expecting her divorce proceedings to be settled at the end of June when she could give up her house, leaving Helen without a home or employment. Despite her unconventional Bohemian views, Mrs Logan strongly advised the young couple to marry. So did Harry and Janet Hooton, who offered their home in Gipsy Hill to Helen after marriage.

Edward was sorely pressed by the practical problems ahead. How to secure Helen's legacy; how to persuade his father to continue his allowance; and how to make adequate provisions for Helen and a child. He discussed his future prospects with Haynes and Morgan. The older Morgan—already a graduate from the University College of South Wales and Monmouthshire, and recently adopted as a candidate for a Welsh parliamentary constituency—gave Edward sympathetic understanding and some confidence in his future prospects. Haynes, completing his own Oxford career, was destined for a successful legal practice in the office of his wealthy worldly-wise father. Much more experienced in affairs of the heart and the body, Haynes suggested the possibility of an abortion, and deplored any hasty marriage that might injure his friend's prospects both at Oxford and, later, in his choice of a career. He promised to get Edward some vacation tutoring, lent him money for immediate expenses, and offered to obtain a loan from his father, if necessary, to support Edward during his final Oxford year. Helen, secure in her overwhelming love for Edwy (as she had at last learned to call him in her letters) and eager for motherhood as an earnest of the ideal, Eden-like life she and Edward had promised themselves for nearly three years, was happy to find that her lover was vehemently against abortion and committed to the birth of their child. The Oxford life and attitudes of his closest friends were not allowed to encroach on his life with Helen. 'By nature I have something of starch stiffness in me,' he once informed Hooton. It was a quality that came to the surface repeatedly at various crossroads of decision throughout his life.

The resulting strain was inevitable. This division of his life into sharply contrasted compartments had characterized him as a youth, as a potential scholar at St Paul's, and as an idealist lover imposing restraints on his physical desires. And now, despite arguments with the eloquent Morgan, Thomas held firm to a faith he had stated in his first letters to Helen, later enunciated in an early letter to Harry Hooton: 'On earth there is perhaps only one perfection, one beauty, that of the physical and spiritual union of two creatures, man and woman . . . I know I am right . . . I have faith.'

Having decided that Helen should live with the Hootons, while Edward lived at home and undertook some vacation tutoring, they were married on 20 June 1899 at Fulham Registry Office with Harry and Janet Hooton and Mr Potbury (Beatrice Logan's second husband) signing as witnesses. Helen wore a flame-coloured dress embroidered in blue and a coat lined with blue silk, both designed by an artist friend and made for her by Beatrice who discreetly did not sign the register. The wedding ring was bought for eight shillings and Edward gave his occupation as 'tutor'. It was all very secretive.

Previously, at the end of May, Edward had spent a weekend away from Oxford with his father and mother at his grandmother's home in Swindon. He was quite unable to discuss his forthcoming marriage with his father. Instead, the usual arrangements were made for the Long Vacation, beginning on 16 June 1899. Edward was to stay at home and study for a time, then pay a short visit to Swindon en route for a longer holiday with his cousins in Ammanford and Pontardulais.

Helen, with the help of a nurse (and colleague) from her first employment with the Webbs, made enquiries for suitable lodgings in Carshalton, and decided on a modest set of rooms there to be taken in

September. Harry Hooton undertook to inform both families of the marriage as soon as Edward was in Wales, and he did so early in August. The result was quite unexpected. Mr Thomas wrote to his son stating that Mr Hooton had made some revelations, but 'what were the facts?' He was a scrupulous man, and although bitterly disappointed with Edward's obvious lack of worldly ambition, and fully aware of many hasty marriages among his own relations, he recognized that his son had come of age and, as always, he wished 'to do the best' for all his children. Mrs Thomas, with her usual warm affection, at once paid a visit to Helen and suggested that, if possible, the Carshalton plan should be dropped. If the young couple agreed they could live at the Thomases' home until after Edward's Final Schools in June 1900. With considerable misgivings, Helen agreed to Edward's reluctant request that she should consent to live with his parents at 61 Shelgate Road. She could see the advantages in financial and personal terms, but cherished her own independence. Yet she longed for the chance to be with Edward immediately and recognized that 'it might make your perfect reconciliation with your people very much quicker and easier, also with Mother'.

Mrs Noble's reaction had a slight air of sad farce, as Helen recounts it in a letter to Edward in which she agreed to 'do as you suggest about Shelgate Road':

Mother is not yet satisfied as to our June marriage and Mr Hinds rushes about first to this office then to that, unable through some fearful carelessness in the keeping of the registers, to find the record. Today I hope he will be able to. As to the money—of course it is mine absolutely, only as I said long ago Mother would feel the parting with it more than all the rest. I shall get it sooner or later. She explained all to Harry and offered in that interview to let me have the whole. To me also she said several times 'Of course you shall have it tho' I wish you could do without it'.

It was years before mother and daughter were fully reconciled, although Helen retained and enjoyed the goodwill and affection of her sisters, Irene and Mary. Mr Thomas insisted that the previous arrangements for the Long Vacation should stand, perhaps to prevent news of Edward's marriage reaching Oxford. While Helen stayed with the Hootons at Gipsy Hill, Edward set off in early August to visit his dying grandmother at Swindon for a few days before travelling alone to Pontardulais for a three-week vacation. This visit, I believe, firmly established the future role that Wales would play in his personal and imaginative life.

While still in Pontardulais he recorded in his notebook the development of his interest on 31 August 1899:

Day by day grows my passion for Wales. It is like a homesickness, but stronger than any homesickness I ever felt—stronger than any passion. Wales indeed, is my soul's native land, if the soul can be said to have a *patria*—or rather, a *matria*, a home with the warm sweetness of a mother's love, and with her influence, too. Today, for example, what yearning thoughts filled my brain as Janet played the tune of *Y Ferch o Landebie* and *Moli merched Cymru lan!* and when I hummed the 'Gwlad Gwlad' of the national anthem, my heart broke with thoughts of what I might be and am not, of what I may be—ah! the future in some bookish cottage in the pastoral Towy with Helen!

This feeling is not a new one, born of my visit to the Mumbles in 1896. It really did begin with my visit at five years of age to Caerleon and Swansea—remembered for the Usk and Arthur's Table Island near Aunt Margaret's house, the great red apples from the orchard, and the ivy, the snails and the gloomy well there, and the salmon we ate, the idiot at Caerleon, the porpoise hunt, the churchyard and pigs and snow in May, the house on the hill and the Cinderella (Rachel) in its kitchen, the parrot there and the loaf-like stone I brought to Aunt Mary's house from Langland, where I remember the tall pillars of rock on the near side, and the flying fish pickled in her drawing room, the gulls, too. Hill House, Newport, too, with its great palings—its dogs, its fruit trees, and the sense of mother's girlhood there.

Then came the second visit—to Abertillery, when I was eight or nine. I remember the mountain climbing, the drive to Pontypool, the mountain-ash berries, the shallow Ebbw river where I wanted to fish, being already a fisherman.

Then the reading of Arthurian stories. Then the foolish years between 1890 and 1893.

One always spoke a few Welsh words like 'moch' and 'achyfi'. I was proud of thinking that both Father and Mother came from Wales, and the land was always a Something 'beyond these voices'.

Then Father's Welsh studies—the Welsh I heard at Swindon which seemed a little Wales,—then Malory in 1895—then Mumbles and Pontardulais, prepared for by my 'love of Nature' which was *soi-disant* Celtic.

But now I cherish every shred of a reminder—like the old farm of Mother's grandmother at Tydraw. [Near Margam.]

And how glad I am of such experiences as this. In November last year at Oxford, I met in Trench's rooms in College, two Gypsies (Cornelius aged 25—Buckland aged 70), for about an hour they gave Trench a lesson in the Gypsy tongue. Then, for I had just read *Aylwin*, I asked the elder if he knew Wales. He did. Did he know any Welsh Songs (for I still loved *Y Ferch o Landebie*)? Yes—and he sang right through in that mysterious night

> Mae hen wlad fy nhadau yn anwyl i mi
> Gwlad beirdd a chantorion enwogion o fri.

These two Long Vacation holidays at Pontardulais in 1898 and '99—at the home of his father's first cousin, Philip Treharne Thomas—and a subsequent holiday there with his wife and son immediately after his Oxford days, formed the hard nucleus of Edward Thomas's adult love of Wales, providing memories and perceptions that filtered through into most of his narrative-descriptive sketches as well as the first half of his book *Beautiful Wales*. The intellectual influence of Owen M. Edwards and the staunch friendship of Gwili and John Williams sustained these early impressions that, later, introduced a potent realism into his recreation of moments of insight beneath everyday experiences. The small part of Wales he knew so well continued to give him balance when he needed it in later life.

Edward and Helen were to remain at Shelgate Road until early November 1900. They were to test severely the idealism of their courtship, as Edward had once stated it in a letter to Hooton:

Ideals will always fall short of perfection, or else fail: what we have planned we can never entirely achieve; but one ideal is attainable certainly, and as certainly it is perfect, though confined. If I shall speak ignobly or ludicrously, it is because I am ignoble: my subject is not. I mean private life, and particularly domestic life in whatever family we are placed, whether our own or one of which we are a small part. If we despair of everything else, we need not despair here. . . .

The sense and meaning of 'Home' remained a recurrent theme in his prose pieces and flows like an undercurrent through most of his verse. Tenacity of purpose, and of theme, is a constant element in his personality.

The final year at Oxford (1899-1900) prefigured external habits that remained constant for the rest of his life. Puritanical by temperament and upbringing—for instance, a firm believer in cold baths for himself and for his infant son 'that the child in after life should not continually be a prey to slight shocks of weather'—he was frequently driven to excess, drinking hard in order to find himself well-regarded and so encouraged in the extravagant verbal obscenities and occasional blasphemies that gained him an unenviable reputation among some of the dons, and many of the students, in a 'commonplace college where an orthodox muscular Christianity sets the tone'. He was a careful manager of money. His letters to Helen—who was now drawing her legacy in monthly instalments and paying her own expenses to Mrs Thomas—are punctuated by precise instructions in the conduct of all extra-household expenses, or the charges and expenses from his College battels that his mother should meet, presumably out of his scholarship money or his father's allowance. By contrast, he often indulged his taste for wine, fine clothes, expensive books and pictures, and occasionally shared good meals at the end of his long walks with friends. He relied heavily on parcels sent by his mother—fruit cakes, apples, tins of meat, paste, tongue, and sardines—and, during his penultimate term, he attempted for a while to eat only porridge and tea as his mid-day meal, until Helen conveyed his father's wish that he should continue to eat in hall whatever the cost.

During vacations he combined strenuous reading for his tutor with his own writing. He was encouraged by Edwards to increase the time spent on History from six to eight hours daily, and to make sure that he would pass the 'paltry' Divinity Examination. Typically, he failed Divinity yet again in December 1899, because of an irresistible desire to translate the New Testament Greek into somewhat slick journalese. When at last he passed at his third re-sit in March 1900, he confessed to Helen that 'in spite of the absurd system of examination this watching and praying may have done me good; at any rate I know a little more of the literary beauty of the new testament. The system however has so sickened me that by my utterances I have gained notoriety as a reckless blasphemer. I have formulated two new heresies on material and perhaps obscene foundations. In fact the most immoral fellows are shocked by my audacity in dealing with the illustrious, Enigmatic Trinity. This I must get out of, if only because it is so easy and so liable to shock amiable people.'

He was conscious of the difference between his domestic self and his Oxford self and in the Michaelmas Term of 1899, as Helen drew nearer to her time and wrote him reassuring chatty letters about her health, her love of him, and the daily events of life at Shelgate Road, he became increasingly lascivious in his thoughts, 'now in the fiercest ardours of love and now of shame'. His tutor, seeing he was not well and quite lacking in energy, suggested a weekend visit to his family in London, but Thomas decided he couldn't afford it:

Of course I am disappointed. I had looked forward to seeing you and my people, to improving my health, and I can not help saying to the two nights I should have spent with you, for the flesh is very weak, and my desires are simply overpowering at times and I could almost pick up a woman of the streets if it were safe in a pedantic City like this . . . My Health is a little better and I have some spirits. But I suffer from depression and loneliness. I have a craving (which might be misconstrued) for the society of such very youthful, fresh creatures as this year's History scholar [Brook] . . . a strange longing, but unsexual passion. What made these passions so strong was the fact that it was thwarted very much . . . I felt quite some of the pangs of disappointed love. I kept hearing his voice through the wall. Whenever I crossed the Quad I saw him, but dared not speak . . . Still, I have so little flexibility or power of interesting others that I fear he will drift away forever. And all this about a boy—with abundant black hair, pale, clear face, piercing and frank grey eyes, red lips and a boyish voice! Some people made indecent suggestions to explain my liking, suggestions which I trust he will never hear.

This infatuation is carefully chronicled in the Oxford notebook: 'Since November 27, I have seen more of him, but he will not be alone with me, and still avoids my rooms . . . Certain people of the College suspect our relations. Perhaps J. O'Brien [a rowing man] has *warned* Brook. He is still a boy. Yet to be staggered by a first contemplation of the infinite, when he, as I, will be forced to reflect that after all the 6 ft. by 2ft. of one's grave represents adequately enough one's importance and relative size in the universe of things.' A later note dated 16. ii. 1900, follows: 'The Vac. and its Events (e.g. 15. 1. 1900) have quite cured me: I ended by being be-nightmared by his face and the thought of what an ugly man he will be!'

The events of Merfyn's birth, 15 January 1900 are also recorded:

P.M. appeared at 2 a. m. screaming ferociously. H. took the ordeal as an athlete takes a killing race; and was happy enough at 3 a. m. I sat up all night, fortified (?) by laudanum, writing letters, adding something to my paper on the *Books of my Childhood* and reading Hallam's 'Literature', Sir Philip Sidney, and Burton. Thus I reached 7 a. m. when I had the tact to go to Kyrle Road [home of Mrs Noble] and announce things, so making up the breach that had existed since August. The affair did not have any great effect: sometimes the plasticity of the infant seemed terrible in prospect; sometimes I determined to leave to Providence what Providence has so high-handedly begun. He has blue—i.e. 'violet' eyes, plenty of dark hair, a pimple of a nose, well-shaped coral lips, a horribly oblong head, long legs, and feet almost too big for his socks, and weighs 9 lbs. at appearance. I saw Haynes at noon; he is anxious to get the family Bible as godfather. The next day I lunched with him at the 'Cheshire Cheese'. . . . The 15th was a night so clear that the air from height to depth was like one great sapphire: there was a white full moon.'

Fatherhood, it seems, could not break the long habit of nature notes that stretch from *The Woodland Life* to the last war diary he kept in France.

Infatuation with Brooks was replaced in the Hilary and Trinity terms by a more lasting friendship with a freshman scholar called 'Lucy' Elsey. He was a successful cox in the Lincoln boat during the 1900 Torpids and May Week, but quite incapable of sustaining the kind of conversation that Edward was accustomed to with Haynes, Morgan, and a research folk-lorist, P. J. Maine. Yet the pattern of Edward's involvement, and eventual modified disappointment, was intense:

Elsey has just been to tea—and gone. How I wish he had not gone, and that I had the power (that every average schoolboy here possesses) to interest him! So far from receiving some of his freshness and charm, when I am with him, I feel and probably appear much older, stupidly old, ludicrously paternal or avuncular. He is interested in birds and eggs, but even there I can no longer *show* sympathy, though with a desperate hope of interesting him I have given him a copy of *The Woodland Life* which I picked up at a sale. But my methods are too crude: the charm I may possibly have among my equals vanishes when I am with my (intellectual) inferiors.

The brutal frankness with which he reports to Helen these strange fits and moods of passion—often using identical words and phrases from his Oxford notebook—marks the fulfilment of their early pact to be completely honest with each other. As she told me frequently in her last years, she would not have wished it otherwise. At the same time it is a strange way of showing love and affection and a curious testimony to the habit of uncritical self-revelation which became the basic attitude of all his letters to her—as much later in his letters to Robert Frost. He was completely confident that these two could accept him exactly as he was. He hints as much, without being explicit, in his 1913 essay 'How I Began'. The ideal act of writing for himself could never be learned 'in or out of school': the words were to be a direct, inwardly informed reflection of the thought, however wayward or hurtful to the recipient.

At Oxford, now in his penultimate term, he was always short of ready money and aware of the pressing need to sell his articles to the weeklies. Previously, in the summer of 1899 when he did not expect to complete his degree after his marriage, he had visited various editors hoping for reviewing and the acceptance of his essays. Initially, a few papers were accepted by *Literature* and *The Review of the Week*; then the *Speaker* changed editors and H. D. Traill of *Literature* died, and these profitable sources dried up. Two of his more significant papers appeared unsigned ('The Frontiers of English Prose' and 'Nature in *Morte D'Arthur*'). Although he failed to find a place for 'Natural Magic in Shelley's Poetry', the American *Atlantic Monthly* accepted two articles (later reprinted in

Horae Solitariae). The *Review of the Week* published his most recent paper, 'Caryatids': an instinctive reaction to the increasing burden of Helen's pregnancy presented through the martyrdom and sainthood of all anonymous women who carried the ordinary labours of the world without complaint. He reacted to his disappointments with a see-saw existence between excessive work late at night and excessive drinking after dinner.

As the Hilary Term progressed, his tutor plied him with one essay after another: 'This doing of papers in my subject is the best way of getting as much as possible out of me. It is long since I wrote a line.' At first he overworked, on an indifferent spartan diet, and then drank or talked late as a relaxation until he was quite ill with exhaustion and had a brief recourse to laudanum to make his depression tolerable.

John Williams the schoolmaster of Waun Wen, Swansea, and a friend of Morgan's, sent him half a guinea for a christening mug for the baby, Philip Merfyn Ashcroft Thomas. Edward decided to buy a plain, useful, two-handled pewter mug 'in commemoration of 15. 1. 1900' and invited his friends to inscribe their mottoes on it.

He worked this particular celebration into his account of 'The Oxford Day':

Sometimes, in the later evening, the singing is not so beautiful. . . . Perhaps only the broadest-minded lover of grotesque contrasts will care for the ballads flung to the brightening moon among the battlements and towers. But the others should not judge harshly or with haste. These are but part of the motley in which learning clothes itself. Much sound and fury is here no proof of deep-seated folly; nor quietness, of study; nor are a man's age, dignity, and accomplishments in mathematical proportion to the demureness of his deportment. I notice on one little tankard these philosophies in brief, scrawled with a broken pen.

He then gives a list of ten mottoes or quotations (in Latin, Greek, French, and English), some evidently framed with an eye confined to the tankard. His own French device—*Qui vit sans folie n'est pas si sage qu'il croit*—he explained to Helen, 'merely expresses the value—the indispensableness—of fiction, of illusion, of self-deceit to make life pleasant.' As always in letters to her he sought the exact words to convey his inner thoughts: 'When I am well I will write to you dearest as you deserve, and as I would like—or almost, for neither is quite attainable.' In an effort to free himself from 'social habits', at the end of the term he decided to leave Lincoln for comfortable lodgings, shared with Maine, at 17 Worcester Place, and to prepare himself thoroughly and methodically for the Final Schools in June.

As usual he worked through the Easter Vacation in the familiar sur-roundings of his own long room at home. Throughout his life, he remained extremely sensitive to the peace and orderliness of the imme-diate environment in which he worked. He planned to complete his revision a week or two before the Final Schools so that he could be in his best form for the rigorous test of ten three-hour papers spread over six days. Maine was an amiable, loquacious companion and they frequently had visitors to share at least one of their main meals, supplemented by the food parcels from his mother. At first Edward found that with the help of long Sunday walks in the country—with Maine or Elsey or Mor-gan—he could 'jog along without too many dissatisfactions and disappointments'.

His mood is best caught in his notebook account of Mayday 1900:

I rose before dawn when the chill mysterious light without fire comes into the world—but I rose because I had too much whisky the night before. The morn-ing I worked for Schools. The afternoon I walked far up Cowley Road, then turned off on the right; reaching Iffley Church, crossed the mill (where the millkeeper's daughter lets me off the usual ½d), & walked across a big grass field towards Bagley to pick four fritillaries with heavy thoughts of how reverently I used to pick flowers, while now I picked them fearfully. I carried the flowers back to my rooms. This was all by myself. In the evening Elsey, Hodges, & Wrottesley came in to me & Maine. The first went early, the rest stayed & drank Marsala, absinthe, & Whisky. I remained up silently long after they went—ashamed of my May day—anxious to do if I w. calmly enjoy for a few minutes the sight of a beautiful face, the touch of a beautiful hand, the sound of beautiful voices. I went to bed at 1 a. m. reading epitaphs & resolved to com-pose my own. I found Maine's epigram too chilling, tho' he *appears* sympathetic.

But by early May, Helen was missing her periods because (she thought) she had been careless with her contraceptive preparations; and, after consultations with Mrs Potbury, she visited a specialist. He gave her further advice about effective contraception, but refused to undertake an abortion if it were required. Edward's work suffered, and he could study for only four hours a day. He was anxious and afraid of two things: the mental strain of the examination which was just four weeks off and a 'plough'. He and Maine discussed his possible classification in the Schools; without much hope, he agreed that 'a second is always an hon-ourable class'. He became morbid and angry when he thought of the possibility of another child; he felt 'as dull as a wall', and began lugubri-

3. In his rooms at Lincoln College, Oxford, Michaelmas term 1899.

4. Helen Noble, taken at Ramsgate, February 1899.

5. The Lincoln College Torpids crew, Lent term 1899. Edward Thomas is second from left in the back row.

ously to present some of his fine books, suitably inscribed, to each of his friends.

On 20 May he recorded that he was very drunk the previous night, when Oxford celebrated the Relief of Mafeking. The following day he was just able to send Helen this account of it:

I promised you a letter, but I don't see what in my present condition I can write. If I could only give you a description of Oxford on Saturday night you would not be so disappointed with this letter as now you will be. The whole of the City and University were in the streets. Some of the Oxford streets are the broadest in England and there huge bonfires were lit which we supplied with rafters etc. while the city crowd stood peacefully and uselessly by. On such occasions the City acknowledges its inferiority. All the women, married and otherwise, allow themselves to be promiscuously kissed etc. by the University: in fact most men employed themselves in recording as many kisses as possible. Nearly everyone was drunk, except the citizens, who looked on with the utmost complacence; and two of whom brought me home when, after an exciting evening, I at last succumbed to the wine I had taken. For universal good temper you never saw such a night. Although we were very ill and 'cheap' the next morning, few regretted it and I certainly did not though it was an absurd occasion for so unpatriotic a man.

I am going to write a volume of 'Mafeking Night Entertainments' and really such of my adventures as I remember were much like the Arabian Nights.

After this, his letters to Helen ring the changes on irritability, remorse, and uncertainty about his future. Helen had suggested that some of her legacy could be used for a seaside or country holiday for the three of them between his Schools and his viva voce examination. He replied waspishly: 'It would be insanity to go about arcadizing with bankruptcy and the gutter ahead.' Though his work was 'making really great improvements, I have been wickedly idle this last year (except in the vacations).' The next day he answered her gentle reply: 'My hard drinking, blasphemy and ingenuous obscenity are strangely incompatible with my real meek harmless character. . . . Forget that my language was unkind.' He was in poor shape for his Final School.

Thomas was pleased with his performance on the early examination papers but, after that, he grew 'horribly languid' and 'too weary for anything'. He had not heard definitely from Helen about her possible pregnancy and his 'health was getting bad and my eyes almost failed me today'. By 12 June, he wrote, 'the Exam. is finished and so am I—I can merely send you these papers and get to work to recover. I am bound to stay up, but I shall not be dissipated; in fact the Doctor has forbidden me intoxicants. All I can do is look on at the merriments of others tonight.' The doctor had diagnosed a mild form of unidentified gonococcal infection which, according to the symptoms, had been caught during his drunken roamings on the Mafeking Saturday night. He was prescribed strict dieting, a medicine known as 'protargol' then used against gonorrhoea, complete rest, and as much freedom from movement as possible. He was ordered to stay in Oxford, ostensibly to prepare for his viva, reading under the guidance of his tutor, who had hinted that his early papers were good and that much would depend on the result of his viva voce. ('As for the Schools my papers were worse and worse towards the end, and my answers were merely sketches. My class will therefore be a third at best.') His last days at Oxford, now that his friends had gone down, were in melancholy contrast to the grand finale he had planned: 'It is sad and humiliating that in an illness which I cannot control, I am without any tender or even joyous hand and voice. That for one who has been, or tried to be, free-handed and sympathetic with so many, who has almost cried out for pity and endearments, is heart breaking.'

Soon he knew that his disease was 'a painful and lingering one, and I shall not be free of it for a month: so that I ought to keep under the same doctor's hands. . . . It is not really dangerous and it forces me to live an abstemious and simple life.' A week later he returned home, on the mend but suffering from continuous fatigue, and with good news of his degree prospects from Edwards who, earlier, had given Thomas hope of a good post in higher education in Wales if he acquitted himself well in the Schools. His parents were informed that his illness was exhaustion following his preparation for the Schools, and his father—after paying all the doctor's bills—had generously arranged with Helen that they should all three join the Thomas's holiday rooms at Porthcawl in mid-August, and that Edward and his family should then spend some time in August and September in Ammanford, first with Watcyn Wyn, the schoolmaster-bard, and subsequently with cousins at Pontardulais. The news from Edwards must have pleased Mr Thomas, although his son's illness was alarming. As Edward explained to MacAlister at the beginning of the viva week,

I cannot meet you on Friday, the day of my viva, and I can't say how soon after, because I have been in bed ever since I wrote to you, until now, and feel horribly unprepared for the journey and the exam; for I am weak physically and mentally and haven't touched my books; otherwise I had a chance of a 1st or 2nd, since it leaked out that my early papers were 'very good' but fell off just where I was first attended by the doctor—on which I sent a certificate and there was talk of giving me the class earned by my best papers, which meant a long viva such as I could not endure.

The viva was a longish one of thirty-five minutes. Edwards assured Thomas that he had improved his position and informed him, unofficially, on Monday that he had gained a Second Class. Before returning to London he spent the weekend with J. H. Morgan at his Headington digs and agreed to consider joining him on a friend's ship for a cheap sea voyage to Sicily or the Canary Islands. Thomas couldn't decide immediatley, for two reasons: 'i. you [Helen] need a holiday, and I want to take one with you, nor could you come by sea because it is a trading ship. ii. Money.' Judging from her letters to him during the various crises of his last Oxford term and his illness, Helen must certainly have waived the first objection. Presently some cheques arrived from the journals to solve the second objection. But Edward's illness had left him weak and early in August, just before he was due to sail with Morgan on the *Ross,* he was hardly out of a temperature of 102 degrees 'that still prostrates'. Nevertheless he planned to be away with Morgan for a month while Helen and Merfyn spent the vacation with his mother and brothers. Fatherhood, a foolish illness, and academic disappointment notwithstanding, he resolutely followed his own path to renewed health. This determined streak in his nature—a strong reflection of his own father's public life—has been insufficiently noticed in memoirs of Edward Thomas, except by Eleanor Farjeon who also saw how he relied on the strength and generous flexibility of Helen's nature. Helen's one desire for him was complete freedom to write.

In the event the sea-voyage came to nothing. Edward spent the waiting time in Swindon with his grandmother, having refused Morgan's invitation to spend Sunday with him at Wooton Bassett. ('I feel I could write now if only I had a quiet sitting room.') The *Ross* was damaged and he gave Morgan three or four days to find another ship at Cardiff or Newport. Finally Thomas decided to spend his remaining holiday with neighbours of Watcyn Wyn in Ammanford village where he was to be joined by Helen and Merfyn. His last letters to Helen are full of instructions about packing his clothes and his underwear, 'for I am wearing dirty shirts and collars and my very thickest clothes and, you see, my portmanteau is at the station. In any case, you might send me the thin vest and, if possible, a collar *at once* . . . I am full of projects (writing) and long for a quiet room and some roses in whose company to write—and you not far off with Merfyn, if he is quiet.'

The young family settled in with a Mrs Howells at Pleasant View,
Tirydail, near Ammanford from 20 August until 19 September, as
Edward explained in two letters to MacAlister who had now fully
recovered from the typhoid fever that had kept him away from Oxford
the previous session:

> My Spanish trip was abandoned partly because I was kept waiting too long,
> and partly because I wrote an unanswerable hostile letter to Morgan. It was my
> first angry letter. The cause was a lady to whom our friend had made love
> under the pretence of giving her a higher education, viz., literary. Morgan
> made rather a bad figure in a final difference with her, which I witnessed in
> Berkshire during my viva visit. The girl had interested me, and as she had
> seemed to be really passionate while M. was preoccupied, I wrote to her and
> sent her a copy of *Wuthering Heights* to read. After encouraging my correspon-
> dence in an amused way, M. suddenly ordered me to bring it to an end, in a
> tone that convinced me that his attitude was one of patronage, maintained
> with some real friendliness because I had a certain sympathy with his vitals, e.g.
> liver. But let us agree that we were incompatible persons.
>
> After all Wales is good for me. In spite of my accidentally Cockney nativity,
> the air here seems to hold in it some virtue essential to my well-being, and I
> always feel, in the profoundest sense, at home. Anyhow I am vastly better,
> though still unable to walk the three or four miles necessary to reach the
> nearest waterfall among trees or the nearest castle—Carreg Cennen . . . I still
> wait for a visit from my prosaic Muse; and have to fill up my hours of solitude
> with writing scraps of a novel, at which Haynes and I are collaborating . . .
>
> My wife and the child (who bears with some grace the names Philip
> Mervyn) are with me here and afford a constant undercurrent of deep joy,
> despite my weakness, irritability, anxiety, disappointment.

A fortnight later, he planned to meet MacAlister in London and Oxford.
'For things must go very ill with me, if I do not visit Oxford once a
term.' He was to take his degree early in the Michaelmas Term and gave
MacAlister a full acount of his collaboration with Haynes on a novel, to
be called 'Olivia Paterson':

> A genuine 'romance of the commonplace', sans blood, sans thunder everything
> except commonplace. . . . So far I have written 3 chapters, Haynes 1, for he is
> back in the office. The hero, Raymond Paterson, is to be a religious sentimen-
> talist, and the tragedy (if any) is his relation with his mother, an uneducated
> woman of high feelings with whom, despite similarity of character, his Oxford
> career (obtained chiefly through her efforts) causes him to have less and less
> sympathy and finally contempt. He is not the son of her husband, but of the
> dashing Balliol scamp, and when he learns his origin (as far as I remember at
> this moment) comes the only bit of melodrama. These two sentimentalists, the

mother a truly romantic woman, the son merely a romanticist, side by side, ought to give both of us plenty of scope. It is to be written in the form of a biography, as of an actual person, and will not pretend to artistic form.

Collaboration on a novel was no substitute for a steady income. Mr Thomas seemed ready to support Edward and his family at home until he had taken his Oxford degree on 17 October 1900.

Edward had originally planned to go on from Oxford to Broadstairs— to visit Haynes and his mother—but Mr Thomas had decided otherwise, as Edward explained to MacAlister:

I ought to have written to you before I did, but the whole of my time until then was spent on writing urgent business letters and in raiding Fleet Street. The fact is that my pater thinks it would be best for me to go out into the world (i.e. the gutter). Though I was never really averse to work, his decision had made me buckle to in a way surprising to myself. Edwards has written to say he has nothing to offer: nobody else has [E. T. had also written to Gabbitas & Thring, the teaching agency], so I must try journalism. On Monday I visited the Editors of Literature, the Chronicle, Daily News, Star, Academy, Literary World, World, and New Century. It was amusing tho' tiring work. Literature at once gave me one wretched book to review and held out hopes of more. The Chronicle was genial and promised to put me down to review 'poetry', essays, etc. The Daily News has come to no decision. The Star was (of course) rude. Hyne of the Academy was stupid and said he liked 'pawodies' (sic). The Literary World made no promises. The World is still undecided. The New Century is penniless. Thus on the whole I got more than I expected and far less than I needed. It remains to be seen what will come of several introductions that my friends have sent to Ian Maclaren and the like. . . . I leave home on the 27th.

Despite Helen's apprehensions about the effect of Edward's three-day reunion with friends at Oxford, he came away in good spirits, though no better in health than when he left home. 'I am seeing people all day long', he informed her, 'but chiefly MacAlister who is much concerned about my position. His father (don't tell a soul) is thinking of setting up a publishing firm in about 6 months, and MacAlister thinks I might act as reader. It is a kind and practicable suggestion. Meantime nothing is certain. I am behaving quite temperately so you needn't fear.' This attractive plan came to nothing, but on the way home from Oxford he called on the editor of *The World* who gave him

books to review, including Morley's *Cromwell* and promised to consider carefully anything I sent. The *Chronicle* the same day gave me 15 books to review, chiefly minor poetry, and has been encouraged to send me the latest translation of the 'Odyssey' this week. Besides this, I have discovered that Poverty and not

Indigestion is really the Tenth Muse. Consequently I have been writing ceaselessly, including two studies of Oxford Scouts, of which some people approve.
It has come to this. I have decided that I could not afford just yet to leave the
neighbourhood of London. So we are going into a 3-room flat at Earlsfield
(near Wimbledon) next week. My people have generously given us nearly all
the furniture we need, and for a time I do not anticipate much discomfort or
pecuniary hardship. There are several schemes in the air; but unless they succeed, I will not discover them. Our flat, which is 117, Atheldene Road,
Earlsfield, London, S. W. 1 is very comfortable and without any expense we are
having the walls distempered in French grey, a colour I greatly love. I wish you
could come to our housewarming!

After so many ups and downs Thomas seemed at last to be set on the
course he had originally planned for himself. His father, against all
expectation and the rather one-sided legend that had grown around
him, had behaved generously and fairly with the eldest son who had
shown so much promise, but left unfulfilled the possibility of some
vicarious satisfaction for the able, austere, public-spirited man. When
Edward was in severe difficulty Mr Thomas had come to his aid, stiffly
perhaps, and undoubtedly prompted by his wife. Now that Edwy was
'qualified' to find a steady job of some kind, and clearly much better
in health, his father had given him the necessary jolt to make him
stand on his own feet. Although no bond of affection—and certainly no
'love'—grew between them, Mr Thomas continued to extend the hospi-
tality of his home to Edward and his family for the rest of his life; and
when Edward became a soldier, and left for France, his father promised
to look after Helen and her children if the need should arise.

The Oxford experience helped to form Thomas more effectively than
his 1903 study of the University would seem to suggest. Until he became
a soldier, it was the only sustained period in which he tried to come to
terms with the demands of a society that held strong attitudes incompatible with his private world. In a letter to Robert Frost, a week or two
before his death, Thomas summed up his reaction to enlistment, and his
first exposure to front-line warfare, with the phrase 'I think I get surer
of some primitive things that one has to get sure of, about oneself and
other people'. This certitude lies at the centre of his poetry, and the best
of his prose writings. It provides the framework of the bridge along
which his voice passes to us with undiminished clarity, fortitude, lack of
bigotry, and self-assurance. Before he went to Oxford he had set himself
to describe natural things and his own involvement in them. He brought
away from Oxford a greater readiness to understand the interests and

pursuits of the audience he was to address, although he was never able to join wholeheartedly in their manifold activities. He was modified and deepened, but not fundamentally changed. Three months after graduation he concluded his Oxford notebook entries in a kind of end-of-year reckoning: 'One of my greatest regrets is that I did not attend chapel at Lincoln. The lack of it is a loss to my "prospect and horizon": it is comparable to the lack of a mother's sweetness in one's early education.' The tone is echoed in a note on the last page of his War Diary: 'I never quite understood what was meant by God.'

CHAPTER 6

London and the Weald

EDWARD THOMAS spent the six years between November 1900 and November 1906 in five different houses. Two were in London suburbs: 117 Atheldane Road, Earlsfield, S.W., from 2 November 1900 to 12 February 1901, and 7 Nightingale Parade, Nightingale Lane, Balham, S.W. until October 1901. Three houses were then tried in the Kent countryside: Rose Acre, Bearsted, near Maidstone from 9 October 1901 until March 1903, The Green, Bearsted, until February 1904, and Elses Farm, The Weald, Sevenoaks from May 1904 until 26 October 1906. Thereafter he lived in and around Steep, near Petersfield in Hampshire, close to Bedales School, until in October 1916 he moved his family temporarily to High Beech, near Loughton in Essex while preparing for his commission in the Royal Garrison Artillery and overseas service in France. His work as critic-essayist and author of a wide variety of books required frequent contact with Fleet Street and various editors and publishers; his instinct, expressed so forcibly in numerous early letters to Helen from London and Oxford, was to live in the countryside. In 1913, in his little book *The Country,* he allowed one of his numerous semi-autobiographical speakers to elaborate the point:

'There is nothing to rest on,' he said, 'nothing to make a man last like the old man I met in the woods.' This man's story could probably be paralleled thousands of times today. I have given it because unintentionally it refutes his statement that nothing is left for us to rest on. There was something firm and very mighty left even for him, though his melancholy, perverse temper could reach it only through memory. He had Nature to rest upon. He had those hills which were not himself, which he had not made, which were not made for man and yet were good to him as well as to myriads of other races, visible and invisible, that have been upon the earth and in the air, or will be in some other moment of eternity.

To put it less equivocally, he had the country to rest on. For Nature includes Fleet Street as well as the Milky Way, Whitechapel as well as the valley of the Towy or the valley of the Wylye. There are eyes, and at least one pair of human eyes, that look with as much satisfaction on a lamp-post as on a poplar-tree, and see towns as beautiful birds' nests. For most of us this visionary or God-like view is impossible except in a few particular and irrecoverable moments. We cannot make harmony out of cities. . . . We may feel the painful splendour of our humanity in the town, but it is in the country more often that we become aware, in a sort of majestic quiet, of the destiny which binds us to infinity and eternity.

This was written thirteen years after he had left Oxford with the determination to live by his writing. In between he held tenaciously to his dream of the healing way of a country life. The thread often snapped, but he and Helen, equal sharers in this dream, as frequently caught up the ravelled ends and knotted them together.

In their first suburban home the initial obstacle was poverty. In the twelve months after Oxford he earned £52 by writing; in the second year, until September 1902, he earned £116. He had accumulated at least £70 worth of debts—£50 for wine—when he left Oxford: he was frequently dunned for them and at last threatened with an appearance before the Oxford County Court. He sold many of his fine Oxford folios and cleared his debts by September 1902. By then his prospects of gaining work as a reviewer were good, although he discovered that the 'nature essays', which had promised a tolerable living between the age of 17 and 21, were as unsaleable as ever, even in the *World*, the *Globe* and the *New Age*. In 1901 he felt able to spend a fortnight's holiday at Heath Hatch House, Horsmonden and 'try to be healthy and stupid and fish all day long'. He returned to London before Helen and Merfyn, probably to pick up review books. Their delayed return home upset him completely, as he explained to his friend, MacAlister: 'I am awfully sorry if my telegram excited you. I was in a state of alarm and then despair. My wife and child were to have reached here at 12, and I waited for them in vain, until 5. I had concluded that there had been a railway smash. As a matter of fact, the only accident was the non-delivery of her telegram, explaining that she had been forced to wait for a later train. The telegram hasn't come yet. My state is laughable—now. I was reduced to reading the Litany.' MacAlister remained one of a small group of friends to whom Edward could open his mind about the fears that frequently beset him from this time forward.

There were very small reserves of money left, either from Helen's legacy or from the Post Office bank account. Probably Ian MacAlister sent him money in February 1901 to enable him to move house to Balham. A few of Edward's essays were accepted by editors and he enlarged his range of topics a little. He sold books and worked unpaid as probationary assistant secretary to the Charity Organization Committee in King's Road, Chelsea, hoping to gain the post permanently at £100 a year. He turned down a post as a schoolmaster, at £120 a year, and then felt compelled to accept a temporary post at 30/- a week as a clerk with

London University. He discovered that 'regular work seems to be good for me, but it is unusually tiring', and he was disappointed when a suitable post as a librarian and another, as a sub-editor on a weekly, eluded him. Yet his eight months' stay at the much warmer and safer 7 Nightingale Parade brought some good omens. There he had a small study of his own, 'quite full of books, in which I can feel as lonely as an island and I daresay very happy when times improve'. His plan to edit Malory for an American publisher (Houghton Mifflin) dragged on until March 1901, was postponed initially for eighteen months, and was then put off for two and a half years. Strongly encouraged by H. W. Nevinson, his reviewing for the *Chronicle* continued, and he placed articles, not always well paid, in the *Atlantic Monthly, Country Life, Outlook,* and *Crampton's.*

He had found that by assiduous attendance—which he loathed—on editors he and Helen could just about make ends meet. Coal was expensive at 28/- a ton, but in their second home he rented five rooms for 11/- a week. He was still hoping to avoid taking an office post from 10 until 6 or 7 every day, but he wrote in a postscript to MacAlister: 'N.B. I shall go on journalising, and try to save, for many objects, e.g., the education of Philip Merfyn.' Among his see-sawing from one temporary post to another and his ultimate rejection of all jobs as a clerk or a schoolmaster (because they gave him no leisure for writing), he seemed tired but happy in his way of life. Two extracts from letters to Mac-Alister typify his mood in the spring and summer of 1901:

Now that I have a son I realise day by day something (by no means all) of what I used to plan for myself in affections; for as with you, in spite of my ludicrous incapacity for being a guide, it has always been part of my desire that I should control and guide the thing I loved. Briefly, I suppose, I wanted to make him what I should have liked to be myself, but couldn't: I even thought it possible I might succeed. I don't know. I only hope to make a sweet failure of my child. ... I am very happy now and then with some old books of travel I have discovered. I am also still busy with your Elizabethan dramatists and have got almost a volume of notes, etc. There are a hundred things I could do—a dozen things I could do well—but I haven't the pluck, when I know they won't be read, far less be printed. So I just polish essays I wrote months ago, and day by day write a sentence or two as near perfection as is possible for me, to keep my hand in. I read Virgil daily: he is the best training for the ear that I know. (N.B. *Have you got a Claudian?*)

Before Michaelmas 1901 he had to leave the Balham house, which was close to his mother, to Helen's friends, and to the source of journalistic work that was coming his way more frequently. He began looking for a cottage in the country and found it impossible to get the 'old-fashioned cottage' he wanted most. A suitable one at Dorking, at £35 a year, fell through and he then completed an agreement to take a 'pretty house' and garden at Bearsted, near Maidstone. The rent was £32 a year, and Helen and he hoped to make it 'worth any house in the world'. Uncharacteristically he was spending all his reserves in the hope that his luck as a reviewer with the *Chronicle* and the *World* would last. Promise of further work with the *Academy* and with Nelson, for biographical contributions to his Cyclopaedia, gave him added confidence about the new house:

Helen and Philip Mervyn both look forward to the change. The latter is more and more fascinating, and I have just been drawing men and girls and cows and dogs and lambs and birds for him. He doesn't talk much English yet. How he will like the hills and woods and oast houses of Kent. I wish I could feel we were settling there for life. It would make existence much sweeter, to know that the house I lived in would always be mine, to fancy it would be sorry when I was carried out at last. . . . My days are devoted to reading Shakespeare and the drawing of the aforementioned and also to carpentering. Last week I was cycling over Kent for a day or two in search of a house; otherwise I hardly leave my door, for a walk is too tiring. The country will be a remedy for many things, I trust, and I don't think it will separate me from my friends. Will it? (To MacAlister.)

For the moment his career was taking the course he had charted ever since his first acquaintance with Ashcroft Noble. His second-class honours degree had closed one door, on a position in learning, but the alternative, something 'to do with literature', remained possible. His father, with four younger sons still to assist in finding careers, could only help in small material ways. Much of their furniture and furnishings, apart from the substantial amount Edward built himself—some of it still in use in his daughter's home—came from his parents' home. Mrs Thomas provided items of food and visited them whenever she could; Mr Thomas secured an interview for Edward with the solicitor of the Great Northern Railway as a possible opening to a lucrative career. For the rest of his life, Edward always found a welcome refuge at his parents' new, more resplendent house, 13 Rusham Road (later called 'Rusham Gate'), Nightingale Lane, Balham. The move to Bearsted was a clear signal that Edward had committed himself to life as a full-time writer, although from time to time later—especially when his books did not sell well—he toyed with the kind of office job that he had decided against soon after leaving Oxford. At the same time he displayed the craftsman

heritage his own father lacked: 'I have been carpentering', he wrote to
MacAlister. 'I began at 10.30 a. m. and at 8 p. m. I had already finished
the frame of a big lounge for my wife's sitting room. It is to be a sofa, an
alternative for 3 chairs, and in case of need an extra bed. I have now only
to fit it with a mattress, and drape it. It is a great saving of cash and the
making gave me a rest; it also amused Philip Mervyn. P. M. is now
wonderfully well and develops apace. *Nulla dies sine linea.* You should
hear him saying 'Hark'!'

The move into Kent brought no work and much expense. He sent
out twenty articles and twelve came back quickly; even the once favourable *Globe* and *Pall Mall* rejected eight in a fortnight. He put a brave face
on things in his letters: 'I go on smoking clay pipes and playing with
Mervyn who is now going to sleep to the sound of Bearsted bells.' There
was an acre of garden and Edward turned all the soil over, planted roots,
shoots, and bulbs, stole young trees to plant in it, dug a ditch 540 feet
long, and threw up a bank the same length. He was full of plans for
other sources of income besides reviewing. Dent had a new publishing
venture—a magazine called *The Country*—and Thomas hoped for a
favoured place on it. After much correspondence and many supporting
introductory letters, it came to nothing. Attempts to get favourable
terms from the Temple Classics, from Blackwood's, and from Nelson's
new Cyclopaedia, brought no reward. He commented to Jesse Berridge
—a poet and bank clerk, whose verse Edward had praised—'To eat and
drink here I find I must go ahungered and athirst. . . . So you are right in
saying I am "busy enough" but wrong in saying I am "paid for my
imaginings". My imaginings all in a cupboard and only my lies in print.'
In March, having earned little for some time, he sold £20 worth of
books and hoped to have peace from creditors for a while; but already
he was finding that as article after article was rejected the exquisite
country soothed him too much and encouraged his favourite vice, 'a
mild despair'. It was an ominous sign. He was determined to succeed,
partly because of older people who 'are never tired of rebuking me.
They put melancholy down to crumpets and the like and laugh; they fail
to realise the simple fact that "there it is". I know now, of course, that
melancholy is largely due to physical causes; only it doesn't seem to me
any the less psychical for that.'

In late January 1902 he sent material for a volume of essays to
Duckworth, whose reader was Edward Garnett. The volume appeared in
June under the title *Horae Solitariae,* because the first essay was woven
around an old eighteenth-century book of that name. The title Thomas

insisted on keeping, although he was advised it would be against its sale. ('It has come to mean too much to me, however, to be dropped now.') The publisher couldn't afford to advertise it, and Thomas enlisted his friends' aid in selling it. *Horae Solitariae* was well reviewed and eventually brought a small profit to the author; more importantly through Garnett's sympathy, interest, and friendship, Thomas had found a publishing firm that would continue to publish his 'personal' non-commercial prose books for the rest of his writing life. They formed the direct channel through which flowed that undercurrent of prose-poems which eventually emerged as his poetry some fourteen years later.

The first six months of 1902 at Rose Cottage were full of uncertainties and increasing self-doubt. Early in February he knew that Helen was pregnant and once again they seriously considered the possibilities of an abortion, although Helen wished above all to have many children. When she visited a doctor in London in February Edward wrote asking her not to delay her return: 'Unless you arrange differently I shall meet the 5.30 here. I shall order meat and vegetables. Edith [a new housemaid] has done the whole house, including windows. She has been good. I have been unusually un-depressed, considering my loneliness. But I find I can't write when you are not here—except reviews—I wrote a few words on "The lost art of Reading" this morning and sent them off to *The Practical Teacher*; but the review was 3/4 quotation—I gave a string of characteristic sentences.' His financial prospects appalled him and, as his Oxford contemporaries settled into their different careers, and the attempts of friends (and their parents) to find him suitable posts with fixed incomes proved unsuccessful, he could see the wisdom of accepting any post with a settled income and balanced such worldly-wisdom against leaving 'this last blest place'. So far, his regular income from reviewing was insufficient: 'My thoughts are not so much of dissatisfaction because people don't recognize what perhaps I haven't got, but because I have shown an average or more than average gift of reviewing and yet cannot get enough to keep me going.' He had regular connections with the *Chronicle,* the *World* and the *Week's Survey* that certainly brought in more than he could get from schoolmastering (£120 p. a.). His prospects as an essayist, on which he had built so much as a student, were bleak:

No editor will look at me, unless I send something written in 1895 or which might have been written in 1895. Even Haynes tells me that my 'edition de luxe style' won't pay. I suppose I must grind out some fiction, though I don't know if that is much more promising. I am very badly off for plots, and frankly I don't feel justified in writing of men and women whom I have scarcely met and never studied. You would laugh at my efforts to write pot-boilers. I think of a popular subject. I write out a popular title. Then I write in a day or two 1,000 words. Then I correct; and transform what might have been a pot-boiler into something that certainly is not. The worst of it is my conscience may really be a bad one and may reject what is the better of two courses. But a conscience I have. My serious defect is that I have no easy and genial command of nonsense, flowing as from an overfilled pen—thus (blot!).

It was a true assessment of his prose works aimed at a publisher's needs, and remained so. He had been type-cast early on as a 'nature' writer; the subsequent bias of his education, and his experience as a reviewer, moved him inexorably towards a concern with the understanding of poetry. The 'damnable habit' of introspection, frequently condemned in his letters, defined precisely his inability to write balanced dialogue or to remove the centre of his attention away from his own thoughts and reflections. Except for the narrative sketches, and the stray encounters that pepper his travel books, all Thomas's attempts at full length fiction—beginning at Oxford and ending in 1914—confirm the judicious comment of W. H. Hudson to Edward Garnett when he read *The Happy-Go-Lucky Morgans* in December 1913: 'He is essentially a poet . . . and this book shows it, I think, more than any of the others. You noticed probably in reading the book that every person described in it . . . are one and all just Edward Thomas. A poet trying to write prose fiction often does this.' Thomas was aware of his faults from the beginning. When he sent MacAlister the proofs of *Horae Solitariae,* he commented: 'Its only good passages are inessential decorations. . . . I feel I ought to use my *knowledge* more than I do at present. Hardly any of my work suggests that I know anything except my own emotions. It might have been written by the solitary or savage occupant of a Pacific island.'

His social life at Bearsted was neither solitary nor savage. Oxford and London friends, and members of the Noble and Thomas families, frequently visited the cottage, although Harry Hooton recalls it as 'a raw, vile cheap-jack house'. At first, Edward admitted, he dug the garden as if the earth was his enemy until he found it a good friend. But underneath, despite a tepid acquaintance with the rector, he lacked companionship and longed for the cut and thrust of his Oxford friendships:

All the people round here [he told MacAlister] are middle aged, retired and neighbourly, except the labourers. As for them, they distrust me because I am neither a 'gentleman' nor a labourer, in their eyes. And of course I am to blame in not chucking off my shyness and speaking to them. But if I go into a village pub they are silent at once and seem half surprised and half resentful. And yet I have many dear acquaintances in Wales and Wiltshire who are labourers, miners, etc. You used to laugh when I talked of shaking the horny hand. And now I am growing a horny hand myself and in fact—especially when I compare myself with [J.H.] Morgan—I am on a fair way to becoming a solid, fairly sensible man. If I drank as much as the labourers I should soon be on equal terms, I expect. Shall I try?

His apprehensions about employment as a reviewer were not justified. When books came in batches he overworked to meet various deadlines, occasionally relying on laudanum to carry him through the effects of fatigue and the nervous bouts which he could not control, even if he could describe them: 'I am all right, except that a sort of nervousness, a continuous palpitation and sense of something approaching that never comes, prevents me from writing. I don't mean a sense of approaching good or bad luck, but merely a sense of *something coming*, as if I had heard a report and waited for the other barrel. . . . So all I can do is to resolve myself into an ear that listens to ceaseless rain and an eye that merely watches the fire. It is hard to write even this.' But he was not as miserable as he sounded: he never was. In the warm March weather all three of them spent hours 'at gardening' until he began to feel he had acquired a thicker skin: 'I have had two papers in the *Illustrated London News* and one in the *Academy* this year. That is all. And yet it is more painful to write this down than the actual experiences, because I have learned to drift. Nevinson of the *Chronicle* tells me that my position (or rather, he spoke of a position similar to mine) is "unendurable". I believe it and ignore it.' Occasionally, after a morning hard at a review, he would seek a distant pub or, on one of his 'mad days', return home after half a mile and empty the remainder of a brandy bottle left over from a weekend visitor, because he was 'unaccountably nervous and anxious, as if something were going to happen'. And yet he knew from 'endless experience' that his fears were groundless.

Like MacAlister, Haynes maintained close touch with Thomas: these were Oxford friendships that never faltered. They seemed to sense that Edward needed the support of their practical down-to-earth advice. Haynes had often counselled Edward against the resort to laudanum and had received his assurance (in late 1900): 'I appreciate your alarm at my taking laudanum. However, I could not unintentionally take too much: with a phial that holds only 100 drops, and visibly divided into strata of ten, that is impossible. Perhaps what you mean is that I may abandon myself at some moment of critical depression: I grant I had considered that, but the memory of a dose of 300 drops I desperately took a week ago is so terrible in my mind and disgusting to my palate that an increase would demand superhuman audacity—the flavour haunts me still.' And now, eighteen months later, Haynes advised him to cut through his financial difficulties and 'plan some critical or autobiographical work'. Thomas and Haynes had once before attempted a novel together but that, too, had collapsed as Edward explained to Haynes: 'Dialogue will be my difficulty. If I do it at all, the most important speeches will have to be autobiographical in which I am least bad. I shall also have to use my recollections of Balliol [Haynes's College] and steal some epigrams from Maine.' Despite his love of company, which he sought out from time to time in London, Thomas was not a natural clubman; nor, in his own chosen work of words, did he become involved in dialogue or the interplay of fictional characters against each other. He was a born observer and could freeze into silence like any professional naturalist. In his *Memoirs,* Julian Huxley records similar bouts of silence, in writing about his brother Aldous, as 'sometimes embarrassing to the company. . . . Their basis could have been . . . an unacknowledged desire for spiritual privacy.'

Overwork and excessive solitude sometimes plagued Edward beyond control; and the effect of his erratic swings of mood on Helen forced from her, on 7 June 1902, a sad confession to her oldest friend, Janet Hooton:

I never in my life desired solitude, complete isolation of body and mind as I desire it now. Two great facts are always before me. First as I expect you know I am to give the world another baby in October. This alone is terrible for no one wants the poor wee thing, no one looks forward to its coming, and I least of anyone. I know I shall love it when it lies in my arms, perhaps all the more because I know it will have only me to depend on for love: but now I cannot have any bright thoughts of it, I think of it only with tears in my eyes and a fierce pain in my heart, an intolerable aching which wears me out body and soul. It is terrible to me more than to most people perhaps for down crash some of my purest ideals: I feel accursed because of this sweet thing lying near my heart. You ask why I do not want it? Because we are very poor; because it means more anxiety for Edward, and more worry for him. Home will become unendurable to him. Even now poverty, anxiety, physical weakness, disappointments and discouragement are making him bitter, hard, and impatient, quick to violent anger, and subject to long fits of depression. . . . He cannot have the quiet he needs, and anxiety and discouragement are not fit fortifications against the little worries and irritations that occur where there are young children. How then will it be with two? We cannot afford any extra help; there are no prospects of being less poor. He is selling some of his dearest books to pay for baby clothes and doctor etc., and as he packs them up I know he is rebelling at fate. How hard life seems to him now, he regrets it all. But on me who loves him more than my life the burden falls doubly. . . . He cannot love, Janet, he cannot respond to my love. How can he when all is so dark, and I, I have deprived him of it all, the joy of life and love and success. . . . I have prayed that I and my babe may die, but we shall not, though this would free Edward. I am as strong as ever. I pile work on work till my body can scarce move for weariness, but nothing lifts the darkness from my soul.

Our little Merfyn is perfect, always happy, always well, and my happiest moments are when Edwy and he play and laugh together. Edwy's gentle word or tender caress are almost more than I can bear now, I faint with too much sweet because I love him so, and because they are so precious being so rare. But O how he tries to be patient through it all: he is so full of good, so sweet, he deserves so much and has so little. . . . Forget all this, perhaps these years will pass and we shall forget them, or remember only the little joys. That I have told you is a proof of my love.

Helen replied to Janet's instant reply, quite unaware of the impact her letter made on Janet and Harry:

Nothing I said in my letter made you think badly of Edward did it? It was a terribly wrong impression if you felt it. For indeed he is not to blame, not one bit. I am more to blame than he because of late I have lost heart and I have had no strength or will to bear up against little things which I should have seemed not to notice at all. . . . he is so sensitive, so nervous that he cannot meet disappointment unflinching as some can. Of the two I am the strongest, it is I who have been weak in allowing him to see that his despair caused mine.

The weeks before the birth of the second child (Bronwen, born on 29 October 1902) were in some ways as clouded as Merfyn's birth two years before. Helen believed she was destined to bear numerous children, and throughout her long life took endless pleasure in the company of the young; she was an approving confidante of older girls. Edward, one suspects, was less happy with small children although an eager instructor of older ones in country lore and skills. (There is ample testimony to this in the written and verbal memories of his brothers, of David Garnett, and the sons of James Guthrie, the artist and printer who had settled for a time at Harting near by, and was recommended to Thomas by Bottomley.) He had acquired from his own upbringing a dislike of the disharmony when father and mother disagreed—but without open discussion—about the role that both nurture and nature should play in the development of their six children. As far as they could, Edward and his brothers had escaped as much as possible from the puritanical ambience of home. In their courtship he and Helen were determined to offer an ideal setting for their own children whose advent, they intended, would be carefully planned. Some of Edward's irritation with his domestic life springs as much from the upset to his ideals for a true 'home' by the unplanned births of Merfyn and Bronwen as from his concern over his financial state which, except in these first two post-Oxford years, was never as desperate as his letters suggest. The riches he sought to provide for his own children—even in his poems to each of them—are of a non-material, fairy-tale kind. He simply wishes them to enjoy a childhood different from his own.

During the late summer and early autumn of 1902, while *Horae Solitariae* was favourably reviewed but reviewing work was not too plentiful, the Thomases were left servantless and Edward helped out with domestic work. He widened his horizons 'by cleaning knives and scrubbing floors' and even began to develop 'housemaid's knee'. Though reviewing picked up, and still more favourable reviews of *Horae Solitariae* appeared, his own essays were being rejected by editors. Most of his friends were away on holiday and fortunately he 'found an inn at the bottom of a hollow of the hills' with good cider, and there, for sixpence, he could make himself 'more sublime than Rothschild [and] Lord Kitchener'. He was pleased that he had the knack of reviewing and that editors recognized it although his one desire was to have unlimited time for his essays and character sketches. 'For though I have to live by reviewing,' he wrote to Bottomley on 17 October, 'I am by nature most uncritical. I read very much as I eat, and all I know is that a book feeds me or it does not. . . . Still, perhaps I know something about technique.'

He was annoyed when his first daughter arrived at 10.45 p. m. on 19 October, 'leaving Helen out of breath but cheerful. Don't congratulate me;' he told Jesse Berridge, who had recently become the father of a second son, 'perhaps in 1920 you may. "It" is an ugly, healthy thing, with a lot of black hair and blue eyes.' At the same time he informed Bottomley, 'I am still excited and can hardly read. Work pours in more often than it used to do, and of a difficult kind sometimes. So the only peaceful task I can enjoy now is reading letters and going over the Christian names of women. I think we shall choose Rachel Mary, especially as both are names which have some call upon me. I should have liked Maudlin but must give it up.' Eventually 'Bronwen' was added to the other two names. She proved a source of joy to him for the rest of his life and, according to Harry Hooton, Bronwen is the child in 'The Flower-

Gatherer' in *Light and Twilight* (1911) around whose imagined death by drowning Thomas wove one of his many fears for the well-being of those he loved most. As he introduces her into this sombre sketch Thomas catches her unspoiled beauty and lively sense of fun.

One child separated herself from the rest, moving down instead of across or up the hill. Often she went on her knees among the flowers, with bent eyes that saw only the hundreds close at hand. But from time to time she raised her head, her delicately browned and yet more rosy face, her gleamy hair, that was as pale as barley on her temples but elsewhere golden brown as wheat, her round and calm yet lively eyes, her restless happy lips—and looked steadily for a moment at the whole of earth and sky, and grew solemn, only to return to the other pleasure of the hundred cowslips just at her feet, the crystal and emerald wings among them, the pearly snails, the daisies, and the chips of chalk like daisies. Tighter grew her hand round the swelling bunch.

On the word of his artist brother Ernest, Edward Thomas was gifted with a pencil, and this sketch of Bronwen shares an atmosphere of affectionate presentation with some portraits of children by Pissarro and Renoir.

Because of his loneliness, tied to Rose Acre by lack of means and Helen's pregnancy, Edward felt physically very tired. 'A three-mile walk tires me just as much as thirty miles with a friend,' he wrote to Jesse Berridge. 'Still, I usually walk twelve miles a day.' However, having cleared his Oxford debts and sold some of his books, his regular income from reviewing began to improve. In December 1902 he reported to MacAlister that he had heard unofficially that he was to receive the review-books from the *Chronicle* which used to go to Lionel Johnson, who had died in November. It was a new beginning that gave him almost ten years occupancy of his 'pulpit' in the *Chronicle* and provided him with at least £200 a year. This letter deserves quoting because it indicates that the underlying source of his discontent with his chosen career as a free-lance writer was not based as much on the meagre financial rewards as on his sense of misdirection in all that he did or was called upon to do:

We are pretty well. Rachel Mary Bronwen (for that is her name) grows more agreeable in appearance. Her eyes are changing in the direction of brown, and her hair is to be dark brown, a contrast to Mervyn, who has conspicuous blue eyes and fair yellow hair in long waves. He is a nice boy at times, and by the way he sends you two kisses. He has already quite a store of knowledge about animals, natural effects and colours etc., and is a good talker and a most hearty lover of life, with just a tinge of reverie along with a short sharp temper. He runs and climbs and walks often five miles a day. He will be three next month. I know you would like to see how joyous we can be while he hears me 'singing' Welsh airs or 'The Old Grey Fox' or 'Widdicombe Fair' or 'The Lincolnshire Poacher'.

Still my progress towards the state of family man is not smooth or invariably pleasant. I often want to go away and walk and walk for a week anywhere so long as it is by an uncertain road. For though I like to stay in one piece of country I don't like (as I have to, in England) to meet continually some respectable acquaintance with whom I must stop to bore and be bored. I am not a bit of a wanderer, but I like to be thought-free and fancy-free as I can't be in this sweet domestic country. Also my melancholy 'grows along with me'.

Everything you say to encourage me in my work encourages me, partly because I know you used to be unsympathetic. I don't despair because my work is unrecognized. What makes me desperate is the little leisure (from reviewing and much thinking about money) left me to write my best in. In the last three months [October–December 1902] I have written about 1000 words exclusive of reviews. Yet my head has been so full that I might have done 10,000 much better than I did 1000, and though some of that was at the rate of 40 words an hour. Moreover, when for a time I am free from all business, though my tendency then is to write, I am not always willing to. For I must have some time in which to be non literary, free to think or better still not to think at all, but to let the wind and the sun do my thinking for me, filling my brain. . . . Well, I seem to have spent much ink in getting myself on paper. I had better have sent my photograph.

Apart from his tales and sketches in *Rest and Unrest* and *Light and Twilight*—both commercially unprofitable—and the numerous prose-poems he inserted from time to time into his commissioned travel books, he had to await the sudden onset of his verse-writing in late 1914 before 'letting the wind and the sun do my thinking for me, filling my brain' became the hallmark of his discovery of a language that would not betray his secret thoughts.

1903 proved a difficult year for Edward and his family. Initially, his good luck in succeeding Lionel Johnson was followed by nearly two months in which he had no books to review for the *Chronicle*. He records, in a notebook dated February, a return of 'the old fatigue'. Edward had already found his parents' spacious new house—with a gas fire in every room and numerous modern conveniences—somewhat too grand for his taste. Yet, on 11 February 1903, he left Helen and the children behind and went to his father's home 'for an indefinite length of time, because I am in debt, and am not earning much or likely to for some months'. Judging by Helen's letters to her friend and her sister, the initiative for this new move came from her. He had only a few shillings left until he got work. Nevinson, instrumental in securing him work on the *Chronicle*, now suggested Thomas as a substitute for himself to write 'a book of 60,000 words on Oxford, to accompany a series of pictures by John Fulleylove, R. I.' The book, which Thomas would have liked to take ten years over, had to be completed by 30 June. He was to be paid £100, with an immediate advance payment of £20. He knew he would have to take extra reviewing during the four months of writing *Oxford*, and this he did.

Originally he had planned to spend at least a month in London, but he was unable to work there. He visited Oxford, met a few old friends, and stayed there briefly, and very soberly, because he had decided to move from Rose Acre, so high and windy, to the village green at Bearsted, eight minutes away and much more sheltered. The move would take place in mid-June when most of *Oxford* would have been written and sent off to the artist and the publisher. The stay in London had relieved his financial difficulties and when MacAlister, now an ADC to Lord Dundonald, General Officer commanding the Canadian Army, sent him a generous birthday present, Edward bought some rugs for the new house. Frequently during April and May he complained of ill-health and of slowness in his work on the book; restless, he visited London and Oxford again for help and background material, and occasionally used laudanum to encourage him to work. On 16 June 1903 they moved into the 'pretty old house on the village green, with a pair of lime trees on the two strips of lawn in front of the house. . . . It is full of old woodwork, which gives the entrance to the staircase quite a monastic look. I expect I shall be able to write there.' *Oxford* was completed a week later in a final flurry of hard writing with increasing irritability in his leisure moments. He expected his friend MacAlister to 'despise it. I do. It is neither good hack work nor good Edward Thomas. . . . It will hurt me very much to see it in print. Day after day I had to excite myself and write what I could. . . . It has left me dried up, and I feel that I shall never do good, slow, leisurely work again. I shall not be happy until I have begun an essay again, at least so I think when I am not quietly happy with a book (which is not often) or with Helen or Mervyn and the baby. The baby, by the way, is now very fair-haired and is the happiest creature in the world.'

Helen regarded the strain of writing *Oxford* as a factor in the intensification of a depressive tendency that Edward had shown since late adolescence, but which was to affect him cruelly and periodically on at

least four occasions in the next ten years, although the illness was rarely
crippling. (Invariably he seemed capable of writing his way through his
bouts.) The favourable reviews that followed later—like the subsequent
reprintings—confirm the posthumous comments of his lawyer-friend
and close Oxford companion E. S. P. Haynes in his *Personalia* (1918) and
Fritto Misto (1922): 'His life at Oxford was, on the whole, happy and
unruffled, and there perhaps for the first time he became thoroughly
interested in his contempories. . . . He was always hyper-aesthetic as
regards impressions, and the beauty of Oxford sank deeply into him. . . .
It was probably the happiest time of his life. The atmosphere of all that
period is admirably expressed in his books *Horae Solitariae* and *Oxford*.
His talk was incomparable—but he was as reticent as he was responsive.'
Thomas, we know, would have liked to take ten years over the book, but
he also knew that concentrated effort brought out some of his best qualities and Haynes was acute to link the leisurely, almost nonchalant,
Pater-tinted approach of the *Horae Solitariae* essays with the more urgent
approach, in all but three blatantly space-filling chapters, of his *Oxford*.
Here are keen humorous descriptions of undergraduate types—and
recognizable figures—with himself woven skilfully in and out. His relish
of good conversation, good living, and sheer fun is shown amply in a
chapter on an Oxford day, at the hard centre of his book. The rest is
crowned by his clearly-observed, well-informed, and variegated
accounts of walks and footpaths that took in Cumnor, Radbrook, South
Hinksey, Headington, Wheatley, Osney, Eaton, Stanton Harcourt, and
Bablock Hythe, with echoes of remembered conversations beside the
Cherwell and Evenlode between Water Eaton and Islip. As he wrote it,
the kind of congenial life that 'success' at Oxford might have offered to
him was out of his grasp. But it is a joyous book that reveals one might-
have-been side of Edward Thomas that always lies just beneath the
smooth surface of his travel-books.

After three days spent with Maine in John Street to attend the graduation ceremony in October 1900, he was an infrequent visitor. Even then
his only really happy hour (save conversations with MacAlister) was in
the churchyard of St. Peter's in the East (Queen's Lane), 'an old resort to
which I went alone,' he wrote in his notebook, 'and enjoyed the almost
vernal and floral beauty of the dainty golden lime leaves overhanging
the tombs and full of sunlight.' He rarely revisited Oxford the place: he
carried its spirit with him for many years on his solitary walks across the
South of England. *Oxford* may have diverted his gift from its true place.
In support of Fulleylove's coloured illustrations, he saw men and things

with a clear eye and recorded what he saw with economy, humour, and detachment. Much later he informed his literary agent that his 'colour books' could stand on their own feet without the crutch of illustrations provided by a fashionable artist-illustrator. Surely, he recognized that the gift for ironic, wry, half-concealed self-relevation, the hallmark of his best work, was already apparent in his first commissioned book. His nature welcomed pricks against which to kick. Even then, in 1903, he could paint himself: 'His one pose is that of plain-spoken, natural man, in the presence of a snob. Everywhere he is as independent as a parrot or a tramp. In life, few are to be envied so much. For he achieves everything but success.' At one time highly valued as a clear memory of pre-1914 Oxford days Thomas's *Oxford* still recalls that age, as well as a much built-over but not completely obliterated countryside. Chiefly, though, it uncovers the intricate byways of Thomas's own mind and attitudes, and underneath the elegant, but not over-refined prose style, lies hidden the tone of regret, already recorded, about his neglect of chapel at Lincoln, comparable to the lack of a mother's sweetness in early childhood.

The aftermath of the hurried work on *Oxford*, together with more frequent book-reviewing and the financial arrangements that went with the change of house, was a period of two months in which he tried some desultory walking along the Pilgrim's Way (for which he was too fatigued), did some necessary bread-and-butter reviewing for the *Chronicle*, and carefully planned and worked in his new garden. ('I find in gardening the properties of Lethe and of Styx.') Early in October he broke a four-months' silence and wrote briefly to MacAlister in Canada: 'I have much reviewing and much misery of an animal and unaccountable kind. I feel quite useless and can't write a line except for an editor, and that very badly . . . for I shall always (I think) be able to do my work somehow, since I have a resigned doggedness in doing what I must to live that might be mistaken for courage—the less work I do the better. In fact, I would take 2 or 3 months off with profit if I could without permanent loss.'

MacAlister had already received two long frank letters from Helen expressing her deep concern and asking for his help. The first, on 4 October 1903, begins formally, and then comes straight to the point:

For some months now I have been very anxious indeed about Edward's health. The Oxford book was a tremendous strain, and that added to anxieties about money and so on, have altogether shattered his nerves. He can now write no more than he is obliged to do, and that with difficulty. His mind once so rich

in thought and idea has become incapable of either, and he sits whole days
doing absolutely nothing. . . . I have just come away from seeing a good doctor
[Dr Segundo] . . . he told me what he told Edward, that he must rest entirely,
that he must mix among people, that he must get out of himself as much as
possible. Edward of course said the first was impossible, for an entire change
and rest would cost a great deal, and we had no money.

Helen then outlined her plan. In January 1904, when her brother came
of age, she was to receive a sum not exceeding £60 from her inheritance. She wished to borrow the cost of a month at least for Edward to
visit MacAlister in Ottawa. She would repay MacAlister when her
money arrived: 'The only way to do this is for you to write to Edward
inviting him over to Ottawa and offering to pay his expenses. . . .
Edward must be taken out of himself, and you more than all of his
friends I feel could do this. He must be with people, he must not be left
to himself. Meanwhile I shall try to arrange a move nearer to town
again. Edward is too lonely in the country. I and the children could
manage very well while he is away, and what little money he can spare
out of what remains of the £100 for the Oxford book would be ample.'
   When MacAlister's reply came Edward was already away from home.
As Helen explained, she had to confide her own plan to 'Edwy's mother'
who approved of the Ottawa visit but strongly disapproved of 'my
money being used without Edwy's knowledge'. Edward refused to accept
the money and feared most the long, cold, lonely sea journey. At the
same time he was afraid—unnecessarily as things turned out—that proposed editorial changes at the *Daily Chronicle* in December required his
presence at home. Dr Segundo urged that something ought to be done
at once and Helen found the strain of Edward's behaviour hard to bear.
Providentially, his Oxford friend J. H. Morgan had business at Warminster and took Edward there with him in mid-October. After a fortnight,
Edward's letters home were cheerful and hopeful: 'We get on very well
and have many long talks, both critical and autobiographical, and I feel
myself stimulated, and am conscious of more purely intellectual power
than I generally am, whether writing or talking. He makes me think
afresh . . . We are seldom dull and never bored.'
   Helen confided to MacAlister—whom she had never met—her intense
desire that Edward should

stay till he is perfectly well, his old self. . . . Of late he has seemed to dislike
home. You see, in his terrible state of nervous tension and irritability things
have occurred here which could not be helped in a household with two young

children . . . It was a terrible time, for the least little annoyance—a thing out of place, the children's chatter—affected him as a fearful calamity . . . For you see Mr MacAlister that Edwy's state at present is really only a terrible exaggeration of what he has been several times since I have known him, since he was 17. His temperament is a morbid one, and introspective. The least physical unwellness makes him at once depressed and irritable.

In reply to MacAlister's question whether money would assist Edwy's chances of recovery, she is quite frank that it would: 'Our average income is at most £130 per year. This year has of course been exceptional for Edwy had all but £100 for the Oxford book . . . Some of that he spent in a visit to Oxford, some went in a useless holiday at Swindon, some on a holiday for me which was a great success, and a great deal in little visits here and there which Edward made in search of health. So in reality we have not been better off.'

The holiday in Warminster was expensive. Special foods were prescribed by Dr Segundo, including 'milk, cod liver oil, and Plasmon Cocoa that is a great part of the cure'. Helen wished Edward to stay away as long as he felt necessary. 'For him to have to hasten back for lack of money (though of course he is reviewing still, and so makes a little each week) would be a thousand pities.' Helen knew precisely how she would spend any money that MacAlister could spare them as a gift. 'A restful chair for him, a curtain for his study door, a few pretty things for flowers, a little new table linen (ours is in a sad way), a warm coverlet for his bed, and—O do not think me flippant—a pretty dress for myself, for I never dress to please him being dependent on gifts of dresses that have been other people's, and very grateful I am for such. But a pretty gown to wear for Edward, when we have leisure and can sit together here in our dear little study, would be such a joy to him.' She now had a really good servant and hoped that 'the inner working of the house would be more in accordance with what I want to make it superficially'. Reading between the lines of these almost heart-broken letters one detects the seeds of much of Edward's occasional bouts of irritable discontent with each of his successive homes. Always, one suspects, he was too ready to judge Helen's unregimented approach to housekeeping against the stricter patterns that his father had demanded (and obtained) from his mother, but in their case with adequate domestic help. Edward's solution now that he was husband and father, as it had been when a youth at home, was to escape, a solution that Helen encouraged him to take.

Letters to Helen in December 1903 suggest that the long Oxford-like debates with Morgan had helped him face his illness more objectively.

He found he could cope with minor irritations. He hoped to stay until 23 December 'though I am continually wishing myself at home'. He had put on 11 pounds in five weeks and planned a visit to London on the 19th for a dinner given in honour of Nevinson who was about to leave the *Chronicle*. He returned from the dinner to Bearsted Green, having met the new editor, James Milne, who received him favourably and was soon insisting that Thomas sign all his reviews.

At Warminster Edward had promised himself to be more careful about excessive exercise and hoped to be wiser, less nervous, more hopeful, and less desperate in future. Within a few days he was 'no better at home. Restlessness becoming a disease with me—I hardly know why.' Despite his approval of Dr Segundo's advice on diet and the organization of his daily routine, he found, even at Warminster, that he frequently had to 'submit to the play of the imps that bring into my mind the most mad and trifling and undesired thoughts'. He believed (he told MacAlister) that he was paying for the wrong pattern of his life until then: intemperance; journalism being allowed to kill his essays; the fear that he was losing his religious attitude towards 'Nature'; and 'the dirtiness and confusion of my house'. He was not surprised that on one visit to London Dr Segundo gave him a 'moral thrashing', after which he asked MacAlister to recognize that Helen's 'point-blankness' in her letters about money was caused entirely by her care for him. As Thomas exchanged Christmas wishes with Jesse Berridge he also confessed to physical weakness: a short review exhausts and dissatisfies him; the thought of an essay is inconceivable; but 'I am glad to say that I brood rather less'.

Helen was now confident that his absence from home was curative and she urged him to spend some time (and part of a £30 gift from MacAlister) in London with her brother-in-law H. V. McArthur, an insurance broker. Edward agreed. He gained more work with the *Chronicle* and *World* as a book reviewer, turned down an offer from Methuen to write a 'colour book' on the Netherlands, and half-heartedly sought a congenial 'Librarianship', while secretly wondering, in a letter to MacAlister, 'whether I shall ever write again for my own pleasure,—especially away from home and books and chairs and pictures . . . For I seem to lose myself in London. Everyone I meet makes fresh demands on my invention: for I can never be myself, and when at last I am left alone, I think of Helen and my real friends, Mac, and feel how unjust I am to them as well as myself. I must be solitary, I think—yet that is just what the doctor says I must not be. Or do you think I am simply changing, and that at last I shall find myself as easily as I used to do out of doors or with you in letters or talk? . . . Splendid reviews of *Oxford,* by the way, continue to come in from friends who watch the papers.'

This experiment in a new working pattern of life, spent away from home, appeared to solve Edward's financial worries, but he was not proof against sudden upsets. After three weeks in London, he returned home for five days and enjoyed them immensely: 'The weather has been a series of pleasant progresses . . . so that I have enjoyed the country as well as home. All are quite well now and I wish you [MacAlister] could see Bronwen who is the genius of smiles. But now I want to work and I rather dread trying to work here lest I should be interrupted by the children, get irritated, and so spoil my holiday.' He returned to the McArthurs in Chancery Lane fully expecting to stay some time, but he got sick of London and people: 'I was oppressed by the crowd—got lost in it—and was lured into things that did not really interest or please me in the least. It is difficult to avoid doing so, because I never meet people whose tastes and life suit me in the least, and, in my fear lest I should appear dull, I am too much inclined to fall in their ways for a time. Well, I suddenly left town and came home, and was enjoying it, when Helen fell ill.'

For Helen had a septic throat infection caused by bad drains and was incapacitated for over a month: Bronwen nearly died of pneumonia and Edward then had his worst fit of fatigue and depression. The doctor condemned the pretty old house on the Bearsted village green and Edward decided to move to Elses Farm, The Weald, Sevenoaks, in Kent, about four miles equidistant from Tonbridge and Penshurst. Moving house and doctors' bills depleted the money sent by MacAlister, but, fortunately, Edward had plenty of work as a reviewer and succeeded in doing it. 'I console myself by working at an essay which I know will never sell. But I am so weak that I can really only work every other day.' For the time being he was ready to acquiesce in the jerky pattern of his working life, shared between London and the country, between reviewing to pay the bills and essays to please himself.

Moving house to Elses Farm brought the Thomases renewed hope and comfort. During the first two months there Edward made only one trip to London and, as was usual in the early summer, his income from reviewing decreased. 'I am very badly off at this moment, with 5/- in hand and a prospect of only £1 this month and debts accumulating.' (To Berridge, 21 July.) Elses Farm proved an ideal house, with large, light rooms, a big country kitchen, delightful country around, and a spare room for guests always ready. 'We spend our time in the hayfields now [late June], and both my babies are as brown as berries and as well as possible . . . Edwy likes it, and I hope he will be well here.' (Helen to Janet Hooton). Edward had tried his hand at a popular tale ('The Skeleton') but his heart wasn't in it and he killed off his hero in mid-July. That and 'a very little complaint about the destruction of an old house near Clapham Junction [? Battersea Rise?] are all, except reviews that I have written this year'. Athough he liked his new house, he was still periodically dejected and relaxed, but now and then he felt much more deeply contented than for some years. Physical weakness led to his feeling dully miserable, but he picked up extra work on the *World* and was glad occasionally to meet sudden deadlines 'because I know I shall have to do something, and when I am not working against time and by order I usually fear I shall do nothing'.

This piece of self-revelation explains, perhaps more than any other cause, why in later years he accepted so much commissioned work for poor pay and against time. For in these early years as a working journalist, picking his careful way, he was to acquire habits and adopt practices that were to lead him into strange decisions, often at variance with the ideals he and Helen had pledged themselves to follow. London visits were financially necessary; but long residence in London digs or at the homes of friends and relatives robbed him of an *élan vital* he believed essential for his creative life, even though his circle of friends in London was widening and he had a ready welcome at various lunch or tea club meetings of fellow writers. He believed that his physical well-being depended on a pattern of life at once close to 'nature' and shared with his wife and children. He had discovered that indifferent health produced irritability with his family, played havoc with his peace of mind, and destroyed his ability to undertake any writing that was not routine—although such 'routine' writing included some of his most perceptive criticism. He needed more money than the average of £130 a year to be earned by reviewing and he constantly varied his methods of earning more. His own predilection was for short prose statements which could either be published independently as 'essays'—his original term for all his personally valued creative prose—or be worked obliquely into books or reviews. In a newly confident mood in June 1904, he affirmed this in a letter to Gordon Bottomley: 'We like this place. I have had terrible moods here and long fits of despair and exhaustion, but the short intervals have been very sweet, though, as I say, I wanted something even then. . . . At any rate, I must avoid long things. Perhaps the "man and landscape" plan has a future for me. It is really my physical weakness that spoils my work. I can't write more than a small page at a time: then I am interrupted for a week: and so I wander and sprawl.'

During the summer of 1904 MacAlister returned from Ottawa and, with Edward's aid, began looking for a career as a journalist. He now joined Jesse Berridge and Arthur Ransome as occasional visitors to Elses Farm, along with older friends like H. B. Davies (ex-Lincoln), Maine, and Harry Hooton. Fishing, haymaking, hop-picking, and berry-gathering filled out the time left free from Edward's receipt of the usual dull books to review and nothing else. ('I am sick of books and am selling many old possessions now (prose, never poetry, I hope). Ruskin is the first to go. I want to begin again and this is my frantic and vain protest.') Earlier in this same letter, after a fit of remorse, he explained his self-doubts to Jesse Berridge who had decided to leave banking and become a clergyman and writer. 'I understand perfectly. No doubt you are busy and poor. I only envy you your will. I ought to be both busy and careful. But I have no anchor or ballast, and I waste time and money on even unpleasant and inessential things.' The changes of house, more secure evenings, and pleasant rural pursuits were not proof against his sudden swings of mood.

At the end of September he decided to take rooms at Arthur Ransome's lodgings at 1 Gunter Grove, Chelsea. He was sorry to leave home, but his work suffered 'from my stupid but unavoidable nervous interest in the children's movements in and out of the house, and my temper suffered too'. He would need £2 extra a week to cover the cost and he felt quite happy in turning down an offer from Methuen 'which I have refused in spite of the opinion of five independent people'. The month spent at Gunter Grove was full of work, distraction, and little joy: 'I have done much work, my room is so hideous and homeless that I have been able to attempt little elsewhere, and after work I have rushed to some distraction, seldom to books, seldomer to writing. And now I am worse off than ever. For I have just been asked to write a book on Wales for Blacks—and I expect to have less than three months for the whole.' Had it not been for the closeness to Arthur Ransome, who was full of plans, achievement, and energy, or the frequent evening visits paid to the Thomas family or to friends like Berridge, Duncan Williams (and his Welsh folk-song evenings), and MacAlister, Thomas might have returned home sooner. MacAlister seems to have written a letter to Helen about his friend's stay in London, probably suggesting a plan—

later put into operation with assistance from A. Martin Freeman, a leisured Oxford friend with strong interests in folk-songs and the theatre—that MacAlister should hire a cheap cottage close to Elses Farm, ostensibly for his own use at weekends, and that Edward could use it during the week. The gentle MacAlister, who had still not settled down with a suitable companion nor found a permanent post, was clearly perturbed that Edward should live away from home and the countryside. Helen sent 'My dear Mr MacAlister' a full and frank reply early in October:

I am very grateful to you for your letter, for I had been thinking of writing to you; for as you say we had no opportunity of talking about Edwy while you were here, and I wanted your advice, feeling that you love and understand Edwy more than any of our friends.

The plan that Edwy is now carrying out is merely the best of two evils, and is done wholly upon my suggestion. I think Edwy's nervous restlessness and irritability has now become a habit more than the evidence of an unhealthy state. That he is not strong of course I know, and that his nerves are his weak point I know too; but he is far better than he was a year, or even less time ago. And I thought that if he went away from home entirely for a few months, the surroundings and circumstances which arouse this habit would be removed, and he would lose what you know Mr MacAlister, not only makes work for him impossible, but wears him out physically, and me mentally. It is not necessary for any one to know to what extremes Edwy sometimes goes when these moods are upon him, but it is necessary to know that the happiness of the entire home is at stake. I mean that after one of his worst days—which have been fewer of late—he is cast into the depths of depression and remorse, and work and happiness are again of course impossible for him. I don't want to speak of myself for my whole hope in life and aim is to make Edwy happy. I tell you this because when Edwy leaves home as now, many quite intimate friends get the notion that he and I are not as husband and wife should be, and this is the bitterest pain to me, and as I am sure you know it is absolutely untrue. When Edwy is away his one theme is the joy of homecoming. But to your plan. I think it is an excellent one. I have always thought that the most perfect arrangement of Edwy's day would be to work away from home, and to come home when he had done at the end of the day. I don't think seeing people makes much difference; when in town he goes about, more because he cannot settle down in his own room, to reading a pleasant book, or otherwise restfully employing his leisure. The only point in disfavour of your plan is this, Edwy is very desirous of getting more work, making more money, in order that we may save a little each year for Merfyn's education. Up to now Edwy's average income has been £3 a week, which you see leaves no margin. Since he has been in town he has made much more than the usual average, and I am sure this has encouraged him. To get work one has to be constantly reminding editors of one's existence, and craving for work. Of course he could go into town once a week—on Wednesday when there is a cheap train—and I should think that would be enough. I quite see that the life he leads now is not good for him, but it has some satisfaction for him. I think the best plan would be for him to stay in town two or at the most three months, and then to take a room near as you suggest, coming home when his work is done. In the three months he might have got a certain footing on the various new papers he is trying to work for; also that time will give him the chance of losing the nervousness which home alone irritates. Then for him to take a room *at once*, so as not to tempt the old devil back by trying to work at home in so short a time.

Will you advise him thus, or any modification of this that you approve. I have no one from whom to ask advice, for you see I cannot ask any solution for myself. But in saner times I realise that Edwy's troubles are of his own making, almost entirely. So please advise me whenever you feel you can.

And in conclusion please remember that I am more than willing to think over any suggestion of yours. Suppose we suggest to Edwy to accept your plan at once, and then mine as above if he feels he cannot return home before giving London a longer trial.

Although this particular plan fell through, these letters became the basis for a secure lifelong friendship between Ian MacAlister (who became Secretary of the RIBA and was knighted in 1934) and Helen and her children that endured for over sixty years. His voluminous correspondence with Edward provides an open door into Thomas's thinking at all key points of decision in his life. MacAlister with Walter de la Mare and Rowland Watson, steered the Edward Thomas Memorial Committee which ended with the placing of the Sarsen Stone memorial on the Shoulder of Mutton Hanger above Steep in October 1937.

CHAPTER 7
Wales and Elses Farm

EDWARD'S agreement to write *Beautiful Wales* put a temporary stop to the amiable conspiracy between Helen and MacAlister. He outlined his immediate plans on 20 October 1904: 'I go to Wales for a short preliminary walk at the end of next week. (I hope Helen may come too). And after that I may find it necessary and best to work at home because for such a theme my old books and notes and a hundred little things which are not here are necessary.' Within three days he, Helen, and Merfyn were in lodgings with Mrs Phillips at Oaklands, Ammanford, close to their old friend the bard Gwili. They spent the entire daylight out of doors; he made a few notes, they read a little, and got very tired to bed. After seven days Helen returned home, while Edward aimed to walk and train into North Wales for a week, carrying a satchel of necessaries and living as cheaply as possible. His plan was frustrated. After three days (and sixty miles) his feet were blistered and strained. He returned to Elses Farm via Ammanford by 11 November. But he was pleased with the outing and was nervously trying to begin to make use of all his recollections and readings in an upstairs room converted into a study. He was 'going to try hard to stay at home, because I want to and also because I can't afford to return to town'. It was a brave resolution. He informed Bottomley: 'You can't guess how the little things of life here trouble me and incapacitate me. Merfyn fidgetting is worse than a brass band practising at Chelsea: truly; though I am not sure why. . . . I hope you will write in spite of all discouragement from me: I believe that I am what I am because I am perplexed by *Wales* and by the reviewing I have to keep up as usual and by problems besides which these are amusements.'

The upstairs study faced north and, reluctantly, he was moving his books ('all my modern poets on shelves over the fire in my study'). There he pushed on relentlessly at *Beautiful Wales* and reviewing, with a series of progress reports to the co-operative Bottomley. When, as usual, the family spent Christmas with his parents, he had completed the first half of the book. In London he and Helen had influenza and he returned alone to Elses Farm for the New Year, 'trying to cook and work at the same time, so that my usual haste and stupidity are doubled. For I want badly to write, but obviously cannot'.

6. With Merfyn on vacation at Ammanford, after Schools 1900.

7. Edward Thomas, regular reviewer for the *Daily Chronicle,* with his son, parents, and paternal grandmother, late 1902.

8. The author of *Horae Solitariae* with Merfyn at Rose Acre Cottage, winter 1902–3.

As usual, when at work on a book, he expressed dissatisfaction with its progress in his letters. But his anger at *Wales* ('infinitely worse even than *Oxford*') went even deeper. In his determination to be something more than a reviewer (however percipient) and a word-illustrator of colour-books, he had published some of his papers and essays as *Rose Acre Papers* (in the Lanthorn Press series associated with Arthur Ransome) and had contributed a story to a new periodical, *The Venture*, with Bottomley. He knew that 'stories' were outside his range, unless they were disguised autobiography: he couldn't hope to meet a popular magazine taste. 'I haven't violence. The nearest approach to it is the sham humour which I insert in order to make it clear that my feeble seriousness is as ridiculous to me as to others. I shall not fight against it.' On the surface, though, the second half of *Wales*, a series of landscape descriptions for each month in the year, should have been a setting for the display of his 'feeble seriousness', yet he couldn't satisfy himself and blamed some of his failure on the deadline: 'Think of me writing often 1000 words a day and then with no correction copying them out, and this too when many of the things are of a kind I should usually—chew for a month or more for each thousand words.' With clarity he could see that these prose pieces came close to Bottomley's own more leisurely efforts in his recent volume of poems, *The Gates of Smaragdus:* 'I have just done a wintry white and lonely mountain. It took 2 hours and is just a series of notes. . . . If I had succeeded the result would have been as much like a poem of yours as verse can be like prose. . . . Honestly, I do think we aim at very similar things and you nearly succeed and I never come even so near as to fail. How I could envy you your leisure if I did not know that I should waste it.'

Thomas knew he was space-filling when he added to his wintry mountain a long quotation from Shelley and an even longer passage from Borrow. His dissatisfaction ran deep, and as he worked at his '25,000 words of landscape, nearly all of it without humanity except what it may owe to a lanky shadow of myself—I stretch over big landscapes just as my shadow does at dawn, right over long fields and hedges into the woods and away!' He was so pressed by work, and unable to acquire concentration naturally, that he took some of the devil—opium—thrice a week to help him and 'if I dally long it is not a help, but a great hindrance, so I must be quick'. In response to Bottomley's warnings, he burned his opium, 'as I often have done', and completed *Wales* by the end of February. He was 'grateful to the Devil' because he was able to act 'the amiable man. Then I threw it off, and such is the value of tradition, I am still amiable, and consequently a more cheerful member of this family . . . My great enemy is physical exhaustion which makes my brain so wild that I am almost capable of anything and fear I shall some day prove it.'

Thomas's first resort to laudanum had been at Christmas 1898 when he spent three days in bed with a severe chill. 'And yet this by the way was not a wholly unpleasant experience: it gave me some very wild enjoyment, which I can only suggest to you by referring you to De Quincey's Opium Eater. Distance—distance took to itself a magic and a terror, a delicious terror—the tempestuous loveliness of terror.' A year later, when he feared he might have to leave Oxford without completing his degree course, he informed MacAlister that at one point in the Michaelmas Term 1899 'I hungered for the indifferentism which opium gives.' Occasionally for some years to come, against the stern advice of close friends, he would resort to the drug, especially in periods of acute depression and anxiety. He never allowed the 'Experiment' to become a habit and as far as one can tell from his letters, he finally abandoned the practice in the summer of 1905.

The publishers of *Beautiful Wales* expected Edward Thomas to conform to the usual pattern of their series of 'Beautiful Books', with page illustrations in colour and advertised under a Ruskin quotation: 'Of all God's gifts to the sight of man, colour is the holiest, the most Divine, the most solemn.' Thomas was to supply the text in auxiliary support of Robert Fowler's seventy-four engraved landscape illustrations. There is no match between text and illustration. The book is divided into two equal parts: the first half is an approach to the Wales Thomas had learned to love in early childhood and, later, during his Oxford Long Vacations; the second half describes the progress of the seasons in Wales, month by month. A series of forays into time and space, it scarcely matches the expectations of the usual reader of Black's series. At the book's centre is a love of the old, the fleeting, and the permanent, with occasional points of momentary stillness. Thomas reveals that he had found silence more eloquent than speech, speech more pliable to the mind than writing, and the imagined memory of things past more true to his present self than legend, or natural beauty, or even his much-admired Welsh folk-songs. 'But by this mountain you cannot be really at ease until in some way you have travelled through all history. . . . And if, as some have done, you go there with willingness and an inability to accept what dreams have hitherto been dreamed, you may seem there . . . to be on the edge of a new mythology and to taste the joy of

the surmises of him who first saw Pan among the sedges or the olives.'
He singles out 'so-called matter-of-factness in combination with a rich
imaginativeness' as perhaps a Welsh characteristic. The combination is
evident throughout his text, even in the second half where he paints the
seasons from Wales (and elsewhere in England) as though in friendly
rivalry with the illustrator.

Rarely, though, does Thomas resort to static descriptiveness. A series
of journeys is energetically presented to the reader, marked by his special gift of direct visual recall, and rarely obscured by the space-filling
rodomontade which may have been caused by resort to laudanum. In
this first half he hangs a necklace of vignettes of people and places around
his memories of holidays spent in the corner of South-West Wales from
which many of his paternal and maternal ancestors had come. He praises
a small river (the Gwili) 'which takes a course like a man's thoughts
when they have the joy of an unknown impulse and no certain aim.' In a
farmhouse which he peoples with half-fictional, half-real Welsh rural
characters he recalls that 'when we are by this fire, we can do what we
like with Time. . . . What I see becomes but a symbol of what is now
invisible. . . . I could see nothing that was there, because I was thinking
of what had been long ago.' It is fire, 'in my memory', that creates the
Welsh characters he has gathered together, among them himself, his
father, and his Pontardulais and Swansea friends, according to a detailed
notebook on Wales in the Colbeck Collection.

What readers did he have in mind as he pursued his half-serious quest
for a new mythology at the time of the Welsh Nonconformist Revival of
1905? 'After all, in matters of the spirit, men are all engaged in colloquies
with themselves. Some of them are overheard, and they are the poets. It
is the Bard's misfortune that he is not overheard, at least by men.' And
then Thomas apologises for using the first person as he introduces a
child who had disappeared after a 'slow process of evanishment. . . . as if
I were addressing, not the general reader, but someone who cared.' His
search for listeners to his words was a life-long quest, a modest reflection
of his father's eloquent involvement in public life. It underlies his valid
objection that the reviewers, although favourable, had missed his purpose in writing *Wales*. Of course, he had given them no clues. The
Colbeck notebook indicates the carefully detailed research into Welsh
history, and contemporary Welsh culture and society, that preceded his
final manuscript. Energetic in his journey, tentative in his reflections, he
shows his awareness that he was concerned with topics beyond his
powers of intellectual formulation at that time. Perhaps, unlike a

modern nationalist or a party politician, he lacked a focal point for his ideas, however strong the influence of Owen Edwards may have been upon him while at Lincoln. Or was this apparent uncertainty of aim a genuine mystic's humility, which he masked by frequent quotations from Herbert, Traherne, and Blake? Thomas asserts that for him 'there is no such thing known to the spirit as a beginning and an end', and in pursuit of this kind of understanding of himself in relation to places, animals, and growing things he displayed his childhood ability to get his own way, even with publishers, to disregard the counsel of others, and to prefer a road not usually taken. As a result *Beautiful Wales* still remains—like the district of Dolau Cothi—a neglected goldmine for any Welshman who wishes to understand his own heritage; but it is undeniably a less satisfactory guide to pre-1914 Wales than Thomas's subsequent articles on 'Glamorgan' (1913) and 'Swansea Village' (1914) collected in *The Last Sheaf.*

In spite of the ghyll-like discrepancy between the Wales he loved and the book he had completed, the four months spent on it influenced his later life as a man and a writer. It reinforced his conviction that task-work was good for him. The regular work he found far easier than the irregular work of reviewing 'which has not been half of it in bulk'. He discovered he was a creature of habit, who could always 'steal a day so long as I leave home or start early for a walk'. Bottomley would be in London for a fortnight; Jesse Berridge would come down to the Weald for a fishing holiday; Martin Freeman or Harry Hooton were available for long twenty-five mile walks; and, under the influence of Arthur Ransome and Duncan Williams, his visits to London drew him more and more into congenial literary circles. At the end of February 1905, sending Janet Hooton some gloves that Harry had ordered, Helen gives a glimpse of the domestic happiness that she and Edward always associated with their life at Elses Farm;

Edward is in town tonight and so the hour of leisure between supper and bed which Edward and I make a point of spending together—that is doing nothing but talking to each other—I am trying to spend with you. It is only when Edward is unwell, and when I have to scold the children that I feel old; generally life is full to the brim of joy, body and soul rejoicing in all good things. . . . of late I have determined simply *not* to worry, but just do my best as wife and mother, and to help Edwy not to worry.

I am busy from early morning till 9 at night, but from 9 to 10 Edwy and I put our work aside and sit smoking by the fire like Darby and Joan talking of our day's work. . . . People ask me if I am not lonely, so far from everyone. But I am not a scrap. This country is perfect, and though I do love very much being with people, yet I am too busy to hanker much after them, and in the Summer our weekends are generally full. Sometimes I spend a day in town with Edwy; just traipsing about, having lunch at Pooles, having a bottle of wine between us, seeing one or two friends perhaps; doing a little shopping with money from the sale of review books, and at any rate enjoying ourselves thoroughly like two children having a holiday . . . I am sure you would love this house, though perhaps the severity of its furniture etc. and plainness of our way of living etc. would not please you so much, after your luxurious suburban ways. We have to save up a long while before we can buy anything other than the bare necessities and, though we are a little less primitive than we were in our accommodation for visitors, we have not all we would like to have. But I do wish in the Summer when they are haymaking you would come with your babies. They could spend the entire day out of doors, for we have fields at our front door, and there they would be safe and happy while you sat under a tree resting to your hearts content.

In his posthumous autobiography, Arthur Ransome testified to the carefree happiness of these London jaunts; and in *The Heart of England*, written at Elses Farm, Edward describes a May Day walk that recalls the more fallow, fragile happiness that kept him and Helen together:

For once more the cuckoo was clear, golden, joyous. When we heard the black-bird again we did not quarrel with the laugh at his own solemnity, since it was not there. It was not memory, nor hope. Memory perished, and hope that never rests lay asleep; and winds blew softly from over Lethe and breathed upon our eyelids, coming as delicate intercessors between us and life. We forgot that ours had been the sin of Alcyone and Ceyx who, in their proud happiness, called one another *Zeus!* and *Hera!* and for that were cast down by the gods. Once again we did so, for this was the wood of youth, and in the old streets of the soul where the grass grows among the long-untrodden stones, and in the door-ways of deserted homes, the sound of footsteps and the click of a frequented latch was heard.

Such happiness he treasured and recalled once again in his poem 'When we two walked'.

His prospects as a journalist were improving. He reviewed regularly for the *Chronicle,* the *Speaker,* and the *World* and some of his best early criticism appeared in extended contributions to the *Academy* between June and December 1905. With *Wales* at the proof stage in March, he hadn't yet learned to be satisfied 'with anything except work and a moment or two (often lonely) now and then'. Martin Freeman had rented the small cottage in Egg Pie Lane for half-a-crown a week, three miles from Elses Farm across the fields, ostensibly for his own use at weekends. Edward went there, as if to business, regularly every day. The weekends were full of visitors with whom he walked in the intervals of proof-corrections and sowing beans, peas, Brussels sprouts, leeks, and radishes—all carefully planned and the dates and positions noted. During April and May he was resisting, half-acquiescing in, the *Chronicle*'s request for short country articles: 'I can't do the usual newspaper country article, and I don't believe I shall be able to hurry myself into doing my best at regular intervals. I want to have subjects given to me *which I must use.*' *Country Life* made similar requests and he pondered his reluctance to accept: 'It is odd that I can do for pleasure what I can't do in answer to a serious call'. Despite a heavy glum restlessness, which never left him completely, he was quite clear about his own desired topics: 'I don't want to write at all, but if I do write, it must be about myself and I had rather do it *à propos* of landscape and imaginary people than popular authors. . . . For landscapes are what I seem to be made for, considering that I have tried for 10 years to do them and am always trying.'

In March 1904 Thomas had already explained to Bottomley his method of composing his 'essays': 'While I write, it is a dull blindfold journey through a strange lovely land: I seem to take what I write from the dictation of someone else. Correction is pleasanter. For then I have glimpses of what I was passing through as I wrote.' Later on, especially in his volumes of essays and sketches, less often in his books of travel, he would use recorded memories of his dreams as doorways into this imagined world of Blake-like provenance. But now, as 1905 wore on and favourable reviews of *Wales* appeared, he experimented more and more with his 'Illusions' or 'Ejaculations' in prose. In this he was encouraged by Edward Garnett, but wryly Thomas noted that none of the reviewers had 'accepted the challenge of my method [in *Wales*] and appraised its results'. In fact his discontent with his published work, whenever he failed to offer the reader precisely what he wished to express, rarely subsided until his poetry began 'to run' in late 1914.

His reputation as essayist and critic was now securely established. By July 1905 he could make £5 or £6 a week. But he resisted the temptation to accept more reviewing, although a succession of visitors had left him more miserable than ever in the intervals of entertaining with 'no money in the bank, and laudanum inside me'. Thomas explained to Jesse Berridge how friends did not appreciate his horrible state: 'I know you are misled by my jesting, my apparent good health, and the many things that ought to make me happy (as you think)'. In August Berridge wished

to re-introduce him to G. K. Chesterton, but a proposed meeting outside St. George's, the vegetarian restaurant in St. Martin's Lane, did not
come off. Thomas explained his refusal to meet G. K. C. just then: 'I am
glad to have your letter though I do not know what is the "one cure" for
me. I can only think about "cures" when I am fairly well and then I can't
think very seriously. The one thought which may in the end be comforting is that there is certainly no hope from myself in the tenderest
friend. . . . What I really ought to do is to live alone. But I can't find
courage to do the many things necessary for taking that step. It is really
the kind H. and the children who make life almost *impossible*.' Even his
long-established palliative of long country walks was denied him.
During 1905—as often for the rest of his life—he complained frequently of a damaged ankle, or of blistered feet, that prevented him
from exploring the Pilgrim's Way with Martin Freeman.

Thomas's moods changed rapidly at this time. In one letter to
MacAlister, early in August, he doubts everything: 'Nothing is worthwhile, and it is really wonderful how I persuade myself to work
regularly. I have no joy, no hope, no responsibility; no certainty. Which
is odd, as I have lived unusually carefully this summer.' A fortnight later
he returns to the same theme: 'I have been better for nearly a week now
and more sensible. . . . Exercise is fatal. During a long hard walk I am
splendid, but the moment I stop I am at my worst and the effect may
last a week. . . . Perhaps, though, I have an exaggerated reverence for
steady work, but so genuine that I always do my six hours a day at the
cottage; I start off with a satchel of books as if going to business and
delude myself with the absolute necessity of work.' Not surprisingly, he
would sometimes hint to some correspondents that he did not possess a
small fixed income—as so many of them did. He never broke free from
the principle of Samuel Smiles, enshrined in the practice of his own
father. The best he hoped for himself from his own dance with words
was to be 'Fixed and free, In a rhyme, As poets do.'

The letters he wrote from Elses Farm suggest that he was beginning
to understand, and partially to accept, the twists and turns of his own
temperament and the direction in which his special gifts would lead
him. He found exact words for this progress in self-understanding in
Chapter XVI of *The Heart of England*. The chapter is entitled 'One Green
Field' and it is opened with a reverie which comments on his life on the
Weald:

Happiness is not to be pursued, though pleasure may be; but I have long
thought that I should recognize happiness could I ever achieve it. It would be

health, or at least unthwarted intensity of sensual and mental life, in the midst of beautiful or astonishing things which should give that life full play and banish expectation and recollection. I never achieved it, and am fated to be almost happy in many different circumstances, and on account of my fore-thought to be contemptuous or even disgusted at what the beneficent designs of chance have brought—refusing, for example, to abandon my nostrils frankly to the 'musk and amber' of revenge; or polluting, by the notice of some trivial accident, the remembrance of past things, both bitter and sweet, in the com-pany of an old friend. Wilfully and yet helplessly I coin mere pleasures out of happiness. And yet herein, perhaps, a just judge would declare me to be at least not more foolish than those men who are always pointing out the opportuni-ties and just causes of happiness which others have. Also, the flaw in my happiness which wastes it to a pleasure is in the manner of my looking back at it when it is past. It is as if I had made a great joyous leap over a hedge, and then had looked back and seen that the hedge was but four feet high and not dangerous. Is it perhaps true that those are never happy who know what happi-ness is? The shadow of it I seem to see every day in entering a little idle field in a sternly luxuriant country.

This concern with the nature of true joy and happiness is a constant theme.

In the autumn of 1905, at Ransome's prompting, Thomas asked C. F. Cazenove to act as a literary agent on his behalf. It was an uneasy, mutu-ally satisfying, but unprofitable arrangement that stood for nine years or so. In constant demand as a reviewer, Thomas wished to supplement that income (even, he hoped, to abandon it altogether) by finding more congenial work. For a time, with Martin Freeman, he had met with a small group of writers on *The Academy* to help shape the paper's policy. He found that the policy was not to his taste: 'their matter is critical in the narrowest sense', and there was no place there for his short prose illusions set in natural surroundings. Nor would *Country Life* accept them. He was still resisting editors' attempts to type-cast him as a country writer. He was zealous with advice and assistance to MacAlister, now regularly employed as a sub-editor or leader-writer, and in October 1905 Thomas found a new friend with whom to play the congenial role of patron as he had done with Jesse Berridge, MacAlister, and, to a lesser extent, Bottomley: 'I met a poet the other day, William H. Davies, Farm-house (lodging house) Marshalsea Road. His book is *The Soul's Destroyer* which is full of things that nobody else could have written in twenty years. Try to see them or him.'

In one of his notebooks devoted to 'Men', with scattered snippets stretching from 1899 to 1909, Edward Thomas records his first meeting with Davies:

11. x. 05.   11.30 p. m.   Farmhouse (Harrow St.), Marshalsea Road, S. E. Called and saw William H. Davies author of 'The Soul's Destroyer'. A small narrow-headed blackhaired Monmouthshire man, with the childish slightly uncomfortable smile (with the mouth) of Welsh people, and still a Welsh accent. One leg: the other lost on railway in U.S.A. He is of Maindee near Newport (where Mother lived) and was a picture-frame maker, but had and has eight shillings a week left by his sea-captain grandfather, and left Wales ten years ago, and spent five years in U.S.A. and Canada, doing odd work—fruit farming and railways, and then five years in London.

12. x. 05.   He showed me his library—Dick's Wordsworth and Shelley; Enfield's 'Speaker', some of Tutin's reprints sent him by Tutin lately; 2 of St. John Adcock's ditto; and (a recent purchase) a book published last year on 'How to write verse'. I gave him an Oxford Wordsworth in exchange for Dick's—of which the print is cruelly small for a man to read by a coke fire.

He is in Pinker's hands [the literary agent] and apparently neglected—i.e. robbed. He has quite the shy manner of a Welshman who has just come to London, and he looks and speaks as if quite unspoiled by experience or by the glory of a review by Arthur Symons. He talked freely and easily with me about early truancy in Tredegar Park—visits to the Ebbw—England v Wales at Swansea five years ago—working his passage across Atlantic eight or nine times in cattle boats—about 'Gambling Fred' who now holds the man who wouldn't lend him sixpence is now in debt for about £50 (because the sixpence was to go on a horse that won and the fifteen shillings thus made would have gone on another and so on.) He paid £19 for printing his book.

Thomas had already reviewed Davies's first poems favourably and these visits marked the beginnings of a close friendship between both writers and an ever-welcome home for the 'tramp poet' when he needed most support. The notebook entry is typical of Thomas's careful determination to base his own essays, notes, and sketches on exactly recorded conversations and sayings. He regarded himself as a sounding board for the unrecorded life and language of ordinary people, while reserving for himself the Olympian role of observer and chronicler.

Until mid-November, weekends at Elses Farm were filled with visitors, as his reviewing increased. He spent a week in Swansea with his old schoolmaster friend, John Williams, and renewed his links with family and friends at Pontardulais and Ammanford. He met W. H. Davies who was full of plans for his 'autobiography', and finally returned to the Weald, conscious that he had earned £20 less during this last quarter of 1905.

He was now eager to increase his income sufficiently to put by money for Merfyn's schooling and, with Cazenove's support, he accepted two contracts far removed from his earlier pattern but closer to his renewed determination—after *Oxford* and *Wales*—to undertake a reasonable amount of task work. He described one job to Bottomley: 'Hodder and Stoughton have asked me to edit a list of popular natural history in twelve monthly parts and I am going to accept because I believe it will be a discipline—(this is hypocrisy).' And a fortnight later (11 January 1906) Thomas explained his half-humorous aside: 'I have accepted the position of collaborator [E.T. later said 'Ghost'] with Frank Podmore in a series of articles on "Apparitions", "Thought Transference" etc. for *The Grand Magazine*. He exudes information and I string it into ropes and coils of pearls. For this humble office I am paid 31/6 a 1,000 words. There was no choice: I cannot pay my rent or anything but daily expenses just now, and my prospects—since Harmsworth bought *The World* and *The Academy* took to the paths of virtue which lead but to the grave—are bad.' At the same time Fisher Unwin, the publisher of Thomas's *Poems of John Dyer* (1903), wanted a book from him immediately, and he toyed with a 'book on the South Country—with more landscapes and persons—but after all, why should I?' Instead he accepted an invitation from Ernest Rhys to introduce Borrow's *The Bible in Spain* for the Everyman Library, which led to five similar commissions in the next eight years. Above all, through the influence of Edward Garnett, he established a business relationship with Dent and Co. which lasted until *The Heart of England* (1906) and *The South Country* (1909) were published.

As an editor and regular reviewer, Thomas extended the range of his London literary colleagues. Besides accepted naturalists, like G. A. B. Dewer and W. H. Hudson, he had commissioned articles for his Natural History list from Martin Freeman, Gordon Bottomley, and Arthur Ransome: these supplemented his own essays on Gilbert White, Richard Jefferies, and 'Some Country Books'. While staying in London to work at the British Museum, he was welcomed at the homes of established older men like Ernest Rhys, Nevinson, and Hudson. On his flying visits to meet Fleet Street editors and publishers, he often joined Edward Garnett who has recalled how W. H. Hudson 'formed the habit of lunching with me, nearly every Thursday at the Mont Blanc in Gerrard Street. Literary acquaintances that I made about this time [1905–6] would also come to the Mont Blanc, and in this way a small circle of habitués was formed, among them Thomas Seccombe, R. A. Scott-James, Stephen Reynolds, Edward Thomas, W. H. Davies, Hilaire Belloc, Muirhead Bone, Ford Hueffer, Perceval Gibbon, occasionally Galsworthy, and rarely Joseph Conrad.' Thomas became a member of a small group who met with Hudson for tea on Wednesdays. When he became a vegetarian for health reasons, he gathered around him his own group of friends, journalists, and writers, upstairs in St. George's Restaurant in St. Martin's Lane.

At home Thomas had established a set working rhythm. Depite some alarms and excursions with the landlady, W. H. Davies 'took possession' of Egg Pie Lane Cottage, sharing it with Thomas, in early February 1906. Davies was at work on the *Autobiography of a Super Tramp* when his artificial leg was broken in late July. A replacement fashioned locally—by a craftsman who believed it to be a 'curiosity cricket bat'—cost £12 and Thomas was able to raise the sum from his old friends and new literary colleagues. For Davies (named 'Sweet William' by Bronwen) spent many evenings at Elses Farm yarning and reading aloud to Helen and Edward the uninhibited memoirs that appeared later in bowdlerized form. A glimpse of the ballad-singing Edward Thomas is recalled by his friends from gatherings in the Chelsea home of Duncan Williams. This Edwy who would 'drop into the Welsh Club for an hour' was so unlike the subdued melancholic he loves to portray in many letters. Perhaps the melancholic portrait was painted half tongue-in-cheek, as it is in his comment to Bottomley on his new life as an editor: 'I have lost my very last chances of happiness, gusto and leisure, now. I am swallowed up. I live for an income of £250 and work all day and often from 9 a. m. until 1 a. m. . . . I use boot trees now—also plates with Monograms. If I live twenty years longer I shall be well-dressed. The pity of it is that I don't sincerely want to be. I am buying a dinner gong with my last sovereign.'

Feeling himself hemmed in by the respectability born of routine work and regular payment, Thomas, stormily at first, entered into an agreement with Dent for a book of 60,000 words on 'Rural England' at 100 guineas. Thomas attributed his touchiness over the terms (originally pounds instead of guineas) to being overwhelmed by work at the time and to his anxiety about taking more, especially when it 'would have had to be very careful and in my most difficult vein'. So he arranged to pay a long-deferred visit to Gordon and Emily Bottomley at Cartmel, near Carnforth in Westmorland, from 5 to 15 March 1906, because his work was puzzling and he hoped 'to get material and to get out of perplexity if possible. I have prepared a synopsis for Dent (who is truly a Rogue) and have not yet formed a plan'. Despite this hesitant beginning, he delivered the manuscript of *The Heart of England* to the publishers on 2 July and, the next day, he was in the British Museum mapping out the outlines of yet another undertaking: a long troublesome arrangement with Grant Richards to edit an anthology of ballads and songs for the open air.

This prospect of pleasurable hard work—'a large number will be such things as I like to think about when sitting down or walking in the country'—had come at a propitious moment. Helen and Edward had known for some time that the lease on Elses Farm would expire at Michaelmas (29 September) 1906. Edward wanted to rent another farm-house on the Weald, but he recognized that he was too impatient to supplement Helen's education of Merfyn and that 'she must have the responsibility shared by a schoolmaster: Yet we cannot really afford a good school and so far I have not heard of a house near Bedales'. As he signed the contract for *The Pocket Book of Poems and Songs for the Open Air,* Helen had found a house at Petersfield for occupation in November, with the inevitable 'two months existence in other people's houses after Michaelmas'. They also arranged for W. H. Davies to have a room in their new house, if he were not allowed to stay on at the cottage in Egg Pie Lane.

The decision to undertake the anthology was not entirely a financial one. *The Heart of England* had proved as difficult and perplexing to write as to plan, and although it was generously received by reviewers when it appeared in November 1906, Thomas complained that only Arthur Ransome had discovered some of his most treasured passages. 'I feel that perhaps they are really good and I am almost sure they are new. But who knows.' He was completely dissatisfied with the last three sections, which formed a third of the book and contained much tired, over-elaborate, space-filling description, some of it taken from early notebooks and from essays rejected while at Oxford. The remainder of the book combines a series of short evocations of response to moments of percep-tion in natural surroundings. There are six highly-charged descriptions of rural scenes, in and out of doors, that are immersed in his love of the Kent countryside. Some briefly recorded encounters anticipate his sub-sequent concern for the vagabonds, tramps, underdogs, and social failures whose company he would seek in his wanderings and whose life-stories were to find a ready place in his prose books and his early poetry.

Thomas never abandoned his belief that many inarticulate country folk sustained traces of a much earlier way of life that, rightly interpreted, might help him to understand the satisfaction he himself had experienced in contact with 'Nature' after boyhood. His friendship with Dad Uzzell had encouraged this belief and further acquaintance with W. H. Davies had convinced him that his own affinity was with men in rural byways rather than in Fleet Street. He also knew that he was trying to handle material for which he had not found the appropriate form. The vague concept of 'men in landscapes' was inadequate. He was confident that in *Oxford* and parts of *Wales* he was breaking new ground, but in each case he was disillusioned, and some of that dissatisfaction reappears in *The Heart of England*. However, some of its landscapes (for example, 'Metamorphosis', 'The Pride of Morning', 'A Golden Age', 'Poppies', 'An Old Farm', 'March Doubts', 'One Green Field', 'Faunus') are pieces of concentrated writing between four hundred and a thousand words, that merit the name of 'prose poems'. A handful of longer pieces ('On Leaving Town', 'Earth Children', 'The Village', 'No Man's Garden', 'An Old Farm', 'Old-Fashioned Times') mix description of places with observations of people and records of sustained monologues. These anticipate his subsequent approval of Robert Frost's poems in *North of Boston* and seem, with hindsight, to adumbrate the initial poetic impulse that was later transformed into such poems as 'Lob', 'Man and Dog', 'May 23', 'The Chalk Pit', 'Head and Bottle', 'Lovers', and 'House and Man'. There are also about ten imperfect short pieces in the large 'Lowland' section, but these are chiefly landscape sketches inexpertly wedded to a vague observer or to a short undeveloped episode. They are strung like beads on an abacus, but presented in a plain manner quite distinct from the over-sumptuous style (modelled on Pater) that makes the last third of the book difficult to read without impatience. For there Thomas is reverting to a way of writing he had already exhausted in *Horae Solitariae* and the more recent *Rose Acre Papers*.

At his best in *The Heart of England* Thomas combines country scenes and country people, who seem to have survived from Richard Jefferies' day, with his own specialized insight. Introspection, he was told by others, was a danger sign, a warning against excessive melancholy and possible nervous breakdown. However, as a student of Burton, he recognized that informed self-analysis could lead to imaginative truth. Some such awareness is scattered throughout the early part of *The Heart of England*, though never integrated into its rudimentary structure:

The past day is long past. . . . The moon reigns; you rule. The centuries are gathered up in your hand. . . . You exult because you are alive and your spirit possesses this broad, domed earth. Poor thing as you are, you have somehow gained a power of expression like the nightingale's, a pure translucency like the petals of the flowers; and as never before to man or woman you open your eyes widely and frankly, even the limbs move with the carelessness of the animals, the features lose the rigidity that comes of compromise and suppression.

Walking slowly thus, with a bowed head, you find an image of yourself and the universe in a shallow pool among the trees. The pool is your own mind.

I dreamed that someone had cut the cables that anchored me to such tranquillity as had been mine, and that I was drifted out upon an immensity of desolation and solitude. I was without hope, without even the energy of despair that might in time have given birth to hope.

. . . trees and their shadows, not understood, speaking a forgotten tongue, old dreads and formless awes and fascinations discover themselves and address the comfortable soul, troubling it . . . in the end it settles down into a gloomy tranquillity and satisfied discontent, as when we see the place where we were unhappy as children once.

But I know well that long hopes and wide, vaulting thoughts are not usually nourished by lane and footpath and highway, on and on; and probably I shall stop at 'The Black Horse' over the next hill, where a man may always lighten his burden on a Tuesday by hearing the price of beasts.

Himself a busy reviewer, he was inured to some critics' misunderstanding of his real aim in the best half of *The Heart of England*. The *World* and the *Standard* recommended him as a cheery companion for a day in the country; the *Academy* complained that people did not speak as he reported. He hoped he had found an acceptable framework for his essentially brief but intense lyricism. 'I ought never to do colour books again. People can't believe there is anything in them at all.'

During his last three months at Elses Farm, Thomas was busily happy. He completed the proofs of *The Heart of England* and sent them on to Bottomley, with whom he also corresponded about words and tunes for his new anthology of Poems and Songs. He kept up a large correspondence with writers and publishers asking permission to use their work, and he made all arrangements for the move to Petersfield and the in-between stops to be made in Wales and at his parents' Balham home. He continued his reviewing and his final work on the Natural History project. Above all, Elses Farm, so accessible to London, remained a constant open house to his friends. Numerous weekend visitors came, ranging from Nevinson to the young David Garnett, Edward's son, and the collection for Davies' new wooden leg was completed quickly. Thomas was especially solicitous for the Welsh poet. On his penultimate day in the Weald he wrote to Bottomley: 'Elkin Matthews is to publish William Davies' second book of poems early in November so the poor bard was not utterly sad when we left him, especially as his leg and his Rent are fully paid up. Did I tell you Bernard Shaw is reading his Autobiography and will introduce it if he likes it?' Thomas still had a crowd of letters to answer and proofs to correct before he and Helen left to spend a fortnight with John Williams at Waun Wen School, Swansea. This was followed by ten days at 13 Rusham Road and the final move to Ashford.

Edward and Helen were studious to keep both their London and Welsh friendships in good repair as they set off for their new home, Berryfield Cottage, which was part of the Ashford Chase Estate, near Petersfield. It was a four-bedroom house with an additional bedroom annexed, a 'back kitchen' which he used at first as a study, and a large store-shed in the adjoining farmyard. He held it at a rent of £25 a year under quarterly tenancy. Thomas was always anxious about financial probity, but he was not incompetent in business affairs. When he clashed with editors and publishers, he could become tenacious in self-defence and unwilling to lower his terms. He failed to judge the audience for his preferred kind of prose, but he doggedly pursued his own chosen themes. He was equally intransigent about the best conditions necessary for his creative work. Before Oxford he had treasured his long study-bedroom at home, with its reproductions of classical paintings and sculptures, and the collection of books that soon outstripped the collections of eggs and butterflies. His mother, a natural home-maker, had always helped, as later she assisted in his attempts to create ideal surroundings at his Oxford lodgings and his college rooms. His father, like Ashcroft Noble, had a large room set aside as a study-library, though neither man kept its use exclusively to himself. Helen's letters in 1900 mention that she and Merfyn occupied the study at Shelgate Road during the day and the early evening.

Edward's mother was an active household manager, with at least one full-time housemaid and often a daily help. Helen was much more easy-going in household matters and, with a succession of girls (or daily women), never seemed to provide the smoothly running environment that Edward expected if he were to work at home, which he always wished to do. This fundamental clash of attitudes, even allowing for the extreme irritability caused by his occasional depressive bouts, must lie behind his readiness to change house and start again. Helen for her part remained unchanged, at all times giving priority to her husband and children as companion and helpmate before the minutiae of household management. While not improvident and with a real horror of being in debt, she never apportioned her expenditure with the precision that her young husband expected. The spontaneity with which she would give up entire days to long walks with Edward, or to rambles with Merfyn, or to haymaking and flower-gathering—some of the expedients adopted by her to counter Edward's disappointments with his writing—was not proof against the accumulated irritability of his sudden swings of mood. Their mutual understanding and love underwent severe strain and suffered many sea-changes between 1895 and December 1916, but the severest test was to come early in 1908.

They resorted to many devices in order to maintain the ideal home they had planned for themselves during their fierce courtship. Helen was emphatic that he should remain true to his vocation as a writer. Whatever the cost to herself, she frequently urged him to leave home in order to find peaceful conditions to meet publishers' deadlines. Except on three occasions, when he was acting strictly under medical advice, Edward rarely allowed these absences to extend beyond a fortnight without a visit home or a visit to him from Helen. (The memoirs of a few friends recall his ironic portrayal of himself as Hawthornden in *Light and Twilight* 'who always returned home for tea'.) A thorough scrutiny of hundreds of his letters, with source and date always given, confirms the point. Helen held that their life together could thrive only in the country without regard for suburban standards or bourgeois domestic luxuries. Edward knew that his best means of regular liveli-hood lay in a frequent presence in Fleet Street and Bloomsbury. Conversely, he demanded a rural upbringing for his children, and direct access to the 'heart of England' for his own well-being as a man and writer.

Eventually the reader of his voluminous correspondence is compelled to reflect on Bottomley's comment in a letter to C. C. Abbott in 1935: 'Yes, he was difficult, but not impossible . . . To a Cambridge man, I would say he delighted in assuming an Oxford surface—but that was partly because he was shy, sensitive to shrinking, taciturn, retiring, and the surface was a convenient help to him to indulge (or accommodate) all this. Yet he was also merry and humorous: a moody Celt, but one who could find solvents for his moods when he was not anxious or over-driven. . . . If he had been sure of a modest competence that would have let him write when he wanted, and sojourn with mountains and peasants when he wanted, I believe all would have been well.' After the first two post-Oxford years, Thomas's fight was rarely against indigence, and never against poverty: the fight was to find ways of communicating his moments of heightened awareness of unity with the natural world. Although Bottomley, and many others, believed that his 'marriage put him for ever out of his right road because it was premature and never let him have leisure and energy of spirit to find himself', the record of Thomas's prose, his reviews, his chameleon-like correspondence and, of course, his poetry, indicate forcibly that there never really was a 'Road not taken' in Edward Thomas's evolution from prose writer to poet.

To become a poet, it seems, Thomas required the forging experience of a life strewn with surmountable setbacks, rather than an easy competence and unfettered bachelorhood. There are many clues to the measured growth of a pilgrim poet in his letters to Bottomley, but two quotations show how resolutely he was set on course, even in 1905: 'The fact is that you want me to use what experience I have had more explicitly than I do, don't you? But I must learn to do so by growth, not by executing poetic justice upon the remnants of a childhood that never existed. How important it sounds!' A few months earlier Thomas has been quite frank about his attitude to money: 'In fact I have had little to think of, except the reasons for and against making over £5 a week, as I easily could. I have decided not to try to make more now, chiefly because it would be murdering my silly little deformed unpromising bantling of originality, and take away the one thing in my life that resembles a hope—a desire, I mean. So I nobly remain moderately rich.' When not suffering from depression, Thomas did not waver in this: he continued on his course, with the proviso that his family should be spared any cost that ensued. To that end he was ready to write more books than his friends thought wise. The puritan element in him responded to the challenge in much the same spirit as the young writer—'a poet of a kind, who made a living out of prose'—in his tale 'The Pilgrim', who was carving a cross on a boundary stone near St. David's, and talking about the faith of the medieval pilgrims to the now empty shrine:

I tried to think in what spirit one of them would have carved a cross. Perhaps just as a boy cuts his name or whatever it may be on a bridge, thinking about anything or nothing all the time, or sucking at a pebble to quench his thirst. At the sight of this stone—I may have been a fool—I thought—I had a feeling that while I was doing as the pilgrims did I might become like one of them. So I threw off my knapsack and chiselled away. . . . Please don't apologize. In any case it would have been no good. The knife was already too blunt, and I was cold and aching and also thinking of a wretched poem. Do you think a pilgrim ever had such thoughts? If there was such a one he would never have got far on this road.

The move from Elses Farm on the Weald to Berryfield Cottage, Ashford, near Petersfield, was another station along this road.

CHAPTER 8
The Middle Years

THREE needs prompted the decision to leave Elses Farm and settle at Berryfield Cottage: a good progressive mixed-sex school, Bedales, for Merfyn and, later, for Bronwen; a place in the country, but not too far from railway contact with editors, friends, and family in London; and the possibility of friendships and social interests for the gregarious Helen who, apart from frequent long tramps with Edward, and the precious evening hour spent together whenever he was at home, was often desperately lonely. They decided to devote weekends to visits from friends and relations and, for some years, continued to maintain the pattern of life established on the Weald. Bedales School lived up to its reputation. Merfyn joined the Preparatory School in December and was much happier there than at home. At the end of June 1907, Edward sent a progress report to Jesse Berridge, who was thinking of a school for his son: 'We have had no disappointment, and you know we had formed great hopes of it. Helen has taught at the Prep. School here for two terms now (an hour or so a day). The headmaster Russell Scott and his wife are both admirable.'

Initially Edward enjoyed the stimulus of the many 'good people' at Bedales; but his shyness, and dogged determination not to compromise his own manner of life, diminished his involvement with the school activities. Helen found there companions who shared her enthusiasm for the activities of the 'Women's movement'. She exchanged tea-parties with wives of the staff, played tennis, and attended meetings and dances at the school throughout her ten years there. Within a few days of taking over Berryfield Cottage, Edward had planned the garden and explored the surroundings: 'This house and the country about it make the most beautiful place we ever lived in. We are now become people of whom passers by stop to think: How fortunate are they within those walls. I know it. I have thought the same as I came to the house and forgot it was my own.' When the 'big house' and the estate around Berryfield Cottage were up for sale in March 1908, the Thomases were invited to buy their house. He told MacAlister that he had 'written to ask the price demanded and to ask a Building Society to send a valuer and say what they will lend—a nuisance as I feel worse than ever—weak, depressed and stupid. Why I have no idea.' His offer was not accepted

but the new owners allowed them to remain at Berryfield. All through
their married life Helen and Edward lived in rented houses.

The nearest railway station was two miles away at Petersfield. Close
friends like Arthur Ransome, MacAlister, and Davies made their way to
Ashford at weekends after the New Year for long walks (including mid-
day rests at inns off the beaten track) and longer evenings of
conversation, gossip, and singing. On one of his visits, MacAlister
accompanied Edward and the young David Garnett, who became a
frequent visitor. Edward was still heavily engaged with his editorial work
preparing *The Book of the Open Air*—four separate parts of it appearing
during late 1907 and 1908—and *The Pocket Book of Poems and Songs for the
Open Air* (1907), which gave him a chance to include out-of-the-way
poems and little-known airs that reflected his own taste and that of his
friends. His selection drew on contemporaries like Yeats, de la Mare, T.
Sturge Moore, Masefield, Noyes, Davies, Houseman, Charles Dalmon,
Bottomley, and a dozen others. He fulfils his claim to have 'gathered
into it much of the finest English poetry . . . and . . . added about sixty of
the sweetest songs which it seemed that a wise man would care to sing,
or to hear sung, in the fields, at the inn, on the road at dawn or nightfall,
or at home.' (It is no surprise that he and Belloc walked and sang
together.) The anthology, too, demonstrates the mastery of the whole
range of English poetry that lay behind his now established reputation as
the leading young critic of contemporary verse. The volume was a
permanent shift of his interests (and public reputation) from an exclusive concern with nature and the countryside towards a professional
involvement in the presentation of English literature to a new audience
fed by the reprint industry, of which Dent's Everyman's Library, edited
by Ernest Rhys, was the most significant. Seven volumes edited by
Thomas were included in Everyman between 1906 and 1914. As we
know, he had resisted offers to become a regular 'country correspondent'
from editors who valued his book-reviews, although he needed the extra
money.

Instead he persisted with his personal writing; and, when many more
papers were being rejected than in his undergraduate days, he put them
into a book loosely strung together as *The Heart of England*. There were
many favourable reviews but, so he believed, little direct perception of
what he was about. 'I am so solitary in my work,' he complained to
MacAlister, 'and no one is interested enough in it to criticize or even
laugh at it (except reviewers who unfortunately don't read it.)' It first
appeared in a De Luxe edition with coloured illustrations by H. L.

Richardson and later in a cheaper, unillustrated edition. Edward then summed up his three full-scale books so far in a dismissive comment to Bottomley: 'You alone know how I felt at your words of praise and happiness after getting my book. All other copies ought to have been destroyed, for *World* and *Standard* have been saying what a cheery knowing companion I am for a day in the country and *The Academy* that I am affected and that in "the heart of England" people do not speak so. I ought never to do colour books again. People can't believe there is anything in them at all.' But the rest of the letter is full of joy in his *Pocket Book*, then being sent to the printers. 'The songs are glorious.... It will be the best short collection in the world. I wish I thought as well of the poems.' In his endeavour to keep clear of what E. V. Lucas and other open-air anthologists had used, he admitted that the 'poetry is not all good and not all popular enough and I shall not make £1,500 out of it as Lucas did out of his genial *Open Road* anthology.' Nor did he, although the *Pocket Book* survived until 1950 in Jonathan Cape's *Travellers' Library* series, and remains as an expression of one side of Thomas—boon companion and ready singer of songs among friends—that has often been overlooked.

Most of his friends recall the exceptional quality of his talk: its range, insight, admirably varied phrasing, and, not least, the disconcerting interjections of mordant wit. The baldest summary of his activities during the first two years at Berryfield Cottage—the only one of his houses never complained of in verse and prose and the only one that he made some effort to purchase—exemplifies the double-sided nature of the temperament he strove to understand. First there was the constant reviewing, to meet weekly or monthly deadlines which varied only according to the publishers' seasonal activities (for example in August 1907 he notes, 'for a month I haven't written a review even'). Then, having sent off *The Pocket Book of Poems and Songs* to the publishers in December 1906, he busied himself until March with various monthly parts that appeared as *The Book of the Open Air* a year later, alongside his introduction to some poems of George Herbert in Everyman's Library. In March 1907 he was restless to begin another book and aware that not a hundred people would be interested in what he wished to write around his 'chiefly pathetic memories of the suburbs'. Staying with his parents for a short time, he decided to visit the Weald and see Davies, who had sounded in a poor way but proved to be fit; and after a 'nice review' of *The Heart of England* he suddenly took an unplanned short holiday with Stephen Reynolds (one of his Mont Blanc friends) at

Devizes and then returned to Ashford after four days in Chepstow. In April Helen spent time in London, visiting relations with Merfyn and Bronwen, while Martin Freeman visited Edward, who suffered two bad spells of languor and melancholy after cutting down from eight to two pipes daily. Then, as his reviewing picked up, he arranged with Hutchinson's reader, Roger Ingpen—an old pre-Oxford acquaintance, now brother-in-law to Walter de la Mare—to write an 80,000-word biography of Richard Jefferies for a £100 advance. In the summer term of 1907, Helen was teaching at the Bedales preparatory school from 9 to 10.30, and Edward was making elaborate plans for his study of Jefferies, who had meant so much to their early life and loving. Amidst the preliminary reading for this at home and in the British Museum, the reviewing, proof-reading, and correspondence with people in and around Coate, he spent a fortnight with Bottomley at Cartmel. He returned, so Helen said, 'nicer and cheerfuller' to a great muddle of 'proofs, letters, carpentry, gardening, reading' and a special London dinner with Galsworthy, Nevinson, Garnett, Muirhead Bone, Laurence Housman, A. H. Bullen, Edgar Jepson, Norrey Connell and 'certain *Daily News* lights'. He visited Jefferies' widow, and after the interview walked the twenty-two miles home to Ashford via Hazelmere.

When the summer term ended Helen went away with the children for a fortnight; the maid, too, was away for a time, and Martin Freeman came to stay once more, 'helping, walking and talking'. As usual, when left on his own, Thomas had 'the damned blues'. Without the apparently stable domestic life to support him, he made endless notes in four volumes, could find no possible outlet or framework for them, and the work on Jefferies stood still. At this time, too, he spent some of the money collected from friends for W. H. Davies and had to call on MacAlister as a temporary banker. He and MacAlister met at a teashop at the corner of Bouverie Street and settled the tramp-poet's affairs before Edward set off for Broome Farm, near Swindon, in search of yet more Jefferies material.

In Wiltshire he spent three profitable weeks in August 'busy all day long, walking until nightfall and then reading and writing' and reported a little progress although, despite masses of notes, he realized that he must 'use Jefferies' books chiefly as my sources, and quote more than I like doing. 80,000 words will not be hard to write'. Planning to begin to write in January 1908, he intended to finish the biography by May. As October 1907 closed in, and reviewing increased, he found less time for walking 'except just to get warm and a little less muddled in the mornings'. As always he kept his garden in good shape and spent any spare time at the British Museum. 'For in London I can be sure of having a good talk at any rate.'

Outwardly, as his frequent letters show, the months of August, September, and October 1907 had been busy ones. The contract for *Jefferies* was signed and, after the usual August lull, reviewing abounded; Grant Richards wanted a book from him on English literature; his visits to Wiltshire and then to the British Museum advanced the research on *Jefferies* and left him confident that he could write the new biography in a few months. Despite his usual expression of misgivings, his approach to the book was more hopeful and clear-cut. On this topic, he knew, he would not have to resort to the space-filling devices so obvious in *Wales* and *Oxford,* so loathsome to him as he wrote against time, and so detestable when proofs were read. His professional self-assurance is evident in his short tussle with Shaw over W. H. Davies' autobiography: 'Shaw has been making Davies an excuse for humiliating publishers (by insisting on terms that will allow Davies to sell to Times Book Club), so Duckworth have returned the MS. But I have written to Shaw saying that I think Davies an unsuitable battleground.' Thomas was seeing much of his chosen friends in town, either at lunch or for tea, especially Mac-Alister, Garnett, Hudson, and H. E. Mann, a civil servant who had been his senior at Lincoln and had introduced Thomas to the convivial gatherings of the Square Club (in memory of Fielding).

Yet his inner world was severely troubled, as the following notes show. They were written in October 1907, preserved by Helen among his papers, and never before published.

9. x. 07. Disappointed because Helen said she would return today now puts it off till tomorrow—which throws me out and gives me no relief for my read-ing—[and] also I may have smoked and taken tea too much—. So I sat thinking about ways of killing myself. My revolver has only one bullet left. I couldn't hang myself: and though I imagined myself cutting my throat with a razor on Wheatham I had not the energy to go. Then I went out and thought what effects my suicide would have. I don't think I mind them. My acquaintances—I no longer have friends—would talk a day or two (when they met) and try to explain and of course see suggestions in the past. W. H. Davies would suffer a little; Helen and the children—less in reality than they do now, from my accursed tempers and moodiness. It is dislike of the effort to kill myself and fear that I could not carry it through if I half did it that keeps me alive. Only that. For I hate my work, my reviewing: my best I feel is negligible: I have no vitality, no originality, no love. I do harm. Love is dead and lust almost dead.

N.B. These thoughts have come to me at least once a week for three or four years now and frequently during the last seven—except as to lust.

x. 07. Now and then for about a minute nearly every day and rarely for perhaps a quarter of an hour on end I enjoy perfect happiness—I am without any thought, my body is painless, I am unaware of it,—I move easily and I sing or hum a song or a fragment of one.

x. 07. I wonder how many people [who] are as impatient of impermanence as I am, and who go away from an evening in company with such regrets not so much because it has been pleasant (it seldom is) as that it might have become so. Why when I am on my way to London I always run through all the engagements ahead that I have made and imagine them finished and my return journey begun and as I enter the Mt. Blanc with Hudson and Garnett, see the clock at 1.30 I reflect that at 3 all chances of making myself happy with them will be over and I shall have to look about for others.

How I admire direct expressive natures. This morning I went into —'s bedroom as he was dressing. He had been rather ill and was not over cheerful but as he was pulling a shirt over his head he talked easily and rapidly in a clear voice, expressing likes and dislikes right out of his heart, without any of the hesitations which I have so often that I really never ought to say or write anything.

x. 07. I am interested in nothing and would for ever sit still and seek nothing if I had to be continually nailing my mind to something with nice docility. And yet unawares I am lured into interest as when I found myself today near crying as I read the Iliad to Merfyn.

x. 07. I believe I can be perfectly humble with a very young child, with no condescension or mere curiosity, simply responding to his emotions as he shows me a picture or a map, and suggesting things to him which are inspired by him and would be impossible to me in a man's company, believing in what I write or what I say to Garnett, for instance.—This imitativeness goes far. I was with an ordinary 2nd. year undergraduate today and found myself sharing his experiences in talk as if I were in my 2nd. year too. Nor does this come from a desire not to displease, though that is (unconsciously) often so strong that when a man opens talk with a remark implying that I know e.g. a certain book I nod assent. Yet again much as I hate argument and am unfit for it I am often lured in talk into an attitude, by some slip of speech or even the other man's misunderstanding, and I keep up the attitude so long that when at last I am beaten I am mortified as I should not have been were I upset in an argument on something I care about. For most people argue to defeat their opponent and not to get at truth.

———

There are many horse chestnuts by roadside at Ashford and today (9. x. 1907) many 'conquers' are falling in rainy wind and they strew the road. I feel a pang as I walk over them and do not like to crush one if I can help it, for thinking of the time when I should not have left the place till I gathered them all,—15 years ago at Cannon Hill, Merton.

In early November he spent a fortnight at the British Museum staying one week with Helen's sister and another with his parents. His evenings were occupied and he kept in touch with his friends by arranged meetings in and around the Museum. He found time for an enjoyable few days with Helen's sister, Irene, and her insurance-broker husband who had persuaded Edward to take out two insurance policies, each with an annual premium of ten and a half guineas. After two short visits, one to Wiltshire staying with Reynolds at Devizes, and the other to Suffolk with the Hootons to make arrangements for a prolonged stay in the New Year while writing the *Jefferies,* he settled down at Ashford 'to reviewing and moderately easy work' until 28 December: 'I could hardly touch the Jefferies till [the reviewing etc.] was done, so I put it off and pleased Helen who likes me to be home at Christmas time! Strange taste.' MacAlister, when he received this letter, would have known how to discount its mock-serious foreboding. Gordon and Emily Bottomley, who had recently visited Berryfield Cottage during one of their rare visits to the south, were not to be deceived either, as the letter sent to them on Boxing Day—while the Thomases were expecting a visit from James Guthrie—suggests: 'I am glad to hear I was enjoying life. Perhaps my melancholy delusion of the surface, a term mistakenly applied by one who is after all only a ½d. critic. I did enjoy yesterday though because Bronwen excelled herself in joy and expressions of joy and even Merfyn was never peevish. We did not over eat, touched no alcohol and I actually laughed as I was going to bed.'

His mind was now fully turned towards *Jefferies.* The next day in London he visited a specialist in neurasthenia en route for the coastguard's cottage near the Aldis family (the parents of Jane Hooton) in Minsmere, near Dunwich, Suffolk. He had decided that although his book would be accurate, and complete in its reference to all Jefferies' works, he would not bother to unmask the pervasive vulgarity of an earlier biographer. On 26 February he hoped 'to finish the draft of *Jefferies* by Friday when Helen comes for the weekend to recover from nursing the children through measles. The book is not, cannot be organic. It may have a lot of small lights, but no light on the whole man.' He intended to put it by for a few months, to think about his projected book on Borrow, and to begin 'a smaller book (without pictures) like *The Heart of England.* . . . and as it must very likely be the last of its kind for me I want to make an effort.'

He felt much better for being at Minsmere but in spite of the strict regimen advised by Dr T. D. Savitt—abstinence from alcohol and sugar and almost complete abstinence from tobacco—he confided to Jesse Berridge, 'I can't expect the effect to last long after I leave.' For he had found writing a biography the most taxing commission he had ever undertaken and he knew that he could not go on for ever 'turning out lengths of Jefferies almost every day. . . . I fear quantities of books would soon reduce such quality as I have. So I hang about the skirt of the ½d. Press.' When the initial spurt on *Jefferies* was over, he resumed reviewing on a slightly restricted scale. In mid February he completed a contract with Dent for *The South Country*. By then external events had broken into the cocoon-like life he was creating for himself, his wife, and his children, profoundly disturbing him.

For in December 1907, when returning books on Christian mysticism to Jesse Berridge, just after he had seen his new doctor, he commented: 'My own soul remains a blasted heath'. This remark may have been a partial response to the new doctor. He certainly followed the severely abstinent regimen prescribed for him with careful regularity until mid-June 1909 when he reported to Harry Hooton, 'I have given up my marvellous doctor'. Whatever the causes of this 'cure'—whether it was the diet, the healthy air of Suffolk (as Helen believed), or the freedom from irritability and moodiness now associated with him, or whether the re-assurance was gained from his sudden absorption in a seventeen-year old girl, Hope Webb—he continued on a fairly even temperamental keel until mid-1911 when he reported to MacAlister, 'I have not been myself this year. Partly this is a physical fact because I am one of a strict sect of vegetarians. . . . I am writing many books but not prospering.' Until his depression once more seemed to overwhelm him later in 1911, it appears as if he had learned after Minsmere, that his descents into the Slough of Despond need not be permanent.

The stay at Minsmere was a decisive watershed in the domestic happiness of Helen and Edward. As reflected in her letters to him, she shared uncomfortably in the bitter wrestle for self-knowledge that accompanied his confrontation with Jefferies—his youthful idol—and his infatuation with Hope Webb, one of Helen's charges in 1896 when their friendship had turned to love. Thomas's stay in Minsmere had a promising start, as Helen describes it in early 1908 to Janet Hooton:

My one delight in my lonely evenings is pretending I am talking to this one or that, and I can pretend best with my pen in my hand. Of course my best letters are from Edwy, and never have I had such cheerful healthy sounding letters from him, no never since I have known him. [None of these have survived.] . . .

the dear people who are being so kind to him: the people so different from humdrum me, and the number of them, and their lightheartedness, and their unconstraint. . . . the whole is different in every detail from life here; and I think a downright change like that is good for everyone, especially for (poor?) Edwy. I wish sometimes that I might go and renew my youth in that gay kindly family; but at present I am filled with deep content, a glad thankfulness that all is so well with my dear old boy. Every day he surprises—I and the children laugh at his strange doings: dancing, playing whist having Molly and Chub in to tea and getting on splendidly. My only fear now is that lack of funds will prevent him staying there till he's done the book. We are very hard pressed at present, and of course it is an expense but I daresay he'll manage it somehow. He seems so hopeful about his book, too, and the writing of a book is generally accompanied with groans of despair, fits of depression, fits of anger. Let us hope the book will not suffer; but I'm sure it won't.

Helen was keen to visit Minsmere, to renew acquaintance with her former charges and, above all, to be seen as Edward's wife among people who knew them both, and not to be regarded, as she feared she was among many of his literary London friends, as a mere domestic appendage. Edward sent frequent letters to the children, a birthday present and a 'poem' for Merfyn, and spent one night home at Ashford (26 January) after a visit to his London doctor. But the plans for Helen to spend a long weekend at Minsmere early in February were upset because measles spread from the school at Bedales, first to Merfyn and then to Bronwen. Edwy was advised not to visit home and eventually Helen spent the last weekend of February with him at Minsmere. On her return to Berryfield Cottage she described her visit to Janet Hooton:

My weekend at Minsmere was perfect . . . I enjoyed it every minute. It was lovely seeing again the Webbs whom I had not seen for 12 years, and their warm welcome for me, and evident affection for me after all this time delighted me more than I can tell you; for it always comes as an almost un-believable surprise that anyone can care for me . . . I should have known Phillis, though Alice not at all . . . It *was* a pity that Hope could not be there. As a child, dark haired and dark eyed, different from the others in everything, she was my favourite, though not nearly such an attractive child in those days as either Phillis or Alice. She was the odd one of my quartette as there is in a family always an odd one, who no one knows quite why it's there, or who it's like, or what the use of it is, and it's certain to be under a cloud, be it ever so light. Hope was that child just as I loved her best, because I understood her, and she and I were very fond of each other. I saw her photograph and see she has a serious, almost melancholy face, different still, and much more in her now than the others, but still perhaps not so loveable on acquaintance. . . . Mrs. Webb just the same as ever, very dear to me, and she too so warm in her welcome, so much the same kind woman, that it was not difficult to unroll the years and fancy myself again 19, and again just beginning life away from home. I saw very little of her, for she had to be away. Mr. Webb I saw is very changed. He is much older, but still as ever he reminded me of a bird, though not any longer the dapper, sharp-eyed robin. . . .

It was pleasant to see the way Edwy went among them, and liking to be with them and getting on so well with them. I get very solemn in my old age—I wish that I could have carried away with me some of the laughter and the genial atmosphere of those cottages. It was lovely to see Joan [Janet Hooton's daughter] too following Edward about, wanting to be 'with Uncle Edward' all the time. The love that children have for him is to me the most beautiful and convincing proof of the fineness Edward possesses, and that whatever else can be said against him, *for* him is the great fact that children love him. I tell him this when he is painting himself black, which he often does. . . .

William Davies's Autobiography of which Edward has just corrected the proofs is fine; the work of a genius of rare power, you must buy it when it comes out, and get anyone else you can to do the same. G. B. S.'s introduction is good too.

Since returning from Minsmere Edwy has been terribly nervy, depressed, desperate, as bad as ever and all my hopes have fallen into many fragments. In fact I've gone I feel just lately through a crisis in my life, and I *think* I'm wiser, and I know I'm sadder. In trying to look into things I believe it's my ideal that has smashed; it was so high and shining and fair, but it was not useful—so it fell. And I wept, but with tears and toil I have built another not *so* high, nor shining nor fair, nor can I worship there, but if I can rest there when I am tired, and let my soul wander in it and make it familiar to me, then perhaps I shall come to love it more than the other. (15 March 1908.)

The crisis was a genuine one. Hope Webb was a mature schoolgirl of seventeen as Thomas described her to Bottomley in four letters between 7 February and 21 May:

Among few disturbances here I got very fond of a girl of 17 with two long plaits of dark brown hair and the richest grey eyes, very wild and shy, to whom I could not say 10 words, nor she to me. She used to milk the two cows her father owned, but has now (7 February) gone away to school. She is a clever child who has begun to write verses. But I liked her for her perfect wild youthfulness and remoteness from myself and now I think of her every day in vain acquiescent dissatisfaction and shall perhaps never see her again, and shall be sad to hear she ever likes anyone else even though she will never like me.

What girl of 17 or 18 could express anything in letters to one wholly unknown and not loved? She is infinitely kind (and mildly wondering), yet her letters can barely kindle a response from my very ready pen and ink: so that self-deceiver and denier of what is though I may be, I dimly foresee a guttering candle, a flicker, another flicker, a smell and an awakening to find the fire as well as the light gone out, the house cold and dark still.

Also the night before I left Minsmere I was pedantically asked not to go on writing to the girl who was away at school. Off my guard, I promised simply to obey: she is reputed to be obedient to the point of indulgence. So there is a more unhappy raw truncation, and though one heals like a dock root it does not feel easy or simple.

Hope Webb is not mentioned in the letters to MacAlister, and the letters to Helen have not survived. The references to Hope in four letters to Harry Hooton bring us closer to Thomas's feelings about her, for he and Harry rather prided themselves on their open-handed, somewhat playful, directness of speech about their feelings:

. . . with my medicine and abstinence I have got wonderfully better: chiefly too, through everybody's kindness. Mr. Aldis and Hope have quite reached my 'art and I don't know what I shall do when Hope goes away on Monday for the term. I have become deeply corrupted, so far as to play Animal Grab and to write verses in Alice's Album. My wife and family are quite forgotten among these delights. But *Jefferies* gets on very steadily. (18 January.)

I was sorry to lose Hope and have hardly done any work since. It is a good many years since I felt such a strong unreasoning liking for anyone. As for getting to know her, I couldn't even make an effort, and she would naturally not help me. Will you promise to tell me when she comes to see you in London if ever? for I can't think I must not see her again. She was Helen's favourite as a child. (28 January.)

I am very much better for being here and for having a good doctor but I can't lose sight of the plain fact that the world is not made for me. . . . I sent Hope (through Mrs. Webb, decorously) my *Pocket Book* but have not even had an indirect word in reply. (30 January.)

When we meet you can help me still more. I greatly fear that will never be at Minsmere. For my folly in concealing (or rather in not proclaiming) my letters to and from Hope procured me an awkard interview in my last evening and unhappiness ever since. I was asked not to go on with the correspondence and I am febrile enough to acquiesce and so throw upon myself various burdens of the imagination, of regret, of scheming, of vaguest hope. I know I was foolish but the punishment as it always is is excessive. It is small consolation that perhaps Hope is serene enough and even that may not be true. Don't talk about this. (7 March 1908.)

It was part of Thomas's nature to accept things as they are. When his idealized views clashed with mundane opinion, he learned slowly to

modify his expectations without abandoning his ideals. The consequence of the nine weeks at Minsmere was the emergence of a more
flexible, less idealistic, but essentially loving relationship between Helen
and Edward which provided Helen with a more identifiable role to fill
in the home, at Bedales, and in the neighbourhood. She found an outlet
for her enthusiasm and her energies in Bedales activities; and now that
her mother had died (in January 1907) she frequently travelled, with or
without the children, to visit her mother-in-law or her sisters and
brother, often taking one of her children and a niece to the seaside, and
at times spending longish holidays with a sister while Edward and the
maidservant coped at home. Although Edward, too, went off separately
on tours or visits lasting six to fourteen days, their correspondence
shows that after Minsmere they planned to spend together at least one
short holiday—and frequently two separate weeks—each year, while the
children stayed with grandparents or uncles and aunts. And as
Merfyn approached his tenth year he, too, spent time on holiday with
his father. This was later converted to longer cycling trips together,
dutifully logged by Edward in long factual statements sent home to
Helen.

Her account in *As It Was* does not attempt to describe the minutiae of
the changes that occurred after Minsmere, although her book catches
the spirit of them. A few quotations from her often undated letters to
Edwy at Minsmere—tentatively placed in correct order—round out the
intensity of 'the crisis' she referred to in her letter to Janet Hooton.

I read [your letter] to the children. They *did* laugh about your dancing and
treading on people's toes and turning the wrong way. They loved that, and the
squirrel, too . . . To me it was a splendid letter: it sounds so well and cheery . . .
Has Hope still large brown eyes, and a skin the colour of Bronwen's, deep red.
She was rather like Bronwen; healthy and rollicking and wicked, yet so tender,
a dear little child, different from the others who were fair and rather angelic. (4
January 1908.)

Your letters amaze me as much as they delight. A miracle is being worked, and
what I have longed and tried for so long has come at last, and you are happy
and content and well. I can't grasp it, though I am just full of rejoicing over it.
. . . . I wish I could put myself out of my thoughts altogether, and just be
perfectly, serenely content and thankful, and never anything else. I wish I could
feel that it satisfies me utterly to know of your well being, and of how your
work goes and your health, and your free time all so splendidly just as I have
wanted it to go. But it doesn't. I thought my love was the kind that could be,
but I find that I'm aching for something else; some suggestion for instance that

it will be wholly sweet to you to be here again; and that after your day of work it would be good to have me with you. . . . I want to see you so well, so content, so happy; I want to join in it with you, but can I, shall I ever, or will it be different when you come back, without all that has done this for you. (15 January, Merfyn's birthday.)

Its so unsatisfactory this letter writing, for by the time a miserable letter gets to you it's quite untrue for my mood has changed, and by the time the happy one gets to you to make up for the unhappy one, you've forgotten about the unhappy one, and its all no use. I think I ought to leave myself out of my letters and just write an essay, on the children, the weather, housework, on acquaintances, on quite impersonal affairs. I'll try that if you like, for why should you be plagued with my moods when they are part of the life you've gone away from on purpose to work in peace and quietness. Goodnight dear heart. The children send you love and kisses and I am ever wholly yours. Helen. (17 January.)

If I was the Webbs, I'd be proud to think that you loved Hope, for they might see with half an eye that you are not the sort to enter her room at night, or kiss her behind the door—unless she wanted you to. Well never mind sweetheart, perhaps she loves you—in her way,—she's reading Jefferies, that's something isn't it? (18 January.)

When I got over my sulks this afternoon I realized how difficult I must be to live with; all emotion and sentiment and things in the air, no sense in me, nothing to hold on to. Or else this weekend would not have shone out like a great light, like a shining palace that I was to reach soon. I should have regarded it as a few hours of happiness, very enjoyable no doubt, but still not to break one's heart over, and planned a nice treat for the children instead, brightened by the knowledge that you and Harry were quite content, in having a long tramp thinking of anything in the world but me. . . .

And Hope's written again to you, and you to her I suppose. I wonder (I do really so please tell me, I'm quite serious) what you want her to develop into, or what you want 'it' to develop into. You are fond of her, but you can't make her fond of you without making it difficult for her. Is it to be the friendship of a middle aged man, a man of letters etc. etc. and of a simple schoolgirl, the sort of idyllic affair that your biographers will dote on—a passionless, innocent, intimate, uncleish, loverish affair that makes one wish in reading the biography that 'I' had been the girl. Is it to be that sort? Or is she meant to slip unconsciously into something more, with sentiment in it, and heart openings, and in fact a love affair, or what? It puzzles me. I mean your attitude to her, what you want, what it's all about. What it will mean for her, what for you. Do you merely want her to get fond of you in the vague way you are fond of her, just so that she will be pleased to see you, and not to be shy with you. Do tell me.

How horribly far from you I am; today I have felt so far from you, that I thought 'I can never get near to him.' . . .

P. S. Another reason why I was keen on the weekend [put off because the children had measles] is that it is most unusual for us to be together among outsiders, in any society but that of neighbours etc. You go away here and there, on work and pleasure, meeting people of all kinds who I hear of but never meet. There are huge slices of your life that I never know of, I am quite shut out of. I try to imagine it, and know that you are being delightful in manner, in speech, in everything, just as I love you to be, and people like you to be there with them. But it's poor fun for me, and besides it hurts what I suppose is my pride that no one ever connects us at all. Some who know you are married guess that as I never appear I'm in my true place the HOME. But now these people knew me before they ever saw you. I am more to them, or was, than you. They think of me as 'Helen', as someone they can picture—plain, untidy, not a bad sort. They'd like to see me again, I to see them, and be seen with you, your wife, not only your nurse, housekeeper etc. heard of in a dim way.

So there. I don't know if I'm any the better for having written this letter, or if I'll cry myself to sleep. (19 January.)

Yes, I am being careful about their manners now, for I get jealous of their being compared unfavourably with other children in any way, so I'll try to attend regularly to those items. But you know, dear, it is a bit difficult for me to be both Father and Mother to them. Your way with the children is far better than mine in lots of ways, and it's with regard to them that I miss your help always. Still, I'll try as hard as I can to be firm and regular, for I should love you to think that I have managed well. (29 January.)

I don't think you could ever know my feelings, because your being is spread out over different causes, while mine is all gathered together, with only one support. I wonder will woman ever change herself so utterly that this part of her is part no more, and that they will look back at us with our one support and say, 'how narrow, how mean, how poor, how weak' and be as men are now not knowing that fine ecstasy, that primitive joy, that divine 'love' which can make a woman's life now so perfect, so hopeless, so happy, so despairing, so full, full of all that her nature desires, so utterly empty sometimes too. I shall not be one anyway. If you were here tonight, if you could speak all across to me I would that you spoke, not love of me, but just some simple word of encouragement, of praise that a child must long for having tried to do its copy well, though it had got blotted somehow. And like a child I cry for the impossible, for you will not know how I longed for this silence to be broken, till I have forgotten too that I cried for the sound of your voice when you were miles and miles from me. I suppose I must be tired too to write like this; tired after a very busy but very happy sunshiny day . . . [Merfyn]'s got the letter

9. A studio photograph by Frederick H. Evans, July 1904.

10. The author of *Oxford* and *Beautiful Wales* at Elses Farm, *c.*1904–5.

[from E.T. with jokes about measles] under his pillow to read 'if I wake up in the night'. And I had my letter to laugh over, too. So you are quite set up now with a letter from 'her', and the hope of another. But seriously you will be careful won't you; she's so very young, so very ignorant, and you don't know her a bit, what she is at all, only that she's different from the others, dark haired and dark eyed. Only make her laugh happily, or think happily, never set her wondering about herself, or you or things she will not have known yet. Don't awake anything in her that sleeps yet awhile will you. Don't let her know at all of "feelings". Her mind could be opened much wider for her good and happiness; her shyness overcome, let it be very happy for her, not anything that she might vaguely feel is strange, that she would hesitate at all even in thought though not in act to tell her mother or sisters. (5 February.)

My love for you is real, I know that. That's all I know, there's nothing else in my life but that, that and the children who are part of it. And now I know what's been on my mind all day; it is that I don't want anything else at all if you'll love me. I don't want to come for the weekend, nor to let them see us together, nor for other people to know it. I got so lonely that is why. I want you to love Hope if you'll love me, too. But I'm so different I don't see how you can. And you see it's always that I want your love; perhaps I can't let anyone in. I don't know. No if I said your love was inferior it was not true. It's different. I see now that if a man's love was like a woman's the world would have come to an end long ago: there is work to be done.—I see, I think that if he felt as a woman feels, jealous of anything that seems to put love on one side, then love would burn out love—there'd be none left. If it was pain for me to hold you in my arms against my body, I would do it just the same; it would only be pain instead of pleasure to express my love for you. Pain would be better perhaps, because pleasure sometimes gets called love, and it's not, but only a public way of expressing it; but sometimes a pressure of the hand, or a glance is the same, or a step. I see your face and know that I know you, and love you knowing all. I have failed miserably in that I have made you feel I have loved a someone who wasn't you; it angered you that I was so blind, but I was not. It is hard for you, it is hard for you, I see that, to have me always getting everything from you; if I drink with you out of happiness it is well, but one must be able to keep bitterness to oneself. I have failed because my love is no help for you, I love wrongly somehow; if I could understand how perhaps after all I could be of some use. . . . If at the end of this long day you will kiss me because I'm sorry for all I've done, then it will be easier tomorrow to live and be happy and then earn your love. Helen. (13 February.)

I've been thinking that I'm 30. I don't know if it would be possible for my character to change so much as to be useful to you now the children are here. I can't leave them, or else my desire is that you should begin over again. I have been imagining glorious possibilities for you. You may be bad as you say, but there's good too, fine good. I could not love only badness, but you have so much in you that is splendid. But you are the bad and the good I'd do anything for that I could; the greatest thing I could do for you would be to slip away, but the children hold me. It's queer that I with my love could do that feeling it was the best for you, but I can't endure the thought of you slipping from me. Yet of course to make it all complete both would have to happen. But that can't be. I will do absolutely anything you suggest. I swear I will try to be less selfish; I'll not drag you into my sorrow. I'll not have any sorrow. All that was only because I was so tired that night and lonely, and I thought afterwards when I wished I had not sent it, that you would make allowances for that, knowing how weak I am. That's it. I'm so weak, you are strong, your very egoism is strength; it is finer far than my adoring weakness, that puts itself under your heel. I am waiting for a letter, feeling that perhaps it will be comforting, but not knowing. . . .

It's a lovely day. I am full of hope. I would have written yesterday, to post yesterday, but I couldn't. You'll get these now at noon on Saturday. Don't misunderstand will you; I'm not sure what I've written, but I know there's nothing that I would wish unsaid, nothing that is meant to hurt you in any way. I am sick of giving you pain.

Won't we ever forget these years. There has been joy, hasn't there. For me, there has—lots of it, till sometimes—Oh sometimes it's been not earthly, no, not that I can't find a word for the joy I have felt sometimes with you. I wish I could have brought you it too. I drag you into my sorrow that is all. However, all this is no use. I am struggling not to wish vain things, not to regret vanity, but to look forward, and out of everything try to learn something, and put some sense into me, into my love, my work, my joy, my sorrow.

Have I made you understand that I never doubt your love. I would not have lain in your arms, or been happy that Sunday with you, if I had not known as I have known long ago and now and always that you love me. I don't deceive myself, don't say I do. I am stupid and don't understand often, and then I get tired too, and things distort themselves. I'll not let it bother you again. Don't put down my ideal. . . .

P.S. My thoughts come in fits and starts. It has just occurred to me that perhaps you will feel I abase myself too much, that that hurts you more than anything. . . . You have told me often that my love has not only been wasted, that it has been a real true thing to you, and again that I know you more than anyone else, and that I was best for you. All these things I remember and treasure. So there is pride in me, dear, it is not all humility. In all I have not failed: I will not say that for the honour of our love. Let us curse ourselves when the fit is on, but our love is pure and true and splendid always, and not to be brought low. (14 February.)

I'm just counting the days till that Friday comes when I shall set out early from here, no one happier in the whole world. I hope the Webbs won't be away for that weekend. I should like to see them, so tell them I'm coming, and *of course* they will put off all their engagements to see the beloved Auntie Helen. What a pity Hope won't be there; do try and get her to stay here in the Easter holidays . . .

No dearest, I won't keep sorrow from you if you don't want me to. I'd rather share every thing with you, but I can't bear to make you unhappy . . .

. . . I think it is very wonderful for me that I have you to love and your love to cherish. Perhaps it is best for you dear after all to have so simple a soul to help you through life. You are so complex, your brain, all your being is just the reverse of simple. I do wrong to hold my mirror up to you. You hate and laugh at, the words, 'genius', 'artistic temperament' etc., but I know that you are one of those who dwell apart. I do look up to you dear, though I don't often 'pat you on the back' and only tell of my pride in you in laughter because else I should weep. (Written on 15 February after two notes of loving reassurance from Edward and a decision for Helen to visit Minsmere at the end of February.)

In the eight letters that remain before Helen left for Minsmere there is no further reference to the cloud of unknowing that had come between them during Edward's longest absence from home since he was an undergraduate. Helen had returned to the chatty, pell-mell, off-the-top-of-her-pen style that characterizes the hundreds of letters that Edward preserved. In her heart, before Minsmere, she wished their relationship, their love-making, their mutual self-revelations to remain exactly as they had been between 1896 and 1902. After Minsmere she became more self-critical about herself as mother, housekeeper, and wife-companion without diminishing one iota of her love for him and her determination to create the conditions for his genius to burgeon. Her letters to Edward in Wales with Merfyn (for ten days after Easter 1909), or to him in Cornwall (for ten days with Haynes in June 1909), or to Edward at home in Ashford while she spent a fortnight at Sandown with Bronwen, Merfyn and a niece (in late August 1909), are quite free from self-pity, full of tolerant concern for, or immediate response to, his well-being, and free from any detailed expression of her physical tension. There are no letters while Edward worked in London as a civil servant in the autumn of 1909: they saw each other every week either in London or at Ashford. When he returned to full-time writing at home in January 1910, Helen's letters show that they had already decided to have another child—their first to be premeditated. She had accepted that her own 'nature' (a much used word in their household) would not change and seemed determined to reduce the causes of irritation. 'I wish

I never angered you with my muddling ways and my foolishness', having 'failed so often'. She becomes more involved with the school, with neighbours, with the Suffrage movement, and sees herself with her usual comic, self-deprecating eye: 'I am trying to finish one of the outrageous cotton dresses I wear.' She gives him a careful account of her expenditure, and relies on him for her weekly housekeeping money and for her own small but regular allowance. She is meticulous in apportioning necessary expenditure between them and invariably loads him with errands to bring household supplies from London or Petersfield.

There is one slight but significant difference. Before Minsmere, one of her tasks was to send on to him, unopened, any parcels of review books and all official correspondence. After Minsmere, she was entrusted to open parcels and—a considerable change this—to record all the cheques sent to him from editors and publishers, before placing them in the special drawer reserved for his bank books. There were other locked drawers to be opened only if he sent specific requests for a notebook or a manuscript. (He kept all her letters to him in one such locked drawer; she was aware of them only after his death.) This change was a conscious attempt by Edward to bridge the gap that he had allowed to grow between her role as housewife-helpmeet and her secret ambition to become an invaluable practical assistant in his work. (Later still she learned to type, but found the process too slow and inhibiting. Consequently, when he asked her to transcribe selected passages for a book on Borrow she resorted to a careful longhand quite unlike her usual epistolary rush.) After their third child was born, and gardening absorbed much of her time, energy, and interest, Helen became more content to fulfil her domestic role—seasoned by frequent spells as a teacher at Bedales—and to recognize that while Edward would never abandon her and her children, nor seek extramarital sexual satisfaction, he would seek out intellectual stimulus with a widening band of friends. Edward found the words for their mature love in his letter to her on 24 January 1916: 'Fancy your thinking I might have someone in view in those verses. . . . Oh, you needn't think of another lady. There would have to be 2 to make a love affair and I am only one. Nobody but you would ever be likely to respond as I wished. I don't like to think anybody but I could respond to you. If you turned to anybody else I should come to an end immediately.'

CHAPTER 9

The South Country

AFTER Minsmere, Edward and Helen decided to settle permanently near Bedales School. When they returned to Berryfield Cottage in March 1908, the entire Ashford Chase estate (of which they were a part) was up for sale. Edward made detailed enquiries with his brother-in-law Hugh McArthur about the cost of mortgages in order to buy Berryfield Cottage. The asking price was beyond him, but when the estate was sold it was made a condition of purchase that the Thomas tenancy should remain unchanged. Much of the land around the manor house was sold in separate lots. Geoffrey Lupton, a friend of Thomas, an old Bedalian, a maker of furniture and disciple of William Morris, bought nearly thirty acres on top of the hill above Ashford Hanger, adjoining his own house and workshop which Thomas often visited. The Thomases had been a little unsettled by the failure to buy Berryfield Cottage which was commodious, had a mature garden, and gave access to some fishing, to watercress beds, and good walking country. In May 1908 Lupton suggested building a new house for them on the crest of the hanger. The fittings and furnishings would conform to William Morris designs and the Thomases would rent it. In late June Lupton and Thomas undertook a five-day walking tour in Cornwall—sixteen hours each day from 5 to 9—and the plan for the house, later called Wick Green, was fully elaborated. By late August Thomas could report to Bottomley that the house would be begun in the spring, 'on the hilltop half a mile away and 400 feet above us, just not in sight of the sea and Isle of Wight—but rather far from Mervyn's school'.

There was little change in his moods. His letters refer to bouts of weakness and depression, seasoned by sustained desk-work and frequent walks into the South Country, often with a night spent with the artist-printer James Guthrie at Harting. He continued to review hard: forty-one reviews between May and June, and forty-three between August and October. On a conservative estimate he earned in this way at least £150 in a half year. Unfortunately, as he reported in late March to his agent Frank Cazenove, there was nothing left of the advance he had received for *Jefferies*. He was beginning to farm out to dailies and journals (especially the *Saturday Review*, the *Nation*, the *New Age*, the *Daily Chronicle* and the *Daily News*) short pieces that were later included in *The South Country,* which now occupied much of his interest and hopes as he worked on the final stages, and the laborious copying, of *Jefferies.* He also made plans for the typing of selected letters of George Borrow in preparation for a book which, he believed, would bring together many of his own interests in the gypsies, in nomadic life and, above all, in Wales. After his Cornish holiday, in an exceptional spurt of energy, he sent off the completed manuscript of *Jefferies* on 17 July, and began the final draft of *The South Country* two days later. It was completed on 6 November when, to the amazement of close friends, he was in London working as a disillusioned civil servant.

He was now past thirty and at Berryfield Cottage he had established himself as a successful reviewer and critically acclaimed essayist. His income was more than adequate for his needs and he was happy with the school and the countryside around. His father was well known to Liberal politicians and, through his influence, Edward was offered, and accepted, a post as Assistant Secretary to a new Royal Commission on Ancient Monuments in Wales and Monmouthshire. It seemed an attractive prospect, but he had some misgivings. Six months before, MacAlister had been appointed Secretary of the RIBA, which he held for life. Perhaps Edward hoped to free himself in a similar way from multiple reviewing and, like many other civil servants, to find enough leisure to develop his writing and supplement his income. He now gave Mac-Alister the news: 'the job is apparently not going to be very pleasant or profitable.' He expanded his fears to Bottomley, who was reading proofs of *Jefferies*: 'It certainly means much of London and I dread lest it means daily office hours. If it does I must chuck it soon.' For the first six weeks or so he lodged with his engineer brother, Theodore, from Mondays to Fridays, although initially he had thought to travel daily from Petersfield. He kept up his reviewing, continued his proof-reading, completed *The South Country,* and at the British Museum prepared for the book on Borrow. After a month he began office work at 10 and worked at his brother's home until midnight: 'The town work is poor because of the air. The evening work is poor because I am half done. Still, I shall stick at it if possible for the sake of the years of Welsh walking or driving. . . . I must carry a half-plate camera and a measuring rod and tape. Cycling I hate and it is no quicker on mountains. I don't know how the Treasury will like paying £1 a day for a pony and trap.'

By early October he had decided to give up this first regular office job for eight years. The prospect of autumn outdoor work in Wales appeared less than he had thought and, as he resumed his London contacts, he realized that he could find plenty of work (chiefly as a reviewer). Even though he was dissatisfied with *Jefferies* in proof, he believed that *The South Country* 'may have got me nearer to real book form. Yet it is made up of separate parts' and this, he thought, augured well for his deep desire to publish many more of his short pieces. This growing certitude about the direction his prose should take increased his dislike of his own time-wasting appearances at London literary gatherings, at a time when he was also seeing more of Guthrie, de la Mare and his modest, hardworking brother, to whom he confided that he was not really earning his stipend and was secretly grieved by it. On medical advice, too, he was advised to take things easy, with longer week-ends at Ashford from Friday evening to Tuesday morning, and with occasional free days to enable him to complete his reading around Borrow in the British Museum. But in deference to his father's influence in gaining him the post, he agreed to stay on until Christmas 1908. Before he finally left the Commission, he spent a week in Swansea gaining a brief taste of the work he had hoped for, at Penard Castle in Gower and, particularly, at Carreg Cennen Castle in Carmarthenshire, which had gripped his imagination eleven years before. As always when he was shut up, as though condemned to be a life-long office slave, his letters during late October and November refer frequently to the desirability of death: 'if only we could know we were dead'. During the Swansea visit he cuts through such fantasies (which he often indulged in as literary tropes in various scattered parts of his prose) with the usual cool robustness that marked his conduct at all times: 'Nor will I, intentionally, die just yet, as I want to see my Castle among the sandhills tomorrow and my lake among the mountains soon after. I return to town in a week.'

The prospect of the new house above Steep now clarified the relationship between Helen and Edward, which had been greatly strained during his two months at Minsmere and the preceding months at Ashford. As Wick Green was being built they decided to have a third child.

During the eight years after Minsmere only three long letters—and numerous detailed notes, almost diary-like—survive from Edward to Helen: one in July 1908 from Crantock, near Newquay, one in late August 1912 from Earlsdon while on a cycle tour with Merfyn, and one in February 1913 when he was staying with Clifford Bax at Wells. All three are full of details of routine affairs, showing a keen interest in Helen's doings—which can be filled out from her letters to him—but with no indication of his own moods, although these abound in simultaneous letters to Bottomley, Berridge, Hooton, MacAlister, John Freeman, and, occasionally, Harold Monro. Writing to his closest friends about himself, he warns them against telling Helen if he is in a bad way. (This note of solicitude runs, too, beneath the last batch of nineteen letters he wrote to Helen between November 1916 and the day before his death in France in April 1917.)

Despite the later open-hearted flow of her two books about their life together, Helen remained reticent about her own response to the changes that came about. In 1931, after the publication of *As It Was* and *World Without End,* she gained the friendship of Sylvia Townsend Warner and occasionally, writing late in life, she would slightly lift the veil of reticence. She was eighty-five when she wrote in 1962:

> Now I know for sure that you count me as your friend and it gives me deep joy. I can never quite believe it because I know that lovers of Edward's poems and other work must have formed some idea of 'Helen' and I *know* (don't contradict) that I fall far short of what they imagined. In fact it must be a shock. Not now so much perhaps as I am old, but when I was young this was an agony to me. That Edward loved me never ceased to be a wonder to me and I knew how inadequate was the girl I was and the wife I longed to be. But no more confession.

Even more revealing is Helen's letter to Sylvia in her eighty-ninth year:

> A propos our little talk on the telephone, how I do realize in myself a terrible fault. It arises from my earliest years when my two brilliant sisters—at school, not afterwards,—dominated me and crushed me into a wormlike state of lack of confidence etc. in myself. That is not to excuse it at all. . . . And I also know that people do love me and I have *great* need of love. And almost Edward's last letter to me was so full of love, so urgent in his longing for me to be sure of it, and his utter dependence on my love, that I *was* sure, and so I can think of him calmly as my lover whom I adored and no Why? comes into it. But it took these almost last words, Sylvia, to make me sure.

As Helen explained, this childhood unhappiness was alleviated first by her father and then by Edward—but late in life 'it still lies bitter at the bottom of my heart and will not—try as I will, knowing its evil, disperse'. With some success, Helen and Edward had decided to build a new pattern of life together, however shaky the foundations may have appeared to outsiders. When *The South Country* was reissued in 1938 Helen described it as 'one of the happiest of the prose works of Edward Thomas . . . written at a period of comparative ease and tranquillity'. She believed that during his walks in Kent, Surrey, Sussex, Hampshire, and Wiltshire 'his soul was revived when it was faint with despair, and comforted as some are by religion or music'. At that time Helen possessed all his notebooks and the entire correspondence that had passed between them throughout their twenty-one years together. Her words substantiate the degree to which they understood each other: 'Here he lived the life he had chosen, often suffering despair and humiliation, but always in that country finding the comfort he so passionately sought, to lose it again and find it ever again.'

For in contrast to the introspective asides in his letters, *The South Country*—on the surface a book about selected parts of rural England—defined consistently the kind of writer Thomas wished to be and laid bare the topics that absorbed his attention when he was free from what he termed the 'unskilled labour' of reviewing:

For what I have sought is quiet and as complete a remoteness as possible from towns, whether of manufactures, of markets or of cathedrals . . . I never go out to see anything. The signboards thus often astonish me . . . The truth is that, though the past allures me, and to discover a cathedral for myself would be an immense pleasure, I have no historic sense and no curiosity. . . . I have read a great deal of history . . . but I have forgotten it all, or it has got into my blood and is present in me in a form which defies evocation or analysis. But as far as I can tell I am pure of history . . . And so I travel, armed only with myself, an avaricious and often libertine and fickle eye and ear, in pursuit, not of knowledge, not of wisdom, but one of whom to pursue is never to capture.

His mind refuses to deal with the topics that absorb the superior and the intelligent man; instead he appeals to the unfortunate, superfluous men who have been saved by modern social science from the fate of the cuckoo's foster-brothers. He expects that the critics will misunderstand what he is about. He has acquired a hopelessly inadequate way of expression, 'but still gradually as fitted to the mind as an old walking-stick to the hand that has worn and been worn by it, full of our weakness as of our strength, of our blindness as of our vision—the man himself, the poor man it may be. And I live by writing, since it is impossible to live by not writing in an age not of gold but brass.'

His domestic wayfaring, undertaken at random in a circle from Ashford that would eventually bring him back to Steep in time for tea, enabled him to include conversations and incidents observed on his wanderings. A grandmother of eighty smiling at a cottage door is sharply contrasted with a girl of sixteen who is

lost in her laughter and oblivious of its cause . . . this is her hour. That future is

not among the dreams in the air today. She is at one with the world, and a deep
music grows between her and the stars. Her smile is one of those magical
things, great and small and all divine, that have the power to wield universal
harmonies. At sight or sound of them the infinite variety of appearances in the
world is made fairer than before, because it is shown to be a many-coloured
raiment of the one. The raiment trembles, and under leaf and cloud and air a
window is thrown upon the unfathomable deep, and at the window we are
sitting, watching the flight of our souls away, away to where they must be
gathered into the music that is being built. Often upon the vast and silent
twilight, as now, is the soul poured out as a rivulet into the sea and lost, not
able even to stain the boundless crystal of the air; and the body stands empty,
waiting for its return, and, poor thing, knows not what it receives back into
itself when the night is dark and it moves away. For we stand ever at the edge
of Eternity and fall in many times before we die.

These are the experiences he most wished to share with his readers,
and had failed to convey in his earlier prose books, because he wavered
from direct statement into mannered artifice and back again. Towards
the end of his first half-year at Berryfield Cottage he had complained to
Bottomley how his self-consciousness

grows and grows and is almost constant now, and I fear perhaps it will reach
the point of excess without my knowing it. . . . Only reviews and nature make
me think at all and that in a way beyond my control—things occur to me and I
think for about the length of a lyric and then down and blank and something
new—if the old idea returns it will not grow, but is only repeated. Perhaps we
worry less about [our] conclusions, generalizations nowadays, in our anxiety to
get the facts and the feelings down— . . . I am by the way going to plead for a
little more playfulness and imagination (if to be got) in archaeology, topography and so on.

Many spurred lyrics—his own phrase—in prose are strewn throughout
The South Country, in that cadenced manner with which Thomas sought
to pay the debt of imitation to experiences he believed he had shared
with Sir Thomas Browne or Traherne:

A house is a perdurable garment, giving and taking of life. If it only fit,
straightway it begins to chronicle our days. It beholds our sorrows and our joys;
its untalebearing walls know all our thoughts, and if it be such a house as
grows after the builders are gone, our thoughts presently owe much to it; we
have but to glance at a certain shadow or a curve in the wall-paper pattern to
recall them, softened as by an echo, and that corner or that gable starts many a
fancy that reaches beyond the stars, many a fancy gay or enriched with regrets.

It is aware of birth, marriage and death; and who dares say that there is not kneaded into the stones a record more pleasing than brass? With what meaning the vesperal beam slips through a staircase window in autumn!

From this mannered prose, recalling Haynes' remark that at Oxford Thomas could insert passages of his own into his reading of a seventeenth-century passage without detection, he moves easily in the same chapter to quote some ballads and to comment upon desirable trends in modern English verse:

Can [the recovery of old ballads in their integrity] possibly give a vigorous impulse to a new school of poetry that shall treat the life of our time and what in past times has most meaning for us as freshly as those ballads did the life of their time? It is possible; and it is surely impossible that such examples of simple, realistic narrative shall be quite in vain. Certainly the more they are read the more they will be respected, and not only because they often deal with heroic matters heroically, but because their style is commonly so beautiful, their pathos so natural, their observation of life so fresh, so fond of particular detail—its very list of names being at times real poetry.

These typical extracts from the same chapter of *The South Country* illustrate two sides of Thomas's scope, and aim, as a prose writer. He wished, in his reviewing of much inferior contemporary verse, to have an effect 'beyond the entertainment of a few scientific men and lovers of what is ancient, now that the first effects upon Wordsworth and his contemporaries have died away'. To this end he treasured his place as a reviewer with the *Daily Chronicle* and was despondent when he lost or seemed about to lose it. Equally, he revealed another side of his temperament in the Wiltshire Outcast described in Chapter XV:

I dare say modernity was in his blood, but no man seemed to belong less to our time. Of history and science he knew nothing, of literature nothing; he had to make out the earth with his own eyes and heart. He had not words for it, but he felt that whatever he touched was God. No myth or religion had any value to him. There were no symbols for him to use. The deities he surmised or smelled or tasted in the air or upon the earth had neither name nor shape. Had he been able to think, he was the man to put our generation on the way to a new mythology. For all I know, he had the vision, the power of the seer, without the power of the prophet. A little more and perhaps he would have invaded Christendom as St. Paul invaded Heathendom. Yet I think he was not wholly the loser by being unable to think. The eye untroubled by thought sees things like a mirror newly burnished; at night, for example, the musing can see nothing before him but a mist, but if he stops thinking quickly the roads, the walls, the trees become visible. So this man saw with a clearness as of Angelico . . .

And this he had at no cost. He employed only such labour as was needed to make his bread and occasionally clothes and a pipe. . . . He did not stay long in the village. He was shy and suspicious of men, and except by the younger children he was not liked. He set out on his travels again . . . perhaps the wisest of men, indifferent to mobs, to laws, to all of us who are led aside, scattered and confused by hollow goods . . .

This outcast, 'who loved Nature because she had no ambiguity, told Jones no lies, uttered no irony', is an extreme caricature of at least half-a-dozen characters and their stories brought intermittently into *The South Country*. They had been accumulated in notebooks for two years at least before the book was prepared for publication. The stories are varied and their conversations are enlivened, not by dialect, but by a naturally flowing command of dialogue (or monologue) that clearly reflects educated speech and echoes the tone of his familiar letters. As the notebook sources indicate, Thomas recalls incidents in his own style with occasional direct quotations from conversation but with no attempt to use dialect forms. In each case the speaker has rejected the normal assumptions of ordinary urban ways of living and earning, and frequently he questions sharply the devotion to causes of those around him.

These narrative interludes represent a conflict between Edward Thomas the journalist-reviewer and the artist within, determined to find adequate words for the vision of a man in uncomplicated communion with the natural world. The tension of this inner conflict perplexed and debilitated him, often when he least expected it. The onset of his bouts of depression continued to puzzle him throughout his life and at times he attributed it directly to his 'writer's melancholy'. He hints at this in a letter to Bottomley on 21 May 1908:

> Walking you will perhaps see suits me. Really I am never so well as when I am rid of the postman and all company walking 20 or 30 miles a day. I was as well as ever I hope to be in my week's walk, and its effect has lasted over another week. I get as depressed and irritable as ever but seem to recover faster. Five months purgation of course has something to do with it.—On the other hand I can't say I feel any 'mad pride of intellectuality', tho a feeling of extreme virtue after 5 months teetotalism and almost abstinence from tobacco is hard to avoid. But seriously I wonder whether for a person like myself whose most intense moments were those of depression a cure that destroys the depression may not destroy the intensity—a *desperate* remedy?

Thomas was fortunate in his friends and they treasured his company especially since, at this time, few of them were aware of the excesses to which his temperament could drive him. In their separate ways, Edward

Garnett, James Guthrie, W. H. Davies, and de la Mare strengthened Thomas's determination to continue with his own, financially unprofitable writing experiments when the advice of editors, publishers, and his agent was pushing him towards a less conscience-ridden acceptance of a well-rewarded journalistic career 'which would conflict inevitably', he believed, 'with my own view of truth, which would be so confused by reservations and afterthoughts that it could not please'.

Helen was fully occupied as mother, teacher, housewife, and prompt domestic help when illness came to her sisters and her mother, who died suddenly in January 1907. Although Bedales was now responsible for the full-time education of Merfyn and Bronwen, she and Edward continued to share with them their own knowledge of nature, believing with Traherne that 'there was never a tutor that did professly teach Felicity, though that be the mistress of all other sciences'. Edward introduces his own ideal at length into Chapter VIII of *The South Country*:

Nature-study is inevitable. Literature sends us to Nature principally for joy, joy of the senses, of the whole frame, of the contemplative mind, and of the soul, joy which if it is found complete in these several ways might be called religious. Science sends us to Nature for knowledge. Industrialism and the great towns send us to Nature for health, that we may go on manufacturing efficiently, or, if we think right and have the power, that we may escape from it. But it would be absurd to separate joy, knowledge and health, except as we separate for convenience those things that have sent us out to seek for them; and Nature-teaching, if it is good, will never overlook one of these three. Joy, through knowledge, on a foundation of health, is what we appear to seek.

Thomas's belief in the trinity of joy, knowledge, and health was an intellectual conviction often denied in daily life. His letters to regular correspondents—at this time, and later—often refer to the 'damned blues that are on me again and will never go'. But these are balanced by others stating 'we are all glad to be back together again', after one of his many absences from home. Helen's teaching—and her acceptance of boarders from Bedales during the holidays—gave her a much-needed sense of identity. Bedales was expensive and Edward's income from reviewing alone—apart from the quickly-spent bonus derived from the sale of review copies to Thomas Thorpe—was rarely less than £250 a year between 1906 and 1911, and often close to £400. But this was not a stipend, and the fluctuation caused by seasonal lists always gave Edward a suspicious anxiety. (He had a pathological fear of being in debt, his first cousin once told me.) Helen's wages took care of school fees while

Edward, with the assistance of Frank Cazenove, sought out commissions for books on literary topics or searched for editors who would accept the tales, sketches, and 'landscapes with human figures' that he now preferred to write. The correspondence (in Durham University Library) between him and his agent testifies to his incessant demand for freedom and independence in his manner of working and choice of topics. Cazenove must have found him an unusually prickly client, however haphazard his daily routine may have seemed to others. Thomas's constant search for a way of life that was at once 'fixed and free' underlay much of his discontent.

W. H. Hudson was surprised that Thomas should take on so many commissions and the resolute, self-contained but not very successful James Guthrie noted that he was too easily diverted from his writing by things that occurred in his immediate surroundings. The memoirs recorded by three of the Thomas brothers emphasise, as we have seen, the degree to which 'Edwy' followed his own devices in youth, adolescence, and manhood. As a boy, he records himself, he persistently got his own way: as a man he evinced a stubborn determination to shape his life precisely in a manner suitable to his inner prompting. (And in this Helen unquestioningly abetted him.) He exercised an iron will in meeting deadlines at all times, whatever his moods. Although the result was often nervous exhaustion and extreme physical lassitude, he was still capable of working for days on end either at his desk or in the British Museum Reading Room. *Letters from Edward Thomas to Gordon Bottomley* gives evidence enough of the care and critical perception he brought to the journalism and reviewing that provided a regular, modest income from 1903 to 1911. His critical output is notable both for the literary judgement displayed and the academic thoroughness with which he reviewed—and placed in historical content—English poetry from *Bēowulf* to the early years of the twentieth century.

At Oxford in his day the study of English literature—as distinct from the pursuit of English and Germanic philology—was a necessary adjunct to the study of history; and as a reviewer of innumerable reprints of earlier English classics Thomas was extending a study that had become more and more congenial to him. The knowledge he displays in his *Daily Chronicle* reviews of the successive volumes of the *Cambridge History of English Literature,* reveals him as a thoroughly competent literary historian, admittedly with a strong bias towards poetry and drama, but away from fiction. His self-confidence in reviewing, like his belief that his future success as a writer lay more with books about literature than about nature topics, was enshrined in the new house built on the Shoulder of Mutton slope above Ashford Chase, which he later referred to as Wick Green, Petersfield.

The new house was not ready for occupation until December 1909 but the separate study—now known as the Bee-house—was ready for Thomas to use in April. Earlier in the year he had had a sudden spell of creativity during which he had written twenty or more stories—'all sorts of sketches', he told Harry Hooton, 'that I manage to put something into, but not one have I sold since I began'. Was it the expense of the new house, or the euphoria of this free burst of writing, that made him give up his 'marvellous doctor' in June 1909? Later he sent further progress reports to Harry, writing on 30 June 1909: 'I am discovering that I do very bad reviews now that I give as much time as possible to my sketches which are so far unprofitable. There is a chance that Harper's will print one. I shall wait a year or so and then if I can't get them into magazines see what I can do with a book of them.'

On 16 September 1909 he promised Harry a copy of *The South Country*, 'a patchy book that I ought never to have done . . . I have had a good deal of rheumatism and my temper doesn't improve, but I have done a lot of (unprofitable) work this summer.' He was very conscious that Harry had run into bad luck in his financial affairs, but was as ready as ever to rely on the older friend's judgement. 'I go on writing', he wrote on 2 December. 'I am glad you think I get closer to things, as I sometimes think I am merely getting rid of some of my futilities, and that when I get rid of the last there will be a blank.'

A similar wry note marks his simultaneous correspondence with Gordon Bottomley during 1909. The twenty notes or letters accompanying the proofs of *The South Country* and the collected sketches, *Rest and Unrest*, confirm that when Thomas kept at reviewing he was easily able to earn the modest competence of £250 a year that he had set as his annual financial target. The concentration on sketches in January and February 1909 was his excuse for not attending MacAlister's wedding, where Bronwen was an admired bridesmaid. Soon after the wedding, his *Jefferies* was well reviewed, but brought no offer of acceptable work. Nor was he quite certain in which direction he was heading:

I have done a great deal at first under a real impulse but latterly (the long frost having quite undermined me) by force of daily custom as much as anything. I can do almost anything if once I start doing it every day at a certain hour . . . I feel sure it is better work or in a better direction than all but the best of the old but it is even less profitable and quite impossible to palm off on a publisher as part of a guinea guide book.

He was stimulated by the proximity of Arthur Ransome, now living at Froxfield with his eccentric first wife, Ivy. In spite of the occasional references to sudden listlessness, his life at this time in 1909 (viewed from the outside) was full of variety and interest. An Easter trip to Wales with Merfyn—which fed into many of the sketches later included in *Rest and Unrest* and *Light and Twilight*—concluded with a visit to Davies at his cottage on the Weald, interrupted by a sudden call home 'to do some work for the *Morning Post* which was hard up for copy and wanted me to manufacture it as they know me for a punctual bloke'. Reviewing for the *Daily Chronicle* as well as the *Post,* he was able to praise Ezra Pound's *Personae,* against the trend of other fashionable critics, and Edward Garnett's play, *The Feud.* He and Helen saw its first London performance, followed the next day by *The Playboy of the Western World.*

Thomas assured Bottomley that Garnett's play, which was based on an Icelandic Family Saga, would in no way detract from the success of Bottomley's new volume of poems (based on the Saga of Burnt Njall), *The Riding to Lithend.* Thomas had read the book in proof, and he and Helen very much approved of the dedicatory 'poem to Edward Thomas in both ways, as a poem and as an expression of friendship'. Bottomley's poem gives a happy glimpse of Thomas as friend and companion: the kind of friend that Walter de la Mare had sought out that summer when he spent some time at West Harting, near Petersfield, and was thinking of settling there. This was the side of Edward's nature that Helen could enjoy only by reflection in the happiness of others and, unselfishly, she urged him to seek out his friends. She also knew a severer side of Edward, so clearly glimpsed in his stilted acceptance of Garnett's proffered friendship: 'The man who readily sympathises with my work and says he likes it, I am with instant cussedness, on the other hand, inclined to suspect.' Much of this side of Edward she kept to herself.

Bottomley's poem 'To Edward Thomas', composed at Cartmel on 30 June 1908, is a fine tribute to Edward's ability to gain the ready friendship of many gifted men—and women.

> Here in the North we speak of you,
> And dream (and wish the dream were true)
> That when the evening has grown late
> You will appear outside our gate—

As though some Gipsy-Scholar yet
Sought this far place that men forget;
Or some tall hero still unknown
Out of the Mabinogion,
Were seen at nightfall looking in,
Passing mysteriously to win
His earlier earth, his ancient mind,
Where man was true and life more kind
Lived with the mountains and the trees
And other steadfast presences,
Where large and simple passions gave
The insight and the peace we crave,
And he no more had nigh forgot
The old high battles he had fought.

———

Because your heart could understand
The hopes of their primeval land,
The hearts of dim heroic forms
Made clear by tenderness and storms,
You caught my glow and urged me on;
So now the tale is once more done

———

I bring my play, I turn to you
And wish it might to-night be true
That you would seek this old small house
Twixt laurel boughs and apple boughs;
Then I would give it, bravely manned,
To you, and with my play my hand.

Throughout the summer of 1909 Thomas was actively engaged in proof-reading and in various business attempts to find a suitable publisher for a congenial book that would supplement his income. Even more ambitiously, he wished to see his sketches and tales published separately, and not in a series along with *The Road Mender* and *The Grey Brethren* by Michael Field and *A Modern Mystic's Way* (dedicated to Michael Field) and so 'designed to depend on its superficial resemblance to that work for its success with the Tooting public'. Bottomley, who had read the proofs of *The South Country* and *Rest and Unrest*, suggested that Thomas relied overmuch on his notebooks and that this showed in his continuous prose. Thomas admitted the fault but, in self-defence, argued that he would never abandon his notebooks. The habit of note-taking on local walks and longer journeys was too ingrained. Thomas agrees with

what you say of note books. But I shall not burn them I expect. Only I shall certainly use them less and less as I get more of an eye for subjects. Among my bad habits was that of looking through old note books of scenery etc. in order to get a subject or mood suggested to me. *I now use the note books more and more exclusively for the details of things conceived independently.* [My italics.] Also I am casting about for subjects which will compel me to depend simply upon what I am—memory included but in a due subsidiary place. I think of Welsh legends. As to modern subjects I can do little with more than one character and that one is sure either to be a ghost (of a pretty woman or a nice old man) or else myself. So far the best things I have done have been about houses. I have quite a long series—I discover, tho I did not design it. The house in 'Sand and Snow' is one.

The autumn brought no immediate prospect of a satisfactory commissioned book. Helen returned to teaching at Bedales and Edward turned 'to all the reviewing I can get . . . I have to give up [town] more and more. I have had to give up dining in London altogether—bad hot city air, smoke, smell of food and alcohol etc. makes me bad for a week after these few hours.' For while he had been in London, in late 1908, he had visited his doctor regularly; and Dr Savitt had convinced Thomas that he suffered not from his stomach but from himself. 'He hopes to cure me of the elaborate self consciousness which he says is at the root of everything wrong in me.' After giving up Dr Savitt in June 1909, he records a sudden return to 'a languid desperate condition'. Referring to his diaries he found, what he had long suspected, 'that I get periods of depression particularly once a month for a week or so'. This mood seemed to pass, as he reported later to the ailing Bottomley from his new house in December 1909:

I was glad to have some news of you though it was bad. I guessed it would be. This must have been a deadly year for you. It has been a great weight to bear continuously and I hope for a crisp winter to clean the earth and help you. For two months nearly I have been better, chiefly because I have had to work hard and regularly in the new garden clay. I don't really care about it, but it had to be done and I kept at it day after day and it did me good almost against my will. I got a hard hand and my fatigues were more purely physical than usual. I had to do my reviewing badly and to do very little else. Still, one or two stories I worked at did not turn out badly. I used some old Welsh fragments of legends. You shall see them some day. I always feel that when I treat these *external* things my approach is very literal and matter of fact, but I hope not.

Perhaps I am not quite just to myself in finding myself very much on an every-day ordinary level except when in a mood of exultation usually connected with nature and solitude. By comparison with others that I know—like de la Mare—I seem essentially like the other men in the train and I should like not to be. This is quite genuinely naïve and will amuse you. It may be only because I am inarticulate and that I can usually only meet others on ground where I have no real interest—as politics, social and current literary affairs.

I am perhaps about to begin a book on poets and women. Originally it was to have been the influence of women on English poets. But that is too difficult: so it will be mainly the attitude of poets to individual women and the idea of woman and so on. . . . I have been dangling after publishers with all sorts of proposals but could not come to terms. This looked bad and I was willing to accept anything especially as our move means an increased expenditure and Helen talks of having another baby. [Their third child, Myfanwy, was born on 16 August 1910.]

His letters to and from Cazenove fill out this second paragraph. Cazenove became his chief literary agent in 1906 with the publication of *The Heart of England*. He discovered early how idiosyncratic Thomas could be. After finishing that book, punctually, Thomas commented, 'By the way I am not in a hurry to do more books that are to have pictures and cost £1 or so. The work seems thrown away on them and I get branded almost as if I wrote advertisements.' A little later he was grateful to escape, temporarily, from a Methuen agreement about a book on Borrow—promised for late 1908. Then, side by side with writing *Jefferies*, he insisted on having 'a free hand to go my own way with people, sea, downs and valleys and gardens' for *The South Country*. Thomas fully expected to be better off in 1909 and agreed to Dent's terms of a £30 advance, £15 on delivery of the manuscript in six months, and 15 per cent royalties from a book sold at 2/6. As his sketches and tales continued in early 1909, he used Cazenove, as well as his own earlier contacts, to place some of them with various journals. The agent had little success and returned most of the papers in August. By then Thomas had already agreed, after much resistance, to accept Methuen's terms (£80 for 60,000 words) for *Maurice Maeterlinck*. He found the prospect daunting and thought the terms low: '*Jefferies* is I believe just in a second edition and I am either going to get a good price for commissioned work or to give it up.' In the end, he made the length of the book (60,000 words to be accepted without comment) his chief bargaining counter and agreed to accept the contract under protest. ('I am not a starving author but I would rather be than accept the terms Methuen

wants.') At this time Thomas believed the writing of books could supplement and then, possibly, replace the steady income he had gained
from reviewing. The ease with which he had written the sketches and
tales had upset his calculations when first discussing *Maeterlinck* with
Cazenove: 'I must have £100 on delivery, in advance of a fair royalty. If
this seems unreasonable I am sorry. The fact is I am reluctant to take up
the work as it would mean putting aside for a couple of years a great
many plans which would produce better if not immediately profitable
work.' In August, when it seemed perfectly clear that nothing could be
done with his tales, Thomas suggested that he and Roger Ingpen should
arrange a book on Lafcadio Hearn 'on something like the same terms as
my *Jefferies*'. After many letters he agreed that Cazenove had a right to
his agent's percentage on this small deal with an old schoolfriend. Then,
through Edward Garnett, he allowed Duckworth to bring out a short
selection of his tales. Thomas had hoped for something larger and urged
Cazenove to arrange with Dent for

a series of my sketches and stories, without calling them such, as a new country
book. I would select the best, the most rustic, and the more cheerful as a rule,
and call it Country People and Country Places. Probably it would be best not
to offer the information that they are all—or nearly all written. If this is at all
likely I might hit upon some sort of framework—if it were only to hitch them
on to the months of the year—that would make them more acceptable.

Dent, however, was disappointed with the sales of *The South Country,* and
the idea fell through. As a result Thomas returned to two previous suggestions made in September: an idea for a book on *Poets of Nature,* and
the possibility of a book for Grant Richards about 'living poets', with a
supporting anthology. ('There has been nothing since Archer's fat book
of the Yellow Book age.') As Thomas saw the final stages of his new
house being completed, digging in the hard clay of his new garden and
believing that Helen would soon be happy carrying another child, he
began to urge his agent to push the idea of a book on *Poets of Nature*:
'You have no idea how I dislike writing such books after *Jefferies*—in
which case I knew my subject fairly well and yet made a very dismal
unnecessary book out of it as I most plainly perceive now.'

Thomas's last letter to Cazenove from Berryfield Cottage—containing
a 10 per cent agent's fee from a payment by Goldring (editor of *The
Tramp*) and a 6/11 fee for £3.8.0. paid by the *Nation* for one of the
sketches—shows that he was beginning to think about accepting reduced
terms for a book on 'Women and Poets'. He wished to run two books at

least in tandem during his first six months in the new house. He moved in on 18 December 1909 and, initially, using an old map reference he gave his address as Week Green, Petersfield (later altered to Wick Green). The need for more work, now that Helen was pregnant, is implicit in his first letter to Cazenove from the house he was later to make the centrepiece of his poem *Wind and Mist*: 'Of course my material must be books. Believe me I do not write or feel defiantly. I want money but I can only write what I am able to write.'

His certainty about the direction his writing should follow, whatever the verdict of publishers, is the core of the 'Note on Edward Thomas' contributed by Bottomley to the *Welsh Review* in September 1945:

Those middle years of his brief career were not happy. At least enough has been written about his manifestations of unhappiness. He was naturally a moody man . . . In the world of his daily work its impact was different. He was a highly skilled craftsman, who rarely earned his just remuneration, or one that was more than barely equal to his commitments in daily life . . . I have heard him say that he was more afraid of being in debt than of anything else he could conceive. In time he became tormented by neurasthenia; and a diabetic tendency developed in the years before 1914 . . . [Bottomley here confirms a statement made to me, by Thomas's first cousin, that Edward had suffered from diabetes.] A change in his character at this time has been suggested in some writing about him; but I do not believe this. Through all the years in which I knew him, he was visibly and intimately the man who was to write the poetry of the last two and a half years of his life.

Helen and Bottomley agree, from different standpoints, that the prose master of *The South Country* and Edward Thomas the poet were recognizably the same person: there was no surprising metamorphosis in between.

Edward Thomas felt welcomed in the South Country. 'Yet is this country, though I am mainly Welsh, a kind of home, . . . These are the "home" counties. A man can hide away in them. The people are not hospitable, but the land is.' It suited him to remain there until he became first a poet and then a soldier.

CHAPTER 10
Wick Green

No intellectual journey undertaken by Edward Thomas ever followed a simple, direct route. Whatever the cost to his family or himself he wished, at all times, to be 'fixed and free', and the three and a half years spent in the William Morris-style house built for him by Geoffrey Lupton at Wick Green above Steep offered as unsatisfactory a place of rest on the way as many of his previous abodes. Two poems (*The New House* and *Wind and Mist*) suggest the failure of the hopes he had woven around this particular symbol of his success as a reviewer-journalist in the preceding three years at Berryfield Cottage. Having resigned from the Civil Service post, he was determined to make his way as a full-time writer. He was satisfied with the education offered to his children at Bedales, while Berryfield Cottage had proved an ideal centre for the long and short rambles that were so necessary for his physical well-being. Ceaselessly he explored the Hampshire countryside within the lozenge bounded by Alton, Selborne, Liphook, Greatham, Petersfield, South Harting, Butser Hill, the River Meon, Froxfield Green, and Bramdean. Inevitably this particular countryside became the backcloth for nearly half his poems. (In July 1911, he could write to Hugh McArthur: 'I find the same magic hereabouts as ever—which compels me simply to work. Therefore I am working.') The oak timbers and furnishings of the new house creaked and groaned in the excessively wind-exposed site above the Shoulder of Mutton, but the stone-built study slightly below and in front of the house—redolent of honey and the hum of bees, as Ernest Rhys recalled it—was an ideal work-refuge with its magnificent vista and its offer of peace for writing, yet not too far from Lupton's workshop, or the lanes immediately around Froxfield, whenever he wished to relax temporarily away from his desk. His tenure of the study from April 1909 until June 1916 was the longest tenancy of his professional life and in this study many of his pre-enlistment poems were written in 1915.

Like the study bedroom at 61 Shelgate Road, or the attic workshop he was later to occupy at Selsfield House in East Grinstead, this Bee-house study provided the secure base necessary for probes into his innermost thoughts. From time to time his attachment to such refuges seeps into his stories. Writing of 'The Maiden's Wood', for example, in *Rest and*

Unrest— 'I had been there a score of times without making anything like a full survey and inventory of my kingdom. It was becoming part of me, a kingdom rather of the spirit than of the earth, and I was content to see what I had seen on my first visit.' Or in *The Happy-Go-Lucky Morgans*: 'Up there, said his mother, he hoped to learn why sometimes in a London street, beneath the new and the multitudinous, could be felt a simple and pure beauty, beneath the turmoil a placidity, beneath the noise a silence, which he longed to reach and drink deeply and perpetuate, but in vain. It was his desire to learn to see in human life, as we see in the life of bees, the unity, which perhaps some higher order of beings can see through the complexity which confuses us.'

In the Bee-house, I believe, he taught himself to unlearn the Paterian influence on his early descriptive writing and to concentrate more intently on the hidden truth beneath obsessive perception, or the implicit meaning that underlies explicit statement; but, above all, he confronted there the dilemma of an artist who finds himself cut off from the aspirations and social expectations of potential readers. The tortuous process of self-discovery and readjustment was extended over four years before he emerged as a poet fully confident, for the first time since pre-Oxford days, that he had found his vocation.

In the new house, the first quarter of 1910 was full of purposeful activity. W. H. Davies spent the New Year with the Thomases before leaving his Egg Pie Lane Cottage for Sevenoaks. Helen now knew she was pregnant and had decided to continue her teaching. Edward resumed his contest with the clay soil of his large new garden and, reluctantly, wrote a short picture-book on Windsor Castle in four weeks. Afterwards he made plans to write three books in the course of a year. Two of them were actually written: *Feminine Influence on the Poets,* between April and July, and *Maurice Maeterlinck,* with growing distaste, between November 1910 and January 1911. A third book was offered to J. M. Dent: 'a country book with houses—cottages, farms etc.—as centres, and dealing more than ever with people. If he will let me—and let me bring in Wales as well—I could make a good book of my kind.' Eventually Dent found the idea 'too nebulous' and turned it down; Thomas incorporated some of the material in *The Icknield Way.* February passed with a visit to Windsor Castle, the publication of *Rest and Unrest,* the planting of his garden, and the tending of a 'beautiful great bush' of Old Man beside his study door. In March, though, in preparation for his long tussle with *Maeterlinck,* he consulted Jesse Berridge yet again about books on mysticism and asked him—as well as Davies, Bottomley, de la Mare and others—some intimate questions about the precise relationship between love poems they had written and 'the circumstances under which each was written.' (Some of the replies, suitably disguised, were incorporated in *Feminine Influence*.)

The new house, and the prospect of a third child, occasioned some economies. He was glad to allow the childless McArthurs to foot the nurse's bill during Helen's confinement. ('It goes to my heart to pay large sums for necessaries especially when I haven't got large sums. . . . There seems no literary work for me. It looks like going back to the land in the form of manure.') He made fewer trips to London and was delighted that de la Mare was staying near to give him a substitute for the London company. It was not all gloom. Some of his short sketches—later to appear in *Light and Twilight*—were accepted by editors and Cazenove's records show a series of payments for them. In July, he worked hard at *Feminine Influence* in 'a kind of suppressed panic' and completed the book a month before the contract date which coincided with Helen's confinement. He excused his own haste: 'I believe I am justified in not doing as well as possible a piece of work I never could do really well with my powers. That is provided I do not harm my ability to do other things more natural to me.' Already he had discovered that the compulsive need to write the stories later published as *Rest and Unrest* and *Light and Twilight* was more satisfying than commissioned literary studies.

He gave Berridge news of the birth of his second daughter, Helen Elizabeth Myfanwy, born 16 August, 1910: 'another girl I am glad to say, and Helen and she have done very well from the start though the birth itself was a laborious one.' Before the birth he had set off on a leisurely walking tour into Kent with Merfyn, visiting Harry Hooton, exploring the Pilgrim's Way, and calling on Conrad. Merfyn was left with the Hootons for a month at Minsmere while Edward returned to tidy up his correspondence about *Maeterlinck* and to arrange a ten-day visit to Wales in September. There he first stayed with the 'Deacon' (John Williams of Waun Wen) at Swansea and with Gwili at Cardiff and Pontardulais. Subsequently he wandered 'in all directions' from Tregaron as a salve for 'all this muddled and hurried reading and writing'. The wilderness country around Tregaron bog, like the creeping industrial spoilation of Swansea, still held its strong fascination for him, 'especially during the first stages in the growth of a place in Pontardulais—when it is being transformed from a village with a fulling-mill and an inn to a Hell, fully equipped'.

On his return to Steep in late September he found Helen fully recovered and overjoyed to be once more nursing an infant. As the proofs of *Feminine Influence* came in, Edward slowly screwed up his resolve to begin writing *Maeterlinck*. He had sought assistance from Hooton, Martin Freeman, Bottomley, A. D. Williams (an undergraduate 'fan' from Worcester College), his brother Julian, and the McArthurs to whom the book was dedicated. He also responded to an invitation from Rupert Brooke—who had been an earlier visitor to Bedales and a caller at Wick Green—and spent a weekend at Grantchester where he was somewhat dismayed by the argumentative brilliance of Brooke's friends. More congenial were motor car excursions with Ashley Gibbons that included visits to Belloc, Hodgson, and Garnett. But these jaunts, like his Tuesday visits to London—often spent in the company of Ralph Hodgson (who shared his love of dogs)—were the temporary diversions his nature seemed to demand before he could settle down to any sustained piece of work. When *Feminine Influence* appeared in November 1910 and was 'killed by its price (10/6) and the General Election', he set grimly to meet his target dates for *Maeterlinck,* escaping to his study in gratitude when the children caught scarlet fever in early December.

After almost a year's concentrated reading in French and English, he completed his *Maurice Maeterlinck* in five weeks on 16 January 1911 and set off for a three-day visit to old friends, Davies, de la Mare, and Garnett. With Garnett he fulfilled two pleasant tasks: the final selection of the stories and sketches later published as *Light and Twilight,* and the preparation of an eventually successful petition for the award of a Civil List Pension to Davies. He did some lobbying of Liberal MP friends of his father and sought the assistance of Belloc and Edward Marsh. As a result, he and Garnett were made trustees of the award to the tramp-poet and it was Thomas who delicately handled the monthly pay-out of £4. At this time, it would appear from his wide-ranging correspondence, he had no doubts that his own prospects would continue to flourish although, wistfully, he often regretted that he was considered too young for patronage of any sort.

His life was a busy one. He expected the proofs of *Maeterlinck* and *Light and Twilight* together in February. He agreed to write, in addition to the short study of Lafcadio Hearn, a collection of Celtic tales rewritten 'more or less' for schools. Through his agent he negotiated a travel book which became *The Icknield Way.* With a splendid if windswept new house and the extra expense of a third child, his need for profitable escape routes from fixed routine dominated his correspondence with Cazenove throughout 1911. Clearly the bold attempt to change the pattern of his earnings had slowly sapped his will for further change and driven him more into himself. His successful career as a reviewer, he found, did not help him to become a popular writer. His cherished tales and sketches were highly praised, but brought small financial reward.

This is the period when, in the retrospective view of his friends and contemporaries, Edward Thomas had become a hack-writer condemned to write books for publishers, against his will, solely to meet the needs of his family. The evidence is conflicting. He was certainly displeased with his two literary studies: 'I am doing this book (*Maeterlinck*) just as I did the *Feminine Influence*, forcing it through to get rid of the beastly thing.' 'Everything that goes down has to stay down and all afterthoughts are afterwritten. What a trade. What I dread is getting to like it.' Yet his real concern, in late February 1911, was with his state of health: 'I am at the end of a second week of extraordinary weakness, unable to work in the garden or to walk, and considerably dejected therefore, but not quite so frantic as I should have been a few years ago in such a case.'

The favourable critical acclaim of his two volumes of tales undoubtedly balanced his acute disappointment with *Feminine Influence* and *Maeterlinck* whose muted reception enhanced his reputation neither with publishers nor the reading public at large. He knew that both books were eventually finished at great speed—that was the way he had always worked best. He also knew that each book was begun in order to answer certain questions about language and thought that absorbed his attention increasingly until finally he found release in writing poetry. At this deeper level he was a slow worker and publishers' deadlines did not apply. Naturally at the proof-reading stage, his correspondence records only his dissatisfaction with the tired passages and the unpretentious paraphrases of other people's views and opinions. As in his trenchant reviewing of inferior writers, he was merciless with his own faults, although fully aware of the good things that remained. This private knowledge, surely, barbed his self-discontent.

Feminine Influence, for example, is an informed literary study based on a judicious reading of poets from Chaucer to Browning. It shows an alert response to Sidney, Shakespeare, Donne, Burns, Coleridge, Wordsworth, Shelley, and Keats and a detailed knowledge of most poets, particularly of Herbert, Milton, Prior, Cowper, Clare, Byron, and Browning. David Garnett wrote in *The Golden Echo*: 'He was the most catholic of all critics of poetry I have ever known: he admired and appreciated *all* the poets of the past I had ever heard of, could pick out their best work and praise it.' In addition, Thomas notes the altering social place of women since Elizabethan times and relationships between poets, wives, mistresses, and patronesses. He outlines the conflict between public practice and private conscience in sexual matters, and writes magisterially of the interaction between Nature and women as symbols of ideal love and as the inspiration of poems of all ages. The book, like their letters, reflects the poetic ideal of love on which Helen and Edward founded their lifelong partnership. It reveals their shared pro-feminine opinions on domestic and public affairs, and is a clear statement of Helen's tolerant acceptance of extra-marital Platonic affections as one element in a true poet's source of inspiration. For Helen never doubted that Edward was 'a genius' and at all times she believed his true vocation to be that of a poet, however the word was defined by him. And yet, in a sympathetic study of Shelley, Edward denies special concessions to genius: 'There is no privilege in these matters except the lack of conscience, and Shelley had not that. The desertion [of Harriet] was consistent with his character, and so far as can be seen, it did not weaken his character nor weigh heavily in the scale against the later acts of his life.' For Thomas was particularly aware of uncritical judgements based upon irrelevant biographical discovery and advises the reader to recall the actual poems of love, best exemplified by Shakespeare and Donne, 'on which biographers can throw not even a marsh light'. Donne shares with Shakespeare, Burns, and some ballads the essence of love poetry as Thomas conceived it: 'This love, it may be seen, has little to do with Petrarch, little to do with Cupid . . . it must be an expression of the inexpressibility of love, the craving for he knows not what, which is beyond sense and understanding . . . One of the rare qualities of [Donne's] love poetry is that the woman is apparently the man's equal.'

Behind the study of the nature of poetry—the true subject of *Feminine Influence*—was his determination to understand his own gift of words. In the fourth chapter, 'Women, Nature and Poetry', he turns aside from quoting John Clare in order to probe the nature of poetry:

['Love lies beyond the tomb'] and perhaps all of his best poems show Clare as one of those who have in them the natural spirit of poetry in its purity, so pure that perhaps he can never express it quite whole and perfect. They are songs of innocence, praising a world not realised, or, it is more reasonable to say, a world which most old and oldish people agree to regard as something different. For such a writer the usual obstacles and limits are temporary or do not exist at all, and as with children the dividing line between the real and the unreal, either shifts or has not yet been made. No man or woman is a poet who does

not frequently, to the end of life, ignore these obstacles and limits, which are
not just and absolute but represent the golden mean or average, and have less
reality than the equator. . . . And so it is that children often make phrases that are
poetry, though they still more often produce it in their acts and half-suggested
thoughts. . . . What [poets] say is not chosen to represent what they feel or
think, but is itself the very substance of what had lain dark and unapparent, is
itself all that survives of feeling and thought. . . . If this is not so, and if we do
not believe it to be so, then poetry is of no greater importance than wall-
paper. . . . Hence the strangeness and thrill and painful delight of poetry at all
times, and the deep response to it of youth and of love; and because love is
wild, strange, and full of astonishment, is one reason why poetry deals so much
in love, and why all poetry is in a sense love-poetry.

He extends the argument further, with similar authority of tone,
when discussing Maeterlinck's first volume of poems, *Serres Chaudes:*

Each man makes his own language in the main unconsciously and inexplicably,
unless he is still at an age when he is an admiring but purely aesthetic collector
of words . . . Any writer whose words have this power may make a poem of
anything—a story, a dream, a thought, a picture, an ejaculation, a conversation.
Whatever be the subject, the poem must not depend for its main effect upon
anything outside itself except the humanity of the reader. It may please for the
moment by the aid of some irrelevant and transitory interest—political interest,
for example; but sooner or later, it will be left naked and solitary, and will so be
judged, and if it does not create about itself a world of its own it is condemned
to endure the death which is its element. These worlds of living poems may be
of many different kinds. As a rule they are regions of the earth now for the first
time separated from the rest and made independent. . . . Anything, however
small, may make a poem; nothing, however great, is certain to. Concentration,
intensity of mood, is the one necessary condition in the poet and in the poem.
By this concentration something is detached from the confused immensity of
life and receives individuality, and this creativeness brings into my mind the
inhuman solitariness of the world at the moment when Deucalion stooped to
make the first men out of stones; and the waste of waters when the dove bore
an olive-leaf into the ark out of the monotonous waste.

Thomas was learning to build a bridge between the intense self-
absorbed activity of a writer and the normal everyday expectations of
the receptive reader. His full-hearted approval was given to poets who
crossed this bridge, men who could free themselves from the trappings
of literary conventions. Particularly, in *Feminine Influence*, he praises
Burns, Byron, and Keats for their ability to keep verse in touch with the
actual world and to deal frankly with physical love and courtship. He
had given the best part of a year to these two books, and though neither
brought him critical claim or financial reward they indicated repeatedly

a change in his view of language that would lead in time to the sudden development of his poetry. For the time being he continued to write numerous sketches and tales as a necessary outlet for that side of his nature in rebellion against the timetables imposed by publishers. Some of these sketches, too, were remote from popular taste, like *The Chess-player* with its eerie dream-sequences and its chilly Olympian detachment from the sufferings of ordinary people. Relying more on his own vivid dreams as a source of fabling, he was coming face to face with the [occasional] fits of depression that frequently unnerved him but never completely incapacitated him.

The radical stocktaking that had begun after Minsmere had been subdued by the plans for the new house and by the abortive five months as a civil servant. He adopted two typical stratagems for avoiding fundamental decisions: to change house or to wear the temporary harness of regular hard work. Self-examination began again during 1910 with Helen's third pregnancy, and the first year of hard reading and writing. It was not a straightforward progress. So far, it is true, he had chanced on the nature of the fruitful interaction between written words and living speech which eventually led to his own poetry in November 1914. Some new correspondents (Harold Monro, John Freeman and, later, Eleanor Farjeon) reminded him of his critical standing among younger writers who required his help in shaping the forward movement of poetic taste. Such appreciation neither enhanced his financial prospects nor matched his compulsive, half-comprehended needs as a writer. Nor, one suspects, did it soothe the bruised sense of inadequacy he was subjected to by the sudden ups and downs of his temperamental moods so injurious to his ideal of harmonious domesticity. He was more inclined to express these doubts to his long-standing friends and, during 1911, he discussed with them yet again the feasibility of a routine editorial job—which could provide the steady income he had once gained from reviewing. Alternatively he canvassed plans for leaving the new house—with its aura of a successful writer who would soon have two children as pupils at the fashionable Bedales school—and sharply reducing his expenditure.

Frequently, in letters to Frank Cazenove, he suggested plans for travel books at home or abroad that would enable him to escape from Steep, his publishers' demands, and from himself chained to his desk, as he worked away at proofs of *Maeterlinck, Light and Twilight,* and the *Celtic Tales,* as he prepared a collection of Norse Tales for children, did the reading necessary for the early chapters of *The Icknield Way,* or produced synopses that his agent could submit to publishers for books as diverse as a large-scale study of Shakespeare or a study of twentieth-century poetry supported by an anthology. No disappointment from publishers could stem the flow of tales and sketches and, despite his worst fears, his reviewing continued (and never earned him less than £1 a week). Eventually publishers accepted his terms for books, to be written with a cash advance against certain royalties, and some even agreed to accept his work in longhand, instead of the now-expected typescript. His articles, sketches, and tales were slowly finding a moderately-priced acceptance in different journals. To economize, he spent only one half-day a week in London, using a cheap railway ticket, but he still met his friends at the St. Martin's Lane restaurant run by the vegetarian lawn-tennis champion Eustace Miles. He followed the strictest regimen throughout the year and, as in many other periods in his life, he became a teetotaller and even tried to cut out tobacco.

As always when he suggested that events were eluding his control, he made elaborate plans to overwork, punctuated by plans to escape from his desk. Work on *The Icknield Way* was carried out at home, with brief visits to the British Museum in early February and March 1911. He planned a few short expeditions along his conjectured path of the prehistoric way and explored it more fully by bicycle in April and May, and again in June and July. Late July and August were spent at Steep, writing feverishly on the book, and making plans for three further studies of Pater, Swinburne, and Borrow. In early September 1911 he turned once more towards Wales. Finally, he completed the writing of *The Icknield Way* at the Dolau Cothi Arms, Pumpsaint, Carmarthenshire and dedicated it there to his old walking companion, Harry Hooton, on 19 September 1911. Having concluded the book with the statement that 'the utmost reward of this conjecturing traveller would be to find himself on the banks of the Towy or beside the tomb of Giraldus at St. David's itself', he continued his own journey for a time, as free as possible, 'walking about with nothing but comb, toothbrush, maps, and Shakespeare's *Histories*'.

In the middle of this strenuous summer of walking and writing he sometimes felt weak and 'good for nothing', and 'more oppressed by necessity and *the consciousness* of it'; yet he could often surprise his family 'by signs of good temper', and seemed eager to convince his friends that he was beginning to see his true self and to justify his excessive undertakings: 'The only chance is that in the haste and pressure of much work I may stumble upon myself again and a stronger self.' As always, he was confident that a visit to Wales would 'soon put me right'. For his oft-paraded bouts of melancholy concealed a resilient constitution. As a youth, growing up in an austere household, he had learned how to escape from domestic involvement. The society depicted in *The Happy-Go-Lucky Morgans* was such an escape route. Another was the explorations of the suburban 'Wilderness' with Hardy, so effectively woven into *A Sportsman's Tale* at this time and, later, more clinically recalled in *The Childhood of Edward Thomas*. At other times, friends and family in South Wales, or Bottomley's quite different, refined society in Cartmel, served as retreats where he could display different facets of his nature.

Thomas was clearly over-driven during the autumn of 1911. His plan to substitute commissioned books for reviewing had not worked He was quite unable to settle down to a sustained piece of work spread over a year or more. He was at his best in intense short bursts—and he knew it. For example, in September 1910 Cazenove reported that Dent would accept the book about houses and their occupants, if he would also undertake a large book on Shakespeare. Dent, pessimistic about the 'Homes' book, was 'willing to advance him £50 on receipt of half the Shakespeare book, and £50 for the rest, and probably £50 on publication'. Cazenove urged Thomas to accept: 'Now that really is not bad, and I think we ought to close. I think he wants a big book, and you could take your own time for writing it.' Thomas dithered, sent an indifferent synopsis which Dent feared might lead to a vague book, and then, claiming over-work, went no further. Six months later Cazenove could report that Dent 'still wants to get a book from you' and was toying with the Shakespeare book on different terms. By then Thomas had settled, as always, for short-term solutions which rarely brought him complete satisfaction. As W. H. Hudson recognized—'Thomas never lets the grass grow under his feet.'

When he returned from Wales in late September 1911, four of his books had appeared (*Maeterlinck, Lafcadio Hearn, Celtic Tales*, and *The Isle of Wight*). Arthur Waugh of Chapman and Hall had agreed to accept a book on Borrow with £50 on account for 75,000 words, followed by royalties of 15% and 20%. Secker had asked for two books on Pater and Swinburne, each of about 50,000 words, with £45 on account for each book, the first to be completed in the spring, the second in the autumn, of 1912. Cazenove pointedly remarked that this would mean three books in a year. He was strongly in favour of the *Borrow* with Chapman and Hall—'a nice clean firm and they always treat one decently. Judging from our reception elsewhere, I doubt if we shall do better.' Cazenove would have preferred Thomas to follow up an idea for a travel book instead of these literary studies. He felt that Thomas was losing his way: 'We are never drawn towards chasing round at random among publishers, trying to get proposals out of them in a haphazard fashion.' The literary agent understood the advantages of Thomas's frequent change of publishers. Did he ever understand why Thomas clung desperately to such vestiges of independence?

A travel book was one avenue of escape that Edward toyed with repeatedly as he prepared, and then furiously completed, *The Icknield Way*. The idea took many forms: a book on houses in the South Country; footpaths anywhere in Britain; castles in Wales; the banks of the Severn from the source to the sea; a tramp-steamer from a Welsh port to the Mediterranean—a belated copy of his crisis plan with J. H. Morgan in 1900. These alternatives to further literary studies crop up constantly in the 1911 correspondence between Thomas and Cazenove, but no publisher would accept Thomas's outlines and, for a time, the agent tried to steer him towards a more acceptable programme that would provide material for a book from which excerpts could be sold separately to journals:

Why not offer a book on South Wales. An impressionist study of the people and the way they live. In a word, such a book would explain why Tonypandy had its own private hell for nearly a year. After all, people don't go on strike for nothing*. . . . I hope I am not trying to switch you on to work which is in any degree uncongenial. As a general rule, I fancy, most people would rather read about Welsh colliers than—shall we say?—about Milton and Keats. At any rate, from the point of view of immediate pecuniary returns, I feel pretty sure I am right.'

In November 1911, the better-off Harold Monro had offered Thomas the use of his own house in Locarno. Thomas was tempted by the idea, but confessed that he couldn't leave England and journalism without a job. His self-defensive mechanisms went deep. The clearest statement of his reluctance to leap in the dark was made two years later to Cazenove:

'Can you conceive of me going to Australia or New Zealand or Canada and writing a book about what I see of men and places and also getting people to read it? . . . I am quite prepared to go but chiefly because I want work. I would much rather go about England or Wales, which however nobody wants me to do. What about a compromise.—Sending me to a Welsh coalfield or an English pottery district and letting me suffer to the tune of 80,000 words? That

---

* In the autumn of 1910 there was a long coal strike in the Rhondda with a bitter clash between strikers and police, much mis-reported then and since.

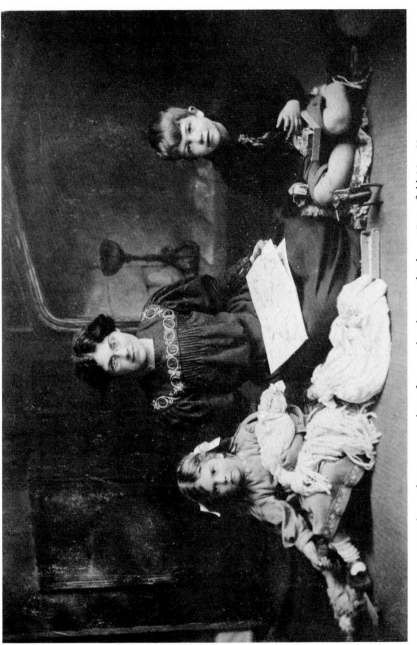

11. Helen with Bronwen and Merfyn, a studio photograph taken at Petersfield, New Year 1907.

12. In dejection at Berryfield Cottage, October 1907.

I should in some ways very much like to do. You once spoke of Tonypandy. P. S. Dent wouldn't, I suppose, care for me to do what I might have done in *The Heart of England* and give a really conscientious picture (not for agriculturalists) of England as it is and call it 'This England', showing what England means as one might show what 'The South' or 'The East' means, but using chiefly the visible things.'

The effect on his taut temperament of these changing patterns of work was severe. He best defines it himself in Poem 115 of the *Collected Poems*:

> And what was hid should still be hid
> Excepting from those like me made
> Who answer when such whispers bid.

He was beginning to interpret the whispers. *The Isle of Wight*, in Blackie's *Beautiful England* series, was quickly dashed off in early 1911 without the usual interposition of irony between the reader and the rare moments of self-revelation. In it Thomas allowed his fancy to play around a dark house which a young Oxford student and would-be artist had planned to leave in order

to go to London but not to return, no matter how long she would wait for him looking into the fire o'nights. . . [The house] looked solid and without life, and the twittering of the sparrows reminded him of the flocks of wild and groundless fancies that fly into the brain to harry it when it has fallen before some agony or grief . . . Nor could he tell why he was setting his mind this task, except that suddenly the house, crouching there like a stupid sphinx under the pines, had somehow repeated in a new way and with a new terror the challenge of matter to spirit . . . silence, stillness, solidity, darkness were incarnate there as in a temple . . . He stood motionless, and tried to silence his quick heart lest perhaps he might miss some illuminating whisper from over there. If only sparrows were to cease it would be intolerable. . . . Heaven preserve him from that silence which would rush in like a sea if the birds were to cease . . . I had a superstitious feeling that I had truly divined a tragedy which had been enacted there. At the inn, half a mile away, I enquired about the farmhouse and its inhabitants, but was disappointed. I cannot explain it. Perhaps it was a prophecy.

As many of his sketches written at Wick Green suggest, Thomas was eager to explore the numinous aspects of experience. His account of the prehistoric Icknield Way contained enough facts, place-names, and recognizable settlements or features to satisfy the publishers and their readers; but Thomas, with equal certitude, saw the road in terms of myth and tradition. Other roads—Watling Street, Ermine Street, or the

Fosse Way—made some appeal, however fantastical, to his intelligence; Icknield Street or Way made no such factual appeal: 'We are touched in our sense of unmeasured antiquity, we acknowledge the honour and the darkness of the human inheritance.'

The non-guide-book half of *The Icknield Way,* he said, was 'diluted me'. In it he moved from guide-book to personal essay with felicitous ease:

It was one of those delicious cool ends to perfect days which give a man the feeling of having accomplished something, but by no means compel him to inquire what. The road still possessed the hills even when it was enclosed on both sides, for it kept broad margins, the hedges were low between it and the grass or corn land, and it mounted higher and higher. They were the gentlest of chalk hills crested with trees—Thrift Hill, Gallows Hill, Crouch Hill, Pott's Hill, Rain Hill, Wheat Hill, Windmill Hill, and Weston Hills—and at their highest points there were villages like Therfield, Kelshall, Sandon, Wallington, Clothall, Weston. I had still four or five miles to walk at the feet of these hills, through a silence undisturbed by the few market carts at long intervals. I am glad now that I walked them. It seems to me now that my purely physical discomfort intensified the taste of the evening's beauty, as it certainly made sweeter the perfection of enjoyment which I imagine possible at such an hour and in such a place. . . . I could always see about a quarter of a mile before me, and there the white ribbon disappeared among trees. And this quarter-mile was agreeable in itself, and always suggesting something better beyond, though itself a sufficient end, if need were. . . . The air was silent and still, the road was empty. The birds coming home to the quiet earth seemed visitors from another world. They seemed to bring something out of the sky down to this world, and the house and garden where I stayed at last were full of this something. I heard rooks among the tall beeches of just such a house as I knew I ought to have been able to imagine, with the help of the long white road and the gentle hills, the tall trees, the rooks, and the evening. There were flowers and lawns, beeches and sycamores, belonging to three centuries, perhaps more, and stately but plain red brick of the same date, and likely to endure for a yet longer period, if not by its own soundness, then by its hold upon the fantasy of men who build nothing like it.

Such speculation was not the idle space-filling of a tired essayist: it characterized, too, his next and last travel book, *In Pursuit of Spring,* the half-way house to his verse. *Feminine Influence* and *Maeterlinck* suggest that Edward Thomas respected—if he could not precisely articulate—the non-rational forces that were as much part of human heritage as the rigour of scientific enquiry. He frequently returns to the topic:

Shelley's letters show us portions of the process of dissolving the objects of the outward and visible world into the poet's inner life, so as to form if not a complete and consistent new world there, yet one of great significance which can only die with his poetry.

For [Maeterlinck's] foundations are built upon truths within the experience of all. . . . Every one has come to the edge of a mystery, as of a deep sea for which no experience or thinking has prepared him; every one has used powers of intuition and unconscious hidden activity for which he has no name. We have assurances and consolations inexplicable, the very reason for living is hidden away from many. . . . It can increase reverence where it does not touch understanding. It undermines our more massive and pompous follies. It teaches not by information or by law, but by making men more profoundly aware of themselves and of the world. . . . Gradually the thought has grown that man can achieve the most difficult things by realizing that he is alone, and can depend only on himself, by refusing to settle down under crude codes in civil and private life, by more widely acknowledging mystery, yet more ardently striving to conquer it instead of denying it, by seeking to understand and enlarge the powers which affect our lives more deeply and more obscurely than reason can do . . . [Maeterlinck] met, says André Gide, 'life and Nietzsche' . . . He explains nothing, but he is afraid of nothing, and unashamed of being baffled. He is a materialist in his attitude only towards what is known.

Thomas's encounters with despair had deepened and widened his quest for a manner of writing that understood rather than embroidered the extra-mundane experience he had constantly brought into his own tales since the early pseudo-Arthurian stories of 'Basil in the Woods'.

However, the 1911 September visit to Wales failed to bring its expected healing. He reported to Harry Hooton a return of weakness and a worse depression than ever; and then, a few weeks later, he suggested, 'I may be all right in a short time.' For the rest of 1911 he kept in close touch with Hooton, who was reading the proofs of *The Icknield Way*, and of *Maeterlinck*, and these extracts from their hurried notes between September and December show a rapid deterioration in his health:

Something will have to happen soon. I am trying to make myself fitter—I have given up tobacco now. It is a dirty job. Helen suggests her taking a cheap cottage with the children and their going to a village school and my having a room not too far away, ten miles say. I wish I could hear of something in Sussex or Wiltshire that might do. The opening would then precipitate things.

It was mostly wet—well, what with one thing and another I got to a worse state than I was ever in: had to go to London and there got worse than ever, quarrelled with Haynes in a final manner, threw up an engagement with Watts-Dunton and incidentally a book of £50, very nearly quarrelled with

Milne at the D. C. and very nearly etc. . . . I wish I could escape from book-writing. I shall never have any satisfaction till I do, as my vanity makes me despise myself so continuously for doing what it persuades me is not my best and not worth doing. I never have time now to do any of those things I like doing such as were reprinted in *Light and Twilight*.

Things get so rapidly worse that something must happen soon inside my head or outside. I hope outside.

You don't quite see that having tried Bedales makes it not so easy to take the 'grammar school of ordinary decent reputation' which you seem to think so much of. You also would not quite see that I should try to keep to Bedales without the slightest confidence that the difference between it and the ordinary decent masturbating plutocracy-worshipping grammar school is worth considering. I like the sudden use of 'the careful de la Mare', and the *tu quoque* implied in *your* satisfaction with *your* home influence.

I have somehow lost my balance and can never recover it by diet or rule or any deliberate means, but only by some miracle from within or without. If I don't recover it and causes of worry continue I must go smash. Then I must remove some of the causes of worry. It is not easy as I must either have a remote study or a separate dwelling I think. Greatest difficulty of all is a school we know something about and a master we can trust and low fees as well. Just going to *any grammar school* is abhorrent. Do you know any schoolmasters? Then I ought not to be over 60 miles from London.

Sometimes I feel wellish here [in Laugharne], sometimes very bad; never well, I never can be well again without a miracle. But do not allow Helen to know this as I contrive to write to her at the better times.

The familiar swing of moods and the indecision—except in the determination to keep on writing—are confirmed by similar letters to Bottomley, Berridge, and especially to MacAlister who had tried to get work for him with the *Daily News* and then found that Edward had written a chilly note to MacAlister's helping friend. ('I won't try to explain my sniffiness now, but I think I could. It isn't conscience, anyhow. It is a feeling of helplessness.')

Suddenly his behaviour—and his apparently suicidal despair—alarmed Helen, whose recollection in 1936 lies behind John Moore's statement in *The Life and Letters of Edward Thomas* that, 'at last, in despair, she sat down and wrote a long letter to Edward's old friend, E. S. P. Haynes. She told him everything, her fears for Edward's sanity, even her fears for his life. She begged him to help in some way if he could.' Haynes sent a cheque to relieve any financial worries, and tried hard to persuade Edward to visit a good psychologist. When this was refused Haynes suggested a holiday instead. Thomas dithered between a return to Laugharne in Carmarthenshire and a visit to Wall Nook, a farm near to Bottomley. Finally, after some elaborate abortive arrangements with Bottomley, he decided to settle at Mrs Wilkins's boarding house in Victoria Street, Laugharne, where he remained from 1 November until 17 December 1911. There he brought to an end the long-projected *George Borrow*. At the same time he re-read the proofs of *The Icknield Way* and began preliminary reading for a study of Swinburne. Bottomley was ill once more and Thomas sent his best thanks to Emily Bottomley from Laugharne on 4 November 1911: 'It made me wish again that I had not been in such a hurry. But the fact is I meant to begin my book *before* the end of October. Then came the offer which made it possible to get away and I was itching to begin—not from love of the thing but from a simple desire to prove to myself once more that I could begin a long task. Well I have begun and my wrist is sore with it after three days. . . . I don't know anybody here. But I get out for 2 or 3 hours a day and try not to overwork'. Once more the temporary salve of a place of refuge away from home, and enough paid work to see him through real (or imagined) money difficulties, was tried. In spite of the cheerful exchange of letters between him and Helen throughout his stay at Laugharne, the cure, once again, proved illusory.

CHAPTER 11

Steep

LIFE at Laugharne provided Edward with many of the palliatives he had previously used to ward off severe attacks of depression: freedom from immediate financial worries; absence from minor domestic irritations for which he largely blamed himself; a regular routine centred on a student-like day combining wide reading and rapid writing; and, above all, the necessity to keep in touch with old and new friends by letter. He relied heavily for peace of mind on Helen's regular 'letter days' and, on the surface, their correspondence at Laugharne is free of the tension and soul-searching that marks the letters to and from Minsmere three years before.

Extracts from two letters to Ian MacAlister help fill out his life at Laugharne. The first was sent on 13 November 1911:

I had a very bad attack of whatever it is three weeks ago today and did not know what to do, but someone came along and sent me here where I am not doing much good because I am working hard at a book on Borrow. Things are in suspense now, but I can't help thinking about them. I have lost, I suppose by pure bad luck, all my reviewing except a very little on the *Chronicle*. I can't write 7 books every year, which is what I shall have done by December, and yet it has been my worst year. It is so difficult to accommodate oneself especially in my condition. Nobody can help much except myself. Everyone is kind, perhaps too kind. I sometimes think that if I were left alone and compelled to come to terms with life I should be the better for it after a time. It may come soon now. I hope it will cure my head which is almost always wrong now—a sort of conspiracy going on in it which leaves me only a joint tenancy and a perpetual sense of the other tenant and wonder what he will do. This is a very pleasant place and a decent landlady but I know nobody, and only speak to a publican now and then on my walks, which I make as long as possible to get away from the book . . . please do not mention it to Helen who is I believe cheerful now and hopes I am getting better here.

Three weeks later he has this to add:

I have been up and down but rather often down. In fact I am certain in my own mind that nothing can seriously affect me for good except some incalculable change that may come with time or with some spiritual accident but by no possible deliberate means. Food, etc., I believe matters very little. I eat meat and fish and fruit and when I am out sometimes I drink a pint of ale. I have had some good days but have mostly been immersed in Borrow . . . so firmly had I believed that I should always keep what position I had. However, obviously I shan't . . . I have refused several offers this year which I would not refuse now, because I thought it was a mistake to cheapen myself, and also I still have enough ambition (so to call it) left to find utterly uncongenial work very humiliating. Still, the bed is mainly of my own making . . . Maeterlinck by the way wrote me a nice letter and the book may do some good . . . I expect we shall choose a County Council School, if we can get a low enough rented house nearby to make the move worth while. The school is the great difficulty or we should have gone to a cheap cottage long ago.

Making his arrangements with MacAlister for a meeting in London on 17 December, Edward sends him a short progress report: 'I have broken up my stay here by several excursions of two or three days to St. David's, Haverfordwest, etc., and have contrived to have some most pleasant hours. Whether I am substantially better remains to be seen. So far I haven't got any work but am offering dozens of suggestions for books that I don't in the least want to write.'

Harry Hooton had earlier accused him of being secretive. Was it insecurity and lack of confidence that made him write this cagey last sentence? For he had already agreed in September to write books on Pater and Swinburne and in October he had informed Cazenove that he was going to Wales 'to bring off *Swinburne* and write *Borrow*', although he was not willing, then, 'to do *Pater* in this state'. By 15 December he was asking his agent for the precise number of words required for *Pater*, and discussing articles, if not a book, on South Wales for which he had made 'plenty of notes in the last four or five years'. He was ready to agree that the decline in his reviewing had been a stroke of bad luck, and nothing more. The complete run of the two-way correspondence between Thomas and Cazenove reveals the defensive, almost bare-faced strategy with which he first approached the concept of a book and then hastily withdrew from acceptance, usually for one of three stated reasons (ill health or pressure of work or dire financial need). The same attitude spills over into his letters to close friends whenever he is writing about his commitments to publish. Forthright in comment and puritanical in the conduct of everyday domestic affairs, he was excessively sensitive to hurt on his inability to keep and maintain a 'position' for himself. So, when things seemed to go right for him, he and Helen would set off on short spendthrift jaunts, exactly as they had done in the early days of their marriage.

During his pre-Christmas week in London, he signed contracts with

Secker and delivered the completed *Borrow* to Chapman and Hall, who
paid him £45 on Christmas Eve. The next day he sent off his usual
Christmas letter to Jesse Berridge with apologies for the absence of a
present for his son Dell. 'A very bad year for me and I did not spend
anything at all on Christmas presents. There was no suitable book to be
found. I am writing a book on Pater.' On New Year's Eve he gave Irene
and Hugh McArthur a different glimpse of his social life:

> I did take to the floor last night. Helen and I went as a country couple to a
> fancy dress affair. There were a lot of very nice males and females under twenty
> who made up for my grotesqueness. I had an old Sussex pedlar's smock, black
> hat and red ribbon with a bunch of corn, knee breeches and grey stockings tied
> with black ribbons. Helen had a print dress bunched up behind to show a red
> petticoat and a lot of white stocking, and a sun bonnet on her head. We are
> now recovering. . . . The children are away for a few days with the idle rich of
> Petersfield.

Thomas's last twenty months at the hilltop house recalled in his
poem *Wind and Mist*—from January 1912 to July 1913—saw the beginnings
of a remarkable change in his way of life, in his development as a writer,
in the enlargement of his circle of friends, and (through an impasse with
his agent) a rediscovery of purpose. His activities are fully recorded in
long runs of published letters to his agent and to old friends like Hooton
and MacAlister; and from February 1913 until his death there are the 204
letters and postcards available in Eleanor Farjeon's *Edward Thomas: The
Last Four Years*.

At the beginning of 1912 Thomas had settled down at Wick Green to
begin *Pater* while he awaited the arrival of a new set of Swinburne's
works. (He would not use books from a library service.) He was committed to deliver both critical studies to Secker by the summer. He planned
to spend a few days with Edward Garnett at Crockham Hill immediately before the hard writing began and a few days with the McArthurs
at Crowborough, where his brother-in-law was recuperating from a
serious operation. He continued his regular Monday or Tuesday visits to
London, calling on friends, editors, and his agents. He continued to ply
Cazenove with a wide range of proposals. Chatto had paid him £16 for
his Pocket Anthology of *George Borrow* until a rival biography was over
and done with. Throughout January 1912, side by side with his final
reading of Pater, Thomas floated the idea of a Roman History book for
Methuen, stressing his own Oxford degree in History. Methuen was
'glad to consider a book on Great Episodes of Roman History, if Thomas

will send a synopsis. I think you know the sort of book I want, which must be brilliant, not to say flamboyant, and should run to 100,000 words.' Nothing could be further from Thomas's known style. Cazenove sent a diplomatic covering note: 'I know synopses are not much in your line, but this subject is rather more concrete, and I think you may be able to do it with very little trouble.'

Thomas then settled down to write *Pater* on 15 February. On 19 March he informed Jesse Berridge that he would dedicate his *Norse Tales* to the Berridge family and that *Pater* was roughly finished, but he intended to 'keep it by me for suggestions until after Easter'. The visit to Hugh McArthur was a hurried one because the infant Myfanwy had been taken to Petersfield Hospital with a mysterious stomach trouble and Helen slept at the hospital. 'We had a scare but nothing serious the matter now.' In two days Edward was home with Helen and the baby, but he 'was no good at all' and, having cleared up his insurance premiums with Hugh, he began *Pater*—'so there is no peace for some time'. He was finding it more and more difficult to work in solitude and at speed in his hill-top study and afterwards, in the evenings, to involve himself sympathetically in the household affairs.

His concern for the well-being and health of his children was real in spite of the off-hand tone he used in his letters to describe this sudden illness of Myfanwy; years before he had been in despair when Bronwen was taken ill with suspected diphtheria on the Weald. The two experiences—and the way his fevered mind toyed with thoughts of suicide—were fused in 'The Fear of Death', written probably at this time, and published in *The Nation* on 5 October 1912. The conclusion, like the notes he wrote in 1907, show the intensity with which he fought the evil dreams that came up into his mind and 'disappeared of their own free will and as unexpectedly as frogs in a pond':

The man watched his children. Their eyes were shining with all the fire of the sun and the liquidity of the rain. Sometimes they stayed out through the showers and contented themselves with grumbling. They took no notice of the man watching. . . .

He saw the beauty of the day and the joy of the children as in a mouldering book with no reality. Yet he could not keep his eyes from off them. He devoured every motion and sound they made like a glutton who has no pleasure from the morsel in his mouth for anticipation of the one to come. . . . His brain within his ears ached with the use of his eyes and with striving to recover the old order that used to make the garden and the house full, if not of melodies, yet of snatches of tunes. . . . Then, suddenly, the youngest child came running out and stood under his window, rapt in some thought or imagination . . . She was the happiest of living things . . . The man watched her and his pain ceased. He was nothing but eyes, and they saw nothing but the child. Slowly she moved away, with one, two, three, four, five steps to a gate, opened it musingly, held it open, and with a run let it bang, and herself disappeared. The demon of that day took possession of the man with a swoop . . . It was the spirit of fear that had swooped upon him—the Spirit of the Fear of Death. He feared the death of his child . . . He called silently for the enemy to come up swiftly to the encounter. And it was granted. The Spirit of the Fear of Death stood before him, mighty and dark. His eyes were closed and he could not see it. It was as a tree suddenly apprehended half a pace ahead in the black night. He was waiting in the calmness of power for the conflict; but why was the enemy so still? He waited—how long he could never know. When he opened his eyes the child was at his knee; she had taken his hand and was leading him into the garden to see the snapdragons. And in the evening he remembered the man saying that air and earth were full of spirits, and he believed that he had been the victim of one that was false, powerful, and usurping.

On 22 March 1912 he wrote to Bottomley from Stow-on-the-Wold:

I was alway either busy at Pater and good for nothing else or contending with my usual devils. I was not reborn in Wales. Work is the only thing though when I am at it I don't invariably realize it especially as it's always in a hurry. . . . I am only just learning how ill my notes have been making me write by all but destroying such natural rhythm as I have in me. Criticizing Pater has helped the discovery. But it is too late now, in these anxious and busy times, to set about trying to write better than perhaps I was born to.

Despite the final disclaimer, he was in the middle of a process of self-criticism which extended from the writing of *Feminine Influence* to the publication of *In Pursuit of Spring* and his subsequent exchanges with Robert Frost in 1914. Thomas rarely took hasty steps in significant matters and it is in character that the change from prose-master to poet was spread over four years of hesitant change. His shedding of Pater's influence—a dominant formative influence while Thomas was an undergraduate—subsequently remained a fixed mark in his mind when he discussed the interpenetration of the written and the spoken word.

He returned home from Coventry to correct his *Norse Tales*, to look for (and write) various reviews, and to learn that Secker had agreed to provide a typist for *Pater* and *Swinburne,* if Thomas would correct the typescripts. He now took the decisive step to seek medical advice. He had got to know Clifford Bax during the Winter of 1910/11 when he had printed Thomas's remarkable piece *The Chessplayer* in the theosophical quarterly *Orpheus*. Bax lived in Wiltshire in an Elizabethan manor house at Broughton Gifford and Thomas called on him during a walking tour from a farm near by. Through David Garnett and Haynes, Thomas had already met Godwin Baynes, a member of Bax's wide social circle. He was a young sportsman and doctor of powerful build and radiant personality, much sought after in society, who later became a friend and advocate of Jung, studied hypnotism in Paris at La Salpêtrière almshouse, and worked with Harry Roberts for a time in his Stepney slum practice. In 1912–13, during the Austro-Hungarian annexation of two Balkan provinces, he served with a Red Crescent unit behind the Turkish lines. His effect on Thomas was profound. For the first time his illness was met, not with a violent change of diet, but with discussion and analysis. Although Thomas was never to be quite free of his unpredictable swings of mood, and suffered again from very short periods of debilitating physical weakness, he acquired from Baynes as he did, later, from Robert Frost—renewed confidence in his ability to shape the future pattern of his life and work. In April 1912 he spent about ten days with Baynes and Bax at Broughton Gifford and reported the result to Bottomley: 'This doctor is working magic with my disordered intellect and in a few hours I shall be better able to enjoy [your] *Chambers of Imagery II* than ever before. I shall have something like your own courage . . . But there is such a continuous flow of talk here and out-door adventures to Bath etc. that I can't read anything.' He confirmed the change in a retrospective letter to MacAlister in early August: 'I have been away so much—once with a doctor—and two months to write a book on *Swinburne* . . . I was much better with the doctor—and would have been even better still if I had been safer in the matter of work.'

Despite the £100 gift from Haynes, the signing of contracts for books placed on his own terms, and the faith he and Helen placed in Godwin Baynes, the strain under which they had both lived since the summer of 1910 nearly reached breaking point after Myfanwy's mysterious illness. Edward was reduced to a state of near despair, similar, but not comparable, to the crisis in October 1911. His moods can be caught in twenty-five letters from Helen which, as usual, he preserved and re-read constantly. The letters bubble over with a rapid account of her everyday doings: work in the garden, visiting friends, meeting the children, playing with them at weekends, forwarding review books and letters, keeping the study aired, and, as always, looking forward to his letters and responding to them with a flowing heart twice a week. She was very much at the mercy of her menstrual cycle and found his long absences from home—especially the seven weeks at Laugharne—almost intolerable. At times her excessive care for his health sends him into bitterness and criticism: occasionally, in her apologetic replies, she fights back in self-defence and offers him firm advice. She insisted that she always balanced her books on the £12 a month allowed her, and gives a breakdown of her expenses. She reminds him, 'You have said that money is not so very bad, only it comes in differently which makes it difficult at first to arrange, so there's no such desperate hurry', that is, to change things hastily and leave Wick Green and Bedales before other economies are tried. ('I will try to be economical but you know what a deadly effect continual faultfinding has on me.') What she needs most is 'you at your best without even once that dreadful cold look that is what I cannot bear to see and feel, or that look of absolute weariness of everything which gives me more sorrow than all the sorrows of the world put together'. Helen also suggested a move to a smaller, cheaper house and doing without a maid, so that Edward could still be free to travel and to meet his literary friends in London. She agrees that he should try the Baynes experiment of staying with him and Bax at the Manor House and is eager that Edward should accept an offer to stay with Norman Douglas on Capri, and so use up the remainder of Haynes' gift of £100. 'Baynes is a magician after all. I do quite agree that Wick Green ought to be avoided for the present; that was why I am, or was, so keen on Capri or any similar plan. . . . Farewell, send some magic to me.' She needs reassurance and frequently asks for it in his letters which are often 'notebooky' in form and which she dutifully files for him with the date of receipt for his further use.

I must tell you that I was well again for a time in that last letter. You do believe in me a bit, don't you, that I'm something more than a queer old thing, nice sometimes, sometimes awful, but that there's always something that goes on and on which is good in me and is always something. And fancy you wanting me and I not there, when it so often happens just the other way . . . Indeed I've had that feeling lately of one waiting to begin a race—waiting with all ones ears and nerves and muscles for the word 'go' . . . The North East wind shrivels me up. I want to 'snoodle' into your arms, and forget, as I always do when I'm *there*, everything else.

Above all her letters are intended to renew his faith in himself, to remove all sense that he is tied to a treadmill that will prevent his being 'happy at home with me and the children'. Knowing his proud diffidence, she urges various remedies against his petty worries.

Tell Haynes that what you want to do you real and lasting good all round is a congenial and not too hard job at not less than £200 a year. Surely he hears of jobs of all sorts and might do something for you in that way. But in the meantime Sanatogen and exercises are a good makeshift I expect. Do not write to me one word if it cannot be of hope. See Baynes. Tell him of me if you like. Tell him how it works round in a circle, only so far we have too often turned the wheel the wrong way. Tell him to teach us how to keep it going the right way. Your health, my happiness, my happiness, my health, and back again to your happiness.

Her good health, and joy in practical things in the kitchen, in the garden, in outdoor activities, could not always sustain her. 'Even my profound and unimpaired "Luck of the Nobles" superstition, my damned optimism beginning to waver. Though still I can't quite get out of the feeling that better days are coming. I'm sorry but it's as much me as my hair or eyes.'

The prospect of Edward's repeated absences from home—like the stay at Bath to complete his *Swinburne,* while she was nursing a sister through illness—suddenly forced her to demand that she be considered, too. It was her decisive stand to retain Edward as her dearest friend, lover, and husband. I believe that the letter that follows governed the pattern of their subsequent life together; although he was left free to work when and where and how he best could, he tried to ensure, not always successfully, that she was not left on her own for more than a fortnight until he embarked for France. This undated letter was written around Whitsun 1912 on her return to Wick Green after nursing her sister:

This much I've decided that much more than either you or I know depends on me. I believe I make the atmosphere and tho' I know that hitherto you have been upset by little things I think Baynes has and will help you out of that if I will for you let my natural self come out as I do for others. I've not been well lately, not for some time. I've never felt as I have done of late so without life and energy and interest in things. Its partly because we have been so far apart and all the good in me I do believe most firmly is born of your love for me, and your life with me, and everything that is between us. I cannot live without *you.* That's why I'm so keen, so set on these few days with you. Let me come and get and give back again. Then if you are well, and we are both happy together (and we would be) I can well wait while you do your book and come home afterwards though with Baynes help, and no stranger, to give me what I need to be myself—well, cheerful, careless too perhaps, but happy above all these. Do you see how it all works round. Baynes supplies just what is needed and he will be there to rely on.

Anyway don't give up just yet. Out of pity for me if for nothing else. I have had to work out my own salvation all alone, and against odds so difficult that it is no wonder I have failed often and often. But the most tragic thing that has ever happened to me is that I should have failed now. Oh do give me one more chance. Let us have one little while together. I feel as if my life hung on that. Miss Senior asked me to cycle over to Winchester, but I've just written to say I can't come. I'll just stay here with Baby and work in the garden and type my letters, and get strong in body and mind all alone. I can do it best so.

We'll take our bicycles. Cycling is much more restful than walking and we can just trundle along and rest when we want to. And get tea and watercress at an Inn. And we'll go on with David Copperfield if you like, and I'll take some sewing. And we'll bath out of doors, and be out of doors and pretend we're 18 again. I can so easily be 18. All my real self is only 18, even my body is. Do you know I amazed Mrs. Scott the other Sunday by *running* up the Mutton with Baby in my arms, laughing because she couldn't catch me to carry Baby.

I'm not old or worn out. Youth cries aloud in me often and often and often. Only I miss something of it if you are not there. We grew up together, didn't we and my youth wants its mate that it knew. . . . I will not ask or desire the impossible. So everything I desire now is a necessary part of life, and is ours, if we but go hand in hand to get it. So sweetheart. Out of agony may come joy. *Must* come, and will come. . . .

Now I'll take Baby out. Then the work. And I will make a magic circle round my thoughts, and all within is good and hopeful and strong, and none shall enter but thoughts that are all these three. And they shall be for you as well as for me, for nothing is good for me to have to myself. Farewell sweetheart, Helen.

The early summer was packed with work—always a sovereign remedy with Thomas. On May Day Secker sent a £40 advance on the *Pater* manuscript and promised £5 later when the typescript was corrected. So, on 3 May Thomas took a room at Dillybrook Farm, near Bath, and there, with many short stays at home, he began to write *Swinburne* quickly because Secker wished to forestall a rival publication. Secker was happy to get it by 15 August: Thomas promised (and delivered) his manuscript by 5 June, and received the first payment a week later. He then left Bath to stay, first, with Helen's sister Mary Valon in Chiswick and then with his own parents at Rusham Road, where he corrected the typescript of *Swinburne* by 18 June before returning to Wick Green. Once there, he tackled the *Pater* typescript—'most vilely typed by an illiterate and hurried person'—and reduced the amount by seven thousand words. On 4 July the proofs of *Swinburne* began to arrive at Wick Green. They were completed and returned from Rusham Road a week later. On

18 July Secker's cheque for *Swinburne* arrived at Thomas's bank in Seven-oaks.

As soon as the *Swinburne* manuscript was finished Thomas had again been urging new ideas for books on Cazenove. Simultaneously he hoped to use the good offices of Roger Ingpen at Hutchinson and of de la Mare with Heinemann. But nothing came of either and on 19 July Thomas asked his agent how his affairs stood. 'If you can't get rid of these [ideas] and nothing else considerable turns up I must make some changes of regime and that soon—move to a cheap house and a very simple life indeed etc.'

To Cazenove's surprise, Thomas was commissioned by Batsford to contribute a small book on *The Country* to a new series alongside Bax and others. In August, while he and Merfyn went bicycling through Sussex and Kent, visiting de la Mare, Davies, and Vivian Locke Ellis, his agent made a fruitless round of publishers and reported no luck from Cassels, Chatto, Unwin, or Black. Once more at home, Thomas typed *The Country*, asked Belloc to look out for some kind of secretaryship for him, considered (I surmise) the possibility of applying for a librarianship in a South Wales college, and then set off for Swansea to collect 'impres-sions for an essay on the town which *The English Review* will be good enough to look at'. The Cazenove correspondence confirms a progress report Thomas made to Bottomley on 1 September 1912, with no ironic self-pitying exaggeration and no helpless talk:

Well and I don't know what to think of apart from writing. I occasionally allow my mind to wander towards some such thing as canvassing for advertisements and similar occupations for superfluous people, but not quite seriously yet. Now and then I remember that I am 34 and ought to stand alone, help myself and keep silent, but I really still feel as I did 12 years ago that people ought to help or might help me to solve my difficulties although I have no claims (has any-one?) and although I know that it is really impossible to help the helpless except by a substantial legacy.

His first practical step in self-help was to withdraw from Cazenove and, presumably, to rely on his own contacts with publishers, exactly as he had done from 1901 to 1906. Thomas wrote to his agent from Swansea in September 1912: 'I am sorry, but as you find yourself at a loss and I can't go on making suggestions, I must see what a change will do if anything can be done at all. The combination between us was ceasing to be anything but a friendly one, and I hope you will not feel it an unfriendly act for me to ask you to consider it as at an end except in a

friendly way and in so far as matters relating to certain books will continue to be your concern.' Cazenove replied two days later:

I think you do us something less than justice. You have issued, during the past
year or so, quite a respectable number of books through our intermediary. We
have certainly not been able to find anything to go on with after the completion
of the two Secker books, but that is just, I think, as it has happened. You want to
write books of a certain kind, and to have a commission in each case before you
write. As what you want to say is not of the obvious kind which publishers can
grasp at once, and as you prefer not to write first and sell the book afterwards,
your agent's work is necessarily—please don't think I am grumbling at all—
rather more difficult than is the case with most of the men for whom one
acts. . . . But, if it be possible, do not allow your friendly feeling towards us to
undergo any change; and further, remember, please, that if you like to come
back we shall be very glad to see you again.

During the next nine months Cazenove wrote Thomas a few brief
notes clearing up business items. Then, in early June 1913, he sent
Thomas a friendly note which led to a resumption of their combination
until Cazenove enlisted in December 1914, to be killed in France in the
following year.

In the interval, Thomas did not ignore his agent's practical advice. For
whatever reason, his literary-critical studies were half as well paid as his
early commissioned colour books. Reviewing suited his ability to work
hard, fast, and punctually, in short spurts. When it was regular—and the
sale of review copies brought a bonus for family extras—his acute
anxiety over minor financial matters was assuaged, and his irritability
lessened. Luckily, a new market was opening for him with the appearance
of *New Age, English Review,* and *Poetry and Drama.* Despite his early, proud
refusal to accept payment from|Harold Monro, these new journals paid
better than either his very early 'papers' or such short books of under
20,000 words as *Lafcadio Hearn* (£20), *Keats* (£25), *The Country* (£20), or
the introductions he contributed to Everyman's Library. For example,
Austin Harrison of the *English Review* offered £20 for a well-informed
5,000 word paper on Swansea, and frequently paid £10 for shorter pieces
that were offshoots of the notes Thomas prepared for his travel books.
On his own submission to the Royal Literary Fund (later in 1914), he
was earning about £400 per annum at this time, as he had done for
some years.

But the strain of living at home without a certain regular income
increased his melancholia and irritability. It certainly sharpened the contrast with, say, the Cricket Week spent with Bax at Broughton Gifford,

or the more relaxed social life of the young, moderately well-off and leisured friends of Godwin Baynes and Clifford Bax—the Farjeons, Thorneycrofts, Oliviers that David Garnett describes in *The Golden Echo* and Eleanor Farjeon in *Edward Thomas: The Last Four Years*. She describes their carefree love of amusement and entertainment, their nomadic holidays camping in the New Forest, canoeing in innocent mixed groups in Worcester, or relaxing in cramped quarters on a house-boat on the Norfolk Broads. Eleanor Farjeon had recently found her own way into this sporadic society after a long-delayed adolescent shyness of ten years. She was eager to be taken under Thomas's wing, to seek his advice for her writing, to begin a strenuous course in natural history under his expert tuition, and always to share new-found happy gaiety with him as he responded positively to Baynes's novel treatment. David Garnett, a friend since Thomas's boyhood visits to his home at Limpsfield Chart overlooking The Weald of Kent (and a close friend of his father, with whom he shared the concept of a literary life in a simple rural setting without style or pretension to worldly success), was alert to the change of milieu that these new friendships brought to Thomas. The life he shared with the new friends, as Eleanor Farjeon unfolds it in *The Last Four Years*, was the nearest thing to an undergraduate existence that Edward had experienced since 1900.

In the autumn of 1912, and in stolid defence of his often stated preference for a nomadic life, he decided to give notice to Lupton that he intended to leave Wick Green and to move into one of the smaller semi-detached workmen's cottages which were then being planned in Steep, by a socialist philanthropist, at a rent of three shillings a week. Lupton agreed to his retaining the study at a one-shilling weekly rent. With almost £20 saved annually in rent, he believed he could spend much more time in London, if he could find suitable digs. Initially, as a stop-gap between visits home, he stayed as a paying guest at Selsfield House, near East Grinstead, with the dilettante poet and antique-dealer Vivian Locke Ellis. The rambling house, its well-to-do owners, its proximity within walking distance to many of Edward's friends, corresponded to his deep-seated need for a household that was half-way between the strict pattern he desired for his own home and the vagrant freedom he admired in the life of wayfarers. Not without justice did his new friends call him 'Walking Tom'.

At East Grinstead, eager to augment the earnings made by journalism in Fleet Street, he wrote his novel, *The Happy-Go-Lucky Morgans,* between late October and Christmas 1912. In it he combined some of the rigour of self-understanding, learned from Baynes, with many of the free-running suggestions for books once offered to Cazenove. The manner of narration testifies to a change in his own style that is lucidly charted in 'How I Began', published in *T. P.'s Weekly* on 31 January 1913:

> There is no doubt that my masters often lent me dignity and subtlety altogether beyond my needs. . . .
>
> Both in these letters [to Helen] and in papers intended for print, I ravaged the language (to the best of my ability) at least as much for ostentation as for use, though I should not like to have to separate the two. This must always happen where a man has collected all the colours of the rainbow, 'of earthquake and eclipse', on his palette, and has a cottage or a gasometer to paint. A continual negotiation was going on between thought, speech and writing, thought having as a rule the worst of it. Speech was humble and creeping, but wanted too many fine shades and could never come to a satisfactory end. Writing was lordly and regardless. Thought went on in the twilight, and wished the other two might come to terms for ever. But maybe they did not and never will, and, perhaps, they never do. In my own case, at any rate, I cannot pronounce, though I have by this time provided an abundance of material for a judgement.

He was now finding the natural rhythm that his earlier addiction to notebooks had stifled—a danger he had recognized when discussing Borrow's *The Bible in Spain:* 'Notes made on the spot are very likely to be disproportionate, to lay undue stress on something that should be allowed to recede, and would do so if left to memory; and once made they are liable to misinterpretation if used after intervals of time. But the flow and continuity of letters insist on some proportion and on truth at least to the impression of the day, and a balance is ensured between the scene or the experience on the one hand and the observer on the other.' (Yet he could not abandon the note-book habit, even when on active service in France.) The critical studies of Pater and Swinburne, written quickly to earn £90, were essential to his own development as a writer. They challenge the gibe that he was a mere hack writer churning out books for ready money to meet the needs of an improvident marriage. Previously he had, it is true, salved his writer's conscience by inserting short 'prose poems' at random into the narrative of his extended travel or colour books. In *Pater* and *Swinburne* he sharply attacked disconnected fine writing if it impaired the whole effect of a work of art, however precious the miniature gems. He knew that in meeting his own deadlines he finished books in a hurry and their 'wholeness' suffered. Professional pride in honouring contracts had conflicted with his instincts for a slower, more leisurely approach to his writing. Beneath the surface of some of his letters, too, is the recognition that a Civil List pension would have enabled him to write in closer accord with his inner experience.

For his 'breakdowns' had sharpened his awareness of the mysterious influence of the subconscious mind upon artists. Frequently he turned from his preoccupation with the role of speech in writing to comment on the strange, 'magical' powers that assist the initial impulse towards artistic creation: 'But Swinburne has almost no magical felicity of words . . . No poet could be poorer in brief electrical phrases, pictorial or emotional . . . Too often, if not always, his words are only words, involving scarce even a wish, or a passionate inability, to believe.' *Pater* contains most of the theory he was soon to share with Frost:

It is certain that there is a kind of unconscious self-expression which no man escapes . . . A man cannot say all that is in his heart to a woman or another man. The waters are too deep between us. We have not the confidence in what is within us, nor in our voices. Any man talking to the deaf or in darkness will leave unsaid things which he could say were he not compelled to shout, or were it light; or perhaps he will venture once—even twice—and a silence or a foolish noise prohibits him. But the silence of solitude is kindly; it allows a man to speak as if there were another in the world like himself; and in very truth, out of the multitudes, in the course of years, one or two may come, or many, who can enter that solitude and converse with him, inspired by him to confidence and articulation . . .

The most and the greatest of man's powers are as yet little known to him, and are scarcely more under his control than the weather: he cannot keep a shop without trusting somewhat to his unknown powers, nor can he write a book except such as are no books. It appears to have been Pater's chief fault, or the cause of his faults, that he trusted those powers too little. The alternative supposition is that he did not carry his self-conscious labours far enough . . . The words have only an isolated value; they are labels; they are shorthand: they are anything but living and social words. . .

It is, of course, true that writing stands for thought, not speech, and there is a music of words which is beyond speech; it is an enduring echo of we know not what in the past and in the abyss, an echo heard in poetry and the utterance of children; and prose, if 'born of conversation', is 'enlivened and invigorated by poetry'.

Similar opinions may be culled from his books written after 1910—with the exception of *The Life of the Duke of Marlborough*. He desired a more direct style. To achieve it he was forced to confront his own early experiences in an attempt, partly clinical, to understand the hidden causes of his recurring bouts of ill-health. The immediate result was *The Happy-*

Go-Lucky Morgans, his most engaging and untypical work; later the process was continued in the autobiography known as *The Childhood of Edward Thomas.*

The circumstances in which he wrote the novel were not favourable. Visits to London produced some work, but not enough. Visiting Wick Green he was, by turns, busy at reviewing and small journalistic jobs, or over-anxious as he tried to deal with the practical problems to be faced when eventually they moved to a much smaller house. He had to sell many more of his books. Helen would have to do without a maid, although she would continue to accept Bedales pupils as boarders during vacations. Things were too reminiscent of their first stringent years at Oxford. Edward was conscious that Helen could not soothe and support him as she had done for over ten years. His firm plan, he told Bottomley, was to retain his study and 'live mostly or half my time at least in London here and there' in order 'to give Helen peace', although scrutiny of his letters show that they continued to meet regularly. He admitted to MacAlister that 'we must (I must) live out of town', and that 'Helen could not get anything like as much tolerable society as here [Steep]'. Even when he had settled in at Selsfield House, he was unconvinced about his readiness for the literary socializing that went with his search for casual commissions, and hesitant to accept the ready welcome extended to him by the friends and families of Eleanor Farjeon and Clifford Bax. He lacked social ease outside his own family and a small, rigidly selected circle of friends, although very few of them detected it. The firm of Dent, and especially the Everyman Library, was one source of his small congenial earning, but he told de la Mare of his unease at visiting the home of the friendly Ernest Rhys: 'I wish I could frequent these running gatherings with any nonchalance. I must learn if I am going to live (largely) in town next year'. As a boarder with Ellis, who was shy with strangers but financially secure, he found he could work 'moderately well and had cloistered days'.

A long period of restlessness was about to begin. He was, he felt, the odd man out among his more successful friends, and his own brothers. Yet, in spite of the effort to write nearly seven books in twelve months, his lack of prospects as a writer-journalist was only too clear. Bottomley had come south to stay at R. C. Trevelyan's house on Leith Hill. After a visit to him there in November 1912, Thomas summed up his own state: 'I am not so bad to meet as to have letters from, as a rule. . . . My habit of introspection and self-contempt has at last broken my spirit.'

To his friends, at this time, he presented his absorption in the novel as a time-filling occupation for the unemployed. He knew it was more significant than that. 'The scheme allows me to use all my memories up to the age of twenty and so far I have indulged myself freely.' In fiction, if not in real life, he was starting again. As if to celebrate this fanciful return to school and undergraduate days, he made a sudden, quite uncharacteristic trip to Paris. Thomas sent an apologetic card to de la Mare on Tuesday, 11 November 1912, writing c/o S. Jones, Esq., 32 Rue des Vignes, Passy, Paris, because he had missed him 'by coming here'. He described his week in Paris to Janet Hooton from the same address six days later:

You know how the Joneses would look after me. Paris did the rest. I found it easy to get about alone walking or riding and have been out all day and three times to the Opera and Theatre in the evening. It has been grey and showery all the time which doesn't suit the pale walls of this city, but electric light does. It is a queer mixture of classic design and rustic accidents. . . . They (I mean S. J. and M. J.) did give a good time, left to myself all day and performed and got others (e.g. the Opera Comique, the Opera and the Gaieté Lyrique) to perform for me all the evening. On Saturday we heard Mozart's Magic Flute, the sweetest and loveliest thing I ever heard—and three hours of it. I hadn't a dull moment, nor an unpleasant one. No time for haunts of sin outside myself. Then the three hours railway to Boulogne in light mist was all delicious—equal to any low downland England. If I am asked I shall go again . . . I didn't see—
Napoleon's tomb   Pantheon   Versailles   Sainte-Chapelle   the Bastille
Ransome.

While Thomas was in Paris, a son was born to Ian and Dorothy MacAlister. After a hurried letter card, Edward got round to writing them a letter from Wick Green in early December 1912, explaining his plans for the future and giving financial reasons why he thinks he and Helen will remain in the Steep district: 'The Paris trip was only a digression. Some people who had often asked me over to their Paris flat collared me at a friend's house, made light of my old excuses, and took me off and only released me at the end of the week. I enjoyed it. . . . All well but very little work. I have had leisure to write, and begin copying, a slight loose suburban fiction since the Autumn.'

In spite of visits to Bottomley at Leith Hill, to MacAlister in London, and a weekend visit by Harold Monro, Thomas was ready to send the manuscript of *The Happy-Go-Lucky Morgans* to de la Mare after a Christmas spent at Wick Green, which he described to his brother-in-law on Boxing Day: 'We have had a good time for us and kept it up till one this morning with sea-songs by a new neighbour ['Muffin' Marston] etc—a man who was on the "Nimrod" with Shackleton.' Thomas hoped to launch the novel anonymously and posed his doubts about it to de la Mare, who was now a successful reviewer and publisher's reader. Should its sub-title be 'A True Story of Balham—with a foreword saying all the characters are from life' and should he put his 'ruinous name to it? The unsettlement of these six months or so has almost completed my demoralisation. The last rag is that I (almost invariably) take my cold bath still. I wish myself a better New Year.'

The year 1913 was full of change, turmoil, and uncertainty. One side of it, and the subsequent four years, has been fully chronicled by Eleanor Farjeon who fell quickly in love with Edward, soon made friends with Helen and the Thomas children, and acted as a willing unpaid typist for Thomas until his death. She remained a loyal friend long after Edward had half-withdrawn himself from the free, affluent, and happy-go-lucky circle of her friends. As he moved further into 1913, Thomas succumbed to the desperate need to leave home for 'the good of his family', as he expressed it, after only a six-weeks period at Wick Green with occasional one-day visits to town. He was accepting books to review for Monro's *Poetry and Drama,* but still insisted on non-payment. He agreed to be one of the panel of six judges that would eventually award a *Poetry Review* prize to Rupert Brooke's 'Grantchester', although his vote went to Ralph Hodgson.

By mid-February 1913 Thomas realized that 'things have been very wrong' and he couldn't write. 'My health is now definitely bad,' he told Berridge, 'not mere depression—and I don't know how it will develop.' He spent a few days cycling, and concluded that he was scarcely fit for much exercise. He joined Clifford Bax at Broughton Gifford with a party of friends and spent the time ' bicycling, and walking over Wilts. and Somerset as far as Glastonbury and taking copious medicine'. At this house-party he decided to invite Eleanor Farjeon to Wick Green to meet Helen, and so began a friendship that brought new interests in theatre, music, and ballet, new horizons in popular literature, a wider circle of acquaintances while Thomas lived, and a staunch, sustaining friend for Helen and her children after his death.

While at Oxford he had noted the desire to act as patron-mentor as one element in his attachment to younger undergraduates, and certainly a magisterial tone is perceptible in all his reviews of young apprentice-poets, as it is in his early letters to Helen. This hypercritical, pedagogic side of his nature is clearly displayed in his letters to Eleanor Farjeon, John Freeman, and Harold Monro as they submitted their work to him for professional comment. Yet, on this basis of staunch friendship, un-affected by severely honest criticism as he had practised it earlier with Hooton, Bottomley, and Berridge, he was now adding new younger friends to an already large circle at a time when he was quite uncertain which of the main roads before him he was to follow.

In desperation he may have resorted, temporarily, to a new literary agent, who is unnamed in a sole reference in a letter to Hooton. His brother Theodore found him work writing 'a short series of articles on the country round London for the Underground Railway'. He still reviewed a little for the *Daily Chronicle* and other journals, besides his unpaid work for *Poetry and Drama*. But his principal occupations throughout this restless period were writing *In Pursuit of Spring*, (with illustrations by Ernest Haslehurst), proof-reading *The Happy-Go-Lucky Morgans* with the help of Harry Hooton, and preparing a series of stories built around English proverbs, which after many rejections was eventu ally accepted by Duckworth for publication as *Four-and-twenty Blackbirds* in 1915. His various letters in the spring and early summer of 1913 refer to short periods of intense work in London. There followed a cycling tour with Merfyn in Norfolk combined with some walks with Jesse Berridge, while Helen and the children were away from home, and Eleanor Farjeon and her friends spent a carefree, rumbustious holiday in the house in Wick Green. Returned from Norfolk, Thomas stayed with Martin Freeman in Maida Vale to prepare *In Pursuit of Spring* for the press and arranged a cycling and walking tour with Jesse Berridge over some of the ground still to be covered in that book. On this tour, he discussed the idea of introducing 'the Other Man' into the travel book and pro-mised to collaborate with Berridge in writing a novel. Afterwards he settled down in his study to write, rewrite, and type his account of the journey—usually typing 4,000 words a day—against a constant battle with indecision about plans for the future and his inability 'to be away from home although for many reasons it is the worst place for me'. As an ironic variation, while preparing to sell four hundred of his books, he had agreed with Batsford to follow his monograph on *The Country* with a similar essay on *Ecstasy*.

Behind all this writing—and the constant new suggestions being placed before the reconciled Cazenove—lay the plans for the eighth move of house in thirteen years. Subsequent to the move to Yew Tree Cottage in Steep village on 23 July 1913, there were elaborate plans for the family summer holidays. Helen was spending part of August in Switzerland with her sister Irene. Edward and Merfyn were to spend the

week of 16 to 23 August on a two-cabin houseboat in Norfolk on
Ranworth Broad as guests of Eleanor Farjeon, and Gertrude and Stacy
Aumonier, the painter who was now beginning to write short stories
and novels. Bronwen would stay with Aunt Mary at Chiswick and
Myfanwy would spend the first of many short holidays with the John
Freemans. As always, Helen and Edward relied heavily on parents,
family, and close friends for assistance when the children were on holiday. The children saw nothing odd in this mobility; it was normal
practice among their friends and relatives and Bronwen, in particular,
often recalled these holidays for me with undisguised relish. Neither she
nor Merfyn were aware of any change in the financial circumstances
that brought them to live at Yew Tree Cottage. Their father's absences
from home they had long accepted as part of a writer's life, 'like a sailor'.
In Steep village they were very much nearer their friends and were able
to join in more out-of-school activities. The move took place at a slack
season for reviewing, and for a time Thomas concentrated on typing the
75,000 words of *In Pursuit of Spring*. As he renewed his reading of books
on mysticism, borrowed from Jesse Berridge, and 'quartered' the area to
be covered by his essay on *Ecstasy,* he began a close reading of
Dostoevsky's novels—intended for a long review-article in *The Times,*
accepted but never published.

   The Happy-Go-Lucky Morgans was not the financial success he had
hoped for. It remains too finely balanced—like Thomas himself—
between Abercorran House on the edge of Hammersmith and
Abercorran hamlet in Carmarthenshire. The actions of the characters
are in suburbia; the stories and recollections that form the book's staple
events are mythical, fanciful, Welsh, or wayfaring and idyllically rural
from an England half-way between Cobbett and Jefferies. Successive
chapters return from the circumference of not-so-random memories to
the central hub—the conversations between Ann, the domestic servant
who has stayed in the suburb, and the narrator Arthur Froxfield, a shadowy figure rather like Pip at the end of *Great Expectations.* The chief
characters remain schematic, allegorical figures designed to sharpen the
numinous edge of heightened consciousness as one man becomes aware
of its survival, even in apparently hostile suburban surroundings. There
is little assertion but a great deal of animal delight. The tone of the
novel conveys a sense of happiness and, as the story unfolds, many of his
favourite antonyms are here held in equipoise: rural Wales and Clapham
Junction; solitude and intense social activity; book-learning and untu-

tored wisdom; carefree natural behaviour and sequestered restrictiveness; the world of childhood play and the economic pressures of adult carefulness. To meet Cazenove's warning that publishers were no longer ready to pay well in advance, this novel was written without a publisher in mind. He does not attack the finished book with the usual discontent reserved for books written against a deadline—often a deadline of his own choosing. His only comment, sent to Harry Hooton with the proofs in June 1913, is critical but not dismissive: 'I feel for example that the opening is tangled. Also I find I have duplicated some characters—or part of characters—past helping.'

His brother Julian—and some other old friends I talked to in the late 1950s and early 1960s—identified Aurelius, Stodham, and Torrance as partially modelled on family friends and neighbours from Thomas's own school and undergraduate days. At least two of Edward's brothers shared some of the Morgans' expeditions in London and Swindon. Similarly, parts of the characters of Ann and Jessie resemble the many Welsh maidservants employed at home in Shelgate Road and, even more, his Pontardulais cousins and the sisters of the bard Gwili. Even in this fiction Thomas could not resist his old habit of using notebook material to help fill space. He had accumulated a great many notes on matters of Welsh interest. One chapter in the novel, 'Ned of Glamorgan', about Iolo Morgannwg (already used in *Wales* in 1905), adds little to the novel's texture and does not fill out any character. Another, 'Philip and the Outlaws' is a blatant use of saga material left over from his *Norse Tales,* and quite out of character here. Both chapters could be excised without loss from a novel that has the merest gossamer-like story-line.

For the novel moves in and around many half-concealed themes that recur occasionally in his descriptive and travel books but find a suitable form only in his short career as a poet: what sources of consolation, joy, and worthwhileness were readily available to someone like himself who shared no religious or social-political enthusiasms with his contemporaries? His sudden bouts of illness, and the introspective analysis used by Godwin Baynes, compelled Thomas to tease out the sources of his early adolescent animal happiness, and to present them in the novel in the character of Philip, before he was seized by Shelley's poetry. This, as we have seen, is an event that reads like a shorthand symbol for Edward's own early decision to become a writer. By placing the idealism of Aurelius, Torrance, and Stodham against the dubious financial state of Mr Morgan and the chequered 'working' careers of his many sons—so like the household of Philip Henry Thomas—Edward was free to query the social usefulness of many clerical and administrative occupations in modern cities.

Especially was he dissatisfied with the role of a creative writer in a modern society of anonymous readers, so different from the rapport enjoyed in earlier times between teller and listener in Wales and Iceland. The novel fills out hints in his letters and notebooks that, could he but find a suitable publisher to commission it, he would write a serious book about houses, homes, and abodes. Not a wistful, nostalgic curiosity full of architectural detail, but a personal attempt to understand the nature of the spreading disease of suburbia that was obliterating the London he had once known with its ready access to the life of nature in the commons and the neglected estates. With characteristic diffidence, he was asking questions, not offering Progressive Comte-based solutions (like his father), about the ethos that would prevail in suburban society in the future. In Chapter XV he comes close to a positive statement when Mr Stodham (the Respectable Man) speaks for England: a forecast of Thomas's own attitude to the war, in his non-bellicose wartime anthology *This England*. But this chapter in the *Morgans* ends rather equivocally: 'His [the pigeon-fancier's] patriotism is more like the "Elephant and Castle" on a Saturday than those trees. Both are good, as they say at Cambridge.' (Was this the only faint echo to survive from his weekend stay with Rupert Brooke?)

A sense of wonder, associated with a youthful reading of *The Thousand and One Nights* and *The Mabinogion,* pervades the novel, not merely as a conscious imitation of an earlier, less adult way of thinking, but in fulfilment of frequent hints in all his books after *Richard Jefferies* that Thomas was not prepared to dismiss entirely pre-scientific ways of assessing and interpreting mystical experience. He remained agnostic, I believe, to the end of his life and probably abandoned his thirteen typescript sheets on *Ecstasy* because its drift was leading him away from ecstasy towards a consideration of the relationship between madness and genius. Somehow he could never come to understand 'quite what was meant by God'. Certain elements, I am told, of the poet Charles Dalmon are incorporated both into Mr Aurelius and into an earlier 1911 sketch 'The Friend of the Blackbird':

Clearly he was one who saw invisible things . . . Beauty, genius, or happiness, each in its own way, compels awe akin to fear, in the detached beholder. This man had happiness. Never before or since have I seen happiness so shining . . . Everywhere he found beauty, personality and differences without end. The old simplicity and horror of the world conceived as the abode of evil man and a dissatisfied, incompatible Deity were forgotten. He could speak of God without emotion.

Thomas summed up his pleasure in *The Happy-Go-Lucky Morgans* when he sent a copy to John Freeman in December 1913 and advised him to begin at the end. The last chapter recalls the narrator's response to the incantation of Shelley's poem. ('Life of Life, thy lips enkindle'):

When I first heard them from Philip, Spring was thronging the land with delicious odours, colours, and sounds. I knew how nothing came, yet it was a sweet and natural coming rather than magic—a term then of too narrow application. As nearly as possible I step back those twenty years, and see the beech leaves under the white clouds in the blue and hear the wood wren amongst them, whenever by chance or necessity I meet that incantation: 'Life of Life, thy lips enkindle,' and I do not understand them any more than I do the Spring. Both have the power of magic . . .

In obedience to his self-induced belief that, unlike his father, he had no gift for logical disquisition, Edward Thomas did not pursue, although he undoubtedly did reflect in his novel, the animal spirits of happiness in his earlier days. The last word in the novel is left to Ann, who haunts so many of his earlier tales and sketches in Welsh locations:

Ann became a housekeeper first to the new tenant of Abercorran House, afterwards to Mr Jones at Abercorran Street. Otherwise I should not have written down these memories of the Morgans and their friends, men, dogs, and pigeons, and of the sunshine caught by the yard of Abercorran House in those days, and of Our Country, and of that Spring and the 'Life of Life' which live, and can only perish, together. Ann says there is another world. 'Not a better,' she adds firmly. 'It would be blasphemous to suppose that God ever made any but the best of worlds—not a better, but a different one, suitable for different people than we are now, you understand, not better, for that is impossible, say I, who have lived in Abercorran—town, house, and street—these sixty years—there is not a better world.'

Thomas's late poem, 'The long small room', has no precise location (though 61 Shelgate Road is a possible candidate); for as always with mature Thomas, the thoughts recede quickly from any direct resemblance to precise daily events or remembered images. They illuminate not one incident but his entire life as a writer, and we are left to read between the lines:

> When I look back I am like moon, sparrow and mouse
> That witnessed what they could never understand

Or alter or prevent in the dark house.
One thing remains the same—this my right hand

Crawling crab-like over the clean white page
Resting awhile each morning on the pillow,
Then once more starting to crawl on towards age.
The hundred last leaves stream upon the willow.

Much of the spirit of the mood of *The Happy-Go-Lucky Morgans* is caught in this haunting poem of quiet acceptance of things as they are: 'It would be blasphemous to suppose that God ever made any but the best of worlds.' Selsfield House had given him a refuge that, in some curious fashion, linked the adolescent Thomas with the plain-speaking prose writer and poet he was soon to become.

CHAPTER 12
Walking Tom

In early August 1913 he cycled west to Broughton Gifford for Bax's Cricket Week. Thomas was an indifferent cricketer and spent most of his time in the outfield. 'Third Man or Child' he signed himself in a thank-you letter to Bax. Before leaving Steep he sent the invalid Bottomley a summary of his plans. It was a poor apology for his havering failure to visit Cartmel in June:

> I will not be such a nuisance again just yet, as I am at last realizing I had better fight my battles instead of sending out lists of the opposing forces etc. Things have gone ill and better again—no work, no unusual strength, but a better equilibrium and a certain amount of gain from various studies in Mysticism and Mental Science—browsings not studies. We have moved and are now fairly fitted into our narrow quarters to everyone's satisfaction. The children are at home for 8 weeks holiday and we have begun with bicycle rides, an excursion to Goodwood Races and so on. I go away tomorrow for a few days riding west.

After the Cricket Week, Eleanor Farjeon paid the first of her regular visits to Yew Tree Cottage to make final arrangements for the houseboat holiday and to reassure Helen that her love for Edward would never be allowed to threaten his marriage. From now on she became one of Helen's intimate friends and a lifelong favourite 'Aunt' to the children. She brought an infectious gaiety, a sensitive understanding of childhood fantasies and aspirations, and a sure sense of a wider social and cultural world. For her part she learned and absorbed the deep knowledge and understanding of the natural world which characterized all members of Yew Tree Cottage. She was extremely shy, except with children and close friends, eager for experience, quite unformed as a personality despite her thirty years, full of fun and ready at all times to join an excursion or become one of a party without revealing too much of her inner thoughts and convictions. Like John Freeman, Harold Monro, and the Bedales master and novelist Grant Watson, she was admirably suited to join the growing number of younger writers who had admired Edward Thomas.

Reading through her invaluable *Edward Thomas: The Last Four Years*—side by side with his letters to other correspondents between 1913 and

1917—one sees how Edward came to rely heavily on her services as secretary, literary agent, companion to Helen and the children, or provider of tickets and information about London music, theatre, and ballet. Above all she became a sympathetic friend to help him while away the tedium of his spare hours when in London in search of employment or peace and quiet. Yet he rarely treats her as an intellectual equal. On a few occasions he turns aside to pour out an imperfect explanation of his excessive concern with his own thoughts, as if to explain the sudden, almost contemptuous changes of mood that Eleanor saw visited upon Helen quite early on in their friendship. She rightly recognized the citadel of reserve that only a few entered: Helen, of course; Frost, quite clearly; Harry Hooton; Jesse Berridge, during their brief annual journeys together; and, after initial hesitancies, MacAlister and Guthrie. I doubt whether Eleanor Farjeon joined this select band, but she assuredly is one of the close friends on whom he relied for assistance until the end of his life.

Unlike the idealized women strewn throughout his writings, she shares with Helen, his mother, his sister-in-law Irene, Janet Hooton, and Emily Bottomley one corner of his affection for practical motherhood and domestic workadayness that he praises in sketches drawn closely from the families of Pontardulais. In prose he never quite bridged the gap between the dream women of, say, 'The Castle of Lostormellyn' and the domestic wholesomeness of the eighteen-year-old Olwen, a factory girl like one of his cousins, in *Light and Twilight*. Some of his poems, despite their reticence, seem to cross this bridge with more assurance than he does in his tales, exactly as he himself did with old friends. In his annotations of Eckert's *Edward Thomas,* Harry Hooton remarks on this other Thomas: 'A terribly sad record. One remembers with amazement the many happy occasions when he was lighthearted and full of the spirit of real enjoyment. . . . He laughed heartily in circles given more to laughter than preciousness.' The sensitive Eleanor reacted to his self-imposed reticence and records it, without sentimentality, in the few intimate moments she recalls from her four|years'|knowledge of him.

He was quite unable to settle into the new cottage. While Helen was in Switzerland with her sister, Edward had one or two of the children always with him for a month and he 'had little done'. He had abandoned the book on Ecstasy although he needed the £20; yet again, he refused payment from Harold Monro for reviews contributed to *Poetry and Drama.* In late September, with the family back together in Steep, he worked in his study in the morning and tried to finish off in the evening at Yew Tree Cottage. The 'mere smallness of the house was vexatious', although the garden was quickly got into good shape. He was in between books with a sense of indirection that he loathed. In September he confessed to Hooton that he could cope with uncongenial work if he had 'any spirit left, any conscious or unconscious motive for going on and on, and not a mere powerlessness to shift the collar'.

This was the moment when Clifford Bax and Herbert Farjeon in Venice sent him the bizarre parody of Masefield, 'Walking Tom', which he read with high declamation to Helen and Eleanor. Like similar poems sent to their friends, each of the forty-four stanzas was equally shared between them, with outrageous rhymes and *John Gilpin*-like bravura. The plot was fantastic. In defence of the precious diaries he hoped to publish Tom fought with Ransome, in a drunken brawl, over a lady of easy virtue. In the end, using Ransome's *Oscar Wilde* as a bludgeon, he killed him and fled to his Aunt Hester in Chester who, he believed, was a pious woman who would help save his soul. But she recognized the 'tavern lady' as one of her girls: Hester was keeping a brothel. In despair, Walking Tom set out on his peregrinations throughout England, neglecting his old friends, especially de la Mare and Davies, breaking with Baynes, repelling the sympathetic Eleanor, and finally abandoning his patient wife. At last he gave in to the two writers' entreaties, settled down in the best London suburbs, found a publisher for his voluminous diaries and, we are left to assume, gave up his wanderlust:

> Then Tom raised up his shiny face to God
> 'And thank you, thank you friends' he murmered thickly,
> 'You've made a man of me that was a clod'
> From which time forth, good Tom made money quickly
> By teaching mortal sinners what Hell fire is
> And publishing (with Supplement) his diaries.

Thomas was delighted with the poem, but equally determined to retreat once more into his time past. Fairly soon he was to dispense with his doctor. ('Godwin can't really help me. When he first came to see me he made me feel that I was the most important person in the world to him. As I came to know his world I found he gave the same impression to everybody—and I don't like being one of a crowd.') He decided to try Selsfield House once again as a base for frequent trips to London (and Steep); he found the large attic there better to work in than he had hoped. Somehow he had re-captured the sense of his old study-bedroom in 61 Shelgate Road; he could work hard, or loaf, exactly as he pleased.

But before he set off, he made his usual provision for his family's needs. He had signed contracts for *Keats* and *A Literary Pilgrim in England,* which he always refers to as *Homes and Haunts,* thereby receiving at least the prospect of £105 in future payments. He still hoped for some small return from the novel and *Pater,* and he knew that his trips to town would pay for the additional expense of lodgings, with a little over for the theatrical entertainments that he and Helen now shared with Eleanor and her friends. At Selsfield House he spent five idle days gossiping with Davies who came on an extended visit, kept in frequent touch with old and new friends, and paid a surprise visit to Chiswick to meet Bronwen as she came out of school with her cousin, Margaret Valon. His little book on Keats prospered; his review output sharpened in quality and doubled in amount. His fortnightly visits to Steep often led to irritability, fuelled by silent self-accusation about his empty study up at Wick Green, by the poor reception of his two books, by the obvious toll his own unhappiness was taking of Helen, and, a new worry, his continued failure to understand Merfyn. In his 1950 memoir Merfyn generously takes on himself all blame for their misunderstanding. Extremely practical, he responded easily to his father's out-of-door teaching of country lore and sports, but he had no interest in books or languages. Bedales had fed his own interests but not those his father would have preferred. A quiet, ordinary boy of thirteen, he seemed sullen to his father who gave him up in despair until Robert Frost later suggested that Merfyn should return with him to America. Meanwhile, in remorse, Edward went back to his work in East Grinstead and London, an unsatisfied observer of other people's contentment and his own malcontentedness. Apart from regular visits home—or meetings with Helen in London—he was away from Steep from October 1913 to early February 1914. Two themes are now repeated in his letters: his growing dissatisfaction with social activities because they robbed him of the solitude his nature demanded, and the insistent need to write, whether he was paid or no, because he had come to accept that writing remained his deepest source of pleasure. Eleanor Farjeon, constantly on the move among friends and relations but with a spread of successful literary interests in London, proved an admirable foil and support to the less social side of his vagrant life at this time. From Selsfield House in November he told her that 'despite his state of mind' he was more deeply involved in the short life of Keats; a month later he informed John Freeman that having left home 'to work and give my family peace', he had 'enjoyed being here and have got some peace myself and done a lot

13. Robert Frost, during his visit to England, 30 June 1913. *Courtesy of the Jones Library, Amherst, Massachusetts.*

14. Eleanor Farjeon in 1913.

of work and got well into a tame literal matter of fact absolutely unrhe-
torical autobiography which there will probably be few to see and none
at all to love. . . . So far I think it is novel. It is just to record what has
not perished. Later on I may get beyond 16, but it will become more difficult.' He was now moving like a homing pigeon in on himself and his
early experiences.

His theorizing, especially in *Lafcadio Hearn, Pater,* and the article 'How
I began', had led him to accept the virtue of 'living and social words' that
would avoid the exquisite unnaturalness of Pater and yet support the
view that 'unless a man write with his whole nature concentrated upon
his subject he is unlikely to take hold of another man'. This was one
source of his discontent when *Pater* was attacked by the Paterians.
Thomas believed that, given the right topic, he could offer 'living and
social words' to other men. There seemed precious little chance of
achieving this while his own work was concealed under the persona of
the 'Edward Thomas' known to critics and editors. His concern, later,
that his poems should appear pseudonymously is already taking shape
when he informs Cazenove about his autobiography: 'A dull German
silver-grey thing, at present decidedly not for publication, don't mention
the project.' Despite apparent disclaimers that he was no poet, he had
long known the worth of what he had to say before he began to cement
his friendship with Robert Frost, who appeared in Thomas's life at the
exact moment when the Englishman was resuming control of his own
development. Their first meeting was during one of Thomas's London
visits from Selsfield House, at a lunchtime gathering. The rapid development of their friendship, as we shall see, owed much initially to
Thomas's cultivation after only their second meeting—with John Freeman and other writers present—at St. George's Restaurant in St. Martin's
Lane on 22 December 1913.

Autobiographical writing apart, his need for useful work was para-
mount and these trips to London had produced a steady trickle of small
jobs, though without quite the regularity of his old pulpit in the *Daily
Chronicle*. Cazenove's good offices failed to provide him with a succession of books to replace his earlier regular reviewing income, but there
were momentary windfalls: the sudden Australian purchase of 2,000
copies of his *Celtic Tales* for use in schools, and a grant of £100 from
the Royal Literary Fund to assist him in 1914. Other journals were opening for him, although he was never able, or willing, to exploit them to
the full. His reserve (or was it a form of intense pride in his own worth?)
never left him in his direct dealings with publishers and editors. Neither

Hooton nor de la Mare could share Thomas's own belief that he was in dire financial straits at any time, except for the temporary embarrassing shortages that all three occasionally experienced. In his obituary notice in April 1917, Thomas Seccombe mentioned Thomas's share of 'Welsh pride'. Superficially, Thomas's life during the eighteen months before the outbreak of war does not suggest a man too proud to accept the hospitality and generous support of friends or to make use of offers of help from his own and Helen's close family. He certainly stayed as a guest with Clifford and Olga |Bax in January 1914. Yet, when he left them abruptly after three weeks, he enclosed a cheque ('which is meant to pay for my butter and honey and washing') with his letter of flustered apology for 'treating you like an inn, in spite of the fact that there is no such inn in the world any more than there is such a landlady as Olga'. Mostly, Edward's overnight stays ended at the house of a friend or at 13 Rusham Road; Helen, too, made regular use of her sisters and numerous cousins, with or without her children. They attracted and accepted a great deal of support at all times. This 'Welsh pride' was a flexible and pliable one.

Recognizing the cramped conditions at Yew Tree Cottage, he had insisted on retaining his study and, as always, kept firm control over all business transactions and expenditure. Helen was only too happy to leave such matters to him. On the surface, then, there was nothing to suggest to his friends that his finances were strained or that his epistolary complaints about uncongenial work—or lack of it—were based only on momentary irritation. The cause, they assumed, was temporary indigence not chronic poverty. It was Davies who interpreted the underlying strain and, early in January 1914, urged Garnett to ask Thomas to consider making an approach for support to the Royal Literary Fund. It was an appropriate moment. Ellis and his wife were off to Switzerland and closing their house. Clifford and Olga Bax had readily welcomed him to stay, and, as we have seen, he left them in a fluster and returned to Steep. In his application, from Steep on 16 February 1914, he stated that by 1909 his annual income was £400, and that within the last two years there had been a rapid fall in his earnings and 'my family has become costly and my health has declined'. Latterly, he claimed, his earnings had averaged '£350 about; last year £250'. He was strongly supported by Hudson, Garnett, de la Mare, Belloc, and many others, and in late February the Fund awarded £100 to meet the difference.

Too much has been made of a relationship between his sense of duty as a family provider, his constant 'hack-work', and the late development of his gift for poetry. His progress as a writer was hampered by two demands he made upon his wife and himself; his ideal wish to unite workplace and family home, and his fanatical dedication to the perfection of his craft. He prefaces every visit to a friend, or each planned period away from home, with the comment that he must clear his reviewing before he sets off. He frequently makes it a condition of his stay that a portion of each day must be set aside for his work. When at home he spent regular hours in the garden, and his notebooks record the meticulous planning of it, increasingly shared with Helen. For although both had professional parents, their grandparents and earlier ancestors were craftsmen. Helen's skills were domestic. She was a good plain cook—especially good as a bread and cake maker—and she prided herself on her dressmaking skill. When they settled on the Weald, she threw herself into all rural and farming seasonal activities. At Wick Green, as in Steep, she became a keen gardener and remained so to the end of her long life. Edward, as we have seen, possessed many practical skills, and, like a good craftsman, he enjoyed imparting his knowledge to others. Even the severity of his comments on literary work submitted to him is that of a master craftsman judging apprentice work. There was nothing personal in his comments: he judged the workmanship like an assured foreman. Cazenove never quite grasped this journeyman attitude. For Thomas, like Geoffrey Lupton meeting a request for one of his carved wooden chests or a bed, wished always to agree on a price for his work before he undertook it. He believed (as indeed discriminating critics had confirmed) that the value and quality of his work was well-known without an elaborate sample of new work. A synopsis, he thought, was enough. His word went with it. Like a good journeyman, he fulfilled his contracts to the letter and supplied his promised manuscripts on time.

His regret at ceasing to be a constant reviewer in the *Daily Chronicle* underlies his sharply-worded article on 'Reviewing: an unskilled labour' in *Poetry and Drama*, March 1914. By then his worth as a skilled critic of modern poetry was well recognized by a variety of journals, as a new interest in Georgian verse spread. None of the columns he wrote then are 'unskilled', although there is an obvious lack of urgency when he is asked to comment on, say, eight volumes of verse in one review. His longer articles, however, on a single author or topic, remain authoritative today. Above all, Thomas needed leisure, peace of mind, and a steady income before he could do his best work. Much of the apparent despair in his letters—when it is not comic wryness—stems from his inability, or refusal, to lower his standards. In April 1910, when he had agreed to write *Maeterlinck* and *Feminine Influence,* he informed his agent that 'it seems to me we can take it as certain now that I am done for as far as books of my own kind go. I mean I must not hope to make money by this kind of work except in magazines'. He would never abandon writing 'of my own kind'. To find peace of mind while doing it, he met, with speed and efficiency, the tight deadlines of the various books undertaken to buy the necessary leisure. He may have idealized the custom of work in his scenes of rural life, but few have written with clearer understanding of the dull routine of country employment. He certainly understood the craftsman's welcome relief from paid labour at a day's end:

> And, through the silence, from his shed
> The sound of sawing rounded all
> That silence said.

The zest to follow his own kind of writing (which he still conceived to be in prose) never subsided although he now knew that his tales and reveries would rarely receive the approval of the book-buying public. The grant from the Royal Literary Fund must have encouraged him to continue with them, and may well lie behind his sudden and final return to Steep in February 1914. Narrative was not his strong point. His one novel soon ceased to follow a direct plot and became, instead, a partial anticipation of the autobiography he had begun in November 1913 at Selsfield House as a relief from his sudden discontent with *A Literary Pilgrim in England.* He wished to give a firm shape to his work. As he informed Edward Garnett in February 1913 his original idea with *The Happy-Go-Lucky Morgans* was to be a loose fiction 'something more than a connected series of essays. I wrote it to prove (to myself) that I could do something without being told to and on a fairly large scale.' And to mark its distinction from his other work, he added, 'My idea was to be pseudonymous—calling myself Arthur Froxfield.' For nearly a year before the meeting with Frost, it would seem, Edward Thomas was submitting himself—and the work published under his name—to a new kind of scrutiny. This marks a change in his attitude to writing which could well have produced poetry without the meeting with Frost and the onset of war.

Now—late 1913, early 1914—a third book was going through press. *In Pursuit of Spring,* published in April 1914, reveals more of Thomas's inner concerns than either *The South Country* or *The Icknield Way.* The form was tighter and, in outward structure, kept to its declared aim to be a record of a journey from London to the Quantock Hills on or with a bicycle. It draws directly on encounters made during a few escape journeys that he undertook from Wick Green, either alone, or briefly with Helen, or for almost a week with Jesse Berridge. Having learned something from Cazenove about publishers' objections to his vague way of writing, Thomas fills *In Pursuit* with recognizable place-names, inns, and topographical details in abundance, without sacrificing his sense of the half-veiled world that lies behind. He identifies himself readily with the Chaucer-like variety of representative people encountered on this pilgrimage, with its back turned on Canterbury, in search of spring in the West Country and a new extension of his own writing. When the book appeared Frost was convinced that some of it was poetry in essence.

There was much else besides: Thomas's constant fascination with personal and place names as windows on to the past; his inevitable literary diversions on Cobbett, Meredith, Hudson, Byron, Hardy, Stephen Duck, Barnes, Coleridge, and Sydney; the life-long preoccupation with epitaphs and memorial stones; the wry irony as he talked philosophically of pipes, or with mock-profundity of Stonehenge; the careful record of prices and the quality of accommodation on the way; and as always equally careful set-pieces describing scenes, landladies, villages, groups of children, birds, footpaths, and wayside chapels and cottages, or the eloquent Elian aside on the 'vanity of waterproofs'. The journey from Trowbridge to Shepton Mallet will give the flavour of this low-key style, intended to supply the ordinary tone of a travel book:

The gradient of the hillside was too much for a modern road. The Fosse Way, therefore, had been deserted and a new descent made, curving like an S; yet, even so, bold enough for a high speed to be attained before we got down to the 'George' and the loose-clustered houses of Nettlebridge. The opposite ascent was also in an S. At the top of it we sat on a wall by the larches of Horridge Wood, and looked back and down. The valley was broad and destitute of trees. Gorse scrambled over its sides. Ducks fed across the turf at the bottom. Straight down the other side came the Fosse Way, denoted by its hedges, and round its crossing of the brook was gathered half of Nettlebridge. The rough, open valley, the running water, the brookside cluster of stone cottages, reminded me of Pembrokeshire. There is no church.

From that bleak and yet pleasant scene I turned with admiration to a farmhouse on the other side of the road. It stood well above the road, and the stone wall enclosing its farm-yard followed the irregular crown of the steep slope. This plain stone house, darkened, I think, by a sycamore, and standing high, solitary, and gloomy, above Nettlebridge, seemed to me a house of houses. If I could draw, I would draw this and call it 'A House.' For it had all the spirit of a house, farm, and fortress in one, grim without bellicosity, tranquil, but not pampered.

Presently, at Oak Hill, we were well up on the main northern slope of the Mendips. The 'Oak Hill' inn, a good inn, hangs out its name on a horizontal bar, ending in a gilded oak leaf and acorn. I had lunch there once of the best possible fat bacon and bread fried in the fat, for a shilling; and for nothing, the company of a citizen of Wells, a hearty, strong-voiced man, who read the *Standard* over a beef-steak, a pint of cider, and a good deal of cheese, and at intervals instructed me on the roads of the Mendips, the scenery, the celebrated places, and also praised his city and praised the stout of Oak Hill. Then he smacked his lips, pressed his bowler tight down on his head, and drove off towards Leigh upon Mendip. I was sorry not to have arrived at a better hour this time.

In Pursuit of Spring has more to offer than detached, half-humorous observations. There is the counter theme of the sporadic appearance of 'The Other Man'—in spite of Thomas's request to Jesse Berridge that he should not uncover the fictitious nature of this sardonic alter ego, but whom Harry Hooton annotates as 'E. T. speaking' in his copy of the book. The life story of the Norgetts of Oldhurst is almost ripe for conversion into verse akin to Frost's *North of Boston*. The dream-like opening sequence of a London February day in the familiar 'high, large room with many corners that I had never explored' recalls his best sketches. The favourite Thomas theme of walking out of London to the West is again played with innumerable variations. The long digression on clay pipes is worthy, and reminiscent, of Raleigh and King James I. And always, on the roadside, in public bars or temperance lodging-house bedrooms, Thomas indulges unfettered his fascination with ballads, snatches of rural or popular song, and with the stereotyped pictures that adorned living rooms, saloon-bars, and bedrooms. He is determined to give a sharply-etched account of the seven stages of his journey, full of useful information that surrounded his own response at certain stations along the way.

These injections of pools of silence and reflection create the mood of an alternative route of self-confession and self-revelation along which Thomas travels between the necessary interruptions of bicycle stops and cheap one-night lodgings.

Three such wayside halts which, like the weatherbeaten statue near Cothelstone Manor, had 'long outgrown the original conception and intention, and become a classic-rustical, romantic what-you-please, waiting for its poet or prose poet', suggest how close Thomas's prose had come to the manner and topics that were to characterize his best verse whenever he tried to communicate directly some of these treasured moments which, too often before in his prose, had been overlaid by fine writing:

Motion was extraordinarily easy that afternoon, and I had no doubts that I did well to bicycle instead of walking. It was as easy as riding in a cart, and more satisfying to a restless man. At that time I was a great deal nearer to being a disembodied spirit than I can often be. I was not at all tired, so far as I knew. No people or thoughts embarrassed me. I fed through the senses directly, but very temperately, through the eyes chiefly, and was happier than is explicable or seems reasonable. This pleasure of my disembodied spirit (so to call it) was an inhuman and diffused one, such as may be attained by whatever dregs of this our life survive after death.

I went out into the village at about half-past nine in the dark quiet evening. A few stars penetrated the soft sky; a few lights shone on earth, from a distant farm seen through a gap in the cottages. Single and in groups, separated by gardens or bits of orchard, the cottages were vaguely discernible: here and there a yellow window square gave out a feeling of home, tranquillity, security. Nearly all were silent. Ordinary speech was not to be heard, but from one house came the sounds of an harmonium being played and a voice singing a hymn, both faintly. A dog barked far off. After an interval a gate fell-to lightly. Nobody was on the road. . . . I was tasting the quiet and the safety without a thought. Night had no evil in it. Though a stranger, I believed that no one wished harm to me. . . . The inn door, which was now open, was as the entrance to a bright cave in the middle of the darkness: the illumination had a kind of blessedness such as it might have had to a cow, not without foreignness; and a half-seen man within it belonged to a world, blessed indeed, but far different from this one of mine, dark, soft, and tranquil. I felt that I could walk on thus, sipping the evening silence and solitude, endlessly. But at the house where I was staying I stopped as usual. I entered, blinked at the light, and by laughing at something, said with the intention of being laughed at, I swiftly again naturalized myself.

Through a low-arched rainbow I saw the blueness of the hills of South Wales. The sun had both dried the turf and warmed it. The million gorse petals seemed to be flames sown by the sun. By the side of the road were the first bluebells and cowslips. They were not growing there, but some child had gathered them below at Stowey or Durleigh, and then, getting tired of them, had dropped them. They were beginning to wilt, but they lay upon the grave of Winter. . . . Therefore, I was very glad to see them. Even to have seen them on a railway station seat in the rain, brought from far off on an Easter Monday, would have been something; here, in the sun, they were as if they had been fragments fallen out of that rainbow over against Wales. I had found Winter's grave; I had found Spring, and I was confident that I could ride home again and find Spring all along the road. . . . Thus I leapt over April and into May, as I sat in the sun on the north side of Cothelstone Hill on that 28th day of March, the last day of my journey westward to find the Spring.

This last travel book reaches its point of rest close to the vernal equinox. Yet Thomas knew how to pinprick the balloon of unqualified aspiration:

For I had formerly gone up this cartway on a day so fine that for many nights afterwards I could send myself to sleep by thinking of how I climbed, seeing only these precipitous banks and the band of sky above them, until I emerged into the glory and peace of the Plain, of the unbounded Plain and the unbounded sky, and the marriage of sun and wind that was being celebrated upon them. But it was no use going the same way, for I was tired and alone, and it was near the end of the afternoon, though still cloudily bright and warm. I had to go down, not up, to find a bed that I knew of seven or eight miles from Tinhead and Edington.

Even Salisbury Plain conjured up in him this self-mocking spirit that characterized the Other Man, who supplies the counterpoint to the entire pursuit:

But let the rain fall and the wind whirl it, or let the sun shine too mightily, the Plain assumes the character by which it is best known, that of a sublime, inhospitable wilderness. It makes us feel the age of the earth, the greatness of Time, Space, and Nature; the littleness of man even in an aeroplane, the fact that the earth does not belong to man, but man to the earth. And this feeling, or some variety of it, for most men is accompanied by melancholy, or is held to be the same thing. This is perhaps particularly so with townsmen, and above all with writers, because melancholy is the mood most easily given an appearance of profundity, and, therefore, most easily impressive.

In Pursuit of Spring—like his two strange reveries *The Chessplayer* and *A Sportsman's Tale*—grew out of his friendship with Clifford Bax, the Farjeon brothers, and Godwin Baynes. It shows that at a desperate time in his family relationships, and in his determination to allay the mysterious voices that came into his head, Walking Tom was developing a new purpose in his writing. As he later informed Edward Garnett, when sending him some of his first poems, 'dimness and lack of concreteness I shall certainly do my best against.' Certainly the Edward Thomas whom Frost met and influenced so decisively, late in 1913, was already well along the road to the discovery of his real gift as a writer.

CHAPTER 13
'When we two walked'

WHEN Robert Frost read *In Pursuit of Spring* at Eastertide 1914 he was convinced that Thomas was a poet behind the disguise of his prose. Edward Garnett, who had long championed Thomas's tales and sketches for their poetic vision, reviewed the new book for the *Manchester Guardian*, in June 1914, with an acute awareness of the novel individuality it reveals: a quality much closer to the Thomas he knew well: 'Devoid of the least trace of any tendency to sentimentalise or moralise, he visibly stiffens and draws in at an opportunity for the display of a little expansive emotion, lyrical outburst, or genial fellow-feeling. . . . Every page has some quiet, disconcerting stroke on the fallibility of opinion and the frailty of human feeling, which are exhibited to us in their passing littleness against the background of peaceful landscape and changing heavens.' Garnett understood Thomas's new concern that his writing 'had got up into the air'. Looking back from our knowledge of his poetry, we can see now that Thomas was clearing the ground in preparation for a thorough understanding of the self that, he feared, had gone astray, and that later he was to offer to Helen, 'if I could find Where it lay hidden and it proved kind'.

Much of his uncommissioned writing from 1912 until mid-1914—including the final chapter of his *Keats*—gives unmistakable evidence that he was drawing closer to a way of writing that was, as he later expressed it, 'like me'. A great deal of *Rest and Unrest, Light and Twilight, The Happy-Go-Lucky Morgans* and *In Pursuit of Spring* gave him some joy as he wrote, and seemed to allow him a new freedom in choice of subject and manner of expression. He seemed capable once more—as in his pre-Oxford and Oxford days—of losing himself completely in the act of writing and uninhibited self-exploration. The autobiography—begun at Selsfield House in late 1913 and first published in 1937 as *The Childhood of Edward Thomas*—was an inevitable next station on this progress towards unvarnished self-portrayal.

It was his last attempt to disentangle the incidents, emotions, and circumstances that conditioned what he was at the age of sixteen, when he first began to write for publication and before he fell in love with Helen Noble. During its composition he insisted in his letters that he relied absolutely on things he could remember clearly. There was to be no embroidery, no post-hoc tinkering. 'I don't trust myself to build up the self of which these things were true. I scarcely allow myself any reflection or explanation.' This refusal to use language in an act of self-betrayal—rather to sing as he believed the birds did—became a hallmark of his poetry subsequently, as he continued to explore his life. This was the eventual manner of his desire to use 'living and social words'.

The Childhood was begun as a welcome relief from *A Literary Pilgrim* which he was finding tediously laborious. The theme behind that book had seemed a congenial one—the extent to which certain writers reflected the places where they had grown up. It would enable him to bring together many of his favourite writers and the regions he had visited or hoped to visit; but the terms offered by Methuen (£80 for about 100,000 words) were a clear reminder that his style of writing was much less valued than when he wrote *Oxford* or *Wales*. By 8 December 1913 he had come to detest *A Literary Pilgrim* ('I believe I have been doing it intolerably ill through indifference') and a few days spent at Leith Hill with Bottomley and Trevelyan could not dispel the effect of a few sleepless nights at East Grinstead while the Ellises were away. 'I hate forsaken houses (no fear, just a tendency to wretchedness), I am lucky to have this .... [*The Childhood*] is very lean but I feel the shape of the sentences and alter continually *with some unseen end in view*,' (my italics) he wrote to Eleanor Farjeon in December 1913.

All his letters in late 1913 hint at moods of helplessness that, on previous occasions, would have been followed by one of his 'breakdowns'. This time, surprisingly, he began to act with some decision. He left Selsfield House on 15 January 1914, after Helen and the children had spent Christmas there with the Ellises and some friends, considerably cheered by a sumptuous Farjeon Christmas parcel with presents for every one. Early in the New Year the Thomas family party at Selsfield House split up. Merfyn went to his grandparents, Bronwen, Helen, and Myfanwy (who was ill) went to Chiswick to stay with the Valons, while Edward, after some hesitation, decided to stay with Clifford and Olga Bax at 11 Luxemburg Gardens from 16 January, where he continued to work at the autobiography. Reaching its seventeenth year and recognizing that 'the thing is almost as long as a novel', he asked Eleanor Farjeon for 'a good skeleton for a bad novel'. He agreed to let her type his heavily cross-paginated autobiography from the tangled manuscript and confessed he 'had read positively nothing these three months that I have not had to read except [Eleanor Farjeon's] *Kol Nikon* and the first chapter of *Great Expectations*'. Then, at the end of January 1914, he brusquely decided to leave Luxemburg Gardens. There he felt increasingly unable to work and 'as I depend on work not only for a living but for my principal or sole enjoyment', he planned to stay somewhere in the country for a time, and even considered the possibility of staying near Frost at Beaconsfield. 'It is no use going home without plenty of work,' he explained. Suddenly, in early February, he returned to Steep, which remained his permanent home thereafter until Helen and the children settled in at High Beech, near Loughton, Essex in mid-October 1916 during his final training as a Royal Artillery Officer Cadet. Steep was the firm base from which almost all his verse was written.

Despite a half-hearted attempt to apply for an adult lecturing post in London in the New Year—using Garnett and Hudson as referees but withdrawing before an interview—he knew in his bones that 'changing about doesn't suit me or my work'. He needed a secure domestic base. Probably, too, an increased demand for his reviewing, helped by R. A. Scott-James (at the *New Weekly*), Monro, and the Fleet Street literary editors Robert Lynd and Holbrook Jackson, promised a steadier income—soon to be supplemented by a grant from the Royal Literary Fund. And he certainly needed the notes and books at Steep to complete the tedious *Literary Pilgrim*.

As always when he felt the grinding effect of a duty-book he sought an escape outlet. After leaving London he planned to extend the autobiography beyond the age of sixteen by writing a 'Fiction' (still the title in the notebooks). He had often discussed collaboration on a novel with Jesse Berridge and had sketched an outline story during a lunch with Berridge early in 1914. In late February, Thomas replied from Steep to his friend's suggestions:

I ought to have written at once, but the fact is I was busy with some odd jobs and very impatient to begin my book. That was three days ago. I meant to begin today but simply couldn't even begin to try to begin. So at the end of the day's writing I will write about your suggestion. When I first read it I felt it to be very much impossible, because I had given up that story. I talked it over with several people, including two novelists, and thought I had got it clear, whereas really I had only got it clear enough to see the difficulties. So I was intending to attempt a totally different story. Now I should like to collaborate with you. Should I succeed in getting to work on the *second* story of course I must go on with it. But if I don't I shall be glad to hear what your idea is—or had we better wait till I am up next, in a fortnight or so? I ought to warn you by the way that I didn't mean the lovers to be platonic and they were to get married in a hurry just to make their walking tour respectable—they were regarding that week as their last week of perfect freedom, before entering on their parts in middle class existence. If you want them to remain chaste, do you intend to ignore the sexual side or to assume that they are capable of ignoring it? In a whole book on a honeymoon there must be some sex unless the thing is lightest comedy.

Nine weeks later, together with a copy of *In Pursuit of Spring*, Thomas sent Berridge a short progress report on the Fiction and repeated it in a letter to Cazenove soon after: 'The fiction I spoke of early in the year got started and in fact has just advanced to about halfway, but I shall probably not finish it. I have lately been writing a number of South Wales sketches and wish I could get a book to do which they could be fitted into.' He noted, too, that his writing of proverbs (later published as *Four-and-Twenty Blackbirds*) had now been rejected by four publishers although he thought that, suitably illustrated, it would make a good Christmas book.

His life at Steep had returned to something like an acceptable pattern with alternations between work up at the hillside study and leisure spent in the village of Steep. But there is a subtle change of mood. Looking back in May 1914, his letters to two close friends suggest a brisk new note of confidence. In May he wrote to Hooton:

My work is perhaps a little better owing to the *New Weekly*. Otherwise no change. But I got a grant from the Royal Literary Fund to help me through the year. We are all well, except that Bronwen had got mild deformities through bad habits and I have allowed her to have this term with Margaret Valon for the sake of some gymnastic teaching which is supposed to be good. Please send me some more news and fix up a weekend here. I shan't be up till about the 5th [of June].

A letter to Bottomley a few days later is equally buoyant:

I returned home before the end of February and worked hard. Then all April I was away chiefly with Merfyn and Bronwen in Wales and near Robert Frost in Herefordshire—also near Abercrombie and Gibson by the way. And now I am again working hard, mostly at uncalled for little Welsh pictures, of a plain perhaps lucid kind, in my later manner, if it is a manner. So I have my usual excuse for not writing . . . What imbeciles the Imagistes are. I think Frost will do something. In fact he has done already. One or two things in his first book were very good. . . . I have seen a lot of him. But I can't gossip on paper.

These are not the restless, driven journeyings that had characterized 'Walking Tom' in late 1912 and 1913 to the intense amusement of Clifford Bax and Herbert Farjeon. When Thomas left Selsfield House (because the Locke Ellises had gone abroad) and had then become discontented with a few weeks in London, he could still report to John Freeman, 'Luckily I can now work almost anywhere.' This was a significant advance in self-discipline and a happy practice for the poet who, later, was to write half of his poetry in and out of barracks. It is temptingly easy to link these changes in life and work from October 1913 onwards directly with his new friendship with Robert Frost. To do so is to diminish Thomas's own dogged nature and, possibly, to misunderstand the relative standing of the two men in 1913.

Neither Thomas's early death nor Frost's subsequent reputation can obscure their quite different status when they first met. Thomas was well-established and highly respected in English critical circles, Frost was gradually making his way in England. Superficially, they had little in common at the time of their first two restaurant meetings. Frost was receiving some critical acclaim. Thomas, not for the first time, was in a deep Slough of Despond and living away from home. Frost was in his thirty-ninth year after a wayward, wavering career which barely concealed his iron determination to gain recognition as a poet. Supported by an increased annuity of $800 from his grandfather's estate, he had come to England solely to write poetry. Before he left America in September 1912 his poems were beginning to appear fairly regularly in journals. His first two volumes of poetry (*A Boy's Will* and *North of Boston*), published in England in 1913 and 1914, included poems composed during the previous decade as well as a few written at Beaconsfield where he had first settled, in the country but not far from literary London. The letters sent to his American friends reflect his upsurge of self-confidence, his desire to pay off old scores experienced during the doldrum days of neglect and fancied humiliation, along with his assiduous cultivation of English and American reviewers who might create a favourable critical reception for his books. He had successfully cultivated Pound, Flint, Monro, Wilfrid Gibson, Hodgson and Lascelles Abercrombie to this end and, less successfully, Bridges, Trevelyan, de la Mare, and Yeats. Acquaintance with Hodgson and Gibson had led to his first meetings with Thomas. As far as one can judge from sparse letters between them early in 1914, when they may have met frequently in London, Frost was unaware of Thomas's reputation as a critic and did not include him in his own carefully orchestrated campaign for recognition.

Their friendship owed much to Thomas's initiative after their second meeting on 23 December 1913. A few weeks later he made arrangements for Frost to spend a night at his parents' home in Balham. At the end of

January he asked 'My dear Frost' to look for suitably cheap lodgings near Beaconsfield. Soon afterwards, as we have seen, he decided to return to his family at Yew Tree Cottage and it was from there in February 1914 that he wrote to Frost as though the basis for a close friendship had already been formed:

I have accumulated a press of little things to be done before I begin and am flustered in the extreme. When I am next in London I will let you know. Also I will look up my map and consider the roads between us. But first I must see if I really can write something. I wish you were nearer so that we could see one another easily and our children.

Thomas, apparently, was more concerned to try out his decision to work at home before he involved himself too much with the American's ideas, however fascinating they were and however much he approved of them. On 24 February he apologized to Frost for not yet cycling to Beaconsfield ('I really had some work to do and had decided it was a day's ride'. 'Today I rather think I began a fiction. I won't say positively . . . . When I'm really into the book I will try [the ride]'.) He reassured Eleanor Farjeon about the beneficial move from London to Steep: 'I am glad to be back and to watch the plain and the downs from my study. We are all well and liking one another.' With this letter he sent her *The Childhood* manuscript for typing. At home in Steep many small jobs continued to come his way: eight volumes of verse in manuscript to adjudicate for an unspecified publisher; some articles accepted by the *Manchester Guardian*; articles and reviews for *T. P.'s Weekly, The New Weekly, The Bookman, Daily News* and *Daily Chronicle,* or the *Saturday Westminster Gazette*; and, as always, the demands for his judgement of their work made by Monro, John Freeman, or Eleanor Farjeon. He planned his work methodically—'two pages a day at the Fiction and eight for Homes and Haunts, allowing three hours for each activity.'

After a short stay in town, he set off from his parents' home on 25 March to pay a long-planned visit to the Frosts at The Bungalow, Reynolds Road, Beaconsfield. The Frosts were about to leave there and to join Wilfrid Gibson in Gloucestershire, after a week's sight-seeing in London. Apparently Frost was still to take the measure of Thomas. Writing to Sidney Cox on 26 March, Frost announced the change of English home because 'I have no friend here like Wilfrid Gibson'. Nor does Thomas figure in the *Selected Letters of Robert Frost* until Elinor Frost first mentions him in mid-June 1914.

In early April 1914, after making arrangements for Myfanwy to stay with the John Freemans, Edward set off on a cycling tour in Wales with Merfyn and Bronwen. Their Welsh trip was a mixture of long train journeys and short cycle rides; it ended with a week at Laugharne which the children enjoyed thoroughly. Edward, though, had a cold and had insisted on working every day, 'partly to keep my conscience|quiet|partly because I have so much I want to get on with, especially after spending an awful lot on getting to Wales etc.'. They left Wales by train and spent a week with Frost at Little Iddens, Ledington, near Ledbury. It was here that Edward and Robert began their sustained discussion of the role of speech in the language of poetry which revealed the closeness of their views, independently arrived at, and so added a shared intellectual conviction to the bond of affection that was being forged between them. (Both Helen and Eleanor Farjeon were later to assert that Frost's personality drew Thomas towards him like a magnet.) While the two men walked and talked, their children concentrated on preparing an anthology. As the two writers explored the border country, with its many overtones of Vermont, personal linking and agreement about the nature of poetry came together.

Twelve years after Edward's death, Robert caught the essence of their friendship in 'Iris by Night—The Malverns' which reads as a gloss on Thomas's own warm and balanced verse memory of their discursive perambulations around Ledington in the early days of the war ('The sun used to shine while we two walked'). Appropriately Frost recalls a more numinous scene:

> One misty evening, one another's guide
> We two were groping down a Malvern side . . .
> And then we were vouchsafed the miracle
> That never yet to other two befell
> And I alone of us have lived to tell.
> A wonder! Bow and rainbow as it bent,
> Instead of moving with us as we went,
> (To keep the pots of gold from being found)
> It lifted from its dewy pediment
> Its two mote-swimming many-coloured ends,
> And gathered them together in a ring
> And we stood in it softly circled round
> From all division time or foe can bring
> In a relation of elected friends.

The adjective 'elected' was no haphazard choice. Writing to an American poet, Grace Walcott Conkling, in 1921, Frost is explicit about their friendship:

You will be careful, I know, not to say anything to exalt either of us at the expense of the other. There's a story going round that might lead you to exaggerate our debt to each other. Anything we may be thought to have in common we had before we met. When Hodgson introduced us at a coffee house in London in 1913 I had written two and a half of my three books, he had written all but two or three of his thirty. . . . I dragged him out from under the heap of his own work in prose. . . . The point is that what we had in common we had from before we were born.

There was an empathy between the two men, a readiness to discuss every topic without concealment, that is found nowhere else in Thomas's correspondence except with Helen and, to a slightly less open degree, with Hooton, MacAlister, and (after a few false starts) Eleanor Farjeon. Helen, in a sober retrospective article in *The Times* of 3 August 1963 ('Poets' Holiday in the Shadow of War'), confirmed the close relationship between the two men:

It was at once obvious that Robert and Edward were very congenial to each other. They were always together and when not exploring the country they sat in the shade of a tree smoking and talking endlessly of literature and of poetry in particular. When it was wet we all assembled in the Frosts cottage, and as there were only two chairs in the living room we sat on the floor, talking or singing folk songs in which the children joined.

I never became close to Robert as Edward was. To Edward he was an inspiration. He and Robert had been drawn together by Edward's recognition of Robert's genius. Edward's reviews of Robert's early poetry published in England laid the foundation for Robert's success. And Robert encouraged Edward—who had not written any poetry—to think of himself as a potential poet.

This is an honest tribute, after half a century during which the coolness between Helen and Frost grew. But in 1914 the Frosts were immediately taken with Edward and, to the best recollections of the three Thomas children, the meetings between the two families prospered, as Mrs Frost states in a letter to her sister Leona:

Wilfrid Gibson and his wife live about a mile from us and Abercrombie with his wife and two children are three miles away. We see them all often. We have had quite a little company since we came, and some friends from near London have been down and taken lodgings near us. Edward Thomas, who is a very well known critic and prose writer has been here with his two children and he is going to bring his whole family to lodge near us through August. Rob and I think everything of him. He is quite the most admirable and lovable man we have ever known.

While Edward and the elder children were in Wales and Ledington, Helen was tied to Steep looking after holiday boarders from Bedales. She had a succession of visitors and spent long hours in her garden, reporting her progress in letters to Edward and the children. Eleanor Farjeon had been loaned a house at Kingham in Oxfordshire for a fortnight towards the end of April and early May. She invited Edward to join her, her brother Bertie, and his future wife for the first week there, on his way home from Ledington. After some hesitation, and a few days at Steep, he joined them for four days on condition that he should be allowed to spend his mornings and late afternoons working at his Welsh sketches and catching up arrears of work. He then returned to Steep and to the last stages of his fiction ('crawling tediously towards its chief episode'), to the final push on *A Literary Pilgrim,* and to the exciting preparation of at least two reviews of Frost's new volume, *North of Boston.* Edward and Helen joined the Farjeons in London on visits to *The Magic Flute* and, later, to the Russian Ballet. They both missed Bronwen's engaging company, now that she was away from Steep at school in Chiswick with her cousin, and Helen, less tied (during term-time) on non-teaching days, took frequent cheap excursion trips to London to see her. She and Edward began to plan a holiday together in June before his final assault on two outstanding deadlines: *The Flowers I Love,* a series of twenty-four drawings by Katherine Cameron with an anthology of Flower Poems selected by him (chiefly from the poems of his friends), and *A Literary Pilgrim* which had now occupied him for a longer period than any of his other commissioned works. Eventually their plans fell together. While Helen taught, Edward spent three days with the Bottomleys at Cartmel, working at reviews and an article, walking, taking solitary long-distance swims in the lakes, talking, and listening to Bottomley's harpsichord-playing in a peaceful house where

> all within
> Long delicate has been;
> By arts and kindliness
> Coloured, sweetened, and warmed
> For many years has been.

On 16 June, after an evening at the Russian Ballet, the Thomases set off from London for Ledington (passing through Adlestrop) and spent three days with the Frosts, planning to return with the children for the month of August. Eventually they made their way to Steep via Coventry and London, with visits to de la Mare, the Hootons, and the Guthries. In pursuit of friendship in mid-1914 Edward and Helen were tireless. If there is any truth in a statement by Frost's biographer that Thomas talked of nothing but divorce at this time—an untypical piece of Thomas behaviour—these ten days travelling with Helen either refute the suggestion or hint at a renewed attempt at marital harmony. There is no surviving evidence to support Lawrance Thompson's statement and he does not name his informant.

By now Edward's review of *North of Boston* had appeared. Preparing it in late May, he had assured Robert that he would not hedge his praise although he doesn't want 'to sprawl about before your eyes as I feel I should do, more than usual, just now'. Some of Frost's self-confidence in his own success as a poet—as well as the intense activity of Rupert Brooke, Wilfrid Gibson, Lascelles Abercrombie, and John Drinkwater in producing their quarterly, *New Numbers*—must have stirred Thomas to think of verse-writing, probably after Frost's praise of *In Pursuit of Spring*. For Thomas had written from Steep on 19 May 1914, after completing his review of *North of Boston*: 'I wonder whether you can imagine me taking to verse. If you can I might get over the feeling that it is impossible—which at once obliges your good nature to say "I can". In any case I must have my "writer's melancholy" though I can quite agree with you that I might spare some of it to the deficient.' (The subject is not mentioned again in their correspondence until Thomas sent Frost his first poems six months later.) Meanwhile Frost approved of the 'autobiography' but condemned both the 'Fiction' and Edward's inured introspection, while Thomas continued to meet his deadlines and to write 'something every day. Sometimes brief unstrained impressions of things lately seen, like a drover with 6 newly shorn sheep in a line across a cool woody road on market morning and me looking back to envy him and him looking back at me for some reason which I can't speculate on. Is this North of Bostonism?' Frost's theory and practice had struck a new chord in his friend.

Frost's 'new theory of poetry' is documented in his published letters. The germ of the idea appeared very early in letters written between December 1894 and October 1907 to Susan Hayes Ward, the sister of an influential editor, but the theory began to emerge in its final form in a series of letters sent from England between July 1913 and February 1915 to two younger friends at home, John T. Bartlett (a journalist and former pupil) and Sidney Cox, a younger teaching colleague and subsequent biographer.

A few quotations from Frost's letters will indicate the main thrust of his developing argument:

In *North of Boston* you are to see me performing in a language absolutely un-literary. What I would like is to get so I would never use a word or combination of words that I hadn't *heard* used in running speech. I bar words and expressions I have merely seen. You do it on your ear. Of course I allow expressions I make myself. War on clichés. (To Bartlett, December 1913.)

The living part of a poem is the intonation entangled somehow in the syntax idiom and meaning of a sentence. It is only there for those who have heard it previously in conversation. . . . Words exist in the mouth not in books. You can't fix them and you don't want to fix them. You want them to adapt their sounds to persons and places and times. You want them to change and be different. (To Cox, January 1914.)

I give you a new definition of a sentence. A sentence is a sound in itself on which other sounds called words may be strung. . . . Many of them are already familiar to us in books. I think no writer invents them. The most original writer only catches them fresh from talk, where they grow spontaneously. . . . The voice of the imagination, the speaking voice must know certainly how to behave how to posture in every sentence he offers. (To Bartlett, February 1914.)

Frost then apologizes for this long account because 'it is the most important thing I know. I write it partially for my own benefit, to clarify my ideas for an essay or two I am going to write some fine day (not far distant).'

Frost was warned that if he did not write his own book on speech and literature Thomas would feel constrained to do so as a follow-on from his *Pater*. *A Literary Pilgrim* was nearing completion; the Flower Anthology was sent off on 16 July after three hectic weeks of preparation; and, characteristically, Thomas was already hankering after a new project that would secure at least £100 to meet basic family expenses for the next year. A double approach to Cazenove and to Harold Monro marks the next stage in his progress towards some form of direct involvement in the shaping of a new post-Victorian poetic. With typical caution, his suggestion draws on his dual reputation as a successful anthologist and skilled champion of significant new poets. His two notes to Monro are self-explanatory:

Do you think you could sell a book on modern poets by me and if so do you think it would be worth your while to pay me anything in advance for it? If it does not appeal to you do not trouble to reply will you. (29 June 1914.)

My idea is a series of studies, probably grouped or connected, of from 12 to 20 living poets. I should choose not the 12 or 20 I might think the best, but some because I like them, some because they are interesting, some because people buy their works. I should try to make clear what they do and are and only incidentally why I admire it or not. Wherever possible I should try to get some significant biographical details. I should try to avoid destruction or pooh-poohing in most cases. If I could I should like to make it some sort of an introduction to modern poets, though I should not hamper myself with an imaginary young person to be introduced. . . . A book of 50 or 60,000 words would be long enough. (2 July 1914.)

Thomas and Monro frequently met in London and probably discussed the project then; there is no further mention of it in their letters. Perhaps the declaration of war that finally ended Monro's journal *Poetry and Drama* blocked this promising venture which, in Thomas's case, passed underground for later use. For the outbreak of war sent him off on a tangent for a while, away from poetry and towards a more profitable kind of journalism, some of which is included in the posthumous collection, *The Last Sheaf.*

Thomas was ready for a change. As he explained to Frost in early June:

I have dropped that fiction, so that's two truncated Mss. in a year. I should feel vain at doing unprofitable things if I hadn't added up my earnings the other night. Something has got to happen. I keep saying, why worry about a process that may terminate a kind of life which I keep saying, couldn't be worse. Oh, and £3–3–0 is satisfactory. [The agreed weekly cost of the Thomas's coming stay at Ledington in August.] I will not say we shall come but I feel sure we shall.

A similar sense of futility, combined with dogged persistence, appears in early June in a letter to John Freeman who was to look after Baba while Helen and Edward were away together. Had Freeman, too, suggested that Thomas try verse?

I haven't tried 'Hang it, here goes' yet. The nearest I get is humming tunes over. I expect my difficulty is finding it too easy and having so long stamped on a sort of conscience. And I have a crude plan of turning sensations, etc., straight into prose, or expecting to do it. I could write about that spring for example, just substituting wit for not very cold water. I should think I do remember it. I see it every day practically. . . . I have dropped Shelley for the time being: have done such a mass of descriptions (mostly Welsh) that I have got quite out of the habit of reading.

A planned July meeting with Freeman in London didn't come off. Thomas was busy completing *A Literary Pilgrim* for Cazenove before he and Merfyn set off from Steep:

Work presses—work I don't want to take away with me—and I shall only just finish by the time we (all five) start for Mrs. Chandler's, Ledington, Ledbury, Herefordshire. We expect to be there a month. Merfyn and I are cycling. Baba is almost blind now after the treatment her eyes got before being examined. She does look forward to seeing what things are really like. So should I, if I thought there was a chance. . . . P. S. We go on or about the day after Bank Holiday.

The six months following his return to Steep had been marked by a quiet, persistent change in his attitude to his life and his work, a new sense of expectancy and purpose. Influenced by Eleanor Farjeon, he was much more involved in the doings of his elder children and increasingly attentive to the chatter of the younger daughter. Helped by the Royal Literary Fund grant—a welcome act of official recognition—he had stuck at uncongenial necessary writing jobs. But he had also forged a sparer prose style. Above all, the thrust of Frost's robust manner and theory, together with the interest younger writers showed in Thomas's judgement of their work, helped him to believe in the rightness of that private kind of writing to which he had kept doggedly faithful. Later, he found the words for this experience in *The Bridge*, written on 12 March 1915:

I have come a long way today:
On a strange bridge alone,
Remembering friends, old friends,
I rest, without smile or moan,
As they remember me without smile or moan.

All are behind, the kind
And the unkind too, no more
Tonight than a dream. The stream
Runs softly yet drowns the Past,
The dark-lit stream has drowned the Future and the Past.

No traveller has rest more blest
Than this moment brief between
Two lives, when the Night's first lights
And shades hide what has never been,
Things goodlier, lovelier, dearer, than will be or have been.

To answer one of his own questions: this is not North of Bostonism. Like so many of the first eighty-five poems composed in the seven months before his enlistment, it reflects with subdued technical skill the long process of self-understanding that preceded the sudden outpouring of his verse in November 1914. In the final process the stimulus came from Robert Frost, whom Thomas designated the only begetter of his poetry. Frost preferred to state that they gave each other a boost: his retrospective comment is nearer the truth about a writer who at the age of thirty-six had to double back after twenty years of writing in order to discover what still remained of his childhood self. The single-mindedness with which Thomas undertook this pursuit was the hidden guarantee of its successful outcome. The onset of war, with the immediate prospect of the cessation of large areas of peace-time journalism, certainly jolted Thomas into a new way of thinking about public affairs. There is nothing to suggest that it disturbed his already well-formed opinion about the way he would write in the future. As his War Diary shows, he had found a way to adapt his mature gift of observation to the clear-sighted enthusiasm of the youth of seventeen who had embarked on the publication of *The Woodland Life*.

CHAPTER 14

1914: This England

I WISHED to make a book as full of English character and country as an egg is of meat. If I have reminded others, as I did myself continually, of some of the echoes called up by the name of England, I am satisfied.
(E. T.'s introductory Note to *This England: An Anthology from her Writers*, 1915)

Helen, with her two daughters and Peter Mrosowsky, a Russian boy boarder from Bedales, completed a day-and-a-half train journey from Petersfield, via Oxford and Malvern, to the Chandlers' farm near Ledbury on the fifth of August 1914. The small colony of writers gathered there (Gibsons, Abercrombies, Frosts, Thomases, and, later, Eleanor Farjeon) had settled down to their usual unconventional pattern of daily life. Occasionally the village policeman made them aware of local hostility and suspicion, aroused especially by Frost's obvious Americanism and the presence of the Russian lad. The gamekeepers on Lord Beauchamp's huge estate knew that the English writers had the freedom of his woods and fields: they were less inclined to accept the Frosts as 'gentlefolk'. The women and children picked fruit and lifted potatoes, and played in and around the orchards and fields that separated the cottages, which were about two miles from each other. Gibson and Abercrombie were planning further publications of *New Numbers*. The first number had been printed in Gloucester, assembled at Gibson's house, The Gallows, near Ledington, and sent by post from Dymock to two hundred subscribers during April and May. It had been a communal effort. Frequently Frost and Thomas set off on long rambles across the Beauchamp estate and the surrounding countryside, taking in May Hill and the British Camp at Malvern, and exploring the villages and churches of Kempley, Much Marcle, and Malvern, which had been known to Thomas from childhood visits to his mother's relatives. And always—according to the testimony of Eleanor Farjeon and Jack Haines, a local solicitor and botanist living at Hucclecote who had become friendly with the poets—the endless conversation continued between Robert and Edward as they explored their similar views on the nature of poetry, and felt the powerful magnetism that held them together. If outdoor games or rambles proved impossible, the evenings were convivial and rowdy. There were word games, charades, readings of prose and verse, cards, and the inevitable singing of catches, ballads, and folksongs at which Thomas excelled with his light baritone voice. Cider and country food helped things along.

It was not all play. Thomas explained to John Freeman on 14 August:

I am working as much as I can by finding jobs for myself when even an unpatriotic person can't imagine it is of the least importance or money value. But this morning I have got a headache that keeps me in and also prevents me working. . . . Now that Mr. Chandler (an old soldier of 21 years service) has been called up we are more secluded here from realities than ever. We had our fixed terms for board raised a little. I get no work and discover no likelihood. Otherwise little is changed except in the newspapers.

He was still reviewing regularly for *The Bookman* and, having tidied up the typescript of *A Literary Pilgrim in England*—an assessment of the part various native British environments had played in the development of poets from all corners of Great Britain—he was asking his agent about alternative plans for paid work. Meanwhile, as always, he was alert to the developing verbal skills of his younger daughter. 'She sang four or five verses of "John Peel" the other morning without one line of sense, yet using hardly one word that isn't in the song, just transposing and rearranging, retaining only the tune and the metre. Some lines were better than ever but I can't remember one.' The stimulus of the debates with Frost about speech and poetry had bitten deep.

Reading between the lines of some recently discovered letters from Frost to Thomas, one senses that the two men were uncertain about the outcome of the war. Frost was clear that it meant the end of his English venture into poetry and he decided to return to America early in 1915. Thomas was less sure at first. While replying to Cazenove about points raised by Methuen in his typescript, he returned to the idea of a series of short introductory critical commentaries and texts which would introduce modern poetry to more readers. Cazenove implied that there was now no market for books of his own kind, and Thomas replied immediately: 'I believe you are right. Only the kind I have had to do has paralysed me for original work except in short bursts, supposing I ever could have done more. Perhaps you can do something with the collection of sketches. Call it "Thick and Clear", perhaps.' This, too, proved a fruitless request, but Cazenove quickly seized on Thomas's suggestion, in mid-August, for a 'series of country rides . . . to relate solely to the war's influence'. A week later, Cazenove reported that Austin Harrison (editor of *The English Review* who had published Thomas's 'Swansea Village' in June), was anxious for a careful handling of the theme, but ready to

discuss the idea. Harrison was prepared to pay £25 for 5,000 words
including travelling expenses. The final outcome was three articles for
Harrison—'Tipperary' in October, 'It's a Long, Long Way' in December,
and 'England' in April 1915—and 'This England' which appeared in *The
Nation,* November 1914.

These straightforward journalistic pieces, and others written between
January 1913 and April 1915 (available in *The Last Sheaf*), show how far
Thomas had left behind the Paterian preciosity that had frequently
obscured his finest perceptions. The journalism conforms closely to the
picture I have in mind of the significantly changed, more outward-
looking man he had become after two years of intense heart-searching.
The wartime articles led on directly to his next (and last) commissioned
works—an anthology, *This England*, for Oxford University Press and *The
Life of the Duke of Marlborough* for Chapman and Hall. In the articles
Thomas has a closer relationship with his expected readership: a vital
experience in his ultimate decision to trust himself to write verse in a
language not to be betrayed. In addition, they throw some light on three
questions that he posed constantly, in different guises, in his letters to
friends during the next twelve months. Should he enlist as a soldier?
Should he accede to Frost's belief that he should join him in New
England and attempt a new life there as farmer, summer-school lecturer,
and writer? How could he interpret to others, what 'England' really
meant to him and to them?

Thomas offers no simple answers to any of these questions. The
notion of understanding what 'England' stood for seems to emerge,
partially at least, from his walks and talks with Robert Frost in the
English-Welsh border country that both men found congenial to their
temperaments and purposes. Frost would have recognized the close
similarity between the Hereford-Gloucester landscape and the familiar,
more spectacular townships and hillsides of New England where, even
today, a twenty-mile bicycle ride from Bellows Falls towards the old
Rockingham Town Hall can evoke memories of the Welsh Border
Country. It would not have been difficult for Frost to convince Thomas
that he would find in New England, north of Boston, a familiar extension of his chief form of necessary, health-giving activity. Yet Thomas
rejected the attractive offer to spend some time there with Frost and, for
the rest of his life, the American continued to believe that he had somehow let Thomas down. The ties that bound Thomas to England were
complex but undefined until he decided to enlist in 1915. His
'England'—which at all times included an earlier 'Britain' where his own

mixed ethnic inheritance from Devon and Dyfed could feel at home—
was compounded of present and past, of rural and urban ways and
practices, of high Palaeolithic camps and Pontardulais (or Landore)
metallurgical waste-lands, the valleys of the Gwili and the Evenlode. His
instinct had been to settle in small communities where it was easier to
satisfy the urge to be free, an urge he frequently attributed to his
ancestry of skilled journeymen and seafarers. His own first-hand knowledge of London and industrial South Wales had found readiest
expression in the sketches and tales where he balances rural pity and
cruelty against the miserable condition of urban misfits and social outcasts. In his short note to *This England: An Anthology from her Writers*, he
drily admits a possible objection to his rigid definition of 'English'—
'never aiming at what a committee from Great Britain and Ireland
might call complete'. Perhaps his own borderline attitude is best
expressed in his choice of epigraph from Robert of Gloucester for the
second section of his Anthology, about 'Merry England':

> England is a right good land, as I think of all lands best,
> Set here at the world's end, far in the West.

Frost, equally conscious of his own English and Scottish roots—and seeking like his friend the permanent condition that underlay fleeting
activities—was an admirably sympathetic companion as he and Thomas
walked. The inspiration that Thomas believed he owed to Frost, as he
found his way towards becoming a poet, was many-stranded and,
perhaps, needed the sharp concentration of powers that the sudden
onset of a major catastrophe can bring.

Interpreting the meaning of England as a concept worth fighting for,
is a vital undercurrent to Thomas's pre-enlistment verse. It plays a substantial part in the prose that he continued to write until he joined the
Artists' Rifles in July 1915. His first private thoughts on the subject are in
a letter to Frost from Steep on 19 September 1914:

I had a good ride there [to see James Guthrie at Flansham] and back over the
Downs and a swim too in a cold rough sea rather. But I am tired after it and
have only been able to type and add a little rather dully to an article on the
new moon of August 26 and you and me strolling about in the sun while our
brave soldiers &c. I doubt if I shall get nearer soldiering than I did then, chiefly
for fear of leaving many tangles behind and not being able to make new ones
for perhaps a long time. So I probably shall see you before the year's old. I
might go to you on the way back. But I must first see if there is any paid work

to do. I did my English Review article and have just corrected the proof. Your suggestions for others I scorn. Earning a living is a serious business.

'This England' shows how quickly Thomas's thinking veered from the expectation of his friends that he would display no warmongering, as befitted a 'typical Liberal of the Intelligentsia' (Thomas Seccombe). The article, written in September 1914, concludes with a movement passing from clear description of what he loved to a less assertive comment on the implications of that love for himself:

At one stroke, I thought, like many other people, what things that same new moon sees eastward about the Meuse in France. Of those who could see it there, not blinded by smoke, pain, or excitement, how many saw it and heeded? I was deluged, in a second stroke, by another thought, or something that overpowered thought. All I can tell is, it seemed to me that either I had never loved England, or I had loved it foolishly, aesthetically, like a slave, not having realized that it was not mine unless I were willing and prepared to die rather than leave it as Belgian women and old men and children had left their country. Something I had omitted. Something, I felt, had to be done before I could look again composedly at English landscape, at the elms and poplars about the houses, at the purple-headed wood-betony with two pairs of leaves on a stiff stem, who stood sentinel among the grasses or bracken by hedge-side or wood's-edge. What he stood sentinel for I did not know, any more than what I had got to do.

He had added a similar conclusion to his first article for Harrison's *English Review* ('Tipperary', October 1914):

Probably there are two kinds of patriot; one that can talk or write, and one that cannot; though I suspect that even the talkers and writers often come down in the end to 'I do not understand. I love.' It must happen more than once or twice that a man who can say why he ought to fight for his country fails to enlist. The very phrase, 'to fight for one's country', is a shade too poetical and conscious for any but non-combatants. A man enlists for some inexplicable reason which he may translate into simple, conventional terms. If he has thought a good deal about it, he has made a jump at some point, beyond the reach of his thought. The articulate and the inarticulate are united in the ranks at this moment by the power to make that jump and come to the extreme decision.

'Tipperary' was based on a week's journey talking to workmen in pubs and eavesdropping on them. The warm days and heated pavements persisted through Coventry, Birmingham, Sheffield, Manchester, and Newcastle, which he liked best for its bridges and its riverside. ('In fact I never enjoyed a night in any city so much, just for the city's sake and nothing but the city.') He was eager to get back to Helen and the children and by 14 September he had planned an article on 'War Poetry' for Monro's *Poetry and Drama,* because he was still looking for work he could do better perhaps than soldiering. The other options before him had been stated on 3 September to Bottomley: 'It would be a good time for trying America if I could leave Helen and the children with a conscience, but I can't. I should join the Territorials if it didn't mean asking others to keep my family.' On the same day he told Jesse Berridge, 'I am slowly growing into a conscious Englishman.' He was determined to keep his family by his own literary efforts for as long as possible, but the decision to enlist was always before him.

A few significant sentences from letters written between October 1914 and January 1915 indicate his developing mood as he turned to writing verse:

I wish Harry would enlist with me—I do so dread being the oldest bald head in the battalion. (To Janet Hooton, 12 October 1914.)

I have just made myself almost ill with thinking hard for an hour,—going up to my study and sitting there,—that I ought to enlist next week in town. Now I am so weak I wouldn't show anything but my ear to any doctor. I am just going to do that. I go on writing, unlike all the patriots, or rather as the patriots feel they oughtn't to. (To Robert Frost, 31 October 1914.)

There is little work that has to be done, so I do the other kind. [A first reference to his poetry.] Some day you may see it. I kept making excuses for not trying to join the army and know I am made to believe I should probably be refused, but am none the easier for it. (To Bottomley, 19 December|1914.)

I haven't begun to serve my country yet in any way and have had regular crops of reasons against it ever since I saw you. There is not much work of course but I suppose one unconsciously compares lots with those in France and Belgium and elects not to begin complaining yet. (To MacAlister, 26 December 1914.)

I've given up groaning since the war began, I believe, and have been mainly the better for it. But that is the one good effect of the war. It leaves me otherwise rather stranded, tho habits of work keep me up at my study for almost the usual hours. I travel a little more may be. . . . I don't like Bedales folk. All I like is the hills and my study. I don't know where we shall go. But the American plan is by no means off yet. (To Bottomley, 28 December 1914.)

I know an Oxford man of 42 with a wife and 5 children who is addressing envelopes for the War Office at 30/- a week and hasn't a uniform. That would not suit me. I called at the Duke of York's H. Q. but only found there was a Cyclists' Battalion of Territorials at Putney Bridge. I shall enquire about one at

Andover I have heard of. . . . I have an anthology in hand. . . . These little jobs trickling in distract my attention rather. (To Freeman, 1 January 1915.)

A typical response to Thomas's wish 'to do his bit' was made by Frank Cazenove, in early December: 'You startle me by saying you are not sure whether or not you should enlist. This is a matter which every man must settle for himself: but I should have thought your calls were else-where.' Helen and his parents, one reads between the lines, agreed with his literary friends. Thomas was the man least likely to volunteer, although he might have been expected to seek non-combatant work overseas like Garnett, Masefield, and his friend and neighbour Maitland Radford who spent the first year of the war in France as a civilian doctor with the forces and then returned to recuperate in Steep.

Thomas, as usual, spent Christmas with his parents and returned to Steep on 2 January 1915. Rushing down the path from the Shoulder of Mutton to lunch at home, he severely injured an ankle so that he was compelled to spend the next few weeks either in bed or sitting immobil-ized in a chair downstairs in Yew Tree Cottage. There was something odd about his proneness to foot blisters and ankle strain. Some medical friends have suggested to me an incipient diabetic condition as the cause. His letters show that this was a long-drawn-out injury that didn't heal for four months and continued to plague him. He chafed at the inacti-vity in a tiny house without the outlook of his study and within the sound of his own children and a neighbour's boy, 'very often squabbling and my wife overworked, and worst of all with myself always here'. While he was in bed, 'consciously enduring the dull annoyance', he had thoroughly enjoyed drawing for Myfanwy. When boredom set in, he continued work on his 'England' article, read through all his note-books—Poems 17 to 36 in *Collected Poems* were then written—dipped into the *Compleat Angler,* and read a hundred pages of Dostoevsky. The ankle healed very slowly and because John Freeman (like Bottomley) experi-enced bouts of ill-health, he wrote to him often about his own troubles:

Brooding over it these last few months doesn't convince me I should make much more of a soldier than that [i.e. non-combatant occupation at the front] but doesn't leave me either content to be doing practically nothing, tho labori-ously enough, down here. But I am a fool at moving. If only there were somebody I could start with. (16 January 1915.)

It isn't glory I want, but just to get rid of the thoughts I have had since I first felt I ought to do something tho I never felt I could except under what seems a sort of alien compulsion. I hate all crowds. I hate uncertainty. So naturally I hate the idea of being in the army in any capacity. . . . I wish once again a reviewer I could be for the sake of comfort anyhow. (21 January 1915.)

For six weeks after his injury Thomas was unable to 'walk strong' and a great deal happened around him besides the rush of poems and the inner debate for which he finds appropriate words in 'House and Man'— 'A magpie veering about,/A magpie like a weathercock in doubt.' This poem was written immediately before the Frosts' last visit to Steep to discuss the details of Merfyn's journey with them to the USA where he was to live (and learn) with an old family friend and ex-Bedales master, Russell Scott, nephew of C. P. Scott of the *Manchester Guardian*. Frost was prepared to delay their departure another week if Thomas would agree to accompany them, but Edward had already contracted to prepare *This England* quickly and, disliking more and more the anti-war spirit at Bedales, he was thinking of leaving Steep soon in order to be near 'real friends'. In the end, Helen took Merfyn to Liverpool, via London, and he sailed with the Frosts on the American ship *St. Paul* on 13 February 1915. On Helen's return, Edward felt strong enough to spend a fortnight at the British Museum preparing his anthology and staying with his parents while Helen took Myfanwy on a visit to Ivy Ransome. Edward's mother, awaiting an operation for cataract, was gloomy about the war news and perturbed at first about Frost's plans for Edward's visit to New England. Her own sister, Margaret, was still in Los Angeles and some of her own relations (the Tedmans) had earlier spent some time in the States before returning to retire comfortably near Bristol. Mrs Thomas hinted that, once the war was over, she might wish to accompany Edward and his family to New England. Until his enlistment in July 1915, Edward frequently told Robert that only his mother's fears and indifferent health kept him in England.

However, his letters to other friends, though keeping open the option of joining Frost, leave no doubt that three conjectures dominated his thoughts—and crept into his poems as they continued to flow: that he would not pass an army medical examination, except possibly into a Cycle Corps; that if he were to spend four months with Frost his savings would be exhausted so that Bronwen would have to go 'to some very cheap school' and he would have to let 'Merfyn slide rather, unless I had the boldness to have all my savings used up in one year'; and, significantly, that as a substitute for some form of War Service, he would accept only worthwhile writing jobs. *This England* and the *Life of the Duke of Marlborough* fitted into this necessary category, as did his unsuccessful attempt (there were too many competitors) to join the historical section of the War Office.

He could not deceive himself into imagining he would be a new man, either as a farmer-lecturer-journalist in America or teaching English in a school in Coventry, run by C. F. Hodson, former Bedales master, or as a soldier in the Royal Garrison Artillery which, he was later to believe, would accept him in spite of his weak foot. By mid-June, with the anthology and *Marlborough* behind him, he summed up his feelings for Frost after a talk with his mother:

Frankly I do not want to go, but hardly a day passes without my thinking I should. With no call, the problem is endless. It all comes of not believing. I will leave nothing to chance *knowingly*. But, there, I suppose the believers calculate to the best of their ability—It means stepping out alone into company where I should expect to remain alone, with neither faith nor forgetfulness but just a reluctant admission of necessity—How much of it comes of unwillingness to confess I am unfit. [An interesting gloss on his poem *Health,* written in mid-April.]

As long as the two books were on the stocks, with the usual working pattern of long days at the British Museum, of two-way correspondence about the use of possible material, followed by the hard concentrated writing against a deadline, he seemed able to subdue his doubts and to continue with the poems which often demanded to be written, as he made his way up the Hanger to his study, even before he had lit his fire. He thought he had dried up when he began the twenty-six days of continuous writing of *Marlborough* (completed between 16 May and 12 June), but after a week he wrote *Sedge-Warblers*: 'It came of a Sunday with no work but a cycle ride with Bronwen. It is devilish like habit, but I am all rules and evasions.' (To Frost, 23 May 1915.) By this time, possibly disillusioned (but not downhearted) by the refusal of editors to accept his pseudonymous poems—sent out as by 'Edward Eastaway' from the Farjeon home in Fellows Road—he had let some of his close friends into the secret of his verse-making, so far shared only by Helen, Eleanor Farjeon, and Frost. He was determined to use an assumed name because he wished his poems to stand on their merits. He was confident that they would succeed once the reader 'got at them in the right way' without preconceived notions. In fact a quiet confidence in what he was doing during these first six months of 1915 marks a change in his attitude to himself, his work, and his future prospects. 'I hope you are right about "Lob"', he wrote to Bottomley on 16 June. 'I incline to like it best, but about the others I don't know.... I quite feel though that I may have been in a hurry often and that delight in the new freedom—I hope to God it is freedom—has made me too ready to accept intimations merely. Also there is the writing habit. 75,000 words on the Duke in 26 days. But of course I can't be somebody else.... God bless us all, what a thing it is to be nearing 40 and know what one likes and know one makes mistakes and yet is right for oneself.' The buoyant confidence of this letter, with its tell-tale echo of Dad Uzzell's speech, and of many others when he writes about his verses, is a sure indicator that the decision to enlist emerged from a confident, mature man and not from a vacillating failure driven by despair to seek an easy way out of emotional, matrimonial, or financial difficulties.

Frost was not the best of correspondents, but Thomas, obviously pleased with Merfyn's happy progress and even more eager to keep Frost informed of his own thinking, rehearsed repeatedly (in a series of letters in June) the pros and cons of enlisting or coming to America. Helen was in favour of trying America first and then enlisting if it failed. If he were to accept a post as English master at Coventry it would help break the ice for lecturing in Boston. And so it went on—quite distinct from the letters to his English friends—until the final decision to enlist was reported to Frost on 11 July 1915:

Last week I had screwed myself up to the point of believing I should come out to America and lecture if anyone wanted me to. But I have altered my mind. I am going to enlist on Wednesday if the doctor will pass me. I am aiming at the 'Artists Rifles', a territorial battalion, chiefly for training officers. So I must let them make an officer of me if they can. This is easier to do than to come out to you and see what turns up. But it will train me for the greater step.—I wish I could explain how it came about. But I don't quite know.... If I am rejected, then I shall still perhaps come out in September.

The doctor passed Edward Thomas fit for military service on Wednesday, 14 July 1915. He was to be attested in the Artists' Rifles the following Monday and receive his uniform. The MO kept sounding his left side and asked if he had ever had rheumatic fever. He called in on his parents at Rusham Road, wrote off a long letter to Frost, and then returned to Steep to 'clear things up a little and get a walk with Helen on the downs'. He knew Frost would be disappointed. 'If there is anything to forgive you would forgive me, I believe. But I don't feel inclined yet for explaining myself, though if you were here I should.' Frost replied on 8 August, but by then Thomas was sitting in the King's

15. Near his hill-top study at Wick Green, after *In Pursuit of Spring*, 1914.

16. At Steep between visits to Robert Frost, after completing *The Childhood of Edward Thomas*, midsummer 1914.

17. Helen at Steep, 1914.

uniform in the rain with a bad heel. It began with six hours' drill on Tuesday 20 July with a heavy boot pressing on the tendon at the back of his right foot: his feet gave him trouble straight away and the MO placed him on sick leave for a week which he spent largely at his parents' home. (He was billeted there.) Edward was a little bothered and ashamed of his enforced idleness. As he explained to Bottomley—'I want to mend and get on with this. It was not at all a desperate nor yet a purposed resolution but the natural culmination of a long series of moods and thoughts. . . . I was very happy about it and so was Helen, though she was happy perhaps chiefly to see me so clearly resolved and satisfied at once. And now I dread its being upset. But don't mention this to anyone.' With this letter he sent a group of forty poems by 'Edward Eastaway' from which Bottomley selected the eighteen that were eventually published in *An Anthology of New Poetry* in March 1917.

Three weeks passed before Thomas could wear his army boots and 'become a normal soldier'. Meanwhile, he had two reviews to complete; he wrote three short poems and made arrangements with Duckworth, after so many false starts with other firms, for the publication of *Four-and-Twenty Blackbirds* and for the proof-reading of his two books. He saw something of old friends in the free evenings. At home he argued with his over-patriotic father, and arranged to spend as much time as possible with Helen either at Steep or at Rusham Road. Occasionally he met Eleanor Farjeon for tea if she was not 'distributing herself about the country as usual', as he reported to Frost on 9 August 1915 along with his impressions of his first useless weeks as a soldier:

I am rather expecting to go right through my 3 or 4 months training and already wondering what regiment I shall get a commission in. It seems I am too old to get a commission for immediate foreign service. That is, at present. They are raising the age by degrees. As things are now I should spend at any rate some months with my regiment in England and perhaps even find myself in one only for home service. But I want to see what it is like over there. It has made a change. . . . The training makes the body insist on real leisure. . . . I drill, clean rifles, wash out lavatories etc. Soon I shall be standing sentry in the street in my turn. . . . I stand very nearly as straight as a lamp post and apparently get smaller every week in the waist and have to get new holes punched in my belt. The only time now I can think of verses is on sleepless nights, but I don't write them down. Say Thank You.

The habit of versification had slowed down while he learned the craft of a soldier. From December 1914 to 24 May 1915 he had composed seventy-five poems with some regularity. He then settled down to write the *Life of the Duke of Marlborough* within twenty-six days. His next poem, 'I built myself a house of glass', composed at Hucclecote during a visit to Jack Haines on 25 June, was followed quickly by 'Words', 'The Word', 'Under the Wood', 'Haymaking', 'A Dream' (about Frost), 'The Brook' (about Myfanwy), 'Aspens', 'The Mill-Water', and 'For these (A Prayer)'. This last poem immediately preceded his enlistment. He wrote 'Digging (2)', 'Two Houses', and 'Cock-Crow' while his tendon was swollen, and he completed four more poems ('October', 'There's nothing like the sun', 'The Thrush', and 'Liberty') before his Christmas leave, 1915. The bulk of his verse written thereafter as a soldier (Poems 93 to 133) belong to the first eight months of 1916 which he spent as an NCO instructor before he joined the R. A. School at Handel Street in London as an officer cadet. The tone of his letters to Frost and to Bottomley (whom he saw rarely now he was a soldier) and the memorial reports of old friends all support the change in Thomas as Frost expressed it in a letter to Lascelles Abercrombie on 21 September 1915: 'I forgot to mention the war in this letter. And I ought to mention it, if only to remark that I think it has made some sort of new man and a poet out of Edward Thomas.'

How accurate was Frost's belief? Perhaps the apparent metamorphosis of his friend—'He more than any one else was accessory to what I had done and was doing' (Frost to Amy Lowell, 22 October 1917)—was most acceptable to Frost in terms of soldiering and poetry, because he had known Thomas when the English writer was finding himself and his new voice, after two years of indirection. Thomas as we have seen was a more complex person than Frost implies. The much-reported shyness in company is balanced by the equal testimony of friends to his gift of companionship, his hearty singing, and his ironic quips. He fitted smoothly into the domesticity of the Welsh kitchens and front parlours of his friends and relations. He was no shrinking aesthete. The sensitive, extroverted, but much-knocked-about William H. Davies took to Thomas as a brother, very much as the bluff Frost had done. The warm tributes paid to Thomas by friends of many different natures, who had all known him for at least a decade longer than Frost or Eleanor Farjeon, assert that periods of morbid melancholy, or brooding, formed a tiny part of the complete man they recalled. Some of them, especially Garnett, Bottomley, Ernest Rhys, and W. H. Hudson had long urged Thomas to think of himself as essentially a poet.

The course of his decision to enlist, determined from the beginning to see what it was like 'over there', can almost be charted day by day in

his numerous letters to friends. The final decision was neither as melo-
dramatic nor as simplistic as Eleanor Farjeon's account of his reply to
her question, 'Do you know what you are fighting for?': 'He stooped,
and picked up a pinch of earth. "Literally, for this." He crumbled it
between finger and thumb, and let it fall.' I prefer to accept that his shyness, like his frequent use of irony, was the obverse side of an extreme
caution in arriving at final judgement in practical, intellectual, or emotional matters. He understood only too well how susceptible he was to
the impact of powerful moods of despair, or to sheer natural and human
beauty. There was, too, his pride in his capacity to provide for the needs
of his family. 'Of course I know I shouldn't starve [in the USA] and that
is all I can say of literary life here. I could not ask my father for anything. He has no more than he needs, though it is true that he and my
mother have more or less undertaken to look after my family if—.' (To
Frost, 22 July 1915.) He was not insensitive to the part played by non-
rational forces in reaching decisions. He had spent too many hours in
solitary walking to be immune to the promptings of the subconscious
mind and some of this awareness was shown in his *Maurice Maeterlinck.*
One recalls, too, a 1946 memoir by Jesse Berridge, who had been on a
cycling tour with Thomas between the ending of *Marlborough* and his
enlistment: 'He had the most exquisite expression of thought of any man
I ever knew, but there was something in him ever inexpressible.' This
was a tribute based on the sustained friendship of fifteen years and it is
borne out by de la Mare, a long-standing friend of both men. His closest
friends were accustomed to his forthright denial that he had any gift for
poetry: they were convinced when they saw Thomas's verse that this was
the only medium in which he could possibly give full rein to the qualities of mind they knew he possessed but had rarely seen in his prose.

Thomas's best prose could stand on its own without much support
from narrative or argument. A few passages written in 1909 suggest that,
long before he was a soldier, he had given sufficient evidence of his
move towards poetry:

Some of these scenes [i.e. of different kinds of Edens or Golden Ages], whether
often repeated or not, come to have a rich symbolical significance; they return
persistently and, as it were, ceremoniously—on festal days—but meaning I know
not what. . . . Something in me belongs to these things, but I hardly think that
the mere naming of them will mean anything except to those—many, perhaps—
who have experienced the same. A great writer so uses the words of everyday
that they become a code of his own which the world is bound to learn and in
the end take to itself.

Literature sends us to nature principally for joy, joy of the senses, of the whole frame, of the contemplative mind, and of the soul, joy which if it is found complete in these several ways might be called religious. Science sends us to Nature for knowledge. Industrialism and the great town send us to Nature for health, that we may go on manufacturing efficiently, or, if we think right and have the power, that we may escape from it. But it would be absurd to separate joy, knowledge, and health. . . . Joy, through knowledge, on a foundation of health, is what we appear to seek.

[Richard Jefferies] has mounted from being a member of a class, at first indistinguishable from it, then clearly more enlightened, but still of it, and seeing things in the same way, up to the position of a poet with an outlook that is purely individual, and, though deeply human, yet of a spirituality now close as the grass, and now as the stars. (E. T.'s introduction to Jefferies, *The Hills and the Vales,* p. xxxi.)

Certainly 'joy, through knowledge, on a foundation of health' is a desideratum that emerged after he became absorbed in writing verses with such a sense of freedom. As he said in an off-the-cuff aside to Bottomley—'But of course I can't be somebody else.' At last he had come to terms with his variable moods.

His interest in theories about 'cosmic consciousness' had first been aroused as he prepared his study of Richard Jefferies, then reviewed Traherne's *Centuries of Meditation* and, a few years later, re-read some standard works on mysticism as he wrote *Maurice Maeterlinck.* Thomas never laid claim to any form of mystical experience, although W. H. Hudson wrote in 1922 that 'the chief reason of the bond uniting us was that we were both mystics in some degree'. He was quick to deny Berridge's attempt—after reading *The Stile*—to label him *anima naturaliter Christiana.* However, like Chaucer and Keats he was thoroughly aware of, and at home in, the world of dream experience, and two of his lesser-known prose pieces, *A Sportsman's Tale* (1909–10) and *The Chessplayer,* with its condemnation of the cosmic indifference of the Jehovah-like Chessplayer, read like despair. Yet they celebrate a deep love of the earth.

Every inch of the misty earth was alive, breathing, moving, taking colour, and it crouched there beside the pale quiet sea with looks and speech of unfathomable love. The villages and cities, though they put forth no flowers or songs, sent up something which did not dissolve in the rain as their smoke dissolved, a something that floated up like an *aubade* of earth to heaven, but not to the old man. . . . I knelt there a long age, in the belief that my bent stillness was protecting that sweet moment of earth from his awful hand.

Two years earlier, in *A Sportman's Tale,* Thomas had combined the actual experience of a reunion with his old friend Arthur Hardy, after ten years spent in South Africa, with a dream sequence about the Elysian Fields, where the world of Chaucer's *Book of the Duchess* or *The House of Fame* is tinged with a Darwinian flavour in spite of its Dante-like journeying.

What could men do here? They could not be content to sing and feast with these myriads, so they are turned into flowers and into the wandering clouds and the winds, and so their hot spirits are calmed and cooled and humbled and taught to forget, while those other creatures pass from one world to another as out of one field into the next and are content to know no difference, save that there are few men. Rapt by that unceasing motion of adoration I could have stood for ever as still as the quiet beasts, but the thought came over me to kneel upon the grass, and as I knelt I tasted the scent again of the autumn grass, and burst into tears, falling face downwards upon the earth and lying there listening to the wings. So soft and deep and warm and sweet scented was the grass that I forgot the god.

Thomas's many notebooks confirm that he was early aware of a tenuous connection between his out-of-doors adolescent experiences—which he recognized in Jefferies as some form of mysticism—and the vivid world of his own reveries. He catches one of these experiences in *The Moon* (first published posthumously in *Cloud Castle and other papers* in 1922), as he tries to convey his seeing of

. . . light on a portion of the trunk of one tree only in the dark wood. Low down it was like a fire burning without a sound or a motion, and no figures of men around it. . . . It was a pure accident: there was no one whatever to see, and the moonlight was playing alone among the trees. If I had fancied it was playing for me and that I imagined the playing it would have been different. It would not have been the same if it had amused me: it was no more amusing than the majesty of the moon. I suppose I was near to imagining a deity with as little anthropomorphism as possible, certainly without personification.

These tales, and half a dozen like them, are stations along the road that pointed unequivocally towards quiet-toned unassertive poetry, presented scrupulously in 'a language not to be betrayed'.

In the first autumn of the War, as we have seen, significant changes were noted in Thomas's attitude to his life and work. His eager concern of the previous four years with essays and sketches was put to one side, along with his growing investigation of proverbs as a source of folk memory, his flower anthology, his imaginary Wales, and even his unsatisfactory *A Literary Pilgrim in England* which, he had once hoped, would conjoin his love of poetry with his interest in man in his native surroundings. The new journalist path of his wartime articles, although undertaken for commercial reasons, was pursued in the detached spirit of his early work as a young naturalist in *The Woodland Life*—as indeed it was continued later in France with his War Diary. His powers of observation, with an ear attuned to conversational vitality, seemed to lead him directly to interpret reactions to the wider issues of war and patriotism. And finally, as his poetry gushed out—breaking through a dam of prose description that preceded the composition of 'Up in the Wind' and 'Old Man'—the same enquiring preoccupation enabled him to prepare *This England*, to write articles on war and poetry for Monro, and to complete his life of Marlborough, almost as a substitute for enlistment while his ankle injury was slowly healing. During these early war months his reviews of William Morris, Bridges, Masefield and Gibson—like his memorial article on Brooke for *The Bookman*—are characterized by a sharp, confident tone. There is no suggestion here that he enlisted because he could not make a living as a literary journalist in wartime England.

Frost's repeated request that Thomas should try his fortune in New England had compelled him, as we have seen, to articulate what England meant to him and to others. It was natural to his temperament to regard things (and even to entitle his books) from two contrasting sides. In the end, when he had decided for enlistment and against New England, he seemed taken by surprise. The subsequent change in him surprised all his friends—but only gradually did they discover the change from prose to verse that had preceded the entry into soldiering. There, too, he acted as he had done in 1909–10 when he was 'seized' by the creative urge to write *Rest and Unrest* and *Light and Twilight*. Thomas could not have been blind to the similarity of experience, once his verse 'began to run'. He needed no prompting to continue with the new medium for which he had so well prepared himself. His critical good sense did not desert him and he was rarely diverted by the cavillings of friends or by rejection slips. His only hope was that the urge would continue. An exhibition of his new-found confidence came when he inserted, pseudonymously, two of his own poems—'Manor Farm' (24 December 1914) and 'Haymaking' (early in June 1915)—in order to fill up two extra pages required for *This England*. This was no frivolous decision: he was already halfway through his entire poetic output. Reading both poems today, one can see how admirably they reflect much of his past prose descriptive writing, and give expression to the timeless quality of a Constable painting. The eye sees clearly, as his *English Review* articles did, and the illusory pagan, early British, or medieval dream worlds have been replaced by things one can see and touch and share directly—exactly as his knowledge of Dad Uzzell emerges with clarity from the proverbial character of 'Lob':

> But one glimpse of his back, as there he stood,
> Choosing his way, proved him of old Jack's blood,
> Young Jack perhaps, and now a Wiltshireman
> As he has oft been since his days began.

Similarly, in 'The Combe' he was able to find the precise words that corresponded to the slight dilemma that confronted him when, as a man of Welsh origins, he settled down to compile an anthology of English writers. He defined the badger as 'That most ancient Briton of English beasts'. As he wrote his poems Thomas found no difficulty in maintaining a life-long consistency of attitude: the six months between 'Manor Farm' and 'Haymaking' are irrelevant. They are presented as a matching pair:

> Rather a season of bliss unchangeable
> Awakened from farm and church where it had lain
> Safe under tile and thatch for ages since
> This England, Old already, was called Merry.
>
> ('Manor Farm')

> Under the heavens that know what years be
> The men, the beasts, the trees, the implements
> Uttered even what they will in times far hence—
> All of us gone out of the reach of change—
> Immortal in a picture of an old grange.
>
> ('Haymaking')

Charged with the vision of an imaginative archaeologist, Thomas could see, as from an aeroplane, the pattern of time past leading through the present into the future. The onset of war had compelled him to channel his gifts and brought them rapidly to unforeseen maturity.

CHAPTER 15

Edward Eastaway

In September 1913 Edward Thomas had abandoned an attempt to write a companion book to his monograph *The Country*. Its title was *Ecstasy*. He had begun it in the spirit of *Orpheus: A Quarterly Magazine of Imaginative Art*, edited by his friend and well-wisher, the theosophist Clifford Bax. This was a heady magazine with a quotation from Hafiz on the title page, together with a long dedication of its aims which 'does not necessarily apply to all who contribute to this paper':

We are a group of artists who revolt against the materialism of most contemporary art. . . . We wish to approach with an equal sympathy the methods of East and West; to combat the conception that beauty of theme is essential to art; to find expression for the noblest moods of the modern soul, and thus in a complicated and restless age to create an atmosphere in which the spiritual self may breathe, delight, and grow strong.

There is no contribution by Thomas to *Orpheus* after October 1913 and his initial approach to *Ecstasy*—and his abandoning it—was part of the process of self-scrutiny that preceded his meetings with Frost and the subsequent beginnings of his own verse:

I myself was in favour of ecstasy. It was my name for the faculty in man which came nearest to being, for aught I knew, illimitable and divine. If I envied anyone it would have been the poets who could declare, and that in words capable of making me nothing but ear and soul, as the great Persian did,—that they were neither Christians, nor Jews, nor Moslems: that they were not of country, east or west, not of land or sea, not of this world or the next, of Paradise or of Hell; because their place was the Placeless, and because, belonging to the soul of the Beloved, they were neither body nor soul; they had seen that the two worlds were one, they had put away duality; they were drunken with Love's cup; theirs it was to revel and carouse; if they had ever spent a moment without Love they repented it; they trampled on both worlds, they danced in triumph for ever, they told no tales but of drunkenness and revelry. If I had been so bold, in a world where ideas of perfectability are mawkish, as to imagine a perfect state, I think it would have been ecstasy with its companions liberty, sanguine, generous energy, the 'faith to eat all things', the flow of spirits and speech, alternating with the stillest quiet.

My chief ground and qualification for this choice was my intimate and long-standing aquaintance with the opposite of ecstasy. I knew so well the 'grief without a pang' described with some flattery in Coleridge's Dejection; so often had griefs not without a pang appeared to me almost as delights by comparison; so often had I looked at things, unless I am mistaken, as the poet was doing when he said:

> I see them all so excellently fair,
> I see, not feel, how beautiful they are.

Nor was I entirely ignorant of that extreme lack of ecstasy which, as in this poem, becomes something like ecstasy itself—of the state only a little removed from ecstasy, when that remoteness, real or imagined, produces grief. In that state the soul desires to feel, with a perhaps inhuman, angelic intensity, how beautiul things are. It cries out on Life as Whitman did on Hymen: 'O Hymen, Hymeneall, why do you sting me for one short moment only?' It is willing to change minds with one in Bedlam because of his 'rapt gaze' and his 'dreams divine'.

From there on the manuscript examines the relationship between madness and artistic expression and is much influenced by his concurrent reading of *The Brothers Karamazov* and *The Idiot*. In his usual fashion, Thomas was slowly deciding to change the direction of his work without any clear plan. Staying with Godwin Baynes in early September 1913 he was 'sick of talking books'; when Clifford and Arnold Bax and Bertie Farjeon came to lunch he felt himself 'an elderly literary outsider'. A fortnight later he felt 'cured of the ambition to do Ecstasy and must seek for something more profane and more suitable for a material of insubstantial pen'. But his notebooks for the next few months contain the typescript of an essay on 'Passion in contemporary fiction', dated 7 October 1913, and many short notes that seem to anticipate, or to give in outline and in snatches, the raw material and first drafts of poems that began to flow between December 1914 and June 1915:

The woods only a little darker than bare, as if in another world—a reflection—but darker and clearer than the Downs and winding white hill beyond—between it and which runs pale amount of smoke occasionally. Very silent. I forget all that I know about earth, Grove, Green etc. as I look at this lovely soft sweet remoteness. (18 October 1913.)

How different two days ago when I looked from a highish road (or from railway near Wareham) over a houseless lowish but hollowed wooded country, nothing but graduations of inhuman dark (beginning to get misty at nightfall) as of an underworld and my soul fled over it experiencing the after death—friendless, vacant, hopeless. (17 December 1913.)

One of those eternal evenings—the wind gone, no one upon the road. I grasp the stately tall holly or look over the ploughland to the near ridge, the

crocketed spruces, the dark house mass, and behind them a soft dulling
flame-coloured sky where large shapeless soft dull dark clouds in roughly horizontal lines are massing with one bright star in an interstice—and far behind
me an owl calls again and again and somewhere far to one side in a hid hollow a dog barks and, nearer, one or two blackbirds climb as they fly along
hedges. What does it mean? I feel an old inhabitant of earth at such times. How
many hundred times have I seen the same since I was 15. (18 December 1913.)

These private musings become a habit as he seems to be preparing
himself for poetry. The notebooks cease when he enlists and are replaced
by two hard-covered pocket books, easy to conceal in the rather public
life of a soldier in barracks and better suited to writing in trains. It seems
that the fundamental change of course from his 'own kind of [prose]
writing' to the new habit of versification, which often took precedence
over the bread-and-butter claims of his preparation for his *Life of Marlborough*, was maturing subconsciously for at least a year before he noted
triumphantly to Frost, on 15 December 1914:

> But I am in it and no mistake. I have an idea and am full enough but that
> my bad habits and customs and duties of writing will make it rather easy to
> write when I've no business to. At the same time I find myself engrossed and
> conscious of a possible perfection as I never was in prose. Also I'm very impa-
> tient of my prose, and of reviews and of review books. And yet I have been
> uncommonly cheerful mostly. I have been rather pleased with some of the
> pieces, of course, but it's not wholly that. Still, I won't begin thanking you just
> yet, though if you like I will put it down now that you are the only begetter
> right enough.

Of the nine poems sent to Frost with this letter—'Up in the Wind',
'November Sky', 'March', 'The Signpost', 'The Other', 'After Rain', 'Interval', 'Birds' Nests', and 'The Mountain chapel'—only two are in direct
imitation of Frost's poetry. The remainder can be traced to notebook
prose jottings. Two quotations illustrate the change in attitude that had
taken place in Thomas. One is from 'The Signpost':

> I read the sign. Which way shall I go?
> A voice says: You would not have doubted so
> At twenty. Another voice gentle with scorn
> Says: At twenty you wished you had never been born.

The second is from 'The Other', where the questing speaker comments
on a moment of 'natural magic':

> The last light filled a narrow firth
> Among the clouds. I stood serene,

And with a solemn quiet mirth,
An old inhabitant of earth.

Once the name I gave to hours
Like this was melancholy, when
It was not happiness and powers
Coming like exiles home again,
And weakness quitting their bowers,
Smiled and enjoyed, far off from men,
Moments of everlastingness.
And fortunate my search was then
While what I sought, nevertheless,
That I was seeking, I did not guess.

This last stanza echoes Thomas's constant assertion during his first six months as a soldier that he had never felt better in his life or more balanced. Twice in the course of 1915 he assumed new identities. In late February, the name 'Edward Eastaway' was added in manuscript by Helen, Eleanor, and once by himself, to poems submitted to editors. In August, he reminded his friends: 'I am now Private P. E. Thomas 4229'. Curiously, his earliest nature articles appeared under 'P. E. Thomas', and the fly-leaf of a presentation copy of *Rose Acre Papers* is inscribed 'to E. S. P. Haynes from P(hilip) E(Edward) Thomas'.

During this gradual preparation for a poet's work he relied heavily on his wife and family, and drew on the goodwill of his friends. But once he reached a decision, he held firmly to it. He was pleased with his verse. At first only Helen and Eleanor Farjeon (who typed them and acted as a post-box address when they were sent to editors) knew of them. He read them aloud in the late evening hour with Helen before bed. Subsequently, they were sent to Frost, John Freeman, Monro, Guthrie, Locke Ellis, and Bottomley. Davies read them during a visit to Steep and then Harry Hooton and Jesse Berridge received copies. Thomas was adamant that they should be published anonymously, yet eager that they should be seen by the friends to whom he had opened his heart in recent years. The happy pseudonym Edward Eastaway, a link with the cross-channel Devon–Wales sea-traffic that figures so much in the history of families settled along the coast of Glamorgan and Dyfed, was eventually decided upon. Every poem published during his life-time carried this name, including the first printing of *Poems* in 1917 by Roger Ingpen. Frost was against pseudonymity, but respected it until the poet's father revealed the true name in April 1917. Afterwards Ingpen—and others—followed suit. Thomas's express reason for the pseudonym was that he did not wish his poems to be treated favourably by friends who would review them. His resolve was perhaps stiffened by the cool reception given them by a few editors, by Monro, by Davies and Locke Ellis, and the initially guarded replies of Freeman and Bottomley. He himself was quite sure of their value and was pleased when respected judges like Edward Garnett and Bottomley applauded some of his own favourites.

Somehow, too, the adoption of 'Edward Eastaway' reflected the two-year-long search for a true identity, which, inevitably for him, involved the past of his own family. A pseudonym was linked with the slow process of maturation that was a guiding principle in all his decisions, once some change of direction was necessary. It is difficult to accept immediately this side of his nature because his early biographers, with direct access to people who knew him well, had concentrated on the apparent uncertainty of his two years as the Walking Tom of the friendly caricature. Despite all his own disclaimers, Thomas knew what he was about in his private, life-long struggle to be worthy of the name of poet. It was a title he venerated and he had judged most contemporary versifiers by an idealized conception of what a poet should be. The ideal was given early shape in a paper published in *The Speaker* in August 1899, a paper on 'Natural Magic in Shelley', read before the Davenant Society later that year. The significant passage is a long speech by a dying man about 'Our Lady of Pain':

> That was at the time when I used to pass whole days without a word, except conventional greetings: and when I did speak, that was no exchange of thought. I could only talk in monologue. Secluded and musing on my own central self, and on 'Nature', I was unaccustomed to thoughts. Indeed the artists of my dreams and reveries were painters, not poets; life being rather a succession of pictures than ideas. . . . And when we consider how much of the daytime most people spend in silence, and how much of the night, we must admit the loneliness of men; far far more than half their lives are devoted to silence.

Reading these early papers one wonders at his frequent refusal, during the next fifteen years, to admit that he was capable of writing verse.

Until he met Frost, the assurance of friends was insufficient to induce him to 'let himself go'. When the change took place the assumption of a persona, Edward Eastaway, seemed an appropriate gesture to mark the change. As we can now see, his life as a soldier encouraged his commitment to poetry. He was less happy about his father's attitude to the war. 'My father is so rampant in his cheery patriotism that I become pro-German every evening. We can never so beat the Germans that they will cease to remember their victories. Pom-Pom. I am sorry. The post interrupted this with a letter from Miss Farjeon who is distributing her-self about the country as usual.'

He stood up to daily drill without further problems, and often met friends at lunchtime or for tea before returning to Balham for his evening meal. He completed an index for his *Marlborough* and corrected the proofs of *Four-and-Twenty Blackbirds*. He liked the physical drill and worked hard at an army pamphlet on Company Training. He was anx-ious to get to camp to complete musketry training but, more especially, to get to know better the men he was with. 'They don't seek me more than I do them and I am a good deal alone in our minutes of ease.' But he was able to spend frequent week-end leaves at Steep, to set the garden there, and to picnic with Helen and Myfanwy. At the end of six weeks' training, while living with his parents and spending six or seven hours a day in the drill hall, or in Regent's Park, he found it 'very dull defending ones wives and mothers and sisters and daughters from the Germans'. Except for the Marlborough proofs to correct it was more like a holiday. He still felt himself 'an undigested lump in this battalion' but had no doubts about his decision to enlist. He explained to Frost why he could not accept a proposal by Garnett and others that he should have been seconded to a propaganda lecture-tour instead of enlistment:

They see me as a rather helpless person who needs to make money for a family and I let them go on seeing me so. Yes. I knew right away that for me to act as if I were a smart literary bloke and get my coming advertised as such would be rather worse than being such in fact, I should have penalised my real self heav-ily by trying to live up to it. As a matter of fact I shouldn't have tried. . . . Nobody persuaded me into this, not even myself.

Despite his age, he hoped to be in France, as an officer, in the New Year. He made arrangements for Merfyn to return from the USA in December and he was looking forward to Christmas as never before. He found it 'all like being somebody else, or like being in a dream of school'. Even the country seemed 'a little strange to me. It seems as if in my world there was no Autumn though they are just picking hops in Kent.'

For a time his verse-making had stopped. He had sent poems to Bot-tomley who had shown Abercrombie his 'English Words' and that led eventually to the appearance of eighteen of his poems in *An Anthology of New Poetry*. There were other compensations to set against the dulling routine of early military training. He visited Ian MacAlister, who was now an officer in the Territorials, and gleaned a few tips on drilling a platoon and, when they were not at Steep, his family collected at his

parents' home: 'It is a London Sunday, and the loveliest warm bright
weather after a cold bright hazy morning that ever was in September.
Bronwen and I have just walked 4 or 5 miles of streets and crowds. I
stand it better with her but it is pretty bad—all the mean or villa streets
that have filled the semi-rural places I knew 25 years ago. It is tiring.' He
was ready for a more distinctive change.

The move to a camp at High Beech, in good weather amid the forest
oaks and beeches, soured him a little at first. There was too much un-
military work to be done—'digging drains, carpentering, digging clay
and spading it into a cart, with a bully over us'—when officers were soon
needed in Flanders. 'Apparently any man who will stand up and get shot
is useful however hurried his training.' Letters from Frost, with favourable news of Merfyn and literary gossip, helped to break the solitude
and tiredness he still felt and, although his *Keats* and *Marlborough, This
England,* and 'the Proverbs' were due out in October 1915, he was disinclined to look at print and he didn't write verse: 'Perhaps I should', he
wrote to Frost, 'if I had an interval as I did when my foot was bad. (It
gives me no trouble now except to put on a slight bandage daily.) But
while this work is on I find it hard to do many things I used to do. The
compensation is that I neither read nor want to read.' Because his skill as
a map-reader had already been noticed at the London HQ of the Artists'
Rifles, he reported to Frost a remote chance that he might be used as an
instructor of some kind. 'I am rather loth to entertain the idea, partly
because now I have taken the step the only way to satisfy my vanity is to
become an officer and go out.'

He returned to London HQ in late October. His duties were not
exacting, and along with frequent short leaves at Steep he resumed the
entertainment of old literary friends, either at St. George's Restaurant on
Tuesdays and Thursdays at 5 or in the smoking-room at the back of
Lyons, near Burton Road and Tottenham Court Road. With new confidence he agreed to become an instructor, training young officers for
the Artists' Rifles at the large Hare Hall Camp, near Romford, Essex.
While waiting for the transfer to his new base he began his duties in
London, writing to Frost:

I am a Lance-corporal now, instead of private. This means a schoolmasterish
life. I (and several others) help the men during lectures, explaining, doing their
problems for them &c., and sometimes taking them out on Hampstead Heath
and showing them how to sketch a map with the help of the prismatic compass
and a little mathematics. Thus I got my first practice in giving orders and gradually I get less confidential in tone. Possibly they may want me to stick to this

job indefinitely. Map reading and the use of the compass are very important for tactics and artillery work, and all officers are supposed to be able to do a useful map or field sketch to scale on the spot in quick time, so there have to be instructors and if I can feel myself useful I can (if I wish) give up or postpone my intention of taking a commission. At any rate I shall not be a commissioned officer as soon as I thought. But I expect I shall find it easy to decide before very long to give up the instructor's job and take a commission, unless it seems pure vanity to do so. I mean that strictly speaking it is more reasonable to remain at home doing necessary work that I can do than going out and trying my hand at something that perhaps I can't do. On the other hand it isn't easy to know whether the doubt in mind is due to a feeling that I ought to go out as an officer or simply to the knowledge that most people will think less of me as a corporal at home than a lieutenant abroad.

At Steep, on unofficial leave, he was philosophical about his recently published books. 'They are getting friendly, useless reviews. But who cares?' His mind was on more immediate things and on 6 November he summarized his mood for Bottomley now that hopes of a commission were delayed:

. . . in a week or so we are off to another camp, probably at Romford. Nobody wants to go, least of all I, as I can see people I want to in London. Still, in camp I found I could get on with people I had nothing in common with and almost get fond of them. As soon as we were in London the bond was dissolved and we had blank looks for one another. . . . I am now a lance corporal (L. Cpl. P. E. Thomas, 4229) and an assistant instructor in map-reading. I help to look over men's work and take a squad of 20 or so out on Hampstead Heath to take bearings and sketch a map on the spot etc. The experience is very useful whether I am to stay on as an instructor or to take a commission later. I don't know yet which I shall choose, supposing I am free to choose. . . . Once when I had a bad knee I got 20 lines written and felt as I used to, which is more than I dare do as a rule. It is curious how the mind steadily refuses to hanker after what it knows is absolutely forbidden for (it believes) a comparatively short time. So far I don't think I have resented or regretted anything or longed for the impossible.

At this time Thomas keeps suggesting in his letters that he might well return to peaceful civilian life within a year or so. He expected to profit by his army experience as an instructor, if he joined Frost in New Hampshire. In the same belief, he discussed plans to prepare with J. C. Smith an anthology of narrative verse for the Oxford University Press. He certainly outlined a selected list of poems for such a volume but, once he had settled in at Hare Hall Camp after mid-November 1915, routine tasks absorbed his time and energy and, initially at least, he found the congenial company he had lacked so far and so much desired. He wrote repeatedly that he never was so well or in so balanced a mood and assured Frost he 'was quite vain with satisfaction at doing what I did four months ago: it is just four months. I don't look ahead with any anxiety. I just look forward without a thought to something, I don't know what, I don't speculate what.'

· At this time, the 'Household Poems' (to his family) began to take shape. He was more than ever solicitous for Helen and keenly aware of her deep apprehension. Behind his constant efforts to keep in close touch with all his friends whenever such excursions were possible, Helen at Steep and his mother at Rusham Road remained at the centre of his subconscious concern for the past and his unexpressed hopes for the future. As always, he lifts the veil of privacy a little for Frost:

I wonder would you recognise me with hair cropped close and carrying a thin little swagger cane: many don't who meet me unexpectedly, and they say I never looked so well in health. Now you will think me getting over to the other extreme of complacency. But I am not. Coming in home last night after walking home fast in the rain at 10 and finding the place upside down and Helen almost as much scared and surprised as pleased to see me, I went down plump to the old level. I had been too eager and enjoyed the rain too much—with solitary excitement. Does one really get rid of things at all by steadily inhibiting them for a long time on end? Is peace going to awaken me as it will so many from a drugged sleep? Am I indulging in the pleasure of being someone else?

I have got to be off early tomorrow to pack and get ready and see a little of my mother before leaving her alone. My father is away and the only brother living at home [Reggie] is also in the Artists and going to camp with me on Monday.

The regular pattern of life at Hare Hall Camp pleased him: he had begun real work again. He was in charge of ten to twelve men for five days on end, trying to teach them the elements of map-reading, field sketching (at which he was himself unusually expert and even thought he might illustrate some of his own work after the war), and the use of a compass and protractor. Officer/cadet Wilfred Owen, Artists' Rifles, who arrived at Hare Hall Camp on 15 November, may well have been one of those instructed by Edward Thomas. There was a new intake each week and, until things tightened up in the New Year, Edward had plenty of opportunities for official (and unofficial) weekend leave. Though pay was only one shilling a day, he decided to postpone thoughts of a commission if he continued to like the work and found himself of use. At Steep on weekend pass he did some gardening, chopped wood, and lit a fire in his study. He was able to visit Hodson at Coventry and arrange for Merfyn to live there on his return from America, to attend Hodson's school for two terms before taking up an engineering apprenticeship which would be arranged by his Uncle Theodore. With Helen he spent half a day in late December waiting to welcome Merfyn from his American trip. Merfyn missed the train. Edward was eager to enjoy some leave at Christmas: 'I have never had more than two days at home on end since I joined five months ago, and that only twice.'

He was busy, too, fending off the embarrassing offer of lavish Christmas gifts from Eleanor Farjeon and her family: another sign of growing self-confidence. He was less prickly with some of his literary friends and agreed to let de la Mare and Garnett put things in motion for a grant from the Civil List. Once more he was beginning to write verse, 'as soon as I get really free with nothing close before me to do ... I am always just a little more outside things than most of the others and without being made to feel so at all acutely. They aren't surprised whether I come in or stay out of a group.' He was establishing the pattern of relationship with others by which his fellow officers and men remembered him after his death: the fatherly figure, friendly if taciturn, detached but ready to join in company whenever he felt like it, strict in rebuke, and extremely competent in his specialist and general duties. Life at Hare Hall was congenial to the poet in him. After a slow start in late 1915, he composed over forty poems there before he left in August 1916 to train as an officer-cadet with the Royal Artillery.

The last poem of 1915, like so many of its immediate successors, is a response to an immediate incident that leads back into his past. He gives Frost an unvarnished account of the origins of 'This is no case of petty right or wrong' and 'P.H.T.', which followed five weeks later:

In town I saw my father too, and he made me very sick. He treats me so that I have a feeling of shame that I am alive. I couldn't sleep after it. Nothing much happened. We argued about the war and he showed that his real feeling when he is not trying to be nice and comfortable is one of contempt. I know what contempt is and partly what I suffered was from the reminder that I had probably made Helen feel exactly the same. I came more readily back to camp than ever before. I shall recover; but it makes a difference and I am inclined not to see him again for a time.

The arguments about the war are similar to those in his *English Review* articles and in his letters while preparing the anthology *This England*. The bitterness against his father, and the boomerang-like self-reproach, together with the operation on his mother's eye for cataract, induced the series of family poems that appeared during the next three months. Perhaps the release from the habit of using thinly disguised *personae* in his prose explains the more direct manner with which he manipulated the 'I' of his poems, combining retrospection, and a realistic glance into future uncertainties, with insistent probes into the nature of love, affection, and lust:

> But here I pray that none whom once I loved
> Is dying tonight or lying still awake
> Solitary, listening to the rain,
> Either in pain or thus in sympathy
> Helpless among the living and the dead.

This poem, 'Rain', like so many of his poems at Hare Hall, was sketched out in a notebook and worked over on the way home to Steep in a slow cross-country train. Once a poem had been read aloud to Helen, it was sent to Eleanor Farjeon for her expert typing. Poems like 'Roads', 'The Ash Grove', 'These things that poets said', 'The Unknown', 'Tall Nettles', 'As the team's head brass', 'Bob's Lane', echo experiences in his nature and travel books; but many more seem to spring directly from a dream or from his imagination unobtrusively at work as he settled into the military routine without much immediate questioning or responsibility for the pattern it was following.

Thomas was a conscientious instructor with no intention of staying in a soft option longer than he thought necessary. The poetry began to flow because he had time on his hands, the certitude that he had something worth saying, and the conviction that he had found the appropriate medium for things he had long sought to express. Towards the end of his stay at Hare Hall, his poems deal more directly with the undertones of war. The long shadow of the Battle of the Somme fell soberly upon a camp that prepared young officers in a never-ending stream for active service overseas. A poem written on 23 June 1916 begins

> There was a time when this poor frame was whole
> And I had youth and never another care,
> Or none that should have troubled a strong soul.

and ends

But now that there is something I could use
My youth and strength for, I deny the age,
The care and weakness that I know—refuse
To admit I am unworthy of the wage
Paid to a man who gives up eyes and breath
For what can neither ask nor heed his death.

This seems a morbid exercise in that melancholic introspection that had dogged him in civilian life and, so he believed, earned him the contempt of others:

Weakness was all my boast.
I sought yet hated pity till at length
I earned it.

Here are the first signs of his decision in July and August 1916 to apply for a commission in the Royal Artillery. Our attention is directed to the manner in which he yielded to the imaginative compulsion to use this lattermath growth of verse as an *Apologia pro vita sua,* without rhetoric, in the poem beginning 'I never saw that land before':

and if I could sing
What would not even whisper my soul
As I went on my journeying,

I should use, as the trees and birds did,
A language not to be betrayed;
And what was hid should still be hid
Excepting from those like me made
Who answer when such whispers bid.

There were distinct phases to the life at Hare Hall Camp that corresponded to the ebb and flow of events in the battlefields elsewhere. In mid-January 1916 he was transferred to a new company, had to appear on parade first thing in the morning with pack and rifle, and then move around for an hour before his instructing work began. Thomas was now in complete charge of the twenty men in his hut and soon got into trouble for not reporting the late arrival of the artist John Wheatley from weekend leave. This error cost him his second stripe and probably delayed the eventual promotion to sergeant which might have proved to him that his work as an instructor was valued and was worth doing. Leave thereafter was less frequent and the two mile out-of-bounds rule was more strictly enforced: but he and a few friends found pleasant walks and, when they had a day off, they could visit friends nearby.

Thomas made careful arrangements for his London friends to visit him at camp. His own equanimity surprised him, writing to Frost: 'Until you know a new man fairly well you think of him simply as a soldier. I daresay I have been mistaken for one myself. Well, I can keep step and set a step too, and though I dislike inflicting discipline I can submit to it pretty well and don't ask questions so often as many do or complain of the unreasonableness of rules, of the war, of life and so on.' And there was the added bonus of his good singing voice and love of songs: 'Coming home in the twilight at the end of our day's work, we four instructors march in the rear of the platoon (30 to 60 men) and sing together "Mr. John Blunt" and one or two other songs of mine. They all like "As I was a-walking down Paradise Street" but you can't march to it.' It all helped to relieve the tedium of the weekends spent in camp. 'These are the worse days. The only real cure is to get quite alone and write. I can sometimes get the hut empty and write. Then I sometimes write in the train going home late. I must send you one or two recent verses. "Lob" and "Words" are to appear in a big hotchpotch called *Form* in March. Otherwise I keep out of print.'

He was promoted full corporal at the end of March 1916 and, in spite of eight days of sick leave with a chill—half spent with his parents and half with Helen at Steep—he was growing more confident as a lecturer and had found an easy way to get on with the men passing through his charge in Hut 15: 'I furbish up my knowledge of England by finding some place that each man knows and I know and getting him to talk. There isn't a man I don't share some part with.' During his sick leave he had even begun to think about literary matters. After four months of soldiering, he asked Bottomley for a list of poems to set him going on the proposed anthology of narrative poems. Then he arranged a batch of poems from which Bottomley and others could select the eighteen 'Eastaway' poems that eventually appeared in *An Anthology of New Poetry*. This was a useful diversion from camp during March when there was much uncertainty about his future and leave was cancelled for four weeks. His new skill as a lecturer strengthened his determination—at this time—to join Frost in New England after the war. 'I had an offer the other day to write the history of the regiment. Of course I couldn't take it till the war is over, and then I expect it might be wise not to hang on here picking up odd jobs. If I can and if nothing unexpected turns up, I shall come straight out to you.'

An epidemic of camp measles and the expected reorganization which at last promoted him to corporal produced a series of letters to Frost much more evenly balanced in mood than he had shown in the previous four years. He refused to speculate on the length of the war: 'I hardly go beyond assuming that the war will end.' Part of his minor discontent was delayed promotion—to his annoyance, his younger brother Reggie was promoted before him—part was because of the quarantine that spoiled his birthday visit to Steep on 3 March 1916. But 'partly what made me restless, was the desire to write, without the power. It lasted five or six weeks, till yesterday I rhymed some.'

It was Sunday, always a dreary ruminating day if spent in camp. We got a walk, three of us, one a schoolmaster, the other a game-breeder who knows about horses and dogs and ferrets. We heard the first blackbird, walked 9 or 10 miles straight across country (the advantage of our uniform—we go just where we like): ate and drank (stout) by a fire at a big quiet inn—not a man to drink left in the village, and drew a panorama—a landscape for military purposes, drawn exactly with the help of a compass and a protractor, which is an amusement I have quite taken to—they say I am a neo-realist at it.

The new rigour suited him.

We turn out for physical drill at 6.30. I have made myself fire-lighter now. We are four non-commissioned officers in our hut and N. C. O.'s are not supposed to do anything menial, which is hard on the other men, there being usually only one N. C. O. in a hut of 25 or 30. So to appease them, I light the two stoves while they are still in bed. . . . There is a prophecy abroad that it will be over by July 17. Helen says Why not by her birthday which is a few days earlier? She would be more pleased than I. She has had enough of the war and of comparative solitude.

The reorganized system at camp calmed for a time his occasional questioning of his work as an instructor, which he had partially judged by the award of promotion. He explained such matters best to MacAlister who had had military experience in Canada, but had so far been refused enlistment on medical grounds, and who understood the change from a specialist battalion instructor to that of an ordinary Company NCO with the usual duties outside his 'schoolmastering'. The training given to officers had improved and Thomas welcomed it: 'I shan't take a commission while I can do this work and am considered fit to do it under the new stricter system since we became a Cadet [Officer Training] Unit and things began to hum.' The conflict in Thomas's nature between the need to work intensely to a fixed timetable and then to feel free to wander without restriction had been severely tested during the uncertain period in March while they were confined to camp

by a measles epidemic. As always in his poems after enlistment, he is
able to use a small incident—a restricted stroll within bounds with
chosen fellow instructors—to reflect more widely on his previous way of
life:

> Never a word was spoken, not a thought
> Was thought, of what the look meant with the word
> 'Home' as we walked and watched the sunset blurred.
> And then to me the word, only the word,
> 'Homesick', as it were playfully occurred:
> No more. If I should ever more admit
> Than the mere word I could not endure it
> For a day longer: this captivity
> Must somehow come to an end, else I should be
> Another man, as often now I seem,
> Or this life be only an evil dream.

This poem was written a few days before quarantine was lifted and he
spent a short leave with Helen at Steep. A fortnight later he began the
four poems addressed to his three children and Helen. The Battle of the
Somme had barely begun and his poems are only accidentally occasioned by the war, although with hindsight the 'Household Poems'—as
he termed them—can be made to read like testamentary declarations.

With immediate uncertainties resolved, he gave more attention to
literary matters. He sent his 'Household Poems' to Bottomley, probably
for inclusion as a group in the *Anthology,* and told him that the artist
John Wheatley would like to illustrate them with etchings. Bottomley's
verse-play, *King Lear's Wife,* was about to be performed in Birmingham
and in London, and Thomas made plans to see it in London and meet
old friends. He was toying with an offer to resume some reviewing for
The Bookman, because he found his funds beginning to dwindle and was
uncertain about the Civil List Pension application, although he still had
£100 of War Loan left. The numerous nightingales around the camp
did not compensate for the transfer of friendly fellow instructors, with
the subsequent increase of his own routine duties. As May went by he
saw clearly that the work at Hare Hall was badly organized—more
emphasis on military smartness than efficient training. Dissatisfied, he
applied for some kind of 'Welsh Army job', with the status of an officer
and with access to the fighting in France. Nothing came of it. He was
again writing poems—seven in May and June 1916. He wrote to Frost:

Actually I find less to grumble at out loud than ten years ago: I suppose I am
more bent on making the best of what I have got instead of airing the fact that

I deserve so much more . . . [At Bottomley's play] nobody recognizes me now. Sturge Moore, E. Marsh, and R. C. Trevelyan stood a yard off and I didn't trouble to awaken them to stupid recognition. Bottomley and his wife I just had a word with. I was with a young artist named Paul Nash who has just passed as a map reader. He is a change from the two school masters I see most of . . . Though I am Corporal P. E. Thomas I am not growing so efficient as all that. We don't get a chance. We idle away for days together for lack of organization. Shall I copy out the speech our captain made to the men who were leaving us to go to be finished at the cadet school? 'Pay attention. Stand easy. I just want to say a few words to you men who are going to the school. I wish you all success. I hope you won't get into any trouble at all. Take care to mind your Ps and Qs, and do everything top-hole.' He is a kind huge man with no memory, very fond of the country.

As the demand for officers grew, his unit once more re-organized: he enjoyed longer free evenings but fewer congenial spirits to share them with. He was more involved in routine duties in a larger hut and he found time for verse, particularly on the long train journeys home to Steep during his frequent weekend leaves. Domestic uncertainties were added to his military ones. Merfyn's future training as an engineer had to be arranged and Helen, increasingly anxious and restlessly moving between friends and relations, had become disenchanted with the folk at Bedales School and wished to settle near Merfyn, once the place of his apprenticeship had been decided. Soon Mrs Lupton asked Edward to leave his hilltop study: her husband was at the Front and she wished to let it.

At this time a new factor entered into Thomas's calculations. On 10 June 1916 he was awarded a grant of £300 by the Government instead of a Civil List Pension. Almost immediately he allowed his name to go forward for a Commission in the Royal Artillery and began to make arrangements with his brother Theodore for Merfyn to be trained at the London Transport engineering works at Walthamstow. Helen and her recently bereaved sister, Irene, began the search for a new home convenient for Merfyn and not too far from her family and friends. At the end of June, after a few days' sickness in camp, Edward was granted five days' leave to mark the end of his first year as a soldier. He and Helen set off on a walking tour to see their friends as soon as he had cleared out of his study. Together they visited the Guthries at Flansham, the Hootons at Coulsdon, the Ellises at East Grinstead (where they met Myfanwy), and Eleanor Farjeon in town with tickets for *Boris Gudonov*. Helen then rejoined her children at Rusham Road where Granny Thomas was still seriously troubled with her eyesight and was awaiting an operation for cataract. Edward's father had now retired and was busier than ever with public and political duties. He was soon to fight a local parliamentary election as a Liberal candidate and earned from Edward and Eleanor Farjeon the sobriquet of 'Public Man'.

Three of Edward's poems read like a carefully distanced yet marginal gloss on the decisions he was soon to make. He showed surprise that Eleanor Farjeon, who shared first knowledge of all his verse after Helen, should read more into them then he believed he had intended: 'Is the war preying on you or do you write like that because you are out of tune? [E. F. had a slight attack of whooping-cough.] I wish you could shut your eyes to many big things as I do without trying. If they do prey on me I don't know it.' He was extremely fond of Eleanor and, next to Helen and the absent Frost, she was at this time one of the friends to whom he tried to speak directly about himself. Was he unaware of the way the poetry written between May and August had become—as the Battle of the Somme seeped through—an expression of things that 'preyed' on him without his knowing it?*

Neither his military nor his domestic plans were resolved speedily. At first he had hoped for a commission in the Anti-Aircraft Corps, but he learned that his superiors in the Artists' Rifles lacked the necessary 'influence'. His mathematics were not strong and when two civilian friends—R. A. Scott-James and Blanco White—joined the unit, the latter did his best to coach him in gunnery, especially in trigonometry. Merfyn, too, helped his father with pure and applied mathematics at weekends and later recalled with pride this opportunity to help. Another diversion took place in mid-July, after he had spent a few days at Steep packing his books for sale, burning others, and making a huge bonfire of his correspondence. On his return he was seriously considered for a post on the permanent staff as a sergeant-instructor. The main requirement was the ability to handle squads of men on parade and he doubted if his proven worth as an instructor would tip the balance. From an aside in a letter to Bottomley, informing him that Paul Nash and John Wheatley were leaving the unit, we learn that Thomas might have stayed on with the permanent staff, 'but I have had first too comfortable, and then too uncomfortable a job. I can't imagine regretting the change whatever the end is.' At the end of July 1916, he notified Frost of the impending changes:

A new step I have taken makes a good moment for writing. I offered myself for Artillery and today I was accepted, which means I shall go very soon to an

*See *Collected Poems,* nos. 115–33.

Artillery school and be out in France or who knows where in a few months. After months of panic and uncertainty I feel much happier again except that I don't take easily to the trigonometry needed for artillery calculations. I have done very nearly all that I could do here in the way of teaching, lecturing, and taking charge of men in and out of doors. My old acquaintances were mostly moving out. The speeding up of things left no chance of enjoying the walks we used to have. So I had to go. Now with luck I may find myself at a School in London before my firing course, and in London I can see a few people. . . . When we know where we shall be I will tell you. Meantime *Steep will always be a safe address.*

Things are going right now. We have endured long waiting. I think we can stand anything now, even success. Of course I can't write any more verses just now and have not done for a month or so. The last I did were during a 3 days' walk that Helen and I took at the end of June when I had a few days leave due to me. . . . It was too short. I can only be content now in regular almost continuous work when I have no time for comparisons. . . .

My mother is not happy over my new chance of going out as an officer—I ought to be an officer in less than a few months. Nor is Helen. She is not often happy now. She is tired and anxious.

Once he was definitely accepted to train for the bigger guns of the Siege Artillery he felt at ease again. 'I wanted a change,' he wrote to Bottomley. 'In the Siege Artillery I shall get it. Nobody perhaps is quite as pleased as I am myself and shall be when I am gazetted.' He and Helen had had ample opportunities to discuss the change and, as always, she fell in line with his wishes and failed to conceal her misgivings. A commission would bring them more money, but recently the Civil Liability Commission had allowed them £1 a week as long as Edward had no paid civilian employment and was not a commissioned officer. The expenses of an officer were higher and, apart from the possibility of a better pension, they would have been no worse off had he accepted the job of a sergeant-instructor. Two crucial factors conditioned his decision to train as an officer. If he stayed on the permanent staff of a home-based training unit, he argued, he would never find out for himself what things were like 'out there'. More importantly, he was no longer convinced that his job at Hare Hall was really worthwhile. After his decision to apply, and until he joined the Artillery School, he talked readily of having his 'anchors up'. Two months earlier he had composed his third song, to the tune of Rio Grande:

> No one knew I was going away,
> I thought myself I should come back some day.

· · · ·

I could not return from my liberty,
To my youth and my love and my misery.

The past is the only dead thing that smells sweet,
The only sweet thing that is not also fleet.
I'm bound away for ever,
Away somewhere, away for ever.

It is typical of Thomas that he should first face the future in his poetry and then take two months to act out his decision.

Physically he was run down when he called at his parents' home, after being upset by vaccination and a developing abcess in his right hand. As soon as he was fit enough, he took charge of parades and, during short forty-eight hour leaves in Steep, packed books for sale, and continued to burn correspondence and unnecessary papers. He reveals some of his thinking to Frost:

> Much of the time I spent in sorting letters, papers and books, as I may not have a home for some time to come.... This waiting troubles me. I really want to be out. However, I daresay I shan't be till the winter. I wrote some lines after a period in hospital—largely because to concentrate is the only happy thing possible when one is bored and helpless. Today came a chance of getting a book out. A brother-in-law [Roger Ingpen] of de la Mare's publishes in a small way and I am going to sent him a batch to look at.... Eleanor Farjeon is roaming round in the fine weather. Somebody said today that one realised the blessings of peace and leisure now. I contradicted him. I don't believe I often had as good times as I have had, one way and another, these past 13 months.... Garnett is away [with an ambulance corps on the Italian front]. I have not seen him for 14 months. Bottomley I may see at the end of the month when everyone is away and I may have some leave between leaving my old corps and joining the new. I should like to go up there and bathe in the lake with the bird's-eye primroses and the silver sand. There is nothing like the solitude of a solitary lake in early morning, when one is in deep still water. More adjectives here than I allow myself now and fewer verbs.

As one learns from reading all his letters to friends over twenty years, Thomas was an adept at keeping back part of himself. An outside view of him as an NCO just before he decided to apply for a commission was given in 1947 by R. A. Scott-James, his Oxford contemporary and an editor favourable to Thomas in his worst doldrum days before the War:

> For some weeks we slept in the same barrack-dormitory, he at one extreme end, I at the other. . . . There were some opportunities for outside activity. Thomas was insatiable in his desire for more and more physical exertion. No

longer were the leisurely walks through the country in which he had once delighted enough to satisfy his moods. He persuaded a few others to join him in long cross-country runs. He seemed bent upon acquiring the utmost physical fitness of which the human body is capable. He had escaped from the old literary life, he had apparently weaned himself from the temperament which for him had gone with it . . . He had become the perfect soldier of the State, the contented warrior whom the newspapers loved to depict, more completely than any other serviceman I ever met.

The sharp contrast, so evident in photographs of Thomas as wayfarer in 1912 and 2/Lt. Thomas, Royal Garrison Artillery, before he left for France in late 1916, is clearly marked in his letters to Frost at this time and in the outside persona he presented to colleagues like Rolfe Scott-James. Camouflage was one military art that came naturally to him.

CHAPTER 16

Quo fas et gloria ducunt

THOMAS made preparations for his admission into the Royal Artillery like a conscientious student. He assumed he would be posted to the RA School at St. John's Wood and he asked Eleanor Farjeon if her mother would either allow him to be billeted with them at 137 Fellows Road or reserve a room for him to study there in the evenings. He left Hare Hall Camp on 21 August 1916 and, after reporting to St. John's Wood on the 25th, he found he was posted to the Royal Artillery School, Handel Street, WC to prepare for the big guns of the Royal Garrison Artillery. The Farjeon home was now too far distant and he was once more billeted on his parents at Balham until his unit moved to the Royal Artillery Barracks, Trowbridge on 20 September. Whenever possible, he returned to Steep with Helen to clear up things there, for they had now decided to move to a cottage at High Beech, near Loughton, where he had spent his first camp with the Artists' Rifles in September 1915. He wrote to Jesse Berridge that they were all well, 'though scattered till the moving is over'. Merfyn was in lodgings at Walthamstow, Bronwen was staying with Helen's sister for a few months, and Myfanwy was with the John Freemans, who had taken over Yew Tree Cottage. Helen was with Edward at Balham before setting off for a walking tour in the Lake District with her widowed sister, Irene. As usual, Edward reveals something of his mind to Frost:

We are supposed to be moving to our new cottage in a week or two. I think there will be some delay. Helen runs away so comfortably from affairs, and I am not free to manage them now . . . There is much to learn . . . It is not like camp life. I make no friends. We are treated rather better and have fewer duties and responsibilities, fewer demands on one another than in camp. The result is I am rather impatient to go out and be shot at. That is all I want, to do something if I am discovered to be of any use, but in any case to be made to run risks, to be put through it. I have been saying to myself lately that I don't really care a fig what happens. But perhaps I do. I am cut off. All the anchors are up . . . This is dismal reading. But I don't want money. Didn't I tell you the Government had been persuaded to grant me £300? They would not give me a pension. That £300 might last till the end of the war. . . . Goodbye and try to imagine me more like a soldier than this letter sounds.

Ex-Corporal Thomas did not take kindly to the half-and-half

existence of an officer-cadet at Handel Street and the Royal Artillery Barracks at Trowbridge. He was recovering slowly from his poisoned hand. He found the Statics course rather bewildering and he was surrounded by younger schoolmasters and engineers. The nearness to Steep at weekends emphasized that his years there were suddenly to end. One suspects he didn't mind selling books: it all helped towards the expenses of the impending move to High Beech. But his papers, notebooks (all now neatly documented and dated), letters not burnt, and the final copies and typescripts of his poems had to be made safe and available. Beneath it all was his acute sense of the strain imposed upon Helen and his mother by his decision to become an officer, with the inevitable prospect of active service if he passed the medical examination.

The move to Trowbridge was to familiar Wiltshire country, so important to his well-being. The first weeks were spent under canvas and he wrote *The Trumpet* and then *Lights Out*. Like all OCTU courses, the training was intensive with severe standards of physical fitness, long periods of lectures and exercise classes, and, as a counterbalance, a ridiculously high standard set for turn-out and military bearing. Thomas was amused that he had to wear gloves and spur chains, and confessed to Eleanor Farjeon that at 7.30 p.m., after a long day and rather more formal evening meals than were usual at Hare Hall, he felt disinclined 'to get himself up' in order to leave camp. He preferred to work away at his training manuals or to undertake the duties of a L/Bombardier in charge of guard duty or fatigues. As in his undergraduate days, he was always on the look-out for friendly faces, and on Saturdays and Sundays, when not at Steep, he gathered a congenial group of walkers to explore the surrounding countryside with him.

The train journey home was long and roundabout and two poems at least (*Lights Out* and *The Child in the Orchard*) were worked on in semi-darkness. Until the family moved to High Beech on 8 October he found his reactions were slow: 'I think other people can concentrate more on these things than I can with only a quarter of my mind willing to work at them.' He passed his first examination comfortably and in mid-October he was able to visit his new home at 2 Paul's Nursery, High Beech. He described it in detail to Robert and Elinor Frost in successive letters:

It is right alone in the forest among beech trees and fern and deer, though it only costs 10d. to reach London. Luckily I had a week's leave thrust on me just at the time when I could be of some use. We have fine weather, too, luckily and have had some short walks, Helen, Bronwen and I—Mervyn being still in lodgings 6 miles off, and Baba with an aunt, waiting till the house is ready for them.

It would take me too long to be sure what I think of Rupert [Brooke] . . . I think he succeeded in being youthful and yet intelligible and interesting (not only pathologically) more than most poets since Shelley. But thought gave him (and me) indigestion . . . I think perhaps a man ought to be capable of always being surprised on being confronted with what he really is—as I am nowadays when I confront a full size mirror in a good light instead of a cracked bit of one in a dark barrack room. Scores of men, by the way, shave outside the window, just looking at the glass with the dawn behind them. My disguises increase, what with spurs on my heels and hair on my upper lip. (19 October.)

We like our new home. Except on Saturdays and Sundays and holidays we see nothing only aeroplanes and deer in the forest. Baba has no companions. She goes about telling herself stories. She is a sensitive selfish little creature. Helen has only her, so I suppose she must be spoilt. The others are really only at home to sleep except at week ends. The forest is beautiful, oaks and horn-beams, beeches, bracken, hollies, and some heather. But it is really High Beach not Beech, on account of the pebbly soil. There are 7 or 8 miles of forest, by 1 or 2 miles wide, all on the high ground, with many tiny ponds and long wide glades. We have few neighbours and know none of them yet. But it is easy for people to get here from London. We are half an hour from the station which is half an hour from the city. Helen is going to find it lonely. She does not stand these times very well. If she did, I should have really nothing at all to worry about. (27 November.)

Returning from High Beech to Trowbridge, he made a vital decision, to volunteer for overseas duty. To de la Mare he hoped 'I shall be preserved from Coastal Defence . . . I want a far greater change than I have had so far': in a comment to Eleanor Farjeon about Granville-Barker, who had just been shunted off to a school for Coast Defence, he added: 'I suppose his friends have urged his country not to risk his life. I hope I shall always be as eager to risk mine as I have been these last few months.' He passed his final written examination on 4 November and was then inspected by General Sir William Robertson. There followed a delayed weekend leave, his final week of practical training with the Royal Garrison Artillery at Wanstrow, Somerset, and a leave at home to await his gazetting as second lieutenant. He expected to be sent to a holding unit or, more likely, an immediate posting to a battery destined for France. The full impact of the disaster on the Somme was strongly felt in this mixed gathering of potential officers drawn from old soldiers and new recruits. 'The cinematography pictures of the "Somme Battle"', he told Frost, 'tell you exactly nothing. I went to see them last night. You learn far more from 2 or 3 soldiers talking about women.'

His leave lasted from 18 November to 3 December, when he was posted to the Officers' Mess, Tin Town, Lydd, Kent, presumably for further training on the guns to be used in France. Thomas planned this leave as part of a series of goodbye visits to his lifelong friends. He spent his first night with his parents and then travelled by train to Carnforth to stay with the Bottomleys for three nights and two days. Bottomley recalls his visit

> I have no written record of that time, but the memory of them is still vivid and new. There was talk and music, and he sang (he always sang when he came to us): beside his folk-songs he had acquired a riotous collection of army-songs, which he sang with a mischievous quietness that made the rowdy ones much funnier even than they were meant to be. He went one or two long walks with my wife; at other times he sat with me in my open garden-house. [Bottomley was still an invalid.] One afternoon we spent a long time indoors watching a marvellous storm gather about Ill Bell and High Street and come sweeping down Kentmere and the estuary: the cross-lights among the dark veils were unearthly: he said reflectively 'You are lucky.' I replied 'What, with my health?' He was silent for an appreciable time, then said still more quietly 'Yes'. . . . While he was here I asked him why he had chosen to ask for a commission in the artillery, when that might be thought to be the professional soldier's particular province, with its special training and special risks. He replied 'To get a larger pension for Helen.'

While at Silverdale Thomas corrected proofs of the 'Edward Eastaway' poems in *An Anthology of New Poetry* and returned them to Bottomley with a copy of his 'booklet on Keats' which had just appeared. Ten days later he wrote: 'I am commissioned now. In fact I am in every way ready to go. I wonder will it be Salonica. But it is a worse gamble than ever now everywhere.'

Thomas had returned from Carnforth to spend the night in London with John Freeman who agreed to read the proofs of the Ingpen selection and send them on to Eleanor Farjeon. He was gazetted in the Royal Garrison Artillery on 24 November 1916 and spent the rest of his leave with Helen at High Beech or shopping in London for necessary kit and stores. As much as possible, he visited friends and relatives in and around London. He explained his feelings to Frost the day he was gazetted:

> I want to go soon, to get over the first and worst step (of parting). Even the leave I have got now is not quite satisfactory. I can't think of enjoying it quite. Yet I did enjoy being up at Bottomley's. . . . I have never found what I have to

do too much for me. In the future the worst I shall have to suffer (apart from injury) cold and excitement . . . I think I can be a much more useful person than you would imagine from seeing me amidst ease and comfort. . . . I never spent so much in a week. Clothes! And I always preferred clothes old and loose, and now they are all new and close-fitting.

He hoped he was going straight to a battery and not to any final school. 'So much the better. I have got very sick of school.'

This disgruntled mood extended to the large kit-bag Eleanor Farjeon had had sent on to him at High Beech. He had scarcely time to fill it, nor would he need it at Lydd: 'I am out of sorts with everything except my job now. I am sorry if it made this week worse than middling.' Soon after his arrival at Lydd, he told her, he ached to get on with his job:

This is only to tell you just a few facts. One is that they asked for volunteers to go straight out to Batteries in France and I made sure of it by volunteering. Don't let Helen know. Of course I may not be wanted. I may not pass the doctor. If I do I shall have some leave first. If I go to a Battery in England I may go straight there from Lydd . . . I shan't come home this weekend. I shall just walk over and see Conrad, who is only 12 miles away.

He was pleased with his progress in practical gunnery at Lydd and was used occasionally as a lecturer. His year-long experience as an NCO was impressive among batches of hastily-trained officers and, at the end of his first fortnight, he was posted to 244 Siege Battery, expecting to be in France in January. His first duty as an officer at the new unit was 'to give a man leave to see his wife die in Birmingham'. He found it hard to be 'as judicial as an officer is expected to be' and decided it was time to put away childish things, although he would have liked some Christmas leave.

Roger Ingpen had delayed the final selection for his volume of poems and, now that so much had been decided, Thomas was fretting as always about the uncertainty of immediate events, particularly about the final composition of the officers in his new unit, which had been hastily put together and was soon to be given a new commanding officer just before they sailed for France. An unexpected Christmas leave, Thursday 21 December to Wednesday 27 December, enabled him to spend one night with his parents, to do some last-minute shopping in London, and to see John Freeman and Eleanor Farjeon about proof-reading. He arrived at High Beech in time for Merfyn's supper at 7 p. m. on Friday. Next day he sent Harry Hooton a card (and a copy of his *Keats*): 'They are all well at home. Bronwen is better. I am quite well but impatient to be out. I

18. Outside Yew Tree Cottage with Myfanwy and the son of a neighbour, when the first poems had 'begun to run', late December 1914.

19. Lance-Corporal P. E. Thomas, map-instructor (standing, centre), at Hare Hall Camp, December 1915.

20. Second Lieutenant P. E. Thomas, RGA, photographed by Merfyn at High Beech during embarkation leave, December 1916.

should be much disappointed if peace found me on this side of the channel. . . . I am very sorry I can't send the children anything better worth having.' He was planning to see all his friends during this mobilization leave and wrote his usual Christmas letters to Jesse Berridge and Ian MacAlister with news of the family and the new cottage.

This leave produced his penultimate poem 'Out in the Dark', occasioned by Myfanwy's reaction to the deer in the forest, outside the room with its Christmas tree which owed so much to the kindness of the Farjeons. He sent the verses to Eleanor for typing when he reached Lydd, and added: 'It is curious how I feel no anxiety or trouble as soon as I am back here, though I was very glad to be home.' He summarized his last month of 1916 in a letter to Frost:

I had your letter and your poem 'France, France' yesterday. . . . It expresses just those hesitations you or I would have at asking others to act as we think it is their cue to act. Well, I am soon going to know more about it. I am not at home as the address suggests, but am on the eve of a whole week's continuous shooting. It begins tomorrow. Then at the end of the week or soon after I shall have my last leave. After all we are going to have smaller guns than we thought [6 inch howitzers not 9.2] and we shall be nearer the front line a good bit and are beginning to make insincere jokes about observing from the front line which of course we shall have to do. I think I told you we were a quite mixed crowd of officers in this battery. As soon as we begin to depend on one another we shall no doubt make the best of one another. I am getting on, I think, better than when I was in my pupilage. The 2 senior officers have been out before. Four of us are new. I am 3 years older than the Commanding Officer and twice as old as the youngest . . . It is nearly all work here now and in the evenings, if I haven't something to do with my maps or reading, I am either out walking or indoors talking. When I am alone—as I am during the evening just now because the officer who shares my room is away—I hardly know what to do. I can't write now and still less can I read. I have rhymed but I have burnt my rhymes and feel proud of it.

In the New Year 1917 he began a private diary in cramped handwriting with numerous abbreviations.* When filled out with his last seven letters to Frost, the last eighteen letters to her published by Eleanor Farjeon in *Edward Thomas: The Last Four Years,* and the few extant letters to Helen (out of nineteen sent to her), the War Diary underlines the consistency of the poet's entire writing life, grounded upon his response to the seen world of living, natural, and man-made (and man-destroyed) things. Yet side by side with these laconic jottings, a clear

---

*Printed as Appendix C in *The Collected Poems of Edward Thomas,* pp. 460–81.

picture is given of a self-contained, highly efficient officer who knew how to disguise his fears. He was happiest when working flat out with his gun detachment, or at work in the eerie, dangerous isolation of an Observation Post, acting as the necessary forward-based 'eye' that made efficient the destructive work of his own guns and did its best to provide effective counter-fire against enemy gun positions.

Thomas spent the first week of 1917 at Lydd as fire-control officer or observer with his new battery. They began shooting 15-pounders and then settled into practice with 6″ howitzers of the kind they would use in France as forward support for the advancing infantry in the Arras attack that was to form part of the 1917 spring offensive. He left Lydd on his mobilization leave immediately after duty on Friday and spent the night at Rusham Road with his parents. The next morning his favourite younger brother Julian, still a Civil Servant, came to breakfast. After shopping with his mother, he spent lunch and tea with the Farjeons and then set off for High Beech with Bronwen who had been staying with her aunt at Chiswick. Sunday was a fine day spent in walks with Helen and the children. On Monday Eleanor Farjeon came and spent the night, and Edward 'wrote cheques for the next 6 months'. On Tuesday, after Eleanor left, he and Helen walked alone through Epping Forest. Wednesday meant a visit to town to the dentist, followed by lunch with Harry Hooton and his banker-friend Jones, by tea with Ivy Ransome (Arthur Ransome was by now in Russia), and a drink with Roger Ingpen and W. H. Davies. Before returning home he saw V. H. Collins of the Oxford University Press, probably to discuss the proposed anthology of narrative poetry. The day repeated the pattern of so many of his pre-war 'working' visits to town. The next day, at High Beech, he said goodbye to Helen, Merfyn, and Myfanwy before travelling with Bronwen to Rusham Road. Afterwards he saw Haynes, Berridge, and Tom Clayton and then had 'supper at Rusham Road with all my brothers'. On Friday morning he left Bronwen and his parents, had lunch with Helen's two sisters, and arrived at Lydd to find preparations being made to move the battery to their final mobilization camp at Codford on Salisbury Plain.

Although he was granted a few twenty-four-hour leave-passes between Sunday 14 January and his embarkation on Monday 29 January, he made no attempt to see those closest to him again. He explained his reasons to Frost after a train journey to Gloucester where Jack Haines gave him a spare copy of Frost's new volume, *Mountain Interval*:

I could take a day off so I want to see Haines. I couldn't go and see Helen or my Mother. You understand I said goodbye ten days ago. . . . Merfyn attested on

Saturday but will be free to go on with his work for almost another year. If he has to leave it [which he did] he would choose the Flying Corps, he says. . . . I can ride a motor cycle now. . . . We are off on the 28th and 29th. I have had rather little to do these two days and have had sore ankles from a new pair of boots so that I am thinking that anything will be better than hanging about but I daresay it isn't so. It is always a part of this life to have to hang about in cold and wet and then not to have a minute to spare. Anyhow it is always better to do anything than to 'imagine' what it 'would be like to do it'. Someday we can discuss the difference—that is if you have imagined at all.

The pre-embarkation life at Codford was a testing time for his temperament. On 16 January he informed Helen that 'I shall find myself writing here if we don't get busier' and, four days later, he sent her detailed instructions about household affairs, about the preparation of a duplicate set of verses for Frost, and the nature of his agreement with Ingpen. The men had to be supervised on fatigues necessary for drawing overseas clothes and equipment. He acted as orderly officer in his turn, took pay parade, and gave lectures on map-reading, gun-drill, and general matters of conduct and discipline. When the guns arrived Thomas could ride a motor cycle and he tested (and set) the various compasses that would give the battery their zero lines in action. He learned that *A Literary Pilgrim* was about to appear and, suddenly, he paid the overnight visit to Haines in Gloucester. After his return to camp, when he learned that Myfanwy was staying near at hand with Ivy Ransome, he walked over the Downs from Codford by Chicklade Bottom and the Fonthills to spend his last but one night in England with Myfanwy, who had moved in and out of his verse-making from 'Old Man' to 'Out in the Dark'. From Manor Farm, Hatch, near Tisbury in Wiltshire, he described to Eleanor Farjeon this last English walk:

> Yesterday I walked over here to see Baba and the Downs in the cold sun were so beautiful that I didn't worry till I got here about the blisters that somebody else's shoes gave me. Now I have got somehow to get back. Probably I shall hire a bicycle. We start tomorrow morning [29 January]. It seems certain we are for the Somme, but how directly we don't know yet of course. I have my hands full as I not only have to manage the mess and the cook but have to keep the accounts and pay the bills. How much better to be digging at High Beech or Billingshurst than paying 2d. a 1lb for potatoes. . . . It is nice here and a fine day but I am chiefly occupied (though quite unconsciously I assure you) in being quite patient and not really thinking of tomorrow though it will just flit through my head.

The battery crossed to Le Havre on *The Mona Queen* on 29–30 January, and was spread out loosely at a rest camp outside the town. Thomas was detailed to organize route marches and ice-sliding jaunts, to explain the degree of personal comment in censored letters, and to warn about the dangers of VD in Le Havre. His own reactions to this role are muted in the laconic diary entries, but when, after four or five days near Le Havre, they entrained for their first active service stations near Arras, he noted that on the twenty-four-hour journey via Barly, Alaincourt, Amiens, and Doullens there were thirty-five other ranks in a cattle truck while he and another subaltern shared a compartment. After a one night's stay at Doullens, they moved to a temporary position at Mendicourt. He had the task, once again, of allocating men to their billets. Two days later, when they arrived after long lorry journeys at their first active service stations across the 'Arras Road', Thomas was the first subaltern to explore possible Observation Posts, with his CO Major Lushington, close to the shattered village of Beaurains. His skills were highly valued by the two regular soldiers, Major Lushington and Captain Horton, whose job it had been to forge 244 Battery into an efficient fighting force in less than three months. To his disappointment—he was more than eager to spend his time forward at the OP—they used him to supervise the necessary digging-in of gun emplacements, the provision of camouflage, and the preparing of temporary 'funk-holes' when the battery came under enemy fire. He was relieved to find how much he enjoyed this early phase of his first three weeks in France. His skill as an observer, as a recorder in detailed panoramic sketches, and as an efficient writer of despatches sent back to 35 Heavy Artillery Group HQ at Arras, must have decided the CO to recommend him for duty at HQ as an Assistant Adjutant and Orderly Officer to the Officer Commanding the Group (Colonel Witchall) on 19 February 1917.

Thomas did not relish the change. He expressed his views in letters to Frost, one before and one after the move to HQ:

I left England a fortnight ago and have now crawled with the battery up to our position. I can't tell you where it is, but we are well up in high open country. We are on a great main road in a farmhouse facing the enemy who are about 2 miles away, so that their shells rattle our windows but so far only fall a little behind us or to one side. It is near the end of a 3 week's frost. The country is covered with snow which silences everything but the guns. We have slept—chiefly in uncomfortable places till now. . . . I have enjoyed it very nearly all. Except shaving in a freezing tent. I don't think I really knew what travel was like till we left England.

Yesterday, our 2nd day, I spent in the trenches examining some observation posts to see what could be seen of the enemy from them. It was really the best day I have had since I began. We had some shells very near us, but were not sniped at. I could see the German lines very clear but not a movement anywhere, nothing but posts sticking out of the snow with barbed wire, bare trees broken and dead and half ruined houses. The only living men we met at bends in trenches, eating or carrying food or smoking. One dead man lay under a railway arch so stiff and neat (with a covering of sacking) that I only slowly remembered he was dead. I got back, tired and warm and red. I hope I shall never enjoy anything less. But I shall. . . . I am now just off with a working party to prepare our Gun positions which are at the edge of a cathedral town a mile or two along the road we look out on. We are to fight in an orchard there in sight of the cathedral. (11 February 1917.)

I am temporarily thrust out of my Battery to assist some headquarters work with maps &c. We are living in rather a palace—a very cold dark palace—only 2000 yards from the Hun, in a city which is more than half in ruins already. It is full of our men and no doubt one night we shall know that the Hun knows it. I woke last night thinking I heard someone knocking excitedly at a door nearby. But I am persuaded now it was only a machine gun. . . . But I am very anxious to go back soon to my battery. They are only 3 miles away and when I walk over to see them it is something like going home. I am in a way at home there, but here I have a Heavy Artillery Group Commander to hang about after and do as he pleases and my soul is less my own. You know the life is so strange that I am only half myself and the half that knows England and you is obediently asleep for a time. Do you believe me? It seems that I have sent it to sleep to make the life endurable—more than endurable—really enjoyable in a way. But with the people I meet I am suppressing practically everything (without difficulty tho not without pain). (23 February 1917.)

Thomas remained in this 'safe' office job at HQ—with its numerous inspection visits to all the surrounding batteries (including his own 244) and the constant object of enemy shelling throughout the night—until 9 March, when he rejoined his battery. His most succinct reason for leaving HQ is in the War Diary: 'I am fed up with sitting on my arse doing nothing that anybody couldn't do better.' The Group HQ was never a 'safe billet' and, a week later, the sergeant-major there was killed by a direct hit. Thomas used the night-time bombardment experience at Arras to extend his understanding of the various kinds of shells he would later be subject to. Some of his comments on this subject read as though he were a little scared; one's own view, based on similar experiences, is that he was recording a necessary exercise in self-survival:

I am inhibiting introspection [he wrote to Frost] except when I wake up and hear the shelling and wonder whether I ought to move my bed away from the window to the inner side where there is more masonry—more to resist and more to fall on me. But it is no use thinking like this. I am half awake when I do. Besides I have hardly learnt yet to distinguish between shells going out and shells coming in—my worst alarm was really shells going out. So far it excites but doesn't disturb, or at any rate doesn't upset and unfit. . . . I should like to be a poet, just as I should like to live, but I know as much about my chances in either case, and I don't really trouble about either. Only I want to come back more or less complete.

Thomas's own record of his last month with 244 Battery is sombre. While at Group HQ, he had worked at maps and plans that revealed the artillery's role in the offensive due to begin on Easter Monday. Consequently he knew much more than an ordinary subaltern should. He also understood the essential part played by good ground observation (when British planes were comparatively few) in the effective direction of a barrage, either in advance of one's own infantry or to knock out obstructive enemy guns. He reports to Harry Hooton (16 March 1917) that his earlier impressions of the life were 'far pleasanter than these later ones'. But his diary, and the letters to Frost and to Eleanor Farjeon and Helen, report a keen interest in describing the new tempo of activity at 244 Battery, especially after 18 March when the German lines were straightened out and British troops moved to new front line positions that now included the shattered village of Beaurains from which most of his observations were previously taken.

With the advent of spring he records—as he once did in *Woodland Life* twenty years before—the return of birds and herbs and flowers to the nightmarish landscape. A paraphrase of the War Diary here would dilute its recognizable quality as one more working field-book to add to the eighty others he had arranged himself for preservation—an additional proof, if one were required, of his hopes for personal survival in order to use it. A summary of his military entries between 12 March and 8 April forms a sufficient background to the two long quotations from letters to Frost that help to fill out the Diary. During twenty-eight days, which included a complete change of OPs from Day 9 and entirely new gun emplacement positions on Day 16, he spent two full nights observing in front line trenches, eleven days (or nights) at Observation Posts (first at Ronville but subsequently at Beaurains), five days on routine duties at Battery HQ or as messing officer, twelve days on the battery gun positions engaged in firing practice rounds and then firing on fixed lines as part of the assault barrage, and supervising the digging of new, more effective dug-outs and suitable shallow trenches for emergency use. At

times, too, expecially in late March and in the final days before Easter
Monday, the combination of all-night firing of their own guns and
heavy shelling from the German lines left the entire battery exhausted.
In circumstances like this, it is no surprise that Major Lushington should
recall his dependence on Thomas's all-round reliability and the even-
tempered support he offered to officers and men alike, as he quietly
smoked the York River (or even the free issue) pipe tobacco that he had
once more taken up, as he had done in his earlier undergraduate and
more successful journalist days.

One letter to Frost (dated 8 March) leads gradually into the real
dangers of life at an Observation Post among destroyed buildings:

You sound more hopeful than most people are here. Not that they are
despondent, but that they just don't know what to think. They know that the
newspapers are stupid and the 'Hun wise', and there practically is the end of
their knowledge. We are still fairly quiet here except for brief raids on the
enemy. . . .

I know some things about houses now that you don't know. The houses I
observe from, for example, are all modern small houses, the last left standing
before you come to the front line trenches. In front of them no houses for
about 1500 yards, that is to say about the same distance behind the enemy as we
are behind our troops. No Man's Land is 150 yards wide. These modern houses
have all been hit and downstairs is a mixture of bricks, mortar, bedsteads and
filth. Upstairs you spy out through tiles at the enemy, who knows perfectly
well you are in one of these houses and some day will batter them all down.
One of the houses is at the edge of a suburb of the city. One is at the edge of a
pretty old village. It was being finished when war overtook it. If a shell hits it it
will fall all to pieces, not in huge masses of masonry like the old brickwork at
the citadel. But it is not so much individual houses as streets. You can't paint
death living in them.—As I went to the village house today I heard a very young
child talking in another equally exposed house in the same street. Some are too
poor or too helpless or what to leave even these places. But I positively am not
going to describe any more except to make a living. . . .

I already know enough to confirm my old opinion that the papers tell no
truth at all about what war is and what soldiers are—except that they do play
football close to the fighting line and play instruments of brass too—here we
often hear the bagpipes.

His final letter to Frost (on 2 April) hints at the change of gear before
any major offensive. It is the nearest we can get to his unvarnished
thinking as he prepared for the Arras offensive:

I have seen some new things since I wrote last and had mud and worse
things to endure which do not become less terrible in anticipation but are less

terrible once I am in the midst of them. Jagged gables at dawn when you are cold and tired out look a thousand times worse from their connection with a certain kind of enemy shell that has made them look like that, so that every time I see them I half think I hear the moan of the approaching and hovering shell and the black grisly flap that it seems to make as it bursts. I see and hear more than I did because changed conditions compel us to go up to the very front among the infantry to do our observation and we spend nights without shelter in the mud chiefly in waiting for morning and the arrival of the relief. It is a 24 hours job and takes more to recover from. But it is far as yet from being unendurable. The unendurable thing was having to climb up the inside of a chimney that was being shelled. I gave up. It was impossible and I knew it. Yet I went up to the beastly place and had 4 shell bursts very close. I decided that I would go back. As a matter of fact I had no light and no information about the method of getting up so that all the screwing up I had given myself would in any case have been futile. It was just another experience . . . but it was far less on my mind, because the practical result of my failure was nil and I now see far more from the ground level than I could have seen then from 200 feet up the factory chimney.

Otherwise I have done all the things so far asked of me without making any mess and I have mingled satisfaction with dissatisfaction in about the usual proportion, comfort and discomfort. There are so many things to enjoy and if I remember rightly not more to regret than say a year or ten years ago. I think I get surer of some primitive things that one has got to get sure of, about oneself and other people, and I think this is not due simply to being older. In short, I am glad I came out and I think less about return than I thought I should— partly no doubt I inhibit the idea of return. I only think by flashes of the things at home that I used to enjoy and should again. I enjoy many of them out here when the sun shines and at early morning and late afternoon. I doubt if anybody here thinks less of home than I do and yet I doubt if anybody loves it more. . . .

I revert for 10 minutes every night by reading Shakespeare's Tragedies in bed with a pipe before I blow the candle out. Otherwise I do nothing that I used to do except eat and sleep: I mean when I am not alone. Funny world. What a thing it is. [Two sayings of Dad Uzzell, often used by Thomas.] And I hear nothing of you. Yet you are no more like an American in a book than you were 2½ years ago. You are doing the unchanged things that I cannot or dare not think of except in flashes. I don't have memories such as are involved in the impressions as I see or hear things about me. But if I went on writing like this I should make you think I was as damnably introspective as ever and practised the art too. Goodnight to you and Elinor and all. Remember I am in 244 Siege Battery, B. E. F., France and am and shall remain 2nd Lieut. Edward Thomas. Yours ever.

Thomas knew the chances of war and frequently reminded Helen of the odds. He expands the argument a little in his last letter to his son Merfyn, written four days after his first experience of all-night observing in the front-line trenches:

I brought back a letter from you in the mail bags today and also a new battery for my torch. Thank you very much. Do you know I have been so careful that the first one is not exhausted yet. It must have been a very good one. It is most useful in crossing this dark street when crowded with lorries or columns of horses and limbers and on all sorts of occasions.

I was so glad to hear from you and how much you were earning for Mother as well as yourself. At the same time I am more anxious for you to learn than to earn at present and I hope you will soon be moved to a new shop. You haven't found an O. T. C. yet, have you? I wish you could, though I hope you will not have to go further than that for a very long time! I don't think war would trouble you. I see lots of infantrymen no bigger or older than you. There was one machine gunner doing sentry over the parapet the other night when I was in the very front trench. He had to stand up there behind his gun watching for an hour. Then he was relieved and made some tea for me and himself and turned into his comic little shanty and slept till the next relief. He looked ever so much older as well as dirtier when morning came. He was a very nice bright Scotch boy. Well, I expect you could do just the same. His officer was the same age and very much like him so that I think he had to look unduly severe to show the distinction.

I wonder could you climb that chimney? [At Arras—see War Diary entry for 15 March and letter to Frost.] There were iron rings all the way up and one I knew was loose, but I didn't know which. One bad feature was that you were always hanging *out* a bit, because the chimney tapered. It has been hit three times but only with small stuff. Now I suppose it is likely to survive as the enemy is further off. The crossroads round it became known as Windy Corner because everybody 'got the wind up' as he came near it. Thousands had to go that way and yet very few were injured and only about two killed. Isn't it wonderful how some men get hit and some don't. But it is the same with trees and houses, so that I don't see why it makes some people 'believe in God'. It is a good thing to believe. I think brave people all believe something and I daresay they are not so likely to be killed as those who don't believe and are not so brave.

You would have laughed to hear the machine gunners talking to one another and chaffing the infantrymen as they came along the trench tired and dirty.

The men all think we are fast winning the war now. I wonder if we are: I hope so. Of course I am not a bit tired of it. I want to do six months anyhow, but I don't care how much so long as I come back again. It is going to be Spring soon. Are you glad? Are you often happy and usually contented, not often in despair. Try never to let despair at any rate make you idle or careless. But be as idle and careless as you can when you are happy and the chance comes. If you are troubled, remember that you can do what perhaps nobody else will be able to do for Mother, and Bronwen and Baba: only don't let that make you anxious either. All will come well if you keep honest and kind.

Upon my word, this sounds like a sermon and I do hate sermons, of which it is not true to say that it is more blessed to give than receive, but it is more easy to give a sermon than to receive.

Do you have time to read now? I only read for 10 minutes in bed, Shakespeare's sonnets, with a pipe which I smoke about a quarter through and then put out the light and forget the flash of the guns across the street and the rattle of the windows, everything except the thud of a shell in the marsh behind, but that seems to have stopped now. Goodnight, Ever your loving Daddy.

During the seven days left to him Edward wrote eight letters home. Two, to Bottomley and John Freeman, are consciously written on 'the eve' of his battery's final move to battle station positions and deal with literary matters, especially *The Times* review of his poems in *An Anthology of New Poetry* which Freeman had sent him on Tuesday, 3 April. The same day he began his last letter to Eleanor Farjeon. On Thursday he wrote his last letter to his mother. The remaining four were to Helen.

Thomas was annoyed with the reviewer's charge that his poetry was 'an unconscious survival of a materialism and naturalism which the tremendous life of the last three years has made an absurdity'. He defends himself to Bottomley on Tuesday, 3 April:

I have not seen the *Annual* yet but by the same post as your letter came *The Times* review which I was quite pleased with. I don't mind now being called inhuman and being told by a reviewer now that April's here—that I am blind to the 'tremendous life of these three years'. It would be the one consolation in finishing up out here to provide such reviewers with a conundrum. . . . Why do the idiots accuse me of using my eyes? Must I only use them as field-glasses and must I see only Huns in these beautiful hills eastward and only hostile flashes in the night skies when I am at the Observation Post?

Then, later the next day, to John Freeman:

This is the eve, so I can't write much. I now have a letter, this last note, and the tobacco not to speak of the cutting [of *The Times* review] to thank you for. I do thank you very much. . . . I only live now in the hours when I can smoke. Sometimes all through a wet cold night I do not live, I only smoke. Things have been speeding up and work and some exposure to weather and danger increase. I wonder what these days will bring forth.

I still have your letter unanswered in my pocket. It was a pleasure I can well remember reading it as I came along from where the letters were to my billet. You talked of Mangan whom I never got far into and of Morris whose earlier things and some of 'Poems by the Way' I liked very much—the 'Come back to the inn, love' and a similar one as much as almost anything,—when I last read him. You talked of the *Annual* too which I haven't seen myself. Thank goodness [J. C.] Squire isn't going to sit down upon it hard. I was quite pleased with *The Times* review. It said what they have been saying about E. T. for so long, that he's an inhuman beast. I think they are rather sweeping and I should have thought the things in the *Annual* not wholly inhuman or wholly contrary to 'the tremendous life of the last 3 years'.

I heard you and Joy were at High Beech and am glad you enjoyed it. I enjoyed hearing about Joy and Baba in the forest. My wife sounded so happy to have her and your wife. Give them my love. It is all I can give anyone now.

Perhaps the coolness he had displayed at the OP and as fire-control officer had given him a hint of the 'inhuman' quality others might see in him. The clarity of his vision, and his expression of the seen world, had always been presented with a touch of ironical detachment, and now that he filled his letters home with clear-cut descriptions—best seen in his letters to Eleanor Farjeon—he was amusedly alive to their resemblance to much of his bread-and-butter prose:

The houses and trees dense and then to right and left only trees growing thinner till at last the ridge sweeping away is bare for some miles. But this is E. T.'s vein. . . . I am not pretending I am not E. T.—am not the author of *Horae Solitariae*, although I admit he is a near relative. . . . I am so glad about your cottage and garden. They sound just the perfection of what I am keeping entirely out of my mind.

Helen knew best of all the curbs he had learned to impose on his passionate nature and he confirmed this knowledge in a now missing letter to her, written on 31 March 1917, which described the Beaurains OP where he died:

Imagine me pigging it with chocolate and tinned things and a map and a telephone and a periscope. . . . The hedge I spy through is of elder, but only sparrows come to it, though chaffinches sing near and larks hover above the dry grass just in front. . . . I don't see all the green things here. . . . My hedge is almost the only one in the countryside. . . . Memories I have, but they are mixed up with my thoughts and feelings . . . or when I hear a blackbird. . . . You must not therefore expect me to say anything outright. It is not my way, is it?

Writers on Thomas have occasionally linked these letters with some of his poems, to suggest that he knew he was going to be killed and, in some subconscious fashion, welcomed death in action as a final solution to the melancholy misfortunes that had dogged his life both as a man and as a writer. John Moore records that 'Edward had dreaded it [the OP], had had a queer "feeling" about it, on the very first day he saw it'. The diary glosses this 'feeling' more factually in two entries:

25 March: Up at 5 and to O.P. beyond Beaurains with Thorburn and stood all day in trench behind hedge till head ached with staring at Wancourt and Neuville-Vitasse and the ground between and beyond.
27 March: Rain and sleet and sun, getting guns camouflaged, stealing a Decanville truck, laying out nightlines. . . . Still that aching below the nape of my neck since my last O.P. day.

There are no hints of fatal attraction or dread in the War Diary references to the OP. Thomas used many different OP positions. Everything recorded is severely practical in preparation for the attack to be made north and south of Arras on a broad forty-five mile front:

New zero line, planting pickets. Arranging for material for new OP dugout—old one fell in yesterday. (30 March.)

Up at 5 worn out and wretched. 5.9s flopping at Achicourt while I dressed. Up at Beaurains. There is a chalk-stone cellar with a dripping Bosh dug-out far under and by the last layer of stones is the lilac bush, rather short. Nearby a graveyard for the 'tapferer franzos soldat' with crosses and Hun names. Blackbirds in the clear cold bright morning early in black Beaurains. Sparrows in the elder of the hedge I observe through—a cherry tree just this side of the hedge makes projection in trench with its roots. . . . Night in lilac-bush cellar of stone like Berryfield. (31 March.)

His letters to all his close friends at this time are clearly moulded to recall previously shared experiences and interests. Those to Helen are reassuring but never deceptive. They assume her intense feeling, her love of natural things, her need for support and even that carelessness in trivial domestic affairs that had so often driven him to coldness and near-despair in his irritable moods. He had noted their love-making with a symbol in his War Diary and discreetly asked for confirmation that the fourth child she wished for so intensely had been conceived. The letters he sent to those close to Helen were intended partly to enable her to have a full share of his experiences as far as that is possible to do and, at the same time, to give her more solid grounds for assessing his chances of survival. On 27 March he wrote to Eleanor Farjeon: 'I keep feeling that I should enjoy it more if I knew I would survive it. I can't help allowing it to trouble me, but it doesn't prey on me and I have no real foreboding, only occasional trepidation and anxiety. . . . I wish I could keep back more of what I feel, but you mustn't think it is often fear or ever dread for more than a moment.' Three days later he wrote in similar strain to his brother Julian:

> War, of course, is not altogether different from peace, except that one may be blown to bits and have to blow others to bits. Physical discomfort is sometimes so great that it seems a new thing, but of course it is not. You remember cycling in the rain towards Salisbury [in 1912]. It really is seldom quite a different thing from that. Of course, one seems very little one's own master, but then, one seldom does seem so. Death looms, but however it comes it is unexpected, whether from appendicitis or bullet. . . . I have suffered more from January to March in other years than this. That is the plain fact. I will not go into it any more.

Preparations for the Easter Offensive began in earnest on Monday 2 April when Thomas supervised the reconstruction of emergency dug outs close to the final position of their guns. When they fired 100 rounds for practice, half melting snow began to fall. Tuesday, in frozen slush and with wet feet, was spent filling sandbags to complete the dug-outs. On Wednesday they had fired 600 practice rounds in cold, slippery mud. The day began at 4.30 and finished when they retired exhausted to the sleeping dug-outs at the battery. That night was filled with the flap of artillery, and the next morning he recorded that the 'sods on fire-control officer's dug-out begin to be fledged with fine green feathers of yarrow—yarrow'. The rest of Thursday was spent in firing all day 'practising barrage, etc.'. Friday morning was a lazy half-day. Their billets were shelled, and he and Captain Horton played with an old dog that hung around the ruined cottage before they motored to Fosseux and Avesnes for supplies and mail.

The infantry were already marching up to their final positions wearing yellow gas-detection patches on their backs and the roads were worse than ever—'no crust left on the side roads'. After Saturday spent at the OP, Edward began his last letter to Helen, 'in my valise on the floor of my dug-out writing before sleeping'. He then expanded the laconic diary entry for Thursday:

> When I posted my letter in the morning I thought it would be a bad day, but we did all the shelling. Hardly anything came near the OP or even the village [Beaurains]. I simply watched the shells changing the landscape. . . . But the sun shone and larks and partridges and magpies made love and the trench was being made passable for the wounded that will be harvested in a day or

two. . . . I am tired but resting. Yesterday afternoon was more exciting. Our billet was shelled. The shells fell all around and you should have seen Horton and me dodging them. It was quite fun for me, though he was genuinely alarmed, being more experienced. None of us was injured, and our home escaped. . . . It will be all work till further notice—days of ten times the ordinary work to do. So good night and I hope you sleep no worse than I do. . . . *Sunday*. I slept fairly well and now it is sunshine and wind and we are in for a long day and I must post this when I can.

The last entry in his diary describes Easter Day 1917:

A bright warm Easter day but Achicourt shelled at 12.39 and then at 2.15 so that we all retired to cellar [of the billet]. I had to go over to battery [in their final positions for the assault] at 3 for a practice barrage, skirting the danger zone, but we were twice interrupted. A 5.9 fell 2 yards from me as I stood by the f/c post. One burst down the back of the office [of the Commanding Officer at the gun position] and a piece of dust scratched my neck.

The 5.9 apparently, was a rare dud shell, and as Lushington informed John Moore in 1937: 'in the evening the other officers rather pulled Thomas's leg about his escape. We were all sitting in the mess. Thomas was censoring the men's letters. I remember saying, "Whose turn is it for OP tomorrow?" and he said it was his. Someone else said something about "a fellow who was as lucky as he was would be safe wherever he went".'

The artillery barrage that opened the offensive began at first light the next morning, Easter Monday 9 April. At 7.36 a. m. he was killed by a stray shell at the Beaurains Observation Post.

Helen's last letter to him was on his body when he was killed; like the War Diary and her photograph, it is curiously creased by the shell-blast, and slightly stained. Normally, as one can deduce from his replies to her and to his friends, she sent him a budget of small incidents at High Beech, as she had always done during their peacetime separations. This last letter reads so much like the early outpourings of her courtship letters in 1896 and 1897:

My darling, my own soul, I know that this pain will go and calm and even happiness come again, just as the snow will melt and the Spring come and in the earth is life moving all the time, and in our souls love eternal. And that's all that matters. All that matters: that we love each other and that sooner or later we shall understand as we cannot now.

Farewell sweetheart; and believe that when courage comes back to me as it will you will not find me wanting. This snow must be the last of this terrible winter—that will help me, but more than all your trust in me.

Farewell and God bless you and keep you and bring you back to me whose heart and soul and body are yours ever and wholly.
                Helen.
Baba says 'give Daddy 100 loves'.

To confirm this trust, which she so much desired, he had added the late night postscript to his penultimate letter, quoted by John Moore, but now lost:

My dear, you must not ask me to say much. I know that you must say much because you feel much. But I, you see, must not feel anything. I am just, as it were, tunnelling underground and something sensible in my subconsciousness directs me not to think of the sun, at the end of the tunnel there is the sun. Honestly this is not the result of thinking; it is just an explanation of my state of mind which is really so entirely preoccupied with getting through the tunnel that you might say I had forgotten there was a sun at either end, before or after this business. This will perhaps induce you to call me inhuman like the newspapers, just because for a time I have had my ears stopped—mind you, I have not done it myself—to all but distant echoes of home and friends and England. If I could respond as you would like me to to your feelings I should be unable to go on with this job in ignorance whether it is to last weeks or months or years. I never even think will it be weeks or months or years. I don't even wonder if the drawers in the sitting-room are kept locked!

This hypersensitive, constitutionally diffident man, incapable of speaking outright about his deepest feelings, even to Helen, would have been truly surprised at the reaction of his fellow soldiers to his death. Helen received many letters from his gunners, and Thorburn told me that he could still recall in 1967 one tribute, in a soldier's letter home which he had censored, that confirmed their affection for him. Here are two letters Helen received when the telegram announcing his death arrived at Paul's Nurseries, High Beech, after being forwarded from Petersfield because Edward had officially given Steep as his permanent home.
    The first letter was from Thorburn:

                                        France
                                        April 9, 1917
Dear Mrs. Thomas,
    It is a great trial to me to write to inform you that your husband was killed this morning. As I have been very closely associated with him since we first met at Trowbridge, I thought it would be well to take upon myself the duty of letting you know of his death. It happened this morning, by shell fire, in the observation post.

I think, before anything else, I have to express to you the great debt of gratitude I owe to your husband. He has been so much my support through this
difficult—and to me, uncongenial,—work; and has been so wise and kind in the
help he has given me. His friendship has meant a great deal to me. I don't know
whether you would want me to say this,—but it seems to me he has got on
splendidly,—magnificently,—in the army; as well as much younger men who
have just the knack. And I am sure that his other gifts, and the depth and
strength of his character, have been gratefully valued by all of us who were at
work with him.

I claim, at least, his friendship; and just now I am terribly lonely out here
without him. I hope I may not have given you needless pain by anything I have
said. But will you accept my most sincere and earnest sympathy in your sorrow.

I shall be very glad to look after your husband's personal effects.

I am
Yours very sincerely,
John M. Thorburn.

The second was sent the next day by his commanding officer.

April 10th, 1917.

Dear Mrs. Thomas,

You will have heard by now from Mr. Thorburn of the death in action of
your husband. I asked him to write immediately we knew about it yesterday,
but delayed myself until the funeral, from which I have just returned.

I cannot express to you adequately in words how deep our sympathy is for
you and your children in your great loss. These things go too deep for mere
words. We, officers and men, all mourn our own loss. Your husband was very
greatly loved in this battery, and his going has been a personal loss to each of
us. He was rather older than most of the officers and we all looked up to him
as the kind of father of our happy family.

He was always the same, quietly cheerful and ready to do any job that was
going with the same steadfast unassuming spirit. The day before his death we
were rather heavily shelled and he had a very narrow shave. But he went about
his work quite quietly and ordinarily as if nothing was happening. I wish I
could convey to you the picture of him, a picture we had all learnt to love, of
the old clay pipe, gum boots, oilskin coat, and steel helmet.

With regard to his actual death you have probably heard the details. It
should be of some comfort to you to know that he died at a moment of victory
from a direct hit by a shell, which must have killed him outright without
giving him a chance to realise anything—a gallant death for a very true and
gallant gentleman.

We buried him in a little military cemetery a few hundred yards from the
battery; the exact spot will be notified to you by the parson. As we stood by his

grave the sun came and the guns round seemed to stop firing for a short time. This typified to me what stood out most in your husband's character, the spirit of quiet, sunny, unassuming cheerfulness.

When I get to England again I shall be happy to come and tell you anything more you'd like to know. My address is The White House, Heath End, Farnham, Surrey, and I will write you in case you would like to see me.

Yours very sincerely,
Franklin Lushington
(Major Comdg. 244 Siege Battery, RGA.)

Please do not bother to answer this as I know how busy you will be. I shall understand.

His grave in Agny was re-numbered, as Helen was informed in a neutral pro-forma letter from the Imperial War Graves Commission on 24 October 1924, as Plot 1, Row C, Grave 43. This bleak formal communication seemed singularly remote when it arrived. For some time Helen had been suffering an acute nervous illness—diagnosed later as delayed shock—and was then staying at the home of C. E. M. Joad in Hampstead under the care of a specialist consultant. In the next twelve months she was to begin writing *As It Was,* her sensitive account of her life with Edward, as part of the desperate, but successful, therapy to bring her into renewed touch with her children and their quite different world. Her two books are irreplaceable and no attempt has been made here to paraphrase them.

In spite of Edward's injunction about the use of a pseudonym for his poems, his father had revealed his identity shortly after his death was reported in *The Times* on 14 April 1917. Two proof copies of *Poems* by Edward Eastaway were printed before July 1917, according to R. P. Eckert; *Poems* by Edward Thomas ('Edward Eastaway') was published on 10 October 1917 and was followed, fifteen months later, by *Last Poems.* *Collected Poems* by Edward Thomas appeared in the autumn of 1920 and was followed in 1922 by *Cloud Castle and Other Papers* with an unfinished foreword by W. H. Hudson. Already the interest in the man and his work was concentrating upon his poems and, during the two decades after his death, Edward Thomas, poet, had effectively assimilated most traces of P. E. Thomas, the young nature-writer, or Edward Thomas the influential reviewer-critic and prose-writer, or Edward Eastaway the self-effacing writer of verse. The full significance of his prose works has yet to be assessed with the thoroughness they deserve. One of his closest friends, James Guthrie, made the point twenty years after his death:

It would not be true to say that when he became a soldier, Thomas was
suddenly made into a poet. The poet had already evolved long before. His
poems are little different in texture from the best of his prose.

  He was fortunate in that the climacteric of his intellectual life so nearly
coincided with the war, and that he could face the desperate chances with
untroubled heart. It was characteristic of him that he found to the last the quiet
moment in which he might carry forward his peaceful vocation, to gather from
whatever happened about him some delicate thoughts.

Guthrie extended his tribute in the 1939 August number of the *Welsh
Review*:

We may regret that the world was not kinder than it was to Edward Thomas;
we may feel that he had more for us than he had the opportunity to give; that
here was a life thrown away just when a great talent was at its brightest. Yet this
man did fulfil himself to the utmost, not only as a poet and writer of delicate
prose, but as a stout character and unequalled friend. The events of his life are
his books, done in solitude, and in those we must look to find himself as he
should wish to be found. After many years, those who knew him remember
him as a young man, while they are old and altered. These are indeed not times
for men like him to be living in. His time has gone along with the sweetness
which he drew from it; and in his work we savour it again.

CHAPTER 17

True Thomas

EDWARD THOMAS offers many profiles to those who wish to understand him and the growing significance of his writing for present-day readers. Whichever way we approach him—whether through photographs or letters, the memoirs of close friends, the published records of the two women who loved him, through his enormous output of literary journalism or, more effectively, through his poems—the pattern of recognition changes with the swiftness of a kaleidoscope. Those who knew him best have preserved the sense of a rare quality that sustained him slightly apart from their own concerns with social or literary success. His early death, at the moment of first public recognition of his achievement as a poet, helped create a stereotype that peeps through the material supplied readily to John Moore in 1935 when he undertook to write *The Life and Letters of Edward Thomas* as part of the official celebrations of the Edward Thomas Memorial Committee. The myth is sustained in the numerous unpublished memoirs that were collected between 1945 and 1950 by Rowland L. Watson, the indefatigable secretary of that Memorial Committee which was chaired by de la Mare. The same picture of Thomas emerges from whatever period of his life they recall. Invariably we encounter the tall willowy figure with its slight stoop; the handsome face, piercing eyes, long stride and powerful hands; the mobile, sensitive mouth and the fair (or brown) hair worn slightly long; the distinctive voice, either light baritone or tenor in quality; the countryman's complexion and tweeds so unusual in London streets; the silent listener, in literary clubbable groups or on long cross-country walks, whose conversation was highly regarded if rarely recorded. The debilitating bouts of melancholy are hinted or stated before the consensus settles firmly around the remarkable change in him after he enlisted. His friends and colleagues recall his newly-found freedom from petty worries, the growth of self-confidence in bearing and manner, the ready adoption of a soldier's pride in smart turn-out and attention to duty, and—among those who had known the scholar-gypsy at Lincoln, the hesitant outsider in Fleet Street, and the happy warrior in camp—his excessive concern with physical fitness, his hardened muscles, strengthened limbs, and ready acceptance of tedious yet necessary routine. A few, as Jessie Conrad did, believed that in his last weeks in England in

1916 his face betrayed the marks of a man who knew he was doomed to die, although this was not the 1916 record of close friends who, like Henry W. Nevinson, believed that 'the energy of his soul had found its line of excellence' as a soldier.

Such flickering images and exterior memories, easily produced by a random juxtaposition of snaps of him taken between 1908 and 1916, dissolve like sand through fingers when they are confronted with his poems, his record of childhood, the sharply-etched entries in his War Diary, the plea for an informed awareness of man's place in the natural world that gives backbone to *The South Country,* or the compassionate yet trenchant response to South-West Wales that charges many sketches in *Rest and Unrest, Light and Twilight,* and *The Last Sheaf.* The thrust of all his writing from 1910 conveys a willingness to confront his earlier, self-created world of superfine reverie with the demands being made by an urban-industrial society upon an older way of life: one in which he felt readily at home and which, he believed, reached unbroken into a pre-history he felt compelled to interpret. This process induced a reappraisal of his long concern with the appropriate manner in which to address a present-day reader without discontinuity from the cradling influence of the spoken language. Indeed, the two-way traffic between ordinary speech and the writer's craft had absorbed his attention from early 1908. The wider implications of this personal development were not pursued. They were side-tracked by his stated belief that he lacked the necessary resource for radical intellectual formulations.

This was not an evasive tactic by a solitude-loving thinker who wished to remain free from party labels or the numerous self-perpetuating pressure groups that flourished around him in Edwardian and Georgian London. By temperament, training, and an inflexible habit of self-correction which characterized him from boyhood to his last days in France, Edward Thomas had set out to follow the promptings of his daimon with no consideration of the effect on family or friends. Whatever truths he might uncover were to be the direct result of his own experiences, follies, and errors. J. M. Thorburn—an early disciple of Jung and a fellow-cadet and subaltern during Thomas's last seven months—placed his scrupulous finger on this quality in a letter to John Moore in February 1940: 'I have never read much Thomas, nor when we knew each other was I very capable of appreciating the essentials of his genius (though I think I was aware of this, more or less fully). He was too purely—I do not say outward, but—experiential for me; and my all-too-insistent craving for inwardness and metaphysical depth perhaps too remote from him.' This comment is in tune with a remark by Gordon Bottomley to Clifford Bax in February 1922: 'It was Edward himself who told me you called him True Thomas. I never heard him sound proud of anything about himself, as he told it, save that alone.' Even so, Thomas always kept a tight rein on his fierce urge to speak truth. As we have seen he confessed to Helen in one of his last letters: 'You must not therefore expect me to say anything outright. It is not my way, is it?'

As soon as his poetry began to flow, he trusted himself more and more to this long-sought, newly-found medium. Extracts from two letters sent to Edward Garnett from Hucclecote in late June 1915 underline this readiness to speak out. They follow a sharp verbal exchange of views between them while Thomas was still havering between enlistment, a visit to Frost in New England, and a post as schoolmaster or lecturer. On 24 June, after a four-day cycle ride from Steep to Gloucestershire, Thomas defended his own stand: 'I can't help dreading people both in anticipation and when I am among them and my only way of holding my own is the instinctive one of turning on what you call coldness and a superior manner. That is why I hesitated about America. I felt that unless I could make a friend or two I could do no good. . . . Nor do I think that any amount of distress could turn me into a lecturer. It would weary you if I tried to explain: I don't justify. But these are first thoughts and I am tired rather.' The next day he was

afraid there really is not much I can add to what I said yesterday. . . . But perhaps it is worthwhile assuring you I am aware of my deficiency and that being aware of it only exaggerates it, for it is all due to self consciousness and fear. What you call superiority is only a self defence unconsciously adopted by the most faint-hearted humility—I believe. It goes on thickening into a callosity which only accident—being left to my own devices perhaps—can ever break through. I long for the accident but cannot myself arrange to produce it! However, perhaps landing in New York quite alone, and under some stress, may do the trick, and I almost feel inclined to go if only to see whether it will happen so.

This was a rare moment of self-revelation that anticipates his later attitude towards volunteering for service overseas. Its authenticity is underlined by the first draft of a new poem that ended the letter:

> I built myself a house of glass:
> It took me years to make it:
> And I was proud. But now, alas,
> Would God someone would break it.

But it looks too magnificent.
No neighbour casts a stone
From where he dwells, in tenement
Or palace of glass, alone.

Two days later he began another confessional poem ('Words') during
a cycle ride from Hucclecote to Coventry where he turned down the
friendly headmaster's offer of a temporary post as an English master. A
fortnight later he had decided to enlist in the Artists' Rifles, if they
would accept him. In these poems, and in the letters to Garnett—as in
some later ones to Helen and Frost—we come close to some fundamental beliefs of True Thomas about himself and his chequered career
as prose writer and critic.

The persistent quarrying into his past that marks so many of his
poems was not the result of a sudden road-to-Damascus flash of self-
discovery. The process had been spread gradually over at least five or six
years. The quotation from 'The Outcast', quoted in Chapter 7, reads
uncommonly like a tentative confession of some of his own unrealized
aspirations tacked on to a veiled sketch of W. H. Davies. How much of
Thomas it contains is suggested by de la Mare, who contributed a
prophetic review of the poems by Edward Eastaway in *An Anthology of
New Poetry* on 28 April 1917. The following brief extracts indicate its
quality:

Never lived a man more resolute in fidelity to what he held dear in the world;
and dearest to him were the simplicity, grace, freshness, livingness of what
springs of its own nature, clear and sweet as a wellspring out of the earth, and
as impulsively, out of man's heart and mind and imagination. . . . Most poems
are final and isolated, as it were, in their own form. In these there is a kind of
endlessness in the experience they tell of, and in its expression the desire only
to convey it without friction or emphasis, from consciousness to consciousness,
as in the first of the morning one tells to one's self a dream.

This perceptive criticism, based on eighteen poems and slightly tinged
by an acute sense of loss, catches the timeless quality that marks
Thomas's best prose and verse.

There is no single key to unlock the riches of his mind. His books,
essays, sketches and critical reviews overwhelm the searcher: there are
hundreds of thousands of well-written words to sift, absorb, and overcome. Nor does Thomas help us. He and his friends have recorded too
many slighting references to his works, especially his commissioned
books, without making clear that his dissatisfaction lies in the final

shape of a completed work, tailored to suit a publisher's demands. The initial conception of each book was lovingly forged, scrupulously prepared for, and quickly begun. He knew he was at his best over a short distance. As some books tailed off, the enthusiasm waned and self-loathing took over. Some of the clearest examples of his thinking are scattered in books that brought him little comfort, acclaim, or financial reward: *Windsor Castle* (1910), *Feminine Influence on the Poets* (1910), *Maurice Maeterlinck* (1911), *Algernon Charles Swinburne* (1912), *George Borrow* (1912), and *The Icknield Way* (1913). In particular, the first half of *Feminine Influence* reads like an attempt to present a general theory of the nature of poetry (and its relationship to passion and the love of nature and women) before he began the more anecdotal second half, which displeased him so much.

The nucleus of his life-long desire to interpret Shelley's poetry finds expression here. 'Shelley's letters show us portions of the process of dissolving the objects of the outward and visible world into the poet's inner life, so as to form if not a complete and consistent new world there, yet one of great significance which can only die with his poetry.' Equally, the chapter on 'Women, Nature and Poetry' elucidates an impulse behind much of his prose sketches: an impulse he later repudiated in the poem, 'I built myself a house of glass'. He writes in late 1909 of 'the calm immortal and unchanging world of imagination and of art' which is lovely and desired 'because it is a world inaccessible to age, winter, hatred, tyranny, disease, stupidity, or death'.

This is a significant list, as de la Mare divined. It defines obliquely, as was his way, Thomas's attitude to social problems as they appear in his tales, anecdotes, and sketches. The devastating effect of winter on the misfits, outcasts, and failures of rural and urban society engaged his imagination at all times in his tales (in *Rest and Unrest* and *Light and Twilight*) and in potted biographies scattered throughout his so-called 'travel books' (*The South Country, The Heart of England, The Icknield Way,* and *In Pursuit of Spring*). Yet he lacked his father's Positivist belief in social amelioration and could not admire the fervent involvement in local politics or in the influential Ethical Society that made nationwide claims on Philip Henry Thomas's oratorical gifts as a lecturer. From the early days of his own courtship, too, Edward had supported, but without whole-hearted approval, Helen's tempestuous involvement in advanced social causes and, later, tolerated without objection her share in various socialist activities organized by the staff and friends of Bedales School. His visits to such functions were rare—but much admired, so his elder

children once informed me. He preferred the week-end fireside of his
neighbour up on the Mutton, the socialist doctor and writer Harry
Roberts with whom Baynes had worked. At his home he would talk
endlessly on Welsh and country matters, or sing songs spontaneously as
he had done so often as a boy at home or as a visiting young cousin in
Pontardulais. Apart from one unsigned, damaging, partisan review (in
Orage's *The New Age*) of Thomas's well-argued essay *The Country*, it is
difficult to find comments on his work that identified him as a sup-
porter of any social or political cause. The long correspondence with his
literary agent makes the point repeatedly. This vagueness, or deliberate
refusal to be pigeon-holed, must have earned Thomas the barely disguised disapproval of his father. Certainly, as Edward told Frost during
one period when he was lodging with his parents, he recognized that,
even then aged thirty-seven, he earned his father's contempt. The poem
'P. H. T.', the first of Thomas's series of Household Poems (*Poems* 99–114)
records the bitterness with which Thomas made this discovery; and an
entry in Julian Thomas's 1915 diary about the father's discouraging comments on his son's poems confirms the chasm of misunderstanding
between them that could not be bridged.

Father and son had much in common. Single-mindedness of purpose,
skill in the acquisition of languages, fluency of speech (the one in public,
the other in private), a sustained belief in the social value of a non-
sectarian idealistic education, extreme rectitude in the conduct of
domestic and public affairs, a devotion (without blinkers) to Wales,
punctiliousness in household organization, and a love of reading aloud.
After Helen agreed to the first publication of 'P. H. T.' in February 1944
Edward's remaining brothers and his nephews were bitterly unhappy
about it: they saw no grounds for the poem's cold severity either in their
own memories of their father and grandfather or in their recollections
of the way Edward and his family had always been welcome at the
family home. Their reaction was understandable. Their anger against
Helen implies a suggestion (once made to me) that the poem should
have been suppressed. Helen was surprised at the reaction, as earlier she
had been surprised at the response of Edward's friends to her own two
books which, according to Frost and many others, made Edward appear
a namby-pamby, robbing him of his masculinity. Her defence to me was
that 'Edward was always a truth teller'.

She could have added that she had often experienced this sharper,
impatient, coldly detached side of Edward's nature, which she
smothered with her love for him and her unrestrained faith in his

genius, but which so astounded Eleanor Farjeon on her first visit to their household. Many years ago she allowed me to quote, in a broadcast, a letter she had written to Rowland Watson in July 1946 about this and similar experiences:

What I have out of the love I bore Edward, and the deep friendship he had for me, is not of the past, and our correspondence is only a surface sign of it. I never quite knew what I meant to and did for him—does 'knowing matter'? He, I am sure, never fully knew *all* he meant, and did for me; he probably wouldn't have believed it, any more than he would have believed that he could ever mean what he does to so many of the young generation. One thing I imagine had this value for him in our friendship, that he had no power to hurt me, or any wish to; he never tried to, and it was necessary for him not to be able to hurt everybody he cared for. I think he loved Bronwen so much because she was so airy with him in his moods. On the other hand to be able to hurt a woman as he did Helen, *and not to break her*, to be so sure she was strong enough to bear anything from him, was the most wonderful thing of all. I couldn't have borne it myself without breaking, and often couldn't for her. Yet to die out-right for him would have been easy, if it could have been of any use to him. It is so much easier to die than to live. What a theme to start within the limits of a letter card! Yours and his, Eleanor.

Edward's uncontrollable fits of angry irritation at home seem to be part of the illness for which he sought treatment from Godwin Baynes. Diagnosis of the incidence of any form of mental illness is still as diffi-cult as the prescription of effective curative treatment. Any attempt at retrospective analysis of the long-since dead is full of pitfalls and, to my mind, impossible of useful solution. Some secure basis for any comment on Thomas's 'neurasthenia' rests on the observation of intimate friends, his own partial revelation in letters, and rare comments by Helen. His three children were quite unaware of the strains imposed on Helen. Although her letters and writings are never couched in conventional terms—the Noble family tradition on Merseyside was a distinguished Unitarian one—she had an unquenchable faith in the power of human love to survive as a potent element in some form of future existence. This belief, together with her physical endurance and natural ease of temperament, frequently exacerbated Edward's moments of self-doubt, and led to a deep sense of insecurity and unworthiness. Fortunately, he suffered no process of successive deterioration which might have led to self-isolation from his family or the society of others; but there were short periods when he felt impelled to leave home with a mountain of work to get through. Such absences from family were not uncommon among his friends, especially Hudson, Belloc, Ransome, the Garnetts, and Conrad. Despite his periods of acute depression, he never failed to harness the mental energy beneath his neurotic misery to the task of completing any commissioned book he had on hand.

Solitude had never held terrors for him. His letters to friends are mere interludes of snatched conversation from the lonely work of a writer. Curiously, his view of the special role of the poet, as essentially someone who is chosen by words for their use in a particular way, did not encourage him to think of himself as a poet. Yet he valued his own personal writing in prose and believed himself capable of producing still better work, if only he could find the acceptable way to an audience that would yield him a modest living. His needs were modest and this belief in his own work was never abandoned. Whenever he wrote to please himself—as in *Light and Twilight* or *Rest and Unrest* or the remarkable trilogy, *The Fear of Death, The Chessplayer,* and *A Sportsman's Tale*—he let the words choose him, and he was content. The same confidence emerges repeatedly in the tone of his observations on poems and poets throughout his *Feminine Influence*:

> Love opens the door, but it does not know what is within, whether it be treasure, nothingness or devils . . . The love-poem is not for the beloved, for it is not worthy . . . It is written in solitude, is spent in silence and the night like a sigh with an unknown object . . . Love-poetry, like all other lyric poetry, is in a sense unintentionally overheard . . . [John Clare] reminds us that words are alive, and not only alive but still half-wild and imperfectly domesticated . . . Words never consent to correspond exactly to any object unless, like scientific terms, they are first killed. Hence the curious life of words in the hands of those who love all life so well that they do not kill even the slender words but let them play on: and such are poets . . . Poetry is and must always be apparently revolutionary if active, anarchic if passive. It is the utterance of the human spirit when it is in touch with a world to which the affairs of 'this world' are parochial.

In 1910, when *Feminine Influence* was written, Thomas was deeply informed in English literature and carried with him a ready store of learning. Words, like birdsong or overwhelming sensuous natural impressions, challenged and received his fullest attentive comprehension. His habit of solitary composition corresponded readily to his habit of solitary walking:

> Beautiful as the notes are for their quality and order, it is their inhumanity that gives them their utmost fascination, the mysterious sense which they bear to us

that earth is something more than a human estate, that there are things not human yet of great honour and power in the world. The very first rush and the following wail [of the nightingale] empty the brain of what is merely human and leave only what is related to the height and depth of the whole world. Here for this hour we are remote from the parochialism of humanity. The bird has admitted a larger air. We breathe deeply of it and are made free citizens of eternity. We hear voices that were not dreamed of before, the voices of those spirits that live in minute forms of life, the spirits that weave the frost flower on the fallen branch, the gnomes of underground, those who care for the fungus on the beech root, the lichen on the trunk, the algae on the grave-stone. This hazel lane is a palace of strange pomp in an empire of which we suddenly find ourselves guests, not wholly alien nor ill at ease, though the language is new. Drink but a little of this air and no need is there to fear the ways of men, their mockery, their cruelty, their foreignness.

He wrote often in defence of the virtues of man's wider awareness of his historic role in a slowly evolving world suddenly placed at risk by the mechanical demands of an urban, industrial, and bureaucratic way of life. During many conversations, his daughter Bronwen assured me that such passages constituted a chief part of the 'country creed' with which he imbued his elder children on their long rambling excursions together. For he felt at ease in the domestic role of teacher, as David Garnett testifies in *The Golden Echo,* and we can detect the same urgency to convince in his poems, in many of his short tales, and in his post-1912 concern with the archetypal fables barely concealed behind proverbs.

He remained a dedicated writer until he enlisted, but the act of writing never absorbed his whole life. James Guthrie got it right: 'He was none of your "great" man, bent upon showing his powers at every turn . . . To write of him as a man, tangible, practical, good at all manner of fun, fond of singing quaintly some old song or other, is to describe him better than his art describes him. Yet from his devotion to his work sprang all the rest.' Admittedly, in his early years he had indulged him-self in baroque ornamentation; in his mature prose he rarely employs a careless word or elaborates a trope: each phrase is moulded, like a glove, to the exact flexibility of corporeal sensation. He extended the same good workmanship to his garden, his contracts, the arrangement of his study, his domestic carpentry, and the education of his children in country matters. The orderliness that marked his meticulous knapsack, or the detailed notes made before writing a book, made him, when he had absorbed the necessary theory, into a reliable gunnery officer.

Despite the posed countenance in most photographs, he was given to fun at home, on a farm, on a houseboat, in an inn, at the pantomime, at a boozy sing-song, or at the Races. Could he have drawn more readily on this in his prose, his journalism might have paid better. But a scrupulous pride in the rightness of his daimon governed everything he wrote, certainly after 1911, for private or public reading. He knew 'how frail and perilous and small was the poet's shielded world! The outside world threatened it as the smooth escarpment of tall, toppling water threatens the little piping sea-bird. And yet this poet's world was for the time being my life. Beyond his words there were, perhaps, the gay, the dear, the beautiful persons whom I knew; Nobby, the tinker, and many more; but probably they slept; they were vain if they were not fictitious.'

In his writing, therefore, he was thrown back increasingly upon one highly selective part of himself; and his prose lacks the attractive vein of incorrigible irresponsibility that peeps out readily in his notebooks and in some of his verse. Nothing can detract from his application to the task that mattered most to him as he sought a way forward to becoming a poet: how best to draw finely, unequivocally, the contours of his mind's experiences. The spirit in which he approached his search for the Icknield Way—a not clearly defined ancient British road—is an admirable gloss on his own quest for an adequate means of expression: 'It is not, however, to a man walking for pleasure that we shall go for a sense of roads, but to one like Bunyan. *Pilgrim's Progress* is full of the sense of roads.'

There is an unvarnished description of what Thomas may have experienced on his inspired solitary walks in Edith Wharton's autobiographical *A Backward Glance*:

Yet what I recall of those rambles is not so much the comradeship of the other children, or the wise and friendly talk of our guide, as my secret sensitiveness to landscape—something in me quite incommunicable to others, that was tremblingly and inarticulately awake to every detail of wind-warped fern and wide-eyed briar rose, yet more profoundly alive to a unifying magic beneath the diversities of the visible scene—a power with which I was in deep and solitary communion whenever I was alone with nature. It was the same tremor that had stirred in me in the spring woods of Mamaroneck, when I heard the whisper of the arbutus and the starry choir of the dogweed; and it has never since been still.

Grahame Greene, too, confirms the accuracy with which Thomas found words for experiences that, at first blush, seem bizarre and eccentric. In his personal reminiscences, *Ways of Escape* (1980), Greene quotes 'The

Other' to illustrate his opinion that most writers 'feel the haunting presence of an individual they wish to understand'. Like Greene, Thomas could not rest on a commonsense, clinical acceptance of his own moods and responses. While he denied his own grasp of intellectual formulation, he could turn aside to speculate in a more personal fashion:

He [one of 'the children of earth' in *The South Country*] was a great lover of these things, and to his love for them combined the ecstasy of courtship with the understanding of marriage. . . . It is curious, too, how many different kinds of Eden or Golden Age Nature has in her gift, as if she silently recorded the backward dreams of each generation and reproduced them for us unexpectedly. . . . These things also propose to the roving, unhistoric mind an Eden, one still with us, one that is passing, not, let us hope, the very last. Some of these scenes, whether often repeated or not, come to have a rich symbolical significance; they return persistently and, as it were, ceremoniously—on festal days—but meaning I know not what. . . . Something in me belongs to these things [the recalled scenes], but I hardly think that the mere naming of them will mean anything except to those—many, perhaps—who have experienced the same.

The experiences he treasures were rarefied, but he did not wish to invest them with an aura of mystification. His search for a language without betrayal to himself implied that he had no desire to betray others, especially children and those dear to him.

I still wonder at the self-denigration with which Thomas played down his intellectual ability at the very moment that he asserts, with a critic's practised objectivity, a quiet self-confidence in the value of his private musings. The double vision is present quite early in his life, before he had begun to accept that he had lost his way in the journalistic world or was suffering the onset of neurasthenic illness. Two letters to Ian MacAlister in late 1902, when he had succeeded to Lionel Johnson's place on the *Daily Chronicle,* could have been written at any time in the next dozen years: 'After all my powers being at most very small, it does not matter if I do merely reviewing. For some time, perhaps for ever, I shall be unable to fret that my notebooks and my brain are full of things that will never be on paper. (My vanity does not extend to print, mind you.) [10 November 1902.] . . . When for a time I am free from all business, though my tendency then is to write, I am not always willing to. For I must have some time in which to be non-literary, free to think or better still not to think at all, but to let the wind and the rain do my thinking for me, filling my brain'. (December 1902.)

The desire to be 'non-literary' is a constant refrain in his letters from 1913 onwards. It lies at the heart of his immediate championship of

Davies's early poetry. It governs the special angle of vision with which he presented authors in *A Literary Pilgrim in England*: to show that each writer 'has a country and a topography distinctly its own'. It determines the broad categories within which he confined his selections for his war-time anthology, *This England,* with its non-literary aim. It appears remarkably in his absorption throughout 1913 and early 1914 with his own story versions of well-known proverbs, which later crystallized in his favourite poem 'Lob', and in the renewed interest in the sayings of his youngest child, Myfanwy. Much of his time in camp in England was spent among men of his own background and interests. But when he became an officer he had no difficulty in communicating with his gunners and his batman, Taylor, or in accepting the robust entertain-ment of an active service officers' mess. His War Diary and letters remind us that his response to the natural world was not dimmed.

At no time in his writing did he abandon his preferred observer's position at the point of balance:

> When he should laugh the wise man knows full well:
> For he knows what is truly laughable.
> But wiser is the man who laughs also,
> Or holds his laughter, when the foolish do.

Having lived with his personal papers for so long, I must attempt to sum up his special quality for me. Readers of the prose, as well as the verse, will have learned to create a biography of Thomas for themselves. His words are unequivocal about common experiences. But there are areas of reticence which become clear—as he states so often—only to those who can share some of his intense swings of mood. Yet he offers clear sight, sensitive response to the apprehended world, and an assur-ance that to be in accord with our natural surroundings, even momentarily, is to be offered a measure of peace through self-under-standing. Those who knew him best bear testimony to the assurance he could bring to others. 'His smile and his laugh are things which haven't yet got into the picture for those who never saw him', Eleanor Farjeon wrote to Rowland Watson on 18 January 1938. His cherished moments of solitude—even at the OP in No Man's Land—were instinctive, not selfish, withdrawals from society. He felt compelled to share their value for him in letters home, as readily as he had joined literary clubs and sang songs with his friends. These many sides of Edward Thomas are now widely accessible to a growing company of readers alongside whom, in a companionable way, he continues to walk in step. A passage like the following may be less well known than his poems. It reveals the man who forged for himself, against great odds, the character and language of a poet. The conclusion of this tale, begun in a spirit of irony, opens wide the door to his poetry and the world of experience that lay beyond it:

I found myself saying 'good-bye'. I heard the word 'good-bye' spoken. It was a signal not of a parting but of a uniting. In spite of the unwillingness to be silent with my friend a moment before, a deep ease and confidence was mine underneath that unrest. I took one or two steps to the stile and, instead of crossing it I leaned upon the gate at one side. The confidence and ease deepened and darkened as if I also were like that still, sombre cloud that had been a copse, under the pale sky that was light without shedding light. I did not disturb the dark rest and beauty of the earth which had ceased to be ponderous, hard matter and had become itself cloudy or, as it is when the mind thinks of it, spiritual stuff, so that the glow-worms shone through it as stars through clouds. I found myself running without weariness or heaviness of the limbs through the soaked overhanging grass. I knew that I was more than the something which had been looking out all that day upon the visible earth and thinking and speaking and tasting friendship. Somewhere—close at hand in that rosy thicket or far off beyond the ribs of the sunset—I was gathered up with an immortal company, where I and poet and lover and flower and cloud and star were equals, as all the little leaves were equal ruffling before the gusts, or sleeping and carved out of the silentness. And in that company I had learned that I am something which no fortune can touch, whether I be soon to die or long years away. Things will happen which will trample and pierce, but I shall go on, something that is here and there like the wind, something unconquerable, something not to be separated from the dark earth and the light sky, a strong citizen of infinity and eternity. The confidence and ease had become a deep joy; I knew that I could not do without the Infinite, nor the Infinite without me.

References

The references are to Thomas's published works, excluding published letters. No complete or selected edition of the letters has yet been undertaken.

BW	*Beautiful Wales*
CC	*Cloud Castle and other Papers*
CP	*Collected Poems*
FIP	*Feminine Influence on the Poets*
HGLM	*The Happy-Go-Lucky Morgans*
IPS	*In Pursuit of Spring*
IW	*The Icknield Way*
K	*Keats*
LT	*Light and Twilight*
MM	*Maurice Maeterlinck*
O	*Oxford*
P	*Walter Pater*
PBP	*The Pocket Book of Poems and Songs for the Open Air*
RU	*Rest and Unrest*
S	*Algernon Charles Swinburne*
SC	*The South Country*
ST	*A Sportsman's Tale*
TC	*The Country*
TCET	*The Childhood of Edward Thomas*
TCP	*The Chessplayer and other Essays*
THOE	*The Heart of England*
TIW	*The Isle of Wight*
TLS	*The Last Sheaf*
TWL	*The Woodland Life*

CHAPTER 1

1	SC	8–9, 6–7	8–9	TCET	107–8
5–6	TCET	31–3, 33, 74, 83–4	9–10	ST	15–16, 17–18
7	TCET	102, 104, 107, 106	11	TCET	139
7–8	TCET	17–19	11–12	HGLM	8, 9, 297–8
8	TCET	73, 75, 76	12	HGLM	295–6

12–13	HGLM	286–7
14	MM	267, 260, 312
17	TCET	133, 136
18	TCET	134

CHAPTER 2

21	TCET	142, 143, 144
22	TCET	135, 136, 137
24	TWL	211
26	TLS	19
29	CP	299

CHAPTER 3

| 50 | K | 74, 75, 76, 87 |
| 51 | FIP | 76, 77, 78 |

CHAPTER 4

| 53–4 | O | 11, 250–2 |

CHAPTER 5

70	O	113–14
75	O	115–16
76	O	253–4
85	O	200–1

CHAPTER 6

94	TC	10–11, 12
105	LT	3–4
109	O	129

CHAPTER 7

120	BW	148, 152–3
121	BW	90, 49, 51, 53
122	BW	80–1, 29–30
123	THOE	48–9
125–6	THOE	84–5
132	THOE	147–8, 41, 53, 120

CHAPTER 8

| 138 | PBP | vii |

CHAPTER 9

159	SC	3–6
160	SC	24–5, 243
161	SC	246–7
161–2	SC	259–61
163	SC	147

CHAPTER 10

173	RU	151
	HGLM	100, 101
177	FIP	226, 244–6, 307
177–8	FIP	84–7
178	MM	27, 28, 29
183	CP	311
	TIW	34–5, 36
184	IW	120–1
184–5	FIP	40
	MM	154–5
185	MM	309, 310, 311

CHAPTER 11

200	TLS	19, 20
201	S	96, 205
	P	201, 208, 209, 213, 219
208	HGLM	225
	TLS	205, 206–7, 210
209	HGLM	296–7, 299
209–10	CP	369

CHAPTER 12

218	CP	177
219	IPS	228–9
220	IPS	229, 230, 298

| 221 | IPS | 210, 213, 214, 300–1 |
| 222 | IPS | 171–2, 150 |

CHAPTER 13

| 231 | CP | 371 |
| 235 | CP | 123 |

CHAPTER 14

249	SC	135–6
250	SC	147
	TCP	12
251	ST	37
	CC	195–6
253	CP	167, 57, 49, 227

CHAPTER 15

256–7	CP	23, 31
264	CP	259
264–5	CP	341
265	CP	311
268	CP	287
271–2	CP	333–5

CHAPTER 17

299–300	CP	215
301	FIP	40, 66
304	FIP	76, 85, 86–7
304–5	SC	35–6
306	THOE	141
	IW	5
307	SC	210, 134, 155
308	CP	351
309	LT	50–1

Sources

LETTERS FROM EDWARD THOMAS

The recipient's name is followed by the present known location. An asterisk indicates that a typescript copy is or will be included in the Edward Thomas Collection now being assembled at University College Library, Cardiff. Many letters referred to by John Moore and Rowland Watson have not yet been traced. I have not seen the letters to W. H. Davies.

Clifford Bax, Humanities Research Center, University of Texas at Austin
Jesse Berridge, in private hands.* Ed. Anthony Berridge, *Letters from Edward Thomas to Jesse Berridge*, 1983
Blackwoods, Edinburgh, in the publisher's archives*
Gordon Bottomley, University College Library, Cardiff.* Ed. R. George Thomas, *Letters from Edward Thomas to Gordon Bottomley*, 1968
C. Frank Cazenove, the C. C. Abbott Collection, University of Durham Library
Walter de la Mare, Bodleian Library, Oxford
Frederick Evans, in private hands. *Edward Thomas: Four Letters to Frederick Evans*, 1978
Eleanor Farjeon, Battersea Public Library. Printed in *Edward Thomas: The Last Four Years*, 1958
John Freeman, the Berg Collection, New York Public Library. See John Moore, *The Life and Letters of Edward Thomas*, 1939
Robert Frost, Dartmouth College, Hanover, New Hampshire*
Edward Garnett, Humanities Research Center. *Edward Thomas: A Selection of Letters to Edward Garnett*, 1981
James Guthrie, in private hands
Gwili (John Jenkins), in private hands*
John W. Haines, in private hands. See Moore
E. S. P. Haynes, in private hands. Some at Humanities Research Center, a few printed in Moore
Harry Hooton, the Colbeck Collection, University of British Columbia, Vancouver*
W. H. Hudson, in private hands*
Holbrook Jackson, Lockwood Memorial Library, Buffalo
Sir Ian MacAlister, Battersea Public Library*
Hugh and Irene MacArthur, Battersea Public Library*
Harold Monro, Lockwood Memorial Library, Buffalo
J. Ashcroft Noble, Edward Thomas Collection, Cardiff
Helen Thomas, University College Library, Cardiff.* See Moore
Merfyn Thomas, in private hands

Margaret Townsend, in private hands. Quoted in Robert P. Eckert, *Edward
   Thomas,* 1937. See also the Eckert Collection, Bodleian Library
David Uzzell ('Dad'), location unknown.* See Moore
A. D. Williams, Humanities Research Center. See Moore
John Williams (the Deacon), in private hands*

Letters to Edward Thomas

Those from Helen Thomas are the most numerous and significant. They are in
private hands. I have seen the letters from W. H. Davies (Yale University Library),
Emily and Gordon Bottomley (Berg Collection), Rupert Brooke (Marquette
University Library), Joseph Conrad (in private hands), and Robert Frost (in
private hands*). I have been unable to trace the two-way correspondence between
Thomas and his Oxford friend J. H. Morgan, who told Rowland Watson in 1949
that it survived.

Manuscript material

In addition to the material fully described in *Collected Poems* and *Letters from
Edward Thomas to Gordon Bottomley* I have examined the holographs of *Oxford*
(Lincoln College, Oxford), *Beautiful Wales* (University College Library, Cardiff),
The Heart of England (National Library of Wales, Aberystwyth); the Oxford notebook, begun in 1898 and used until 1907 (in private hands*); a similar notebook
with much Welsh material (in the Colbeck Collection along with many early
papers and essays and a set of the prose works annotated by Harry Hooton); two
early nature notebooks (in the University College Library, Cardiff, with papers,
notes, and family letters for eventual inclusion in the Edward Thomas Collection*). The Humanities Research Center has a rich collection of material by
English writers who knew Thomas. The MS of 'Walking Tom' is there, with some
drafts of Thomas's poems, the original and later versions of *As It Was,* and correspondence accumulated by Moore. The Eckert Collection contains material
assembled by Eckert towards a second edition of his biography.

WALTER DE LA MARE ON EDWARD THOMAS

The following extracts are taken from de la Mare's prophetic review of the
eighteen poems by Edward Eastaway contributed to *An Anthology of New Poetry.*
The review appeared in the *Saturday Westminster Gazette,* 28 April 1917, after the
real identity of the poet had been revealed.

Edward Thomas must have been a critic of verse in his nursery. How much
generous help and encouragement many living poets owe to his counsel only
themselves could say. To his candour, too. For the true cause, he believed, is better

served by an uncompromising 'Trespassers will be prosecuted' than by an amiable 'All are welcome'. Until he became a soldier, and so found a fresh and vivid interest, it had been his fate, day in, day out, to write for a living. To a temperament so independent and so self-critical this experience was little short of purgatory . . . Never lived a man more resolute in fidelity to what he held dear in the world; and dearest to him were the simplicity, grace, freshness, livingness of what springs of its own nature, clear and sweet as a wellspring out of the earth, and as impulsively, out of a man's heart and mind and imagination. . . . Everything which frets and cages and constrains the spirits and bodies of living creatures he hated, and he fought against all that darkens life, denaturalizes, and makes it ugly. Servility, pretentiousness, tyranny, pedantry, officialism, snobbery, dogmatism—such things were to him as evil a blight in human affairs as red tape, corrugated iron, and barbed wire. . . . Virtues attracted him more even than the virtuous, and the instinctive more than the acquired. . . . 'Causes' he was apt to scrutinise a little whimsically and of 'cries' he listened for the echo. . . . His interests, indeed, were not confined to the newspaper, not political, nor what is usually meant by social. . . . To live in content a 'simple life' was perhaps what he desired most of the world, but no man less respected the cant phrase. . . . Most poems are final and isolated, as it were, in their own form. In these there is a kind of endlessness in the experience they tell of, and in its expression the desire only to convey it without friction or emphasis, from consciousness to consciousness, as in the first of the morning one tells to one's self a dream. It is this, one feels—apart from the artist's joy of discovery and experiment—that was the writer's happiness in them. Unforced, unsought, 'unnecessary', they came straight out of himself, from the farthest, yet nearest, verge of experience.

Memoirs

i *Unpublished material* is contained in two typescript volumes of recollections collected between 1949 and 1951 by Rowland Watson. Thomas's family, friends, and colleagues contributed. The material will become part of the Edward Thomas Collection. In addition there is a series of tape-recordings (1964–5), some later broadcast, of interviews I had with Helen Thomas and her daughters, T. T. Thomas the cousin with whom Thomas walked at Pontardulais, Lady MacAlister, and J. M. Thorburn.

ii *Published memoirs and biographies.* The place of publication is London unless otherwise shown.

Clifford Bax	*Inland Far*, 1925, *Some I Knew Well*, 1951
E. C. Bentley	*Those Days*, 1940
Gordon Bottomley	'A Note on Edward Thomas', *The Welsh Review*, Cardiff, September 1945
Hugh Brogan	*The Life of Arthur Ransome*, 1984

Thomas Burke	*City of Encounters*, 1932
Norman Douglas	*Looking Back*, 1934
Robert P. Eckert	*Edward Thomas: A Biography and a Bibliography*, 1937
Eleanor Farjeon	*Magic Casements*, 1941; *Edward Thomas: The Last Four Years*, 1958
John Gould Fletcher	*Life is my Song*, New York, 1937
David Garnett	*The Golden Echo*, 1953
Edward Garnett	*Dictionary of National Biography* entry on Edward Thomas; Introduction to *Selected Poems of Edward Thomas*, Gregynog Press, 1927; 'Edward Thomas', *Athenaeum*, 16 and 20 April 1920
Ashley Gibson	*Postscript to Adventure*, 1930
W. W. Gibson	*The Golden Room and Other Poems*, 1928
Douglas Goldring	*Odd Man Out*, 1938
Joy Grant	*Harold Monro and the Poetry Bookshop*, 1967
James Guthrie	'Edward Thomas: Letters to W. H. Hudson', *London Mercury*, August 1920; *To the Memory of Edward Thomas*, Flansham, 1937; 'Edward Thomas', *The Welsh Review*, August 1939
Robin Guthrie	'James Guthrie: Biographical Notes', *The Amateur Book-Collector*, LV, October 1952
John W. Haines	'Edward Thomas', *The Gloucester Journal*, 16 February 1935; *In Memoriam: Edward Thomas*, No. 2, The Green Pasture Series, 1919
Christopher Hassall	*Edward Marsh, Patron of the Arts*, 1959 *Rupert Brooke: A Biography*, 1964
E. S. P. Haynes	*Personalia*, 1918; *Fritto Misto*, 1924; *A Lawyer's Notebook*, 1932; *The Lawyer: A Conversation Piece*, 1951
Carolyn G. Heilbrun	*The Garnett Family*, 1961
W. H. Hudson	*Letters from W. H. Hudson to Edward Garnett*, ed. with a preface by Edward Garnett, 1928
Edgar Jepson	*Memories of an Edwardian and Neo-Georgian*, 1932
James Milne	*A Window in Fleet Street*, 1931; *The Memoirs of a Bookman*, 1934
T. Sturge Moore	*Some Soldier Poets*, 1939
Henry W. Nevinson	*Changes and Chances*, 1923; review of Moore in *Life and Letters Today*, March 1940
Arthur Ransome	*Autobiography*, ed. with prologue and epilogue by Rupert Hart-Davis, 1976
Ernest Rhys	*Letters from Limbo*, 1936; *Wales England Wed*, 1940
Richard J. Stonesifer	*W. H. Davies: A Critical Biography*, 1963
Helen Thomas	*As It Was*, 1926; *World Without End*, 1931; *Edward Thomas: A Talk*, Edinburgh, 1974; *A Remembered Harvest*, Edinburgh, 1970

Myfanwy Thomas   *One of these fine days,* 1982
Philip Thomas   *A Religion of this World: A Selection of Positivist Addresses,* 1913
Lawrance Thompson *Selected Letters of Robert Frost,* 1963; *Robert Frost: The Early Years 1874–1915,* 1967
Herbert G. Wright *Studies in Contemporary Literature,* 1918 (lectures given at University Hall, Bangor, 1917–18)

Critical Studies

There are two irreplaceable earlier studies of the life and works: H. Coombes, *Edward Thomas,* 1956, and William Cooke, *Edward Thomas; A Critical Biography,* 1970. Other critical interpretations are:

D. W. Harding, 'A Note on Nostalgia', *Scrutiny,* vol. 1, no. 1, 1932

C. Day Lewis, 'The Poetry of Edward Thomas', *Essays by Divers Hands,* vol. xxviii, pp. 86 ff., 1956

F. R. Leavis, *New Bearings in English Poetry,* 1932

Edna Longley, ed., *Edward Thomas: Poems and Last Poems,* 1975

Edna Longley, ed., *Edward Thomas: Language not to be Betrayed,* 1981

Jan Marsh, *Edward Thomas: A Poet for his Country,* 1978

Andrew Motion, *The Poetry of Edward Thomas,* 1980

Vernon Scannell, *Edward Thomas,* Writers and their Work Series, 1962

Stan Smith, 'A Language not to be Betrayed', *Literature and History,* no. 4, Autumn 1976

List of Prose Works

The Woodland Life, two editions, 1897.

Horae Solitariae, 1902.

The Poems of John Dyer (Number 4 of *The Welsh Library,* edited by Owen M. Edwards), edited by Thomas, 1903.

Oxford (Black's Colour Book Series), painted by John Fulleylove, R.I., described by Thomas, with 60 illustrations, 1903. Reprinted, 1911; revised, with 32 illustrations, 1922.

Rose Acre Papers (Number 2 of *The Lanthorn Series*), 1904.

Beautiful Wales (Black's Colour Book Series), painted by Robert Fowler, R.I., described by Thomas, with a Note on Mr. Fowler's Landscapes by Alex J. Finberg, and with 74 illustrations, 1905. Second edition, entitled *Wales* and with 32 illustrations, 1924.

The Heart of England, with 48 coloured illustrations by H. L. Richardson, 1906. Second edition (in *The Heart of England Series*), 1909, third edition (in *The Open Air Library*), with a Foreword and 10 wood-engravings by Eric Fitch Daglish, 1932 and 1934.

George Borrow (Number 151 of *Everyman's Library*), *The Bible in Spain,* with an Introduction by Thomas, 1906.

George Herbert, *The Temple* and *A Priest to The Temple* (Number 309 of *Everyman's Library*), with an Introduction by Thomas, 1908.

Richard Jefferies, His Life and Work, 1909. Second edition, 1911. Re-issue 1978, edited by Roland Gant.

The Plays and Poems of Christopher Marlowe (Number 383 of *Everyman's Library*), with an Introduction by Thomas, 1909.

Richard Jefferies, *The Hills and the Vales,* with an Introduction by Thomas, 1909.

The South Country (in *The Heart of England Series*), 1909. Second edition (Number 12 of *The Aldine Library*), with an Introduction by Helen Thomas, 1932.

Windsor Castle (Beautiful England Series), described by Thomas, pictured by E. W. Haslehurst, 1910; as Volume One of *Our Beautiful Homeland Series,* 1919.

Rest and Unrest (The Roadmender Series), 1910.

Feminine Influence on the Poets, 1910.

Rose Acre Papers, Including Essays from Horae Solitariae (The Roadmender Series), 1910.

Light and Twilight, 1911.

Isaac Taylor, *Words and Places in Illustration of History, Ethnology and Geography* (Number 517 of *Everyman's Library*), with an Introduction by Thomas, 1911.

Maurice Maeterlinck, 1911. Second and third editions, 1912 and 1915.

The Tenth Muse (Number 2 of *The Coronal Series*), 1911. Reissued 1916 and, with a memoir of Thomas by John Freeman, 1917.

Celtic Stories, 1911. Second and third editions, 1913 and 1918.

The Isle of Wight (Beautiful England Series), pictures by Ernest Haslehurst, described by Thomas, 1911; as Volume Two in *Our Beautiful Homeland Series,* 1919.

Lafcadio Hearn (Modern Biographies Series), 1912.

Norse Tales, 1912. Second edition, 1921.

William Cobbett, *Rural Rides,* 2 vols. (Numbers 638 and 639 of *Everyman's Library*), with an Introduction by Thomas, 1912.

The Pocket George Borrow (Authors for the Pocket Series), passages chosen from the works of Borrow by Thomas, 1912.

Algernon Charles Swinburne, A Critical Study, 1912.

George Borrow, The Man and his Books, 1912.

The Country (Fellowship Books Series), 1913.

The Icknield Way, with illustrations by A. L. Collins, 1913. Second and third editions, 1916 and 1929.

The Happy-Go-Lucky Morgans, 1913.

Walter Pater, A Critical Study, 1913.

In Pursuit of Spring, with illustrations from drawings by Ernest Haslehurst, 1914.

George Borrow, *The Zincali, An Account of the Gipsies of Spain* (Number 697 of *Everyman's Library*), with an Introduction by Thomas, 1914.

Four-and-Twenty Blackbirds, 1915.

The Life of The Duke of Marlborough, 1915.

Keats (Number 126 of *The People's Books*), 1916. Second edition, 1926.

A Literary Pilgrim in England, 1917. Second edition (Number 95 of *The Travellers' Library*), 1928.

Cloud Castle and other Papers, with a Foreword by W. H. Hudson, 1922.

The Last Sheaf, Essays by Edward Thomas, with a Foreword by Thomas Seccombe, 1928.

The Childhood of Edward Thomas, a fragment of autobiography with a Preface by Julian Thomas, 1938.

The Friend of the Blackbird [written by Thomas in October 1911], The Pear Tree Press, Flansham, Sussex, 1938.

The Prose of Edward Thomas, selected by Roland Gant with an Introduction by Helen Thomas, 1948.

Edward Thomas on the Countryside, a selection of his prose and verse, edited by Roland Gant, 1977.

The Chessplayer and other essays, with an Introduction by R. George Thomas, Andoversford, 1981.

A Sportsman's Tale, with an Introduction by R. George Thomas, Edinburgh, 1983.

Note. The extent of Thomas's reviews and long articles is indicated in the introduction and footnotes of *Letters from Edward Thomas to Gordon Bottomley.*

Index

Note: Except where indicated, all titles indexed are works by Edward Thomas.